MAKING ADVANCES

A COMPREHENSIVE GUIDE FOR TREATING FEMALE SEX AND LOVE ADDICTS

Edited by Marnie C. Ferree, M.A.
Foreword by Sue Silverman

Society for the Advancement of Sexual Health
Royston, GA

MAKING ADVANCES

A COMPREHENSIVE GUIDE FOR TREATING FEMALE SEX AND LOVE ADDICTS

Edited by Marnie C. Ferree, M.A.

Writers:
Susan J. Campling, Psy.D.
Robin Cato, J.D.
M. Deborah Corley, Ph.D.
Marnie C. Ferree, M.A.
Linda Hudson, M.S.
Alexandra Katehakis, M.A.
Kelly McDaniel, M.A.
Anna Valenti-Anderson, M.S.S.W.
Jill Vermeire, M.A.
Sonnee Weedn, Ph.D.

Society for the Advancement of Sexual Health (SASH)
P.O. Box 433 Royston, GA 30662 www.sash.net

Printed in the United States of America by CreateSpace.

Cover and interior design: Susan Thompson Graphics

10 9 8 7 6 5 4 3 2 1

Society for the Advancement of Sexual Health (SASH)
Royston, GA

Library of Congress Cataloging-in-Publication Data
Making Advances - A Comprehensive Guide for Treating Female Sex and Love Addicts
edited by Marnie C. Ferree

p. cm.
Includes bibliographical references
ISBN 978-0-9857472-0-6
1. Sex Addiction 2. Recovery I. Ferree, Marnie C.

Making Advances is dedicated
to all our sisters in
recovery from sex and love addiction.

Contents

APPENDICES

Foreword

by Sue Silverman

I slump on a couch in a therapist's office in Houston staring at gray walls, staring at a gray, humid sky out the window. I've been diagnosed as "depressed" and am offered a prescription for anti-depressants. Is this my fifth therapist? Sixth? Is this the fifth or sixth prescription for an anti-depressant, another "fix-it" pill that won't fix anything? Why can't anyone or anything fix me? Year after exhausting year I veer from emotionally high to depleted, "hung-over," depending upon whether a man sexually craves me or not. I'm married, another adulterous affair just ended. Yet in the magical thinking of an undiagnosed sex addict, I fail to understand that leading this double life is what debilitates me; I don't even understand that my behavior is inappropriate, unhealthy, or wrong. Gray walls, the gray sky, suffocate me until I can barely breathe.

Back then, in the early 1980s, when few if any clinicians know the label "sex addict," neither the therapist nor I make the connection between this so-called depression and the secret life I live. Well, yes, I suppose I *am* depressed, but no pill will cure a sexual addiction. Sexual sobriety is never prescribed as a remedy for depression, or for my out-of-control life. Unable to diagnose symptoms of a sexual "alcoholic," no one understands the cause or nature of my obsessions. No one, including myself, can see that I'm committing emotional suicide.

In fact, after a man inevitably abandons me, I believe all I need to feel "happy" is another man. Any man. Another sexual fix. I want to believe it is these men who will cure loneliness, fill my emptiness and need. I risk losing my husband, risk losing everything, because only these emotionally dangerous encounters, these risky affairs, make me feel alive. Or so I tell myself. Despite all the evidence to the contrary, I believe that *sex cures all.*

After floundering for another decade – following that gray day in Houston – finally, my eleventh therapist, a specialist in the field of addiction, offers the correct diagnosis. I'm profoundly lucky that I find this therapist; otherwise, my life would have continued to spiral out of control.

Now, in 2012, even though more is known about sexual addiction, there is still too much mis-information, not enough information, about this disease. Additionally, in terms of research and treatment, the focus has traditionally been on male sex addicts. But what about women, also severely affected?

How grateful I am that this invaluable resource, *Making Advances: A Comprehensive Guide for Treating Female Sex and Love Addicts,*is now available. This book explores, among other things, the connection between sex and love addiction: a symbiotic relationship more prevalent among women than men. Replete with therapeutic models that really work, *Making Advances* will make women's journeys through this addiction less lonely and terrifying by providing their therapists a clearer roadmap for the way out. I am deeply indebted to the editor and authors for offering help, offering hope. This important guidebook leads us away from the dark, gray world of addiction.

Making Advances, written for women by women clinicians renowned in this field, really will save lives!

Sue William Silverman, author,
Love Sick: One Woman's Journey through Sexual Addiction

Preface

by Marnie C. Ferree

In 1997, five years into my own healing journey from sex and love addiction, I was driving on the Natchez Trace Parkway close to midnight, returning from staffing one of the first intensive workshops for wives of male sex addicts. It was late spring, and a cold moon was the only light illuminating the road. I hadn't seen another car for over an hour, and I was exhausted, spent with the emotions of the weekend, lonely, and anxious to be home.

Suddenly I felt a palpable presence surround me, and though today I doubt there was an audible sound, at the time it seemed an insistent, but gentle, voice broke the silence: "*You could do this for women, you know.*" I pulled to the side of the road and stepped into the chilly air. Astounded and energized, the path before me was immediately clear. This therapeutic model, which had been proven effective for trauma survivors, male sex addicts, and now their wives, would easily adapt for women struggling with sex and love addiction. I approached the leadership of the church-based counseling center where I worked, and barely eight weeks later, 10 female sex addicts gathered for the first treatment program targeted expressly for their needs and offered in a gender-specific environment. *Healing for Women* was the program's name.

Through the next 15 years I walked with women on their healing journeys and continued my own. Repeatedly, I saw confirmed one of the core tenets of this book: Female sex and love addicts are uncomfortable in the company of women, and the very thing we require for healing, we find triggering, frightening, and almost impossible to embrace.

A few years into my professional work I withdrew from active involvement in the Twelve Step community—at the time an appropriate choice for maintaining professional boundaries since the groups were filled with my clients. I continued to teach about the importance for women to find other women to support their recovery, and I emphasized that need when I first published *No Stones*, one of the earliest books to address sex addiction in women. However,

I was unaware of my own deeply rooted resistance to connecting with women. Raised in the company of men after my mother died when I was three, I had never adequately addressed my profound wounds of attachment, which are foundational treatment issues explored in *Making Advances.* I failed to replace the connections of my S fellowship with vulnerable, intimate relationships with women.

Naively, I thought the pull of addictive relationships was behind me, and professional pride kept me from admitting my own struggles as I increasingly gravitated toward a male sex addict with whom I formed a deep trauma bond. Painfully, I discovered relapse was the price of my failure to surround myself with healthy women, who like a good mother, would nurture and challenge me.

Redemptively, relapse drove me to deeper levels of healing personally and in my private and professional relationships. Restoration also brought a determination to never again be without an intense connection with a core group of recovering sisters. Every week I join an amazing group of women for a closed S meeting in a place I privately call the *women's room,* located stereotypically in a church basement. We've become dear friends, and for many years we've supported and carried each other through the ups and downs of life. *Healing for women.*

I admit, though, I felt the familiar anxiety about being with women as I walked into the first gathering of the Women's Summit Group. These were highly respected clinicians, leaders in the field of sex addiction recovery, seemingly self-confident, accomplished professionals. More intimidating, these were *women.* Would I fit in? Be accepted as an equal? Receive tolerance for my conservative viewpoints I doubted were shared by others in this group? As we got to know each other the first evening, I discovered another powerful women's room—a group of vulnerable, healing women, many of whom had their own stories of recovery from sex and love addiction.

The Women's Summit participants travailed through the predictable stages of any group: forming, storming, norming, and performing (Tuckman, 1965). We had disagreements, splits, and hard-fought repairs. We forged through setbacks and stood together when we had to make difficult changes about our process for the benefit of the final goal. During times of weariness and panic that we wouldn't complete the book on time, we stubbornly refused to quit and found power in our collective strength when personal strength was gone. *Healing for women.*

Professionally, I became a stronger, more confident leader through editing *Making Advances.* Today, I see so many things I would do differently, especially in the beginning around establishing concrete expectations and role definitions. I wouldn't have overlooked the critical process of hearing each other's stories up front, and thus forming a stronger container to hold the energy and challenges of creating this book. Those lessons help me daily in my on-going work with women and for women. *Making advances.*

Personally, I'm richly blessed by the multifaceted fellowship some of us enjoyed. As this massive project unfolded, a few of us moved from professional colleagues to cherished friends. Over the three years it took to birth this book, we buried parents, welcomed grandchildren, supported each other through changes in personal relationships, sobbed in shared frustration at the challenges the book brought, shopped when we gathered for writing weekends, sent flowers, sipped champagne, and engaged in sacred rituals of connection and affirmation. *Healing for women.*

During one of those writing gatherings, I learned my father was seriously ill. The Women's Summit writers rallied around me as I made call after call arranging for his care until I could get home. One week before the next writers' assembly, my brothers and I buried our dad on the sloping hillside where our mother had been laid to rest over 50 years before. As I watched the male pallbearers carry my father's casket to the open grave, I felt the encircling arms of my faithful sisters from the women's rooms, both in person and in spirit. In my mind's eye flashed a long-forgotten scene from an also-forgotten novel, where a tight-knit group of women bore the coffin of a female friend to its final resting place.

Oddly, my next thought was about *Making Advances*, because my own story—and thus eventually my compilation of this treatment guide for female sex and love addicts—began with the wounded, addicted, yet adored father I was burying. Like the compelling scene from a book about a powerful connection among women, in many ways, my sister writers and I have carried and laid to rest the coffin of the heavy shame, personal pain, hurtful "humor" about their plight, and clinical inattention endured by countless women who have struggled—silent and alone—with the darkness of sex and love addiction.

At the same time, our group has been midwives more than pallbearers. I became a *GrandMarnie* during the creation of this book and was privileged to witness my daughter give birth to my first grandchild, a precious, perfect baby boy. That same spring, 15 years after my divine prompting on a midnight road, the Women's Summit writers finalized the conception of a comprehensive, clinical, yet still very personal guide for helping female sex and love addicts put aside their grave clothes and walk into the light as women of grace and integrity.

As I was finishing this preface only a few hours ago, I heard the news of another anticipated baby who will enter my family circle in a few months. Perhaps the coming child will be a girl; for certain, my daughter and her husband will nurture the little one with the attunement necessary for healthy attachment.

Healing for women... we're making advances.

Marnie C. Ferree, Editor
Making Advances - A Comprehensive Guide for Treating Female Sex and Love Addicts

REFERENCE

Tuckman, B. (1965). Developmental sequence in small groups. *Psychological Bulletin, 63*(6). 384-399. doi:10.1037/h0022100. PMID 14314073

Introduction

by M. Deborah Corley

Behind any maladaptive behavior there is always a primary drive for survival. Those of us who have known for years that women, indeed, struggled with sexual addiction because we either knew the fight first-hand or we saw it in our offices were aware of the fierce determination for survival that fueled this misunderstood and misdiagnosed problem in women. We longed for this struggle to be easier for women. Our ambition was for female sex and love addicts to have feminine warriors to fight with and for them. With the publication of this book, we hope we've made advances toward that goal.

Literature Review

In the late 1970s and early 1980s, Dr. John Money, a famous sexologist and professor of medical psychology at Johns Hopkins University, wrote about how one can become "love addicted" (Money, 1980). He went on to propose that paraphilias be classified in the addictions. While John Money, MD, was well respected, very little was made of this proposal, and it wasn't until Dr. Patrick Carnes began to write about sexual addiction in the mid-1980s that the notion took hold that sex and love addiction even existed.

In 1990, Dr. Charlotte Kasl wrote a wonderfully useful book entitled *Women, Sex, and Addiction*. While others had written about women as survivors of sexual trauma, codependents, and even love addicts, Dr. Kasl was the first to speak about women on a continuum between sexual addiction or sexual codependency. She described sex addiction as escalating patterns of obsessive, maladaptive sexual behaviors that reflected more stereotypically male behaviors of aggression, power, and control over others in hopes of relieving the woman's emotional distress - at least for a short period of time until shame, negative consequences, and more anger create a life that grows unmanageable. Dr. Kasl described sexual codependency as a woman's engaging in sex out of obligation, fear for her safety, or fear of abandonment even when she doesn't want to be sexual. The woman feels powerless to say no to others and lets herself be used in order to maintain a relationship. The sexual codependent either uses sex as a way to control men or as a sign she is worthy. Dr. Kasl underscored that few women fit neatly into one category or the other, as many women share a more interwoven way of being (Kasl, 1990).

For many of us, whether we thought we were sexual addicts or sexual codependents or just therapists trying to help women, the work of these early theorists rang true, and we hungered for more research and training. As with most mental health disorders, the research that followed was focused on men as they presented more often for therapy/treatment, were the subjects of forensic evaluations, and seemed to far outnumber the women who had this disorder.

In the 20 years between 1980, when Dr. Money first hypothesized about sex and love addiction, and 2000, only a few articles were written about female sex and love addicts. This small number of articles didn't reflect research, but instead focused on clinical experience about a variety of women's sexual behavior: in prison (Burkhart, 1973), descriptions of nymphomania (Levine, 1982), hypersexual behavior (Mellor, Farid, & Craig, 1988), borderline sexual acting out (Rickards & Laaser, 1999), and one general paper on females' sexual addiction posted by the Society for the Advancement of Sexual Health (Ross, Corley, & Schneider, 1999).

In the last decade, several more articles have been published regarding diagnosis and treatment information (Douglass, 2003, Ferree, 2001; Kasl, 2002; Roller, 2004), experiences of female sex and love addicts within the faith community (Ferree, 2002), impulsiveness and sexual risk taking (Kahn, Kaplowitz, Goodman, & Emans, 2002), resources for female sex addicts (O'Hara, 2002), research on medication use with female sexual addiction (Elmore, 2005), and predictions of risk (Opitz, Tsytsarev, & Froh, 2009). Within the last two decades a few articles (Kalichman & Cain, 2004; Langstron & Haonsen, 2006; Mellor, Farid, & Craig, 1988; Reid, Dhuggar, Parhami, & Fong, 2012) have been published that define what would be considered hypersexual or paraphilic behavior in women and compared those rates to hypersexual/paraphilic men, or compared the hypersexual women to women *not* identified as meeting criteria for hypersexuality. These articles have offered a research base from which to speculate about the number of women within the general population that meet certain criteria for sexual addiction/hypersexual behavior.

Despite the dearth of additional research and articles about women sex and love addicts, a few important books were written for women who were suffering from this issue. Sue Silverman published the autobiographical *Love Sick: One Woman's Journey Through Sexual Addiction* (Silverman, 2001), which was also made into a movie. Next, Marnie Ferree published *No Stones: Women Redeemed From Sexual Addiction* (Ferree, 2002, 2010) as the first self-help book within the Christian community to address the problem in women. Kelly McDaniel (2008, 2012) published a self-help book and accompanying workbook entitled *Ready to Heal: Women Facing Love, Sex, and Relationship Addiction*, that, like Charlotte Kasl's work, looked at women as both love and sex addicts and codependents.

Origin of Focus on Sex and Love Addiction in Women

In 2008 and 2009, the authors of this book and a few others who are considered experts in the treatment of sex and love addiction were asked to come together to share ideas about how this disorder manifests itself in women and what therapists who treat them should do to have the best outcomes. After much discussion about the women we had treated, and for some, about our own experiences in trying to recover from sex and love addiction, three distinct issues surfaced:

1. Women are different than men. Their brains are different, their socialization is different, and the way they interact with others in relationships is different. Women's addiction experiences and especially their treatment needs reflect these differences.
2. Working with women sex and love addicts is different than working with men. Women do best when the therapist is sensitive to their attachment history, injuries (trauma), and attachment needs. Creating a therapeutic environment in which a healing relationship unfolds is required for women to sustain recovery. The client must feel safe, secure, and *heard*.
3. The responsibilities of women to be mothers and care-takers of others impact their ability to enter and maintain recovery. Resources for women seeking help during the recovery process are often limited, especially in terms of support groups. Women need to see other women in recovery from sex and love addiction.

Women's Track

Early in our process, the group established a goal of sharing our collective knowledge about the differences between female and male sex and love addicts, their needs in treatment, and what we thought were the best practices when working with women. One way to share that information was through our professional organization, the Society for the Advancement of Sexual Health (SASH). Our group appealed to the SASH Board and conference program committee about the importance of including a special series of workshops during each annual conference that would address the issues facing female sex and love addicts, their partners, friends, and family. Since 2008, a Women's Track has become an important component of the SASH conference.

Treatment Guide for Female Sex and Love Addicts

Second, several members of the original groups made a commitment to work collectively to write a book for other therapists about treating women with sex and love addiction. We agreed that *all of the proceeds would be donated to SASH* so that continued research and education about women could grow out of our initial efforts. This book is the result of that commitment. Because you've purchased *Making Advances*, you too are impacting the future of research and treatment for women with sex and love addiction. For that investment, we thank you.

Women's Sexuality Survey

We also acknowledged the need for more research beyond our clinical experiences. Our second goal was to start gathering data about women who identified themselves as sex and love addicts and see how they compared to women who identified themselves as non-addicts. In collaboration with SASH, Duquesne University, and Santé Center for Healing, we developed a project called The Women's Sexuality Survey. After obtaining IRB approval, our survey was placed on www.surveymonkey.com for several months in 2010, and almost 500 women completed it. Demographic data about the respondents are shown in the following table.

Data from Women's Sexuality Survey (491 responses)

Demographics

ITEM	FSLA (n=261)	NON-ADDICT (n=230)
Self-identified as sex and love addicts	166	n/a
Self-identified as sex addicts	95	n/a
Average age	33 (range 18-73)	35 (range 18-70)
Sexual orientation	90% heterosexual	93% heterosexual
Committed relationship	55% (avg. 7.2 yrs.)	63% (avg. 10.8 yrs.)
Children	55% no children (mean # children 1.02)	56% no children (mean # children 1.04)

Figure 1

As expected, the impact of sex and love addiction on our addict group was clearly demonstrated in the female sex and love addicts' responses:

- 67% reported feeling bad about their sexual behavior
- 70% felt degraded by their behavior
- 49% of the FSLA group reported they couldn't control their sexual desire, compared to 10% of the non-addict group
- 71% reported symptoms of withdrawal such as irritability, anxiety, and depression when not able to act out
- 45% reported their sexual behavior had interfered with family life and personal responsibilities
- 62% made failed efforts to stop the behavior

There is no longer any question that women who struggle with sex and love addiction are hurting and in need of compassionate therapists who have the training to assist them. More specific findings from the Women's Sexuality Survey are reported in various places throughout this book.

How to Use *Making Advances*

The authors assume that the reader is a trained therapist with a good foundation in clinical work. We approach this problem from an addiction and attachment framework, and we use the shorthand *FSLA* to refer to a female sex and love addict or to female sex and love addiction. *Making Advances* is divided into three primary sections:

1. Part One: Sex and Love Addiction in Women (Chapters 1-3)
The book begins with the definition and presentation of sex and love addiction in women, an exploration of its etiology from a biopsychosocial perspective, and information about diagnosis and assessment.

2. Part Two: Treatment Philosophies and Practices (Chapters 4-9)
Part Two delineates therapeutic considerations when working with FSLAs; describes various treatment settings; outlines best practices for conducting group therapy; for arresting acting out behaviors; and for addressing attachment and trauma; explores systemic issues regarding the FSLA's partner and children; and discusses special populations of FSLAs and special treatment considerations.

3. Part Three: Living in Grace and Integrity (Chapters 10-12)
The final section focuses on a woman's life in recovery and outlines healthy relationships, healthy sexuality, and healthy living practices, including helping future generations of women avoid this struggle.

This book was a collaborative effort, and writers' names for each chapter are listed after the chapter title. In some cases a particular writer wrote a certain section, and a specific attribution at the end of the chapter text indicates that authorship. The appendices include resources such as a list of assessments and sample materials mentioned in the text, contact information for Twelve Step groups, and suggested reading. After an acknowledgment section, writers' biographical and contact information is provided.

The editor and authors of this work appreciate your interest in helping women who struggle with sex and love addiction, and we hope the book is helpful as you seek to ameliorate their suffering and support them as they become women of grace and integrity.

REFERENCES

Burkhart, K. (1973). *Women in prison*. Garden City: NY, Doubleday.

Douglass, M. A. (2003). Understanding the female conceptualization of sexual addiction and the role of addiction treatment (Unpublished Master's thesis). University of Michigan.

Elmore, J. (2005). Psychotropic medication control of non-paraphilic sexual addiction in a female. *Sexual and Relationship Therapy, 20*(2), 211-213.

Ferree, M. C. (2001). Females and sex addiction: Myths and diagnostic implications. *Sexual Addiction & Compulsivity, 8*(3-4), 287-300.

Ferree, M. C. (2002). Sexual addiction and co-addiction: Experiences among women of faith. *Sexual Addiction & Compulsivity, 9*(4), 285-292.

Ferree, M. C. (2002, 2010). *No stones: Women redeemed from sexual addiction* (2nd ed.). Downers Grove, IL: InterVarsity Press.

Kahn, J., Kaplowitz, R., Goodman, E. & Emans, S. J. (2002). The association between impulsiveness and sexual risk behaviors in adolescent and young adult women. *Journal of Adolescent Health, 30*(4), 229-232.

Kalichman, S. C. & Cain, D. (2004). The relationship between indicators of sexual compulsivity and high risk sexual practices among men and women receiving services from a sexually transmitted infection clinic. *Journal of Sex Research*, 41(3), 235–241.

Kasl, C. (1990). *Women, sex, and addiction: A search for love and power.* San Francisco, CA: HarperCollins.

Kasl, C. (2002). Special issues in counseling lesbian women for sexual addiction, compulsivity, and sexual codependency. *Sexual Addiction & Compulsivity, 9*(4), 191-208.

Langstrom, N. & Hansen. R. K. (2006). High rates of sexual behavior in the general population: Correlates and predicts. *Archives of Sexual Behaviors*, 35(1), 37-52.

Levine, S. B. (1982). A modern perspective on nymphomania. *Journal of Sex & Marital Therapy, 84*, 316-324.

McDaniel, K. (2008, 2012). *Ready to heal: Women facing love, sex and relationship addiction* (3rd ed.). Carefree, AZ: Gentle Path Press.

Mellor, C. S., Farid, N. R., & Craig, D. F. (1988). Female hypersexuality treated with cyproterone acetate. *American Journal of Psychiatry, 145*(8), 1037-1054.

Money, J. (1980). Love and love sickness. Baltimore, MD: Johns Hopkins University Press.

O'Hara, S. (2002). Resources for female sexually compulsive clients. *Sexual Addiction & Compulsivity, 9*(4), 297-301.

Opitz, D. M., Tsytsarev, S. V., & Froh, J. (2009). Women's sexual addiction and family dynamics, depression and substance abuse. *Sexual Addiction & Compulsivity, 16*(4), 324-340.

Reid, R. C., Dhuffar, M. K., Parhami, I., & Fong, T. W. (2012). Exploring facets of personality in a patient sample of hypersexual women compared with hypersexual men. *Journal of Psychiatric Practice, 18*(4), 262-268.

Rickards, S. & Laaser, M. (1999). Sexual acting-out in borderline women: Impulsive self-destructiveness or sexual addiction/compulsivity? *Sexual Addiction & Compulsivity, 6*(1), 31-45.

Roller, C. G. (2004). Sex addiction and women: A nursing issue. *Journal of Addictions Nursing, 15*(2), 53-61.

Ross, C., Corley, M. D., Schneider, J. P. (1999). Female sexual addiction. Society for the Advancement of Sexual Health.

Silverman, S. (2001). *Love sick: One woman's journey through sexual addiction.* New York, NY: Norton.

Part One

Sex and Love Addiction in Women

CHAPTER 1

Definition and Understanding of Female Sex and Love Addiction

Kelly McDaniel, Anna Valenti-Anderson
with contributions by Marnie Ferree, Linda Hudson, Alexandra Katehakis

Sex and love addiction is not a new addiction; however, in clinical settings, it's often overlooked or minimized. Programs training therapists do not spend adequate time discussing relational dependency and sexual compulsivity or their devastating consequences. Although sex addiction is getting more attention in the media, the counseling and medical profession suffers from a lack of preparation and training for assisting clients who struggle with addictive sex and love. Problems occur for clinicians and clients when addictive behavior is not properly diagnosed and treated. Whereas sex addiction is receiving attention from the public, the focus is mostly on men. In reality, this problem is not gender specific. Women suffer too. The shame for women who are compulsively sexual or destructively romantic is enormous, so most women don't talk about their private struggle. However, when a clinician is trained to see the signs of addiction and knows the right questions to ask to help a client come out from hiding, the relief is profound. When a clinician asks, "Does your masturbation habit interfere with your time or ability to connect with a partner?" or "When you seduce someone, what is arousing—the power or the person?" the professional indicates a knowledge and understanding of compulsivity that shows a client, "I can trust this person and s/he knows what's going on . . . I don't have to hide anymore."

Sex and love addiction is best understood as a profound inability to bond with others. The pursuit of relationships or sex looks like a search and desire for intimacy, but in fact, the pursuit and high of "falling in love" or orgasm takes the place of connection with a partner. Women use sex or romance for power, energy, or medicine, and lose themselves in the process. In time, what started as fun or easy becomes humiliating and painful. Women find themselves alone and confused.

In this way, we understand sex and love addiction as a problem of psychological isolation. Psychological isolation, different from the human experience of periodic loneliness, is the sense that one will never connect with another, and the reason is intrinsic to the self. Psychological isolation, or "condemned isolation" as Miller (1976) first named the condition, carries both shame and pain as the experience feels unchangeable and unending. A woman or child experiences this type of isolation as an internal defect: something is very wrong with me. For women addicted to sex and love, the sense that "I am bad and unworthy of love" often begins at an early age. Most addicts experienced pathological neglect, and physical, emotional, and/or sexual abuse as children when they were dependent and learning to trust human connection. The attachment injuries at the hands of caregivers altered her developing brain and body's ability to sustain connection with others, setting up a painful template for relationships and intimacy in adulthood.

Additionally, sex and love addiction is a disease of cultural inheritance. McDaniel describes addiction as a desperate attempt to live within "narrow, damaging sexual margins" that define femininity in western culture (McDaniel, 2012, p. 42). Sexuality, understood as a basic human need, is hijacked for women in a culture that teaches her to reject being sexual in order to be "good" or use sexuality as a way to gain "power" which means she is "bad." When one grows up female in a patriarchal culture, the internalized cultural rage becomes part of the self. Kasl describes patriarchy as a "system of social organization in which descent and succession are traced through the male line and the family and culture are ruled by men" (Kasl, 1989, p. 248). The only solution to this intolerable reality is to *act out* the rage or *act in* the rage. The sexual addiction model, designed to treat male sex addicts, is effective for the addict, male or female, who acts out, but it too often fails to reach the unique torture of the female addict who acts in.

In addition to a psychological and cultural disease, sex and love addiction is also a brain disease. In the words of Fisher, a biological anthropologist, falling in love is addictive. Fisher believes, "We're all addicts when we first fall in love" (Fisher, 2009). Her explanation highlights the powerful chemical process involved with mate selection. For women who find themselves addicted to sex and love, mate selection has gone awry. In the brain of a sex and love addict, the relationship is unconsciously formed with the experience of a chemical high rather than an individual. In essence, brain chemistry becomes the mate.

Brain chemistry that facilitates falling in love is designed to bring joy, clarity, and excellence. Love enhances life. For addicts, however, the chemical high of love and sex takes the place of life. Falling in love (or being sexual) is the only time a woman emerges from her otherwise numb or painful existence. She unwittingly substitutes the high of addictive love and sex for real intimacy and connection. A stranger to human bonding and safety, she navigates her compromised brain chemistry as best she can: using the energy from addictive sex and love to medicate her weary soul.

Naming the Disease

As with chemical addictions, sex and love addiction takes different forms, and Patrick Carnes (1991) outlines 11 types/categories of sex addiction. Although some of his categories fit well for women, specifically seductive role sex, fantasy sex, and exhibitionistic sex, others have left women feeling alienated from the diagnosis. Women struggle with the concept of sexual addiction, its application to men, and the cultural double standard for men and women who use sex compulsively. Therefore, naming this addiction, which is critical for recovery, is a fragile process in the treatment of women. How do we as clinicians support our client by naming the disease that is running her life while also acknowledging the shameful patriarchal legacy that set her up for this disease?

For women, the name *sex addiction* misses the important relational component that fuels the disease. Even if a woman finds herself acting out in a specifically sexual way with pornography and masturbation (a traditionally masculine form of acting out that has become more available to women with Internet access), she can name the feelings of loneliness and shame that come from her behavior. At her core, she aches for love. Her human need for intimacy and connection stirs her soul. Therefore, for purposes of inclusion and understanding, in this text we use the term *sex and love addiction*, or SLA, for behavior across a continuum of addictive sex and romance. For convenience, we use *FSLA* to refer to a female sex and love addict.

Patterns of Sex and Love Addiction

Patterns of sex and love addiction are diverse. Historically, women were thought to be more relational in their acting out, and that description fits a high percentage of SLAs, which was supported by the Women's Sexuality Survey (Corley & Delmonico, 2011). Of the 491 women completing the survey, 261 self-identified as SLAs; of that group 64% self-identified as a love and relationship addict compared to 36% who self-identified as a sex addict.

Some women find themselves compulsively attached to someone and unable to separate when the circumstances clearly warrant such a measure. Other women find themselves seeking "the perfect" partner, moving from relationship to relationship without an ability to commit more than a few months to each one. Some women find themselves repetitively drawn to partners who have an addiction to sex in an unconscious attempt to avoid or disown their own sexuality or compulsivity. In some cases, a woman can completely close down her sexuality in an effort to stay safe and feel invulnerable. She may secretly masturbate to pornography while avoiding relationships with another person. Other women, though, don't identify with the "love addict" presentation and are more caught up in specifically sexual forms of acting out. Ferree (2010) describes a broad umbrella of "sexual addiction" comprised of eight presentations that are apt for women: a relationship or love addict, romance addict, fantasy addict, pornography or cybersex addict, masturbation addict, exhibition addict, an addict who sells or trades sex, and one who partners with another addict.

Although many women find themselves in an addictive relationship or pursuing purely sexual activities at one time or another, how do we assess when a woman has crossed over into an addiction? The following questions are adapted from those frequently used in various Twelve Step groups focused on sexual addiction. They aren't meant to be fully diagnostic, but they offer a start in determining the presence of an addiction. It's helpful to keep in mind that only your client can make the ultimate decision about whether or not she is an addict. You can let her know she's showing signs and encourage her to learn about the addiction, but she'll need to own the diagnosis in order to recover.

- Do you change relationships often, sure the next one will be "right"?
- Have you tried to control your relationship or sexual patterns with little success?
- Do you feel shame or fear as a result from your sexual and romantic activities?
- Do you feel empty when you are alone? Or after sex with a partner?
- Do you use substances such as food, work, drugs, or alcohol to avoid shameful feelings?
- Have you neglected responsibilities such as family, friends, hobbies, work, or yourself due to time spent being sexual or preoccupied with romantic partners?
- Do you spend large amounts of time grooming to be seductive, flirting, or seeking romantic partners? Do you wear provocative clothing in an effort to attract?
- Have you been sexual or romantic with inappropriate people: a boss, a married person, your doctor, a person who comes to you for help, or a person in a subordinate position to you?
- Have you experienced periods of inactivity from sexual pursuits during which you were excessive or anorexic in other areas of your life, such as eating or spending?
- Are you spending large amounts of time online in chat rooms, dating sites, or viewing sexually explicit material?

- Are you consumed with self-hatred that you soothe with sexual approval from others?
- Do you blame others for not fulfilling your fantasies or the idealistic role you've assigned to them?

Women who answer *yes* to even a few of these questions would be wise to carefully examine their sexual and relationship behavior.

Definition of Addiction

It's important to understand that there's a continuum to addictive behaviors. A woman may only look at pornography occasionally or infrequently become sexual with a partner more quickly than she intended. At times she may enjoy these behaviors, and at times she may regret them, but she doesn't feel despair about her actions and they don't cause disruptions to her life. So how do you know when a woman's behavior has crossed the line from being occasionally problematic into the realm of addiction? It's rarely possible to identify a discrete point where that crossover happens. Usually it's only with the benefit of hindsight a woman can see she's caught in a pattern of behavior that's progressed into the category of addiction.

In general, addiction specialists agree on certain specific criteria that separate "addictive" from simply unwise or undisciplined behavior. Patrick Carnes (2001) outlines four primary criteria that define an addiction:

1. Obsession

For an addict, the love object or acting out behavior becomes the organizing principle of life. Obsession is an intense, abnormal, preoccupying focus on someone or something. In the Women's Sexuality Survey (Corley & Delmonico, 2011), 68% of the SLAs were obsessed by their love objects compared to 25% of the non-addicts. Addicts' lives come to revolve around fantasizing, planning to act out, engaging in the behavior itself, and hiding and recovering from the behavior. Forty-two percent of the FSLAs in our study indicated they escape through fantasy compared to 17% of non-addicts; yet 70% of the SLAs reported being disappointed in the outcome of their fantasies compared to 30% of the non-addict group.

Female SLAs report spending significant amounts of time online in romantic or sexual pursuits. For example, just over one third of the SLAs in the Women's Sexuality Survey stated they visited porn websites or chat rooms for sex compared to 10% of the non-addict group. The SLAs spent an average of about one hour *per day* at home and almost one hour per week at work on cybersex activities compared to less than one hour *per week* at home and virtually no use at work by the non-addict group. In the survey we didn't separate the impact of cybersex activities from other activities related to sex and love addiction, yet 45% of the SLAs stated their sexual behavior interfered with family life compared to just over 10% of the non-addict group. Of the SLA group, 37% reported their sexual acting out interfered with work compared to 6% of the non-addict group.

2. Compulsion

Compulsion is the hallmark of any addiction. The term describes being compelled or driven to use a substance or participate in a behavior even when the person doesn't want to. In our study, 68% of SLAs compared to one third of the non-addicts were preoccupied with their sexual behavior, and 61% of SLAs compared to 15% of non-addicts stated they were controlled by desire.

Of the SLAs, 49% reported they couldn't control their sexual desire compared to 15% of non-addicts. "I can't stop!" becomes the cry of the addict. "I know what I'm doing winds up hurting me, but I keep doing it." Stopping, though, isn't the problem. *Staying stopped* is the real issue. If a woman talks about continuing behavior she has repeatedly attempted to stop, it's extremely likely she's an addict. In our study, 57% of SLAs felt the need to stop whereas 62% of the SLAs indicated they had made failed efforts to stop their behavior.

3. Continuing despite negative consequences

Persisting in a behavior in the face of detrimental consequences is one of the clearest observable signs of an addiction. An FSLA keeps acting out despite losing a job or experiencing health consequences or negatively impacting significant relationships. She doesn't "learn" from her problematic behavior, and in fact, her loved ones may wonder if she's "stupid." Clinically, you can help her understand it's not about being dense; it's about the power of addiction. When a woman keeps acting out when it's obviously not in her best interest, she's showing the second clearest hallmark of an addiction.

4. Tolerance

The concept of tolerance is most easily applied to the use of alcohol or other substances when repeated consumption requires more and more to get the same results. Although no research to date provides confirmation, clinical observation leads many therapists who treat addiction to believe the same phenomenon also happens with behaviors. The neurochemistry of addiction, including process addictions, explains how the pleasure center of the brain eventually becomes accustomed to the neurochemical bath of dopamine, adrenaline, catecholomines, and other changes in brain chemistry associated with acting out, which requires increased or escalating behavior to get the same high. In our study, just over 71% of the SLAs reported experiencing "withdrawal" symptoms (depression, irritability, craving) when not able to have sex or love object around.

Other characteristics of addiction, again as outlined by Patrick Carnes (2001), include the following: unmanageable, progressive/degenerative, used to escape feelings, fueled by entitlement, used as a reward, and creates a feeling of power. In our study, 57% of the SLAs stated they used sexual behaviors to gain power or control in the relationship compared to 25% of the non-addict group. For women, power is an especially significant component, especially for those addicted to relationships, romance, and fantasy. In Western culture, which celebrates females for their physical beauty, this power factor can be huge. An FSLA learns she's powerful by the influence she exerts over both men and women. Through seduction and provocation, a woman can experience the heady rush of the power of her sexuality.

The Addictive System

Women SLAs report that they experience difficulty in controlling the frequency, intensity, and duration of their thoughts, and subsequently their lack of control over romantic, sexual, or sexualized behavior, and that they continue these behaviors despite adverse consequences. They have, in fact, lost their ability to choose "no." Although lacking an official definition or global uniformity, there are patterns and categories that describe this "addictive experience" for sexual addiction. Patrick Carnes (2001) first identified a cycle of sex addiction that follows a predictable pattern of distorted thinking through despair.

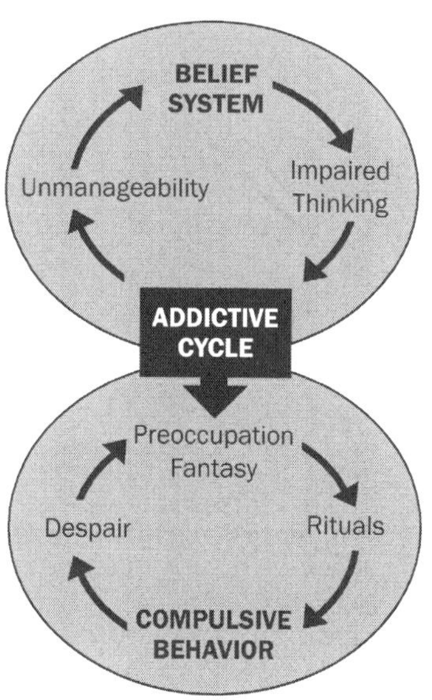

Carnes, P. (2010). *Facing the shadow* (2nd ed.). Carefree, AZ: Gentle Path Press. Used by permission.

Figure 2

Core beliefs

First and foremost the cycle begins with core beliefs that sex addicts hold about themselves (P. Carnes, 1991). These core beliefs are:

1. I am basically a bad, unworthy person.
2. No one would love me as I am.
3. No one will meet my needs.
4. Sex or an intense relationship is my most important need.

These beliefs set up individuals to hold negative views about themselves. Their distorted sense of value, power, and abundance results in perceiving themselves as *not enough* and as unsafe to be who they really are. This shame-based belief system sustains impaired thinking such as "I'm helpless, hopeless, and worthless." Thus, in order to feel or be okay, the woman's unconscious goals tend toward extremes of grandiosity, control, and excessiveness.

Common attributes that all addicts share and that FSLAs subsequently experience as part of their negative self-talk according to Earle, Crow and Osborn (1998) include the following: Having a low opinion of themselves and focusing on their deficiencies; having distorted or unrealistic beliefs about themselves and the world; wanting to escape emotional discomfort; using poor coping mechanisms; having at least one powerful memory of an intense high; and experiencing denial. In the Women's Sexuality Survey, 68% of the SLAs reported feeling bad about their behavior and 70% felt degraded by their behavior, compared to 23% and 32% respectively of the non-addict group. In the shame and guilt subscale, of the 37 items in the subscale, there was a significant difference between the female sex addicts and love addicts (p<.001). Female sex addicts reported *true* on an average of 22 items, and love and relationship addicts reported *true* on 19 items, compared to non-addicts who reported *true* on 12 items on the scale (Corley & Delmonico, 2011).

Preoccupation and obsession

Next, some internal or external stimuli triggers emotional discomfort for the woman (fear, pain, shame, guilt, loneliness, sorrow, etc.). Because she has poor coping skills or can't successfully alleviate her emotional discomfort in healthy ways, she wants to escape the discomfort. Obsessively thinking about a person or sexual behavior provides opportunities to dissociate. This involuntary dissociation moves the woman into an obsessive, trance-like state whereby she separates herself from reality and moves into a fantasy or euphoric state of altered consciousness. This obsession interferes with her ability to remain emotionally present, with her sleep and work, and ultimately her interpersonal relationships.

Ritual and grooming

Ritual and grooming behaviors are those that have become habituated in order for the woman to become more involved in her fantasy. They also intensify her arousal and diminish her emotional discomfort. Preparing for a romantic or sexual encounter enables the woman to continue increasing excitement. In our study of 491 adult women (Corley & Delmonico, 2011), 43% of those who self-identified as sex and love addicts compared to 17% of the non-addict group reported they had spent a large amount of time grooming to be seductive, flirting, or seeking sexual partners. Of the SLAs, 40% reported wearing provocative clothing compared to 18% of non-addicts; 60% of the SLAs reported feeling high when being provocative compared to 22% of the non-addicts.

Rituals can be as varied as women themselves, and one or more rituals are associated with each form of an SLA's acting out. A pornography and masturbation ritual may be very short and only involve creating enough privacy to go online and self-pleasure. An affair ritual may be much more involved and take weeks or months. Connecting with an affair partner may involve increasing amounts of contact through a variety of means (phone, text, emails, social media, etc.), meeting in person, flirting, touching, and exchanging verbal and emotional intimacies before ever specifically connecting sexually. For many FSLAs the ritual is hugely compelling and enjoyable. In fact, many women will say they enjoy the chase or the connection far more than the sexual activity.

Acting out

The bottom of the addictive cycle is the actual behavior in which a woman engages, whether it's a sexual act with herself or another person or via some form of technology-based activity. The acting out is compulsive in that she has lost her ability to refrain from the behavior in spite of commitments to herself or others to stop or despite negative consequences. Myriad examples illustrate women's SLA behavior. One woman describes becoming involved with more than one romantic partner at the same time, although she experiences overwhelming shame when she can't remain loyal to one man. Another states she can't be alone and becomes involved in serial relationships without ever taking time to be unattached. Still another FSLA masturbates at least daily and often several times a day to relieve anxiety and loneliness. Many women spend hours online looking at pornographic websites or engaging in cybersex or chat rooms. Some women frequent bars to hook up for one-night stands. Others don't have sex, but engage in emotional affairs because they're exciting and eliminate the worry about the sexual part of relationships.

Acting in

Some women, though, *act in*, which means they totally shut down sexually and compulsively avoid all sexual thoughts, feelings, and awareness. Acting in is also termed "sexual anorexia" (P. Carnes & Moriarity, 1997), and it represents a full pendulum swing away from acting out. Patrick Carnes defines sexual anorexia as "traumatic abstinence" (P. Carnes & Moriarity, 1997, p. x) and the "emptiness of profound deprivation" (P. Carnes & Moriarity, 1997, p. 1). Sexual anorexia is portrayed as a period of "de-escalation" in which "sex becomes the enemy" (P. Carnes & Moriarity, 1997, p. ix). In addition to shutting down sexually, some FSLAs limit contact with potential relationship partners, because being isolated feels safer than interactions that are wrought with self-consciousness, self-doubt, and apprehension. Acting in sexually gives the illusion of power in much the same ways that sexual acting out gives the illusion of connection.

The term comes from the notion that sexual addiction can be compared to problems with food addiction. Eating disorder specialists understand that instead of being contradictory processes, anorexia (compulsive deprivation) and binge eating (compulsive satiation) represent opposite ends of the spectrum of disordered eating. Their common denominator is an unhealthy relationship to food. In the same way sexual addiction and sexual anorexia are opposite poles of disordered sexuality: One is the out-of-control behavior of the sexual addict and the other is the tight, constrained control of the sexual anorexic (P. Carnes & Moriarity, 1997). If an FSLA is partnered she often becomes sexually anorexic in her primary relationship—a shame-driven reaction against potential closeness—as she continues to act out sexually elsewhere.

Following is a list of the signs and symptoms of sexual anorexia (P. Carnes & Moriarity, 1997):

- A dread of sexual pleasure
- A morbid and persistent fear of sexual contact
- Obsession and hypervigilance around sexual matters
- Avoidance of anything connected with sex
- Preoccupation with others being sexual
- Distortions of body appearance
- Extreme loathing of body functions
- Obsessive self-doubt about sexual adequacy
- Rigid, judgmental attitudes about sex

- Excessive fear and preoccupation with sexual diseases
- Obsessive concern or worry about the sexual intentions of others
- Shame and self-loathing over sexual experiences
- Depression about sexual adequacy and functioning
- Intimacy avoidance because of sexual fear
- Self-destructive behavior to limit, stop, or avoid sex

The cycle of sexual anorexia mirrors the cycle of sexual addiction with only two substitutions: *distance strategies* in place of ritualization, and *compulsive aversion* in place of compulsive behavior. Both disorders start with a belief system that leads to impaired thinking. For the sexual anorexic, the unrelenting core belief of being flawed and therefore unlovable causes her to withdraw from any potential partner for fear of having her beliefs vulnerably exposed. Staying defended against rejection solidifies her perception of being unlovable, which creates a self-fulfilling prophecy of never finding an emotionally available partner who is willing to share an intimate connection. Sexual anorexia may look different from sexual addiction, but they're driven by the same addictive system and have many overlapping features. Frequently an FSLA catapults sexually between acting out and acting in as a way to corral her uncontrollable behavior, and a clinician must be aware that these extremes are flip sides of the same coin lest he or she misses their interconnected patterns.

Relief and shame

Although many women may experience some temporary relief when engaging in the acting out stage, a significant number report that during and after the behavior they feel guilt and shame, especially when they find themselves in the same situation of powerlessness over and over again. This is a type of self-perpetuating abandonment of self, and subsequently the woman is again ashamed of herself, confirms her original negative core beliefs, feels emotional discomfort, and seeks ways to alleviate that distress and unmanageability, which begins the cycle again.

Consequences Without Treatment

The female SLA may find herself experiencing increasingly serious consequences that lead to a variety of problems that are typically clustered in the following areas.

Physical/health concerns include exhaustion, sleep issues, ulcers, high blood pressure, self-injury and injuries from others, unwanted pregnancy/abortion, and sexually transmitted diseases (STDs), including HIV infection, genital herpes, syphilis, and gonorrhea. In the Women's Sexuality Survey, 33% of the SLAs reported having an STD as a result of their sexual acting out compared to 14% of the non-addicts. Twenty-five percent had gotten pregnant as a result of sexual acting out and 18% terminated a pregnancy compared to 13% and 10% of the non-addicts, respectively (Corley & Delmonico, 2011). Additionally, Chlamydia can infect the reproductive system and cause pelvic inflammation, which can lead to infertility. Some studies report a higher risk of cervical cancer in women whose blood tests show evidence of past or current Chlamydia infection. Moreover, contracting various strains of the human papilloma virus (HPV) may increase a woman's risk for cervical cancer (American Cancer Society, 2012). Internal or external injury can occur from rigorous or excessive sexual activity, which may include the use of sex toys or other objects to her breasts, genitals, and colon. A woman who engages in excessive, more rigorous, or even violent sexual behaviors may find herself injuring or bruising the vagina and cervix and may be at a higher risk for cervical cancer (American Cancer Society, 2012). Of the SLAs in the Women's Sexuality Survey, 7% indicated they had experienced infertility as a result of sexual acting out compared to 2% of the non-addict group.

Some women report having nearly caused car accidents when they exhibit themselves to other drivers, or have almost run off the road self-masturbating or having someone masturbate them while driving. Other women report having harmed themselves in order to stop their behaviors.

Emotional and mental consequences include depression and anxiety, paranoia, loneliness, hopelessness and helplessness, self-loathing, and a lack of self-esteem. Many women report such despair and overwhelming feelings of guilt and shame that they have thoughts of suicide or self-harm as a way to escape their pain, shame, and fear. Some SLAs follow through with such acts. Most women experience difficulties in their primary relationships, and some report increased conflict or neglect of their children as they become consumed with their preoccupation and compelled to act out sexually. Additionally, women self-identify more readily with having problems with their sexual behaviors because of their internalized expectation that they should think and act in certain acceptable ways. For instance, women who look at sexual images may believe themselves to be abnormal because culturally they believe good girls don't look at pornography. Women may, however, under-report looking at sexual images because of their internalized shame and the fear of being regarded as more deviant than most women.

Spiritual issues from acting out include conflicts between her value system and behaviors, or struggling with a belief in a god or disconnection from her god. Some women say they feel spiritually empty and experience a lack of faith in anything, or feel angry at God for having abandoned them. Disconnect and shame may manifest in a woman's avoiding spiritually supportive communities and networks. In the Women's Sexuality Survey, 59% of the SLAs reported their sexual behavior had interfered with their spiritual integrity compared to 23% of the non-addict group (Corley & Delmonico, 2011).

Financial consequences are associated with some forms of romantic and sexual acting out, such as the purchase of pornographic materials and sexual aids, buying clothes and costumes, the use of prostitutes and escorts, the fees for phone sex, buying webcams and audio/video equipment, the monthly charge for computer access, and air travel and fuel expenses for the purpose of a romantic rendezvous or sexual contacts. Many women are still paid less money than men in similar positions, and therefore they have less disposable income. The woman SLA who is not earning income may resort to creative ways to find money to support her behaviors if they require payment. She may embezzle money from her children's child support or from her weekly budget for groceries, for instance. She may also find ways to support her own addiction by working as an escort, stripper, or pimp. If a woman is arrested for exhibitionism or soliciting, she incurs the expense of legal representation.

Employment consequences typically involve relationships. Women do not as frequently engage in Internet-based sexual behaviors at work (Corley & Delmonico, 2011), therefore the consequences of being exposed at work and the risk of losing their jobs is less than with men due to Internet access. Unfortunately, women do become involved romantically or sexually with others in their workplace. This may be as a way to earn favoritism, as a way to exploit a subordinate, or as part of the compulsion to seduce or inability to maintain boundaries. Possible negative consequences might include loss of colleagues' respect, possible repercussions from their bosses, demotions (or no promotions), loss of business/clients/customers, tension or loss of work friendships, conflict with lovers at work, stalking behaviors/being stalked, possible termination, and the necessity of changing careers due to an unfavorable reputation.

Legal consequences primarily involve prostitution. Women who exhibit themselves are less likely to be arrested or forced to register as a sex offender for indecent exposure, because Western society is more accepting and often more encouraging of women to show their bodies and are less offended when a woman's breasts, buttocks, or even genitals are exposed in public. Women, however, may be arrested for soliciting as prostitutes and escorts, for voyeurism and inappropriate touching or sexual harassment, and for child molestation. In the Women's Sexuality Survey 7.3% of the SLAs reported they had been sexual with a minor compared to 2.2% of the non-addicts. (Together that was almost 10% of the sample.) Regarding other boundary violations, 54% of SLAs reported having sex with a subordinate compared to 28% of non-addicts (Corley & Delmonico, 2011). Again, we were surprised to see the overall high number of women engaged in inappropriate sexual behaviors with subordinates at work, in school, and so forth.

Moreover, there are countless custody battles in the courts involving women who are regarded as "unfit" mothers due to their romantic or sexual escapades and who must fight to retain their rights to parent or see their children.

Differences in Female SLAs as Compared to Males

Although all sexually "addicted" individuals present with similarities such as decreased control, preoccupation with obtaining and using the substance or engaging in the behavior, continued use despite negative consequences, and resulting shame around their behaviors (Schneider, 1991), women SLAs also present with some differences from men.

An obvious difference involves a greater concern to women due to their ability to become pregnant and an increased consideration for using contraception when being sexually active. According to the American Cancer Society (2012), women who have had three or more full-term pregnancies have an increased risk of developing cervical cancer. Further research shows that more women report having gotten pregnant because of acting out versus men who would admit to having impregnated women as part of their acting out (Corley & Delmonico, 2011). Becoming pregnant, then, subsequently leads to a serious consequence of having to decide whether to abort their fetus, give the baby up for adoption, or keep the child. Depending on the age and socioeconomic status of the woman, or if she is already in a relationship or has children, this presents a substantial stressor for herself and others.

Another difference is that women are less likely than men to self-identify as *sex* addicts. Females will more readily admit to their relationship dependence using language such as "I'm love addicted to him" and acknowledge the use of seductive behaviors. Even after the sexual revolution, women are more comfortable talking about their codependency as it relates to their relationships and to their attachment to men, although many women still find it difficult to admit their *need* to be affirmed as worthwhile. Increased shame exists for the "feminist" woman who *needs* to have a man in her life in order to "be complete." Kasl's early work (1990) described the sexually addicted woman as being driven by the power of sexual conquest and using sex as a way to meet her need for tenderness and touch. She described a sexually codependent woman as one who derives her self-worth from being pursued; she's more the passive partner or recipient in the sexual or relational encounter. Kasl asserted that women in both groups, though, may become addicted to romance, which seems more socially and culturally acceptable than pursuing purely sexual exploits.

Further, a woman may be more comfortable discussing her inability to maintain her boundaries by saying, "I have a hard time saying no" instead of admitting her obsession with sex. Adams (2008) writes that many women who are relationally dependent talk of being hooked on unavailable people, being obsessed to the point of being unable to think of anything else, having that preoccupation interfere with their ability to manage their activities of daily life, becoming involved in serial relationships in order to continually pursue the high of new romance or conquests, or being unable to let go of a toxic relationship. A sexually aggressive woman is still often seen as less acceptable than one who assumes a more passive role.

Sussman (2010) further argues that "love addiction" is an immature romantic love that permeates the woman's daily life, involves repeated out-of-control behavior, and results in negative life consequences. She also notes that women in love addiction-based relationships exhibit more stalking behaviors than men in their attempt to obtain a sense of intimacy, however false that connection really is. Finally, it's not uncommon for women to exhibit a combination of SLA symptoms in order to feel loved and powerful such as being drawn to partners outside their primary relationship while being less sexual in their primary relationship, and also needing the emotional high of sex (McDaniel, 2012).

Both clinical (SLAs) and non-clinical (normal) populations of women report that they "felt degraded" by their sexual behavior and speak of "being" degraded "by" a partner instead of necessarily degrading themselves (Corley & Delmonico, 2011). In our study, 70% of the SLAs reported feeling degraded by their behavior compared to 32% of the non-addict group. This circumstance often reflects their comfort in being more of a passive participant in their behaviors. Although there are some narcissistic women who experience a sense of power in their romantic or sexually predatory behavior, many women are more comfortable talking about "being done to" or allowing themselves to be used, rather than admitting to acting in more exploitive ways or having initiated behavior such as husband-swapping, compulsively looking at pornography or using sex toys, or entering into extramarital affairs and one-night stands. One woman admitted that she didn't feel as bad at having sold herself at auction as she might have had she done the buying. Additionally, women in our study report having faked orgasms to please their partners (37% of SLAS compared to 25% of non-addicts).

Given that many SLA women are more comfortable accepting a codependent/dependent label or even a victim role, women who use the Internet for sexual purposes or engage in a variety of sexual behaviors or have sexual fetishes report a substantial amount of shame because some sexual behaviors are still regarded as more taboo and deviant for women. Because of this added internalized shame, women have a more difficult time talking about their sexual thoughts and addictive behavior, especially if they believe they're going against cultural or religious norms. Ask specific questions about women's romantic and sexual thoughts, fantasies, and behaviors, because women will likely hide in secrecy until they are directly questioned in a non-judgmental way.

Although women report a higher incidence of Relationship Disturbance as a factor of their sexual addiction than men (P. Carnes, Green, & S. Carnes, 2010), ensure you don't make assumptions that a woman can only be addicted to a person as a love object, or that love addiction and sex addiction are mutually exclusive, or that her other sexualized behaviors aren't causing relational upset. You must carefully navigate the path between assessing for distress and dependency related to what's typically considered socially acceptable sexual activities or relationships, not pathologizing what is culturally considered atypical sex or relationship behavior, and helping your female clients acknowledge when their behavior is harmful while avoiding self-loathing.

Just as women in the 1960s made advances in their unfolding as sexual beings, women now make advances in their personal growth as they courageously admit their struggle with sex and love addiction. As clinicians better understand this issue and its treatment, they, too, make advances both in helping women live in grace and integrity and in paving the way for future generations of treatment providers to offer assistance.

Contributing Writers

Marnie Ferree - Definition of Addiction, Sexual Anorexia

Linda Hudson - Sexual Anorexia

Alexandra Katehakis - Sexual Anorexia

REFERENCES

Adams, C. (2008). *Love addiction*. Retrieved from http://www.bluffviewcounseling.com/love-addiction.shtml

American Cancer Society. (2012). *Detailed guide: Cervical cancer: What are the risk factors for cervical cancer?* Retrieved from http://www.cancer.org/Cancer/CervicalCancer/DetailedGuide/cervical-cancer-risk-factors

Carnes, P. (1991). *Don't call it love*. New York, NY: Bantam Books.

Carnes, P. (2001). *Out of the shadows: Understanding sexual addiction* (3rd ed.). Minneapolis, MN: CompCare.

Carnes, P. C., & Moriarity, J. M. (1997). *Sexual anorexia: Overcoming sexual self-hatred.* Center City, MN: Hazelden.

Carnes, P., Green, B., & Carnes, S. (2010). The same yet different: Refocusing the sexual addiction screening test (SAST) to reflect orientation and gender. *Sexual Addiction & Compulsivity, 17*(1), 7-30.

Corley, M. D., & Delmonico, D. (2011, September). *Closing the gap: Results from the Women's Sexuality Survey on Female Sex and Love Addicts.* Presentation at Society for the Advancement of Sexual Health Conference, LaJolla, CA.

Earle, R., Crow, G., & Osborn, K. (1998). *Lonely all the time: Recognizing, understanding and overcoming sex addiction, for addicts and co-dependents.* Phoenix, AZ: Tri-Star Visual Communications.

Ferree, M. C. (2010). *No stones - Women redeemed from sexual addiction* (2nd ed.). Downers Grove, IL: InterVarsity Press.

Fisher, H. (2009, September). *Lust, romance, attachment: Why him, why her?* Keynote address at Society for the Advancement of Sexual Health Conference, San Diego, CA.

Kasl, C. (1990). *Women, sex, and addiction: A search for love and power.* New York, NY: Ticknor & Fields.

McDaniel, K. (2012). *Ready to heal: Breaking free of addictive relationships* (3rd ed.). Carefree, AZ: Gentle Path Press.

Miller, J. B. (1976). *Toward a new psychology of women* (2nd ed.). Boston, MA: Beacon Press.

Schneider, J. (1991). How to recognize the signs of sexual addiction: Asking the right questions may uncover serious problems. *Postgraduate Medicine, 90*(6). Retrieved from http://www.jenniferschneider.com/articles/recognize.html

Sussman, S. (2010). Love addiction: Definition, etiology, treatment. *Sexual Addiction & Compulsivity, 17*(1), 31-45.

CHAPTER 2

Etiology of Female Sex and Love Addiction: A Biopsychosocial Perspective

Marnie Ferree, Linda Hudson, Alexandra Katehakis, Kelly McDaniel, Anna Valenti-Anderson

No woman hopes to become a sex and love addict, of course. Most are bewildered about the origin of their problem and torment themselves for their unmanageable, "bad" behavior. Their shame is overpowering. When you help a woman understand the etiology of her sex and love addiction, you lessen that shame and free her spirit for healing.

To explain female SLA, it's important for you to view it through a multi-faceted biopsychosocial perspective rather than through a single lens. That's because the development of sex and love addiction in women is a complicated process that interweaves neurobiology, environment, and technology. Difficulties in any of these aspects favor the formation of addictive or compulsive behavior, and in combination they increase the chances a woman may suffer from SLA. This chapter discusses all three factors that interact to create sex and love addiction in women.

NEUROBIOLOGICAL FACTORS

First, knowing the basic principles of neurobiology helps you better understand women who struggle with SLA by clarifying a major factor contributing to its development. *Affective neuroscience*—the study of how emotions actually grow the brain and nervous system—shows that most of our psychological, intellectual, and even physical growth depends on attachment patterns we (or more correctly, our brains and bodies) learn during infancy. It also demonstrates how early relational trauma hurts not just our feelings but our cognitive and behavioral capacities as well, making us susceptible later to major depression, posttraumatic stress disorder, schizophrenia, and borderline personality disorder (Roth & Sweatt, 2011). What's more, we now know that such trauma doesn't need to be dramatic to be damaging.

Simple emotional neglect, characterized by repeated breaks in caretaker-child attunement, may actually prove more injurious than violence or abuse (Field, Diego, & Hernandez-Reif, 2006). The integrity of the child's core self is determined by whether her parents validate or deny parts of who she is becoming. By relating solely to features they accept and denying other characteristics, parents negate parts of the child, which they don't or won't recognize. This leaves the child without subjective experiences of those ignored aspects of herself because they couldn't be shared in relationship with others. Such negation of facets of the growing self is damaging and creates developmental or relational trauma (Bromberg, 2011). This early, constant emotional trauma can hobble affective, cognitive, and behavioral brain functions and leave the child less resilient to the varied psychological and social pressures life presents.

This childhood neurological crippling leads both male and female SLAs to disturbed attachment patterns—the hallmark of the addiction and the reason affective neuroscience is so relevant here. But from conception to maturity, just being female seems to increase susceptibility to SLA: Brain structure, physiology, evolution, and sociocultural factors all favor its occurrence in women. So knowing a bit about each is crucial for treatment.

The Female Brain

For the first two months of life all fetal brains have identical neural pathways. But at eight weeks, a testosterone surge in males kills some cells in the communication centers and expands areas dedicated to sex and aggression (Arnold, Xu, Grisham, Chen, & Kim, 2004; Brizendine, 2006). Female brains, though, remain especially structured for social connection. This distinction suggests to some that women are more hardwired than men for empathy, whereas men are more hardwired for reasoning and systematic thinking (Baron-Cohen, 2005). Certainly, though, female infants' greater neurobiological powers of connectivity appear to make them more susceptible to sex and love addiction if early relational trauma leaves them pathologically rather than securely attached.

The Lasting Costs of Girlhood

Possibly because of their greater relational sensibility, girls seem more prone than boys to stress from poor care-giving. An anxious or depressed mother nurtures less, and baby girls appear to incorporate this neglect into their nervous systems, which alters their perception of reality (Brizendine, 2006). Even prenatal intrauterine stress, which affects the neuroregulatory systems involved in addiction and medical illness throughout one's life (Becker et al., 2005; Felitti & Anda, 2010;

Kessler, 1997; see also Meaney & Szyf, 2005) may strongly incline adolescent girls to anxiety (Becker et al., 2005; Phillips, Hammen, Brennan, Najman, & Bor, 2005). Early stress, then, directly impacts females' vulnerability to mental disorders. Their sensitization to tension may be directly correlated with depression at about twice the frequency as in men (Becker et al., 2007; Cosgrove, Mazure, & Staley, 2007), as well as with addiction (Nestler, 2005; Nestler et al., 2002). And if early stress alters neural systems to encourage novelty-seeking behaviors like substance abuse, it's likely that these same alterations might also lead to a compulsive "process addiction" such as SLA.

Neurobiological Damage to the Brain and Nervous System

A brief review of the hypothalamic-pituitary-adrenal system (HPA axis) shows exactly how attachment deficits created by poor care-giving can occur in an infant or young child, how they damage affective and intellectual abilities, and how this damage can manifest as SLA.

The HPA axis comprises the *neuroendocrine system*—the interactions of our nervous and endocrine systems (Solomon & Tatkin, 2011). The interface of the structures and systems comprising the HPA axis lets us absorb sensory information from our central nervous system (CNS) as it's brought to us through our autonomic nervous system (ANS). The HPA axis then assesses this information as a threat or a benefit. If an infant or child senses a threat (and we saw that females appear to sense stress more readily than do males), her HPA axis activates ANS responses. First, the HPA axis tries the active strategy of "fight or flight" by releasing the hormone cortisol. If that response fails to end the perceived threat, the ANS triggers the more primitive, passive mechanisms of withdrawal or even of dissociation.

Activating these emergency responses over and over habituates the girl's developing brain and body to using active anxiety or paralyzing dissociation, and turns these responses into permanent "go-to" traits instead of occasionally useful protective mechanisms (Perry, Pollard, Blakely, Baker, & Vigilante,1995; Schore, 2003). The constant, routine use of these emergency responses to stress physically stunts her growing neuronal paths, and thus her cognitive and affect-regulation abilities. Those more mature capacities include the higher executive functions of emotional self-control, focus, planning, self-monitoring, and understanding others' points of view though "empathic attunement, the ability to read facial cues, vocal tones, and body posture" (Solomon & Tatkin, 2011, p. 208).

Much of this habituation occurs during the first 18 months of life in the affective right brain, which develops long before the verbal/logical left brain. And while the left hemisphere may overcompensate later for these right hemispheric social and emotional deficits, it won't do it as well. This process may explain why SLAs, usually early auto-regulators, often choose isolated self-soothing strategies including sexual fantasy, fantasies of being "swept away by love," and compulsive masturbation.

We have known for decades that infants who have not experienced the co-regulation built on attachment become neurologically programmed to auto-regulate the only way they can, through potentially pathological dissociation (Schore, 2009; Tronick, 2004). Affective neuroscience has now taught us that by the first year and a half of life, poor infant-caregiver attachment not only denies the child the emotional co-regulation she needs in order to develop her self-regulation, but also arrests the physical growth of her structural and neuronal pathways and trains her nervous system to respond to stress with either panic or dissociation.

These findings allow us to understand and treat female SLAs as *regulation-impaired due to a fundamental attachment disorder.* Since early relational trauma likely blighted growth in her right orbitofrontal cortex, its mature executive function of self-regulating and monitoring was never fully activated, so she is often incapable of self-reflection, self-differentiation, somatic awareness, and insight into self or others. Neither can she tolerate long-term intimacy, because being truly known by another (lover or therapist) threatens to bring back the shame and self-loathing experienced in repeated losses of emotional attunement with her caregiver. Without the regulatory capacities of a strongly developed, high right hemisphere to view and regulate her subcortical (below the cortex) primitive impulses, she seeks sex as a substitute for love, in hopes of feeling better. In brief, we can now see that SLA functions like other addictions, and understand it as an effect of the links between poor care-giving, neurobiological deficits in the child's growing brain and body, and psychological impairment in her adult life.

Attachment Theory

If sex and love addiction is best viewed in relation to early disruptions of attachment, it's important to understand the basics of attachment theory. For decades, psychologists (Bowlby, 1969; Schore, 2003; Winnicott, 1958) have recognized eye contact, prosody (the music of speech), facial expressions, touch, and gestures of the caregiver as crucial in creating attachment, which allows babies temporarily to engage in a co-regulatory dance with their caregivers' more mature emotional regulation. This co-regulation shapes babies' emerging right hemisphere and helps them begin to implicitly learn independent affect regulation and relational skills. Secure attachment also provides a basic positive view of oneself and others in the world. The security a child feels, or misses, in such early attachment becomes internalized and life long, though it may be altered by later experiences.

Although others have named varying categories (Ainsworth, 1989; Bowlby, 1969; George, Kaplan & Main, 1996), the four attachment patterns of adults identified by Bartholomew in 1990 are commonly preferred due to their simplicity (Bartholomew & Horowitz, 1991; Flores, 2011). This book uses Bartholomew's quadrilateral format because it's included in the Sexual Dependency Inventory (P. Carnes & Delmonico, 1996), and therefore, many therapists working in the sex addiction field are familiar with it. However, this system has its limitations because it doesn't include the ambivalent or disorganized styles. Originally conceived as a way to work with couples, it nonetheless can be adapted to use with individuals. The four attachment patterns delineated by Bartholomew and others (Bartholomew & Horowitz, 1991; Flores, 2011) are secure; avoidant/dismissing; preoccupied; and avoidant/fearful. Seeing SLA as a problem of affect dysregulation due to insecure attachment means that understanding attachment styles is crucial both for explaining and for treating this addiction.

Bowlby's (1969) formulation clarifies ***secure attachment***. He stated that the *biological function* of attachment was to protect us from predators, making safety its principal role. Next he connected *attachment* and *play*, pointing out that only with a secure attachment to a safe figure can the child afford to turn away from her primary attachment figure to explore the world. Finally, Bowlby believed that this attachment style *persists throughout life*. Therapists know that, like the securely attached child who can look around herself, the securely attached client who feels safe in the therapist's presence can look inside to investigate her inner world. Fortunately, insecure styles of attachment that formed in childhood may, however, be changed through effective psychotherapy to an "earned secure attachment" (Pearson, Cohn, Cowan, & Cowan, 1994).

Let's look at the insecure attachment categories. The ***avoidant/dismissing*** client rarely experienced attunement to her affect, usually from a cold, rejecting mother, so she almost always dismisses her own and others' feelings or avoids relationships altogether. This routine discounting of emotion results from her right-brain deficits and helps her avoid her habitual feeling of threat from others, so her speech may sound blunted as she reports her history without much affect. She may seek substances or risky behaviors, preferring anonymous, emotionless sex, to get the dopamine rush that masks her internal numbness—her early survival strategy. Although she has a positive sense of self, her view of others is negative. Her customary position that other people are untrustworthy or at fault when her relationships fail may make maintaining your empathy difficult.

Raised by an inconsistent caregiver who "blew hot and cold" unpredictably, the ***preoccupied*** child always felt out of control and so never learned how to manage her own impulses—or even that impulses could be managed. That is, her immature right orbitofrontal cortex under-regulates affect and actions, allowing her to speak and behave in an uncensored, unwise way. Unlike the avoidant/dismissing client, she may be very chatty, in part because she relies on others for a sense of value and self-worth, and in part because she doesn't restrain her speech, and instead, uses it as a way to soothe herself from stress. In fact, she carries a negative sense of herself and a positive, if continually disappointed, view of the other. So her uninhibited speech usually fixates on past bad attachments, fear, and anger, which makes her clingy and demanding , which is quite in keeping with her negative-tinged attachment style.

The ***avoidant/fearful*** attachment style, sometimes associated with the borderline personality, is not even *organized* (self-consistent), and so is also associated with ***disorganized attachment*** in this model. A client with this style has a negative sense of self as well as a negative sense of others and presents as both avoidant and ambivalently attached, yet longs to be in relationship. As a child, she received little to no affect regulation from her primary caregiver, who was probably frightening and so was simultaneously the source of protection *and* threat. She very likely has a history of unresolved early developmental trauma. You may observe her ricochet between fear of engulfment and fear of abandonment. She may also use contradictory coping strategies such as seeking negative attention or careening from total silence to rambling monologue. Clients with this attachment pattern often narrate a confused and incoherent history, which usually includes a negative description of herself and of others. She sees herself as a victim (even if she "deserves it"), fears the intimacy that healthy people seek for comfort, and may belittle her relationships because she believes she can never be truly loved.

Recognizing these insecure attachment styles points you along the right (if often challenging) path for treating the female SLA, to be detailed in chapter 7.

Why Turn to Sex?

The female SLA's insecure attachment styles play directly into her addictive cycle. Dopamine in the brain creates an intense euphoric rush, so it makes sense that the female SLA who has limited capacity for self-regulation will gravitate toward the one experience that makes her feel good, if only momentarily. During sexual arousal in women the medial orbitofrontal cortex—the part of the brain responsible for self-reflection—is deactivated, creating a state "generally associated with a more carefree state of mind" (Georgiadis, Simone Reinders, Paans, Renken, & Kortekaas, 2009, p. 3097). Some women report altered states of consciousness during intense or prolonged orgasm (Sayin, 2011). Neurochemicals including dopamine, testosterone, and endorphins flood the brain at orgasm (Exton et al., 1999; Kruger et al., 2006) and powerfully elevate mood. Post-coital release of the neurohormones oxytocin and serotonin create feelings of attachment and well-being and further attaches the female brain to the sexual experience.

Female Physiology and Evolution: Menses, arousal, orgasm, and partner choice

Along with their brain's structure and early relational injuries, women's bodies may also intensify vulnerability to SLA. Every 28–32 days, the menstrual cycle alters levels of neurohormones including estrogen, which shapes brain structure and chemistry and may regulate arousal (Cosgrove, et al., 2007) and make female SLAs more likely to cheat when ovulating (Dixit, 2010).

The female brain seems deeply involved in orgasm as well. In one study, women reported that the more in love they were, the stronger their orgasms were. Such statements are more than just romantic. Using functional Magnetic Resonance Imaging (fMRI) to map women's brain activity, researchers saw left insula activity spike as partners' names were subliminally flashed. The fact that the left insula is involved in the brain's reward center suggests that female orgasm itself might function as an addiction (Wenner, 2008). Thus women's sexual desire occurs through a combination of psychological and physiological arousal rather than as the spontaneous sexual reaction typical in men (Basson, 2003; Hiller, 2004). So psychologically healthy women lose interest in their love objects if not both psychologically and physiologically aroused. But the female SLA, unconsciously schooled by early relational trauma, stays in painful relationships because the *fantasy* of romance is more powerful than her real suffering.

In addition to monthly hormonal rhythms, the span of human evolution seems to encourage women to seek partners, casual or not, whose symmetrical features signal good genetics. Not only single females but married cheaters unconsciously obey evolutionary biology to look for good providers and protectors (Brizendine, 2006; Fisher, 2004). However, women appear fairly flexible about specifics of appearance, with genital responses only modestly related to their preferred type, whereas men tend to be quite preference-specific in their arousal patterns (Chivers, Rieger, Latty, & Bailey, 2004).

Research, then, confirms what many clinicians have long believed: Sex and love addiction is, at its core, a brain disease. Yet at the same time, psychological, social, and cultural factors interact with these neurobiological ones, and those processes also need exploration.

ENVIRONMENTAL FACTORS

A variety of environmental factors play a part in the etiology of sex and love addiction in women. The family of origin environment is the first non-biological shaper, and its influence is profound. As children, most female SLAs experienced harmful dynamics and even trauma of various kinds. In each case, painful emotions gained tenacity due to the absence of caregiver compassion and repair, especially by the mother. Perhaps equally significant is the cultural environment and the powerful messages it sends to women. From false cultural beliefs about females and sexuality to shame-based religious teachings, women are unconsciously and profoundly affected by their environment.

Family Systems

Family is the learning ground for relationships. When families function well, children learn to trust themselves and others. As adults, relationships prove satisfying and enjoyable, and individuals are able to weather crisis and conflict with resilience. For women healing from sex and love addiction, however, their stories contain painful family memories. FSLAs report caregivers who were inconsistently attuned and unpredictably intrusive. These women share many common family characteristics that have been clearly outlined by Wegscheider-Cruse (1989) and other family systems theorists. Ferree (2010) extensively discusses the following material and specifically applies it to female SLAs.

Dysfunctional families operate according to a variety of rules, many of which are unspoken, which means a person only realizes the rule exists when she's broken it. The most common rules in unhealthy families are *don't talk, don't feel, deny or minimize*, and *blame*. Often other rules specific to an individual family are in play, as well. Examples include, "*Mom is always right*" or "*males are more important*." These rules prohibit the healthy interchanges that build robust relationships.

Flawed families also play roles that define the members' interactions and serve to add predictability and stability to family relations. The standard roles most theorists list include *hero* or *heroine*, *scapegoat*, *doer*, *mascot*, *peacemaker*, and *lost child*. While everyone may have talents, gets things done, be funny or diplomatic, these traits become problematic when people are rigidly locked into behaving a certain way. Many female SLAs played one or more entrenched roles in their families, which carry over into adult relationships.

In addition, boundary issues plague dysfunctional families, and problems in this area also form the breeding ground for later detrimental behavior. Boundaries are the invisible force fields that define a person's space: Where "*I*" stop and where "*you*" begin. Boundaries provide structure, safety, and security. Most FSLAs, though, grew up in families where boundaries were too loose, too rigid, or a confusing combination of both.

Loose boundaries fail to equip a child with sufficient safety and guidance. There may be yelling, criticism, or even physical violence. Caregivers don't provide adequate guidance or instruction. When boundaries are too rigid, the opposite dynamics exist. There is little emotional connection, affirmation, or healthy touch. The environment is one of judgment and avoidance.

More damaging still is the confusion of both loose and rigid boundaries. In a two-parent home, each caregiver may practice a different kind of boundaries. Worse still, the same caregiver may have both loose and rigid boundaries. For example, a stepdad may voyeur a daughter or make inappropriate sexual comments (loose boundaries), yet otherwise have almost no interaction with her (rigid boundaries). This duality leaves a child confused and off balance. Without boundaries to protect her and caregivers to engage with her, the sex and love addict in the making is primed for both poor personal choices and exploitation.

Trauma

As if dysfunction in the family system isn't enough, many FSLAs experience some form of trauma. According to Patrick Carnes' extensive early research (1991), which was conducted primarily with males but had a small representation of females, 97% of sex and love addicts experienced emotional abuse in their childhood environments, 81% experienced sexual abuse, and 72% experienced physical abuse. Laaser (2004) divides trauma into two broad categories: abuse (also called invasion trauma) and abandonment (also called neglect), and he further delineates each trauma category into four subsets: emotional, physical, sexual, and spiritual.

Emotional abuse can be quite difficult for people to recognize because it's not as obvious as being physically or verbally assaulted. Designed to belittle, control, and demean the child, emotional abuse as described by Hein (2006) includes verbal *aggressing* such as name-calling, accusing, blaming, threatening, ordering, or even constant criticizing, "advising," or questioning disguised as "just trying to help." *Abusive expectations* are unreasonable demands that are often accompanied by complaints that the victim didn't do "enough." If a female SLA grew up with a narcissistic father who made her always keep him company due to his own abandonment issues, she suffered his abusive expectations that left her feeling responsible for his happiness, which is a perfect set-up for codependency with needy men to whom she will subjugate herself.

Physical abuse is more easily identified and includes acts such as hitting, slapping, pushing, or beating with the hand or an object. A violent environment is detrimental to a child even if she isn't personally attacked. Vicarious trauma occurs when a child witnesses or is aware someone else is being abused or when the perpetrator throws things or breaks furniture or punches walls.

Sexual abuse occurs when a child or adolescent is sexually exploited by an adult (or older or more powerful child or teenager) for the adult's own gratification. Sexual abuse, then, is much broader than acts of penetration. Fondling, sexual kissing, masturbation of the adult or child, oral sex, and other forms of sexual contact also constitute sexual abuse. These acts can create an early sexual awakening and confusion about sex and love, especially when the perpetrator is known to the child. *Covert sexual abuse*, as opposed to overt abuse, doesn't involve touching, but it creates a psychological bond between parent and child that is meant for adults. A mother or a father uses a daughter as a confidant, therapist, or caretaker. A child in this position is confused and misused. The parent's misplaced emotions and actions translate as a pseudo-marriage for the child's relational template, and the child feels wed or enmeshed to the parent. In adulthood, she has difficulty identifying and breaking the bond with her parent in order to be intimate with another. Romantic relationships or close friendships bring a feeling of betrayal or exhaustion, because love is equated with duty (Mellody, 2003). Adult children of covert incest are tired and worn by relationship demands. They tend to avoid commitment and/or search for intensity outside a relationship to maintain a sense of distance from their partner.

Spiritual abuse sometimes happens in "fundamentalist" religious systems that insist on strict adherence to a specific doctrine or behavior. It consists of restrictive and punitive views of "God" or a "Higher Power." Spiritual abusers are often self-righteous and seek to control others through shame-based tactics.

Under the category of abandonment trauma, ***emotional abandonment*** happens when the caregiver isn't attuned to the child's emotional needs. This category is closely related to the disruptions of attachment discussed earlier in the chapter. It is every bit as painful and damaging as more active forms of abuse. Perhaps the perpetrator questions the victim's perceptions, memory, and even sanity. Invalidation and minimizing undermine the child's perceptions and state that any hurts the child reports are due to her being "too sensitive." Sometimes a caregiver gives a child the "silent treatment" of emotional withdrawal. In any case, the child is left feeling on edge and anxious.

Physical abandonment, also called *neglect*, is a passive form of abuse in which a perpetrator responsible for providing care (medical, nutritional, hygienic, educational, safety) to someone who needs it fails to do so (Hein, 2006). Human infants are born completely dependent on their caregivers, and this dependency continues for an extended period of time—longer than for any other mammal. Many women who struggle with SLA weren't provided adequate supervision, instruction, or medical and dental care. They had to "fend for themselves" and even become responsible for the care of younger siblings.

In our sexually saturated culture, the premise of ***sexual abandonment*** may seem ludicrous. Yet many females describe growing up without basic instruction about their sexual selves and sexual processes. Parents abdicate this teaching to schools and religious institutions, which often do a poor job (if at all) instructing about sexuality.

Spiritual abandonment is rarely considered but is also impactful for many FSLAs. This idea is discussed more fully as a separate topic under cultural factors later in this chapter. In simplest terms, spiritual abandonment occurs when the family's practices are disconnected from their value system. Instead, a child is exposed to a divergence between what the family professes to believe and how the family operates. The child is left morally adrift without a guiding light to direct her path.

Mother Hunger and Wounding

Culturally, emphasis has been placed on mothers and sons/fathers and daughters. In patriarchal structures, mothers and daughters are overlooked. However, the bond between a mother and her daughter sets up a child's relational template. It's within this first relationship that a young girl learns to love or to fear, to trust or to hide, to laugh or to cry.

Our mothers are our first love. We are born designed for her embrace. At her breast, we learn the world is either safe and warm or cruel and rejecting. In our first relationship with mother, we begin to form a concept of self. In the words of Hunter, "By using our mother as a mirror, we know what it is to be female" (1994, p. 41). Sex and love addicted women learn how to be female from their mothers, and the lessons are painful. Women in recovery from sex and love addiction often describe their mothers as "rejecting, unpredictable, and/or unavailable."

Barbara, a client in recovery, recalls a painful image of her mother that she revealed in therapy. "I could see her clearly . . . pushing me away from her . . . handing me over to my Dad. She sacrificed me to keep him happy."

Growing up separate and alone, FSLAs long to be held like children even as adults. In addictive relationships, clients struggle to have this craving satiated. FSLAs place impossible, unconscious expectations on one person to fill all needs and heal old wounds (even the ones that are unconscious). This mindset is a set up for failure, and FSLAs regularly feel betrayed, confused, and angry with others.

Mother hunger is the core of addiction to love and sex. Adrienne Rich (1995) says, "The woman who has felt 'unmothered' may seek mothers all her life—may even seek them in men. Some . . . marry looking for a mother" (p. 237). To recover and know healthy loving relationships, FSLAs must heal this pain.

CULTURAL FACTORS

Many women who seek help wonder, "How could I be a sex and love addict?" The answer to this question requires an understanding of cultural issues as well as ones coming from her family of origin. Cultural influences for women often are minimized or overlooked when a woman is facing an addiction. In Western American culture, women inherit damaging images of femininity and sexuality. McDaniel (2012) outlines four cultural beliefs that result from patriarchal images of women. Some clients identify with one or two beliefs; however, many connect with all four. They are as follows:

- I must be good to be worthy of love.
- If I am sexual, I am bad.
- I am not really a woman unless someone desires me sexually or romantically.
- I must be sexual to be loveable.

These destructive beliefs fuel contradiction, confusion, and addictive behavior. They create the shame of a sexual double bind. The *American Heritage Dictionary* (2011) defines a double bind as "a psychological impasse created when contradictory demands are made of an individual so that no matter which directive is followed, the response will be construed as incorrect . . . a punishing and inescapable dilemma." The four cultural beliefs create a "punishing and inescapable dilemma" which leave women no room for healthy sexual development. As a result, the double bind is a set up for sex and love addiction.

In addition to a sexual double bind, destructive cultural messages create shame for women. Both men and women are bombarded daily with pornographic images of the female body in literature, advertising, and film. Eroticized images of women, sex, and love are so institutionalized they seem real, and women often find themselves competing with these internalized images of femininity.

Consider the four cultural beliefs in light of the definition of double bind. To be worthy of love, a woman must be "good." But if she is sexual, she is "bad." Yet she must also be "desirable" to be fully female. So, how can a sexual woman be a good person? The double bind resulting from these beliefs is a painful cultural inheritance. Sex and love addiction provides an escape from this cultural impasse as women consciously or unconsciously attempt to avoid the "punishing and inescapable" cultural dilemma that tells them they are unworthy of love. Understood in this way, sex and love addiction is a survival mechanism that serves as a desperate attempt to live within narrow, damaging sexual margins.

Spirituality

Religious influences frequently impact the development of a woman's self-image and her core beliefs, including about sexuality. The primary religious influence is the family, and Patrick Carnes' early research with sex addicts (1991) found that most described their families of origin as "rigidly disengaged" on the Circumplex Model (Olson, 2000). The Circumplex Model plots a couple or family along two continuums that measure family cohesion (bonding) and family flexibility (adaptability). The rigidly disengaged category reflects an extreme rigidity where one person is in charge and highly controlling, coupled with extreme emotional separateness among family members where individuals aren't able to turn to one another for support. This kind of imbalance in a family's emotional bonding and flexibility goes to the core of two risk factors for later addictive behavior: attachment issues and shame.

In what way? And how does this imbalance influence the development of a girl's spirituality? Theologians have often surmised that a person's view of God is largely shaped by the relationship with an earthly father (Seamands, 1981). If a dad is disengaged, meaning he's not emotionally available and leaves the daughter to fend for herself, she may view God or a Higher Power as similarly unconcerned about her well-being. If she fails to securely attach to her father, she may have difficulty trusting in a Higher Power. Similarly, if her father is rigid and inflexible, the girl learns there is "only one way" that's acceptable, and if she questions that way, she pays the price in the form of moralistic lectures and accusations of failure. With repeated experiences, the daughter begins to believe she is a horrible and terrible person, which is the very definition of shame.

Growing up in a rigid background then, no matter what the brand of religion, has taught many women that they are not good people. Many religions are paternalistic and picture Father God as all powerful and very judgmental. Many FSLAs believe if they displease him, he'll punish them. God may also be benevolent, but it's up to them to keep him happy. Being sexual is a sure way to attract God's wrath, not his pleasure. For many women the fear of failing to do "the right thing" is terrifying, and the shame of going against what they were taught about God is tremendous. Ironically, this overwhelming shame is often a driving factor for medicating through addictive behavior.

Sometimes the shame cycle swings to arrogance, and the FSLA rejects God before he can reject her. If God is like a judgmental, punitive, rejecting or absent father, acting out becomes a way to challenge the authority of the all-powerful source.

The church in many religious traditions sets up a dualist notion of sexuality.

A woman is taught that her body is the "temple of God" and then is encouraged to either cover it up or minimize its sinful appearance. Some conservative groups teach that dancing, drinking, smoking, and especially sex is the "devil's handiwork." Women are encouraged or in some cases required to remain celibate until marriage and stay "pure" for a spouse. In that system it's difficult to express sexuality in any way that isn't considered sinful. Even when adult women have been married and divorced, they're required to eliminate any sexual expression until and unless they remarry within the church.

In more chaotic family and religious belief systems the rules are more diffuse. Women aren't given many guidelines or explanations about ways of expressing their sexuality, and they can easily confuse "loving" with being sexual. Young women are given the mixed message that sex is wrong and you shouldn't engage in sexual practices, but you should "save yourself for the husband you love." Love addiction can easily become the way out of this dilemma. If every man with whom a woman becomes involved is her potential husband, then surely sex equals love. How can she refuse sex with Prince Charming? Surely this man was sent by God to be her partner. When a woman begins to project her liberating power outward onto a man, she loses the ability to claim her true sense of self.

TECHNOLOGY FACTORS

Sexual activities by females in the electronic age are often misunderstood, under-assessed, and under-diagnosed because of the wide-spread popularity of various media and sexual outlets. The fast paced and quick changing world of technology and portable devices provides a broad arena for technology-based sexual behaviors, which include activities such as sexting, chatting, social networking, sharing photos, and streaming real-time video, and so forth (Weiss, 2010). This has changed the landscape of how women define and experience intimacy, connection, and attachment, how they manage social skills, and how females deal with anxiety and self-esteem. Today's technology is a definite factor that can contribute to the etiology of sex and love addiction, especially for women who are at higher risk because of family and cultural experiences.

Sexting

Unfortunately, girls and FSLAs increasingly use their cell phone cameras to sexually and romantically connect with another person by taking photos of parts of their body to tease (Shafron-Perez, 2009). This growing phenomenon is known as "sexting," which combines text messaging and sexuality and automatically makes public the image because these images can be re-sent or forwarded to others. Sexting has become a concern for parents, educators, and law enforcement (Richards & Calvert, 2009) because although the First Amendment protects sexual correspondence between adults, this behavior possibly becomes criminal when an underage minor is the one sending or receiving such a message. More and more incidences are being reported in the media where teens are being arrested for manufacturing, possessing, or distributing child pornography as a result of sharing a sexual image of themselves (as a minor) or re-sending sexual images of their girlfriends, boyfriends, or school classmates.

Additionally, as this form of flirting and courting becomes even more the norm, younger girls will likely continue to increase their participation in sexting as part of their relationship building, part of common dating behavior, or a way to rekindle romance. "Smart" phone software or applications ("apps") are available that include global positioning systems (GPS), which enable users to instantaneously search for sexually oriented material (video streaming) or environments (strip clubs, adult bookstores), or to find others for immediate sexual exploration and hook-ups (classified advertisements, live video, social networks).

Internet-Based Sexual Activity

There is a double standard and misconception when it comes to women and cybersex, which includes accessing pornography electronically, engaging in sexual behaviors in real-time, participating online in sexual conversations with others, and accessing multimedia software (Delmonico, Griffith & Moriarty, 2001). The use of technology is inherently an expectation of instant gratification. Being able to superficially connect with a measure of detachment allows SLAs to experience intensity, which leads to a state of chronic anxiety. The risk taking, consequences, isolation, obsession and escape into fantasy, and thrill of instant gratification easily impedes intimacy and leads to a sense of at least superficial (false) connection, thereby replacing the face-to-face and heart-to-heart presence that can only be experienced between individuals who are exchanging "real" energy and non-verbal cues that support interactive attachment to one another.

One type of cybersex is virtual reality sex, which includes 3-D software and web sites that enable women to participate in a fantasy life online or to "meet and hook up" in a virtual "world" like Second Life. In these virtual worlds there are no limits, and often women spend hours in this fantasy world creating an "avatar" that participates in explicit sexual situations, including prostitution, sadomasochism, and sexual violence. The arousal that exists for women in these virtual sex rooms far exceeds the reality (and routine) of a real live person and relationship. Real people can't compete with fantasy, and women may find they prefer fantasy to real-life partners and physical connection. Writes one woman about her online secret, fantasy life, as reported by Emma Boyes (2009), "I spend two to three hours several nights a week 'working' in Second Life. I dance in escort clubs, and people know what they're coming there for; they know where to find me."

The Internet is compelling because of the nature of its features, which have been termed "interactive, inexpensive, imposing, integral, isolating, intoxicating" (Delmonico, Griffin, & Moriarty, 2001, p. 6). The immediacy supported by various electronic mediums can lead to impulsivity such as sending a sexual text, photo, or video on a cell phone or a posting a sexual image on a photo or videosharing site like YouTube or flickr.

Social Networking

Today's technology has broad implications for social communication and interpersonal relationships and for how girls' and women's attitudes, values, and behaviors are shaped regarding what's considered "normal" and "acceptable" ways of relating, building relationships, dating, courting, and expressing or experiencing sex and sexuality. Boyd and Ellison (2008) describe social networking sites as web-based services that allow individuals to network publicly or semi-publicly, which provides for some women a sense of safety and anonymity. The popularity and far-reaching scope of social networking sites is evidenced by a popular movie titled *The Social Network* (Fincher, 2010). Facebook, founded by Harvard University student Mark Zuckerberg and his fellow collegians, is currently the most used social networking service worldwide. As of May 2012, it has nearly 157 million unique U.S. users with almost 42% of the U.S. population having a Facebook account (Internet World Stats, 2012). Although the site has restrictions on use by children and prohibitions about sexual content, it's still a rich playground for connecting with potential romantic or sexual partners or stalking former love interests. And it's not just adults: A study about youths using social media sites (Moreno, Parks, Zimmerman, Brito, & Christakis, 2009) found that 24% of MySpace profiles referenced sexual behavior.

In the past SLAs may have turned to bars and churches for meeting potential sexual partners. Today, technology provides female SLAs with numerous avenues to find sexual matches. Some online sites include Match, plentyoffish, Yahoo!Personals, zoosk, eHarmony, Singlesnet, OkCupid, True, DateHookup, Chemistry, FriendFinder, date, and lavalife. A female SLA who uses social networking mediums now has a way to reach out to millions of other users online with varying degrees of privacy control and security and with varying degrees of commitment and interests (SeekBuddies, CasualEncounters, SocialFlirt, Whisper-Dating, EliteFling). If she is partnered and is looking for discreet sexual liaisons, there are web sites for her to search specifically for extramarital affairs and casual hookups (Ashley Madison, Married Secrets, lonelyhousewives, ArrangementSeekers, MarriedFlirtation). Carol says of her use of social networking sites, "I have a lot of control over what I want people to know and who I get to screen and have sex with." Even the non-sexually focused website Facebook has been implicated in an increase in divorces due to extra-marital relationships initiated online (Gardner, 2010).

Many girls and teens begin learning about sex and exploring gender norms on the Internet, where their searches are anonymous and there are no limits to what they can explore in a virtual world. Girls as young as 13 are able to join Xanga, a network of blogging and social networking communities for teens, and a majority of its blogs, articles, and advertisements focus on dating and sex. Girls and women also are able to explore or participate in online sex while still being available in real-time through the use of teledildonics or cyberdildonics. High tech sex (e.g., Fleshlight and Sinulator) enables virtual sex to become more real by allowing users to control sex toys via a computer over the World Wide Web. Girls are becoming more aware of vast sexual options and myriad ways to experiment and explore their sexuality. In younger females who begin using technology and pornography, their brains begin to be wired toward what is arousing—what Patrick Carnes (2001) has termed the arousal template—which can lead to an intimacy or courtship disorder. Arguably, exposure to sexual imagery online as well as memories of experiences that occurred at times of emotional arousal may become imprinted on the brain (Cline, 2002). SLAs with an altered sexual and intimacy template will often report feeling uncomfortable outside of cyberspace. Some SLAs will never or have rarely dated, and some will likely experience significant difficulty with close relationships.

Pornography

Although there are many ways that female SLAs use technology as a tool or outlet in their courtship and sexuality, pornography remains one of the most significant forms for women SLAs to become aroused, to explore "what's normal" and to engage with a partner (Maltz, 2012). For mature women, strong in their sense of themselves as women and sexual beings, watching some types of adult erotic videos, whether alone or with their partner, may not be harmful, and they are able to distinguish fantasy and role-play from reality. For some women, though, viewing pornography becomes a significant part of their addiction (Gambotto-Burke, 2012) and leads to internal conflict regarding socially determined rules of female behaviors (Watts & Zimmerman, 2002) and acceptable dominance and violence against women.

Attorneys, educators, and clinicians debate the helpfulness or harmfulness of sexually explicit material. However, those who treat SLAs focus on the harmfulness and damage of the obsession and internal conflict for some women. According to Violet Blue (2007, July) for *Oprah* magazine, a third of visitors to adult entertainment web sites are female, and women account for 56% of Hustler's video store business. As of December 31, 2011, Internet World Stats (2012) reports approximately 273,067,546 Internet users in North America, and 245,203,319 in the United States alone. Twenty to 43% of them are online for sexual purposes. Another study found that 28% of Internet pornography users are women (Cooper, 2004; Internet World Stats, 2012). According to Ropelato (2012), 28,258 Internet users are viewing pornography every second.

In their examination of the cybersex issues in our Women's Sexuality Survey, Corley and Hook (2012) reported almost 14% of the FSLA group reported having cybersex problems. Participants in the cybersex group spent more time online and reported more symptoms than did those in the addicted/no cybersex group, who reported more symptoms than the non-addicted/no cybersex group. Of the cybersex group, 79.3% reported frequently visiting pornographic websites and chat rooms, compared with 20.1% of participants in the addicted/no cybersex group and 6.4% of the non-addicted group. Additionally, 57.9% of the cybersex group reported relying on abusive pornography or fantasies to feel aroused, compared with 16.3% of the addicted/no cybersex group and 9.7% of the non-addict group.

Unequivocally, today's technology provides SLAs ever-increasing ways to act out and more powerful and quicker paths to addiction. When added to neurobiological and environmental factors, technology becomes the great accelerator for women on the road to sex and love addiction.

Writers

Neurobiological Factors - Alexandra Katehakis
Environmental Factors - Marnie Ferree, Linda Hudson, Kelly McDaniel
Technological Factors - Anna Valenti-Anderson

REFERENCES

Ainsworth, M.D. (1989). Attachments beyond infancy. *American Psychologist, 44*(4), 709-716.

American Heritage Dictionary of the English Language. (2011). (5th ed.). Boston, MA: Houghton, Mifflin, Harcourt.

Arnold, A. P., Xu, J., Grisham, W., Chen, X., & Kim, Y. H. (2004). Minireview: Sex chromosomes and brain sexual differentiation. *Endocrinology, 145*(3), 1057-1062.

Baron-Cohen, S. (2005). The essential difference: The male and female brain. *Phi Kappa Phi Forum, 85,* 23-26.

Bartholomew, K., & Horowitz, L. M. (1991). Attachment styles among young adults: A test of a four-category model. *Journal of Personality and Social Psychology, 61*, 226-244.

Basson, R. (2003). Biopsychosocial models of women's sexual response: Applications to management of "desire disorders." *Sexual and Relationship Therapy, 18,* 107-115.

Becker, J. B., Arnold, A. P., Berkley, K. J., Blaustein, J. D., Eckel, L. A., Hampson, E., . . . Young, E. (2005). Strategies and methods for research on sex differences in brain and behavior. *Endocrinology, 146,* 1650-1673.

Becker, J. B., Monteggia, L. M., Perrot-Sinal, T. S., Romeo, R. D., Taylor, J. R., Yehuda, R., & Bale, T. L. (2007). Stress and disease: Is being female a predisposing factor? *The Journal of Neuroscience, 27*(44), 11851-11855.

Blue, V. (2007). *Eyes wide shut.* Retrieved from http://www.oprah.com/relationships/What-Kind-of-Woman-Watches-Porn-Researchers-Find-Answers

Bowlby, J. (1969). *Attachment and loss: Vol. 1. Attachment.* New York, NY: Basic Books.

Boyd, D. M., & Ellison, N. B. (2008). Social network sites: Definition, history, and scholarship. *Journal of Computer-Mediated Communication, 13*(1), 210–230. doi: 10.1111/j.1083-6101.2007.00393.x

Boyes, E. (2009). *Games of love: Virtual sex. I live out my sexual fantasy as an online escort.* Retrieved from http://www.greenpixels.com/articles/features/2256/Games-oflLove-virtual-sex

Brizendine, L. (2006). *The female brain.* New York, NY: Broadway Books.

Bromberg, P. M. (2011). *The shadow of the tsunami.* New York, NY: Routledge.

Carnes, P. (1991). *Don't call it love: Recovery from sexual addiction.* New York, NY: Bantam Books.

Carnes, P. (2001). Cybersex, courtship, and escalating arousal: Factors in addictive sexual desire. *Sexual Addiction & Compulsivity, 8*(1), 45-78.

Carnes, P. J., & Delmonico, D. L. (1996). *Sexual dependency inventory-revised.* Minneapolis, MN: Positive Living Press.

Chivers, M., Rieger, G., Latty, E., & Bailey, J. (2004). A sex difference in the specificity of sexual arousal. *Psychological Science, 15*(11), 736-744.

Cline, V. B. (2002). *Pornography's effects on adults and children.* Retrieved from http://stop.org.za/Victor%20Cline%27s%20Study.pdf

Cooper, A. (2004). Online sexual activity in the new millennium. *Contemporary Sexuality, 38*(3), i-vii.

Corley, M. D., & Hook, J. (2012). Women, female sex and love addicts, and use of the Internet. *Sexual Addiction & Compulsivity, 19*(1-2), 53-76.

Cosgrove, K., Mazure, C., & Staley, J. (2007). Evolving knowledge of sex differences in brain structure, function, and chemistry. *Biological Psychiatry, 62*(8), 847-855.

Delmonico, D. L., Griffin, E., & Moriarity, J. (2001). *Cybersex unhooked: A workbook for breaking free of compulsive online sexual behavior.* Wickenburg, AZ: Gentle Path Press.

Dixit, J. (2010). The cheat sheet. *Psychology Today, 43*(1), 45.

Exton, M. S., Bindert, A., Kruger, T., Scheller, F., Hartmann, U., & Schedlowski, M. (1999). Cardiovascular and endocrine alterations after masturbation-induced orgasm in women. *Psychosomatic Medicine, 61*, 280-289.

Felitti, V., & Anda, R. (2010). The relationship of adverse childhood experiences to adult medical disease, psychiatric disorders and sexual behavior: Implications for healthcare. In R. Lanius, E. Vermetten, & C. Pain (Eds.), *The impact of early life trauma on health and disease: The hidden epidemic* (pp. 77-87). Cambridge, UK: Cambridge University Press.

Ferree, M. C. (2010). *No stones: Women redeemed from sexual addiction* (2nd ed.). Downers Grove, IL: Intervarsity Press.

Field, T., Diego, M., & Hernandez-Reif, M. (2006). Prenatal depression effects on the fetus and newborn: A review. *Infant Behavior and Development, 29*, 445-455.

Fincher, D. (Director). (2010). *The Social Network* [Motion picture]. United States: Columbia Pictures.

Fisher, H. E. (2004). *Why we love: The nature and chemistry of romantic love.* New York, NY: Henry Holt.

Flores, P. J. (2011). *Addiction as an attachment disorder* (2nd ed.). Lanham, MD: Jason Aronson.

Gambotto-Burke, A. (2012, March 24). *Addicted to pornography* [Web log message]. Retrieved from http://www.thisisawar.com/AddictionPorn.htm

Gardner, D. (2010, December 2). The marriage killer: One in five American divorces now involve Facebook. *London Daily Mail.* Retrieved from http://www.dailymail.co.uk/news/article-1334482/The-marriage-killer-One-American-divorces-involve-Facebook.html

George, C., Kaplan, N., & Main, M. (1996). Adult Attachment Interview. Unpublished manuscript, Department of Psychology, University of California, Berkeley (3rd ed.).

Georgiadis, J. R., Simone Reinders, A. A. T., Paans, A. M. J., Renken, R., & Kortekaas, R. (2009). Men versus women on sexual brain function: Prominent differences during tactile genital stimulation, but not during orgasm. *Human Brain Mapping, 30*, 3089-3101.

Hein, S. (2006). Types of emotional abuse. Retrieved from http://eqi.org/eabuse1.htm

Hiller, J. (2004). Speculations on the links between feelings, emotions and sexual behaviour: Are vasopressin and oxytocin involved? *Sexual and Relationship Therapy, 19*(4), 393-429.

Hunter, B. (1994). *In the company of women.* Sisters, OR: Multnomah.

Internet World Stats. (2012). Retrieved from http://www.internetworldstats.com/

Kessler, R. C. (1997). The effects of stressful life events on depression. *Annual Review of Psychology, 48,* 191-214.

Kruger, T. H., Schiffer, B., Eikermann, M., Haake, P., Gizewski, E., & Schedlowski, M. (2006). Serial neurochemical measurement of cerebrospinal fluid during the human sexual response cycle. *European Journal of Neuroscience, 24,* 3445-3452.

Laaser, M. (2004). *Healing the wounds of sexual addiction* (3rd ed.). Grand Rapids, MI: Zondervan.

Maltz, W. (2012). *The sexual healing journey: A guide for survivors of sexual abuse* (3rd ed.). New York, NY: William Morrow.

McDaniel, K. (2012). *Ready to heal: Breaking free of addictive relationships.* (3rd ed.). Carefree, AZ: Gentle Path Publishers.

Meaney, M. J., & Szyf, M. (2005). Environmental programming of stress responses through DNA methylation: Life at the interface of a dynamic environment and a fixed genome. *Dialogues in Clinical Neuroscience, 7*(2), 102-123.

Mellody, P. (2003). *Facing love addiction* (2nd ed.). New York, NY: Harper One.

Moreno, M. A., Parks, M. R., Zimmerman, F. J., Brito, T. E., & Christakis, D. A. (2009). Display of health risk behaviors on MySpace by adolescents. *Archives of Pediatrics & Adolescent Medicine, 163*(1), 27-34.

Nestler, E. J. (2005). Is there a common molecular pathway for addiction? *Natural Neuroscience, 8,* 1445-1449.

Nestler, E. J., Barrot, M., DiLeone, R. J., Fisch, A. J., Gold, S. J., & Monteggia, L. M. (2002). Neurobiology of depression. *Neuron, 34,*13-25.

Olson, D. (2000). Circumplex model of marital and family systems. *Journal of Family Therapy,22,* 144-167. Retrieved from http://onlinelibrary.wiley.com/doi/10.1111/1467-6427.00144/pdf

Pearson, J. L., Cohn, D. A., Cowan, P. A., & Cowan, C. P. (1994). Earned and continuous security in adult attachment: Relation to depressive symptomatology and parenting style. *Developmental and Psychopathology, 6,* 259-373.

Perry, B. D., Pollard, R. A., Blakely, T. L., Baker, W. L., & Vigilante, D. (1995). Childhood trauma, the neurobiology of adaptation, and "use-dependent" development of the brain: How states become traits. *Infant Mental Health Journal, 16,* 271-291.

Phillips, N. K., Hammen, C. L., Brennan, P. A., Najman, J. M., & Bor, W. (2005). Early adversity and the prospective prediction of depressive and anxiety disorders in adolescents. *Journal of Abnormal Child Psychology, 33*, 13-24.

Rich, A. (1995). *Of woman born: Motherhood as experience and institution.* New York, NY: W. W. Norton.

Richards, R., & Calvert, C. (2009). *When sex and cell phones collide: Inside the prosecution of a teen sexting case.* Retrieved from http://www.lawrencewalters.com/articles/AlpertArticle.pdf

Ropelato, J. (2012, March 24). *Internet pornography statistics.* Retrieved from TechMediaNetwork at http://internet-filter-review.toptenreviews.com/internet-pornography-statistics.html

Roth , T. L., & Sweatt, J. D. (2011). Annual Research Review: Epigenetic mechanisms and environmental shaping of the brain during sensitive periods of development. *Journal of Child Psychology and Psychiatry, 52*(4), 398-408.

Sayin, H. U. (2011). Altered states of consciousness occurring during expanded sexual response in the human female: Preliminary definitions. *NeuroQuantology, 9*, 882-891.

Schore, A. N. (2003). *Affect regulation and the repair of the self.* New York, NY: W. W. Norton.

Schore, A. N. (2009). Attachment trauma and the developing right brain: Origins of pathological dissociation. In P. F. Dell & J. A. O'Neil (Eds.), *Dissociation and the dissociative disorders: DSM-V and beyond* (pp. 107-141). New York, NY: Routledge.

Seamands, D. (1981). *Healing for damaged emotions.* Colorado Springs, CO: David C. Cook.

Shafron-Perez, S. (2009). Average teenager or sex offender? Solutions to the legal dilemma caused by sexting. *The John Marshall Journal of Computer & Information Law.* 26 J. Marshall J. Computer & Info. L. 431.

Solomon, M., & Tatkin, S. (2011). *Love and war in intimate relationships.* New York, NY: W.W. Norton.

Tronick, E. Z. (2004). Why is connection with others so critical? Dyadic meaning making, messiness and complexity governed selective processes which co-create and expand individuals' states of consciousness. In I. Nadel & D. Muir (Eds.), *Emotional development* (pp. 293-316). New York, NY: Oxford University Press.

Watts, C., & Zimmerman, C. (2002). Violence against women: Global scope and magnitude. *The Lancet, 359*(9313), 1232-1237.

Wegscheider-Cruse, S. (1989). *Another chance: Hope and health for the alcoholic family* (2nd ed.). Palo Alto, CA: Science and Behavior Books.

Weiss, R. (2010, September). *Sex addiction and the new media frontier*. Presentation at Society for the Advancement of Sexual Health Conference, Boston, MA.

Wenner, M. (2008). Sex is better for women in love. *Scientific American Mind, 19*(1), 9.

Winnicott, D. W. (1958). The capacity to be alone. *The International Journal of Psycho-Analysis, 39*, 416-420.

CHAPTER 3

Diagnosing Sex and Love Addiction in Women

Susan Campling, Sonnee Weedn
with contributions by Deborah Corley, Alexandra Katehakis, Anna Valenti-Anderson

Timely, appropriate, and thorough assessment is the heart of effective treatment whether the presenting problem is physical, psychological, spiritual, or some combination of the above. For women presenting with concerns related to love and sexuality, regardless of the form this activity takes (relational, solo, or a combination of the two), a comprehensive and holistic evaluation is the first step in identifying the problem and developing an appropriate treatment plan. Assessment and diagnosing is essential to this process. Assessment requires questioning in areas of psychological, physical, environmental, social, and spiritual wellbeing. Some clinicians believe that the assessment is best done according to an addiction perspective, whereas other clinicians utilize an integrated model during the assessment phase to evaluate for co-occurring disorders.

At the outset, the client must be given a careful explanation of the assessment process: what it will entail, how data will be gathered, and how it will be shared with her and others once the assessment is complete. The treatment provider must discuss informed consent and obtain agreement (Releases of Information) about collateral data that will be gathered and the assessment results that will be shared with others, including the referring professional, if applicable. Explaining the assessment process helps alleviate the client's inherent fears and concerns and prevents any misunderstanding. Furthermore, it helps reduce the client's shame about problems related to SLA and creates safety for her to talk more openly about her behavior, perhaps for the first time.

The assessment needs to include both structured and open-ended questions to allow for the greatest possible amount of information to emerge. The initial process can require several hours and perhaps multiple sessions. "The therapist must convey an attitude of openness and sensitivity to the client and ask questions from a position of interest and neutrality" (Courtois, Ford, & Cloitre, 2009, p. 88). Developing rapport is more important initially than focusing on specific areas of sexual and love relationship behavior, including sexual history, current behaviors, and consequences of the behaviors. Only once stabilization and safety are achieved is the FSLA likely to fully disclose. It's also important to keep in mind that despite a positive therapeutic relationship, it may only be further in her treatment before the FSLA will disclose aspects of her history. This may have more to do with her readiness to reveal secretive parts of her past, though it may be related to remembering experiences that previously were dissociated, repressed, or forgotten.

Assessing for various types of trauma in the FSLA is also important. Understanding what may activate trauma responses in the client may help to avert any unintentional re-traumatization in the session. In monitoring for trauma responses you avoid placing the FSLA at risk for acting out when she leaves the office or not returning for treatment. If a trauma response does occur, explore with her positive coping skills and other preventive measures that will help avert dysregulated emotions that may threaten to overwhelm her.

Sexual Addiction and the DSM

The current *Diagnostic and Statistical Manual of Mental Disorders* (*DSM-IV-TR*) published by the American Psychiatric Association (APA, 2000) does not include sex and love addiction. After years of debate and review in formulation of the up-coming *DSM-V*, hypersexual disorder may be included in the appendix, but it won't be formulated as an addictive disorder. Instead, the diagnosis will be conceptualized as a behavioral problem similar to impulse control disorders. This lack of recognition of SLA as an addiction in the mental health field isn't unique and may reflect a larger issue regarding addictive disorders in the *DSM* in general. Support for process addictions, including SLA, recently received increased backing, including acknowledgment by the American Society of Addiction Medicine (ASAM) that sexual addiction is an addictive disorder.

ASAM now defines addiction as

> A primary, chronic disease of brain reward, motivation, memory and related circuitry. Dysfunction in these circuits leads to characteristic biological, psychological, social and spiritual manifestations. This is reflected in an individual pathologically pursuing reward and/or relief by substance use *and other behaviors* [emphasis added]. Addiction is characterized by inability to consistently abstain, impairment in behavioral control, craving, diminished recognition of significant problems with one's behaviors and interpersonal

relationships, and a dysfunctional emotional response. Without treatment or engagement in recovery activities, addiction is progressive and can result in disability or premature death. (ASAM.org, 2012)

The *DSM-IV* does, however, include diagnostic criteria for substance use and some behaviors that are often thought of as "addictive." The *DSM* lists nine criteria or signs and symptoms for chemical dependency, for example, with the presence of three establishing a diagnosis. It also uses the term *substance dependence* instead of *addiction* to indicate a maladaptive pattern of abuse resulting in clinically significant impairment or distress during a 12-month period. Many clinicians working with individuals who struggle with substance and process dependency undoubtedly use the terms *dependency* and *addiction* and sometimes *compulsivity* interchangeably, which is a practice used in this text.

The *DSM* also includes diagnostic criteria for not only the use of substances, but also pathological gambling, a behavior that's generally considered addictive. For pathological gambling, the manual lists 10 criteria, with the presence of five or more establishing a diagnosis (see Figure 3). The DSM states that the essential feature of pathological gambling is "persistent and recurrent maladaptive gambling behavior that disrupts personal, family, or vocational pursuits" (APA, 2000, p. 671). Moreover, early work by Schneider (1991) identifies that most of the criteria for diagnosing "dependence" concerns behavior related to decreased control, preoccupation with obtaining and using the substance (or engaging in the behavior), and the continued use despite negative consequences. These characteristics are normally considered the hallmarks of "addiction" and line up with the characteristics that are seen clinically in FSLAs.

DSM Criteria for Pathological Gambling

(5 or more criteria in a 12-month period)

Is preoccupied with gambling
Needs to gamble with increasing amounts of money to achieve the desired excitement
Has repeated unsuccessful efforts to control, cutback, or stop gambling
Is restless or irritable when attempting to cut down or stop gambling
Gambles as a way of escaping from problems or of relieving a dysphoric mood
After losing money gambling, often returns another day to get even
Lies to conceal the extent of involvement with gambling
Has committed illegal acts to finance gambling
Has jeopardized or lost a significant relationship, job, or educational or career opportunity because of gambling
Relies on others to provide money to relieve a desperate financial situation caused by gambling

Figure 3

Source: DSM-IV-R

Sex and love addiction is more closely analogous to pathological gambling, which is also considered a process, rather than substance, addiction. Despite the endorsement by ASAM, debate continues within the clinical and medical communities about whether sexual and relationship behavior can be "addictive" and should be included in the *DSM*. For our purposes in identifying and treating the female SLA, it's safe to assert that no matter if and when the DSM accepts this condition as valid and includes some term to describe it, the problem is real and negatively affects millions of women.

Diagnostic Interview

A structured interview is one assessment method to assist in identifying symptoms and determining whether or not the problem is SLA. What's most important is that the clinician feels competent and skilled in whatever method she or he is using for this process. It is important to conduct an evaluation with an open mind and clinical objectivity at this phase. As part of any clinical assessment, it's also important to fully assess for suicidal or homicidal ideations. Women attempt suicide over their lifetime three to four times more than males (Samoon, 2010) and clinicians need to ask directly if the SLA is having thoughts of self-harm. As noted earlier, it's imperative to evaluate the FSLA's coping skills before delving deeper into the shaming aspects of her addictive behavior and her history of trauma. Remember, addiction is fundamentally a dissociative process and is used to medicate shame and pain. If you target the FSLA's deeply ingrained maladaptive coping mechanism before she's acquired adaptive skills to manage difficult feeling states or behaviors, you may inflict unintentional consequences.

The Sample Forms section of the Appendix provides a suggested questionnaire for a diagnostic interview. These questions aren't exhaustive and are generally close-ended. It's best to reframe them according to both your own line of inquiry and your client's anxiety. Some of these questions can be asked directly or given as an assignment for the FSLA to complete for the following session. Often clients have periods of cognitive blocking when asked open-ended questions, especially as part of an initial session. If you sense this is the case, allow the client time to formulate her answers more fully to yield better results. Workbooks and assessment sheets can also help the FSLA provide information about herself. Be sure, though, your client has privacy and safety at home before asking her to complete information outside of sessions. As you become more experienced with this population, you'll integrate your own wisdom into the process. Using supervisors and consultants is also highly recommended if you don't frequently treat women who struggle with sex and love addiction.

Assessing for SLA

Females who present with distress due to their behaviors tied to sex and/or love often demonstrate common themes found among all addicts. As described in chapter 1, the FSLA engages in continued behaviors despite negative consequences. She experiences shame and a loss of integrity. She lies to herself and others, which is a hallmark of addictive behavior. Frequently she's made multiple attempts to stop the behaviors, and her failure has resulted in anxiety, pain, and further shame. A pattern of mood altering behaviors with failed attempts to stop is a key characteristic of an addictive process.

However, *you*, the clinician, are an excellent informal tool for identifying female SLA. As a guide, remember the directive to "listen, look, and feel." Listen to and look at the client, and notice your own bodily sensations and reactions.

Listen for her mother's psychological state during pregnancy (especially during the last trimester) and the first 18 months of the client's life. Listen also for early attachment problems with her primary caregiver, childhood trauma, continuing attachment problems, or constant indulgence in impersonal or dangerous sexual or romantic behavior. But listen, too, for positive attachments that may have healed some of the damage.

Look at her eyes. While in session, pay close attention to the client's tendency to avert her gaze. She's probably looking away to distance herself from you and her own feelings. Eye aversion often serves as a form of auto-regulation. Ironically, the same mechanism may be going on when she sexually objectifies others. For some female SLAs, "looking at" someone sexually is actually a strategy for emotional distancing, just as looking away is. Both actions come from her need to avoid getting intimately involved in order to protect herself from the hurt she habitually expects from others. You also need to be aware of cultural implications about eye contact and the meaning she attaches to the behavior. It's important to check out your observations and determine if something is a defense mechanism or a cultural response.

Feel your own feelings. Since an SLA usually hides her emotions from herself and others, you need to rely on your own emotional and somatic reactions as well as on your observations of the client. Ask her how she feels in the moment and share your feelings with her. For example, say, "I feel angry and sad that your father beat you. Do you experience any of those feelings, too?" or "My stomach feels queasy as I hear you talk about how horrible your living conditions were as a child."

Although it isn't always stressed, therapists need to use all of their senses, including smell, when present with a client. Notice whether the FSLA wears excessive fragrance. Can you smell alcohol on her breath, or a fruity scent, which can suggest possible diabetes? Does she lack self-care in her basic hygiene? Can you smell fecal odor or anything sour to suggest that she may have purged prior to your session?

Scent and odor can also have significance to the client's overall well being. Ask a client about her sense of smell, which is governed by a cranial nerve which is directly linked to subcortical regions of the brain. Smell can be a significant trigger for clients beyond their conscious awareness.

Assessment Tools

A variety of assessment tools or screening tests have been developed to address sexual acting out. The Women's Sexuality Survey utilized questions from three assessment tools: the W-SAST (P. Carnes, Green, & S. Carnes, 2010), Hypersexual Behavior Inventory (Reid, Garos, & Carpenter, 2011) and the Sexual Compulsivity Scale (Kalichman & Rompa, 1995). The survey also included a number of questions related to love and relationship addiction (www.loveaddiction.com) as described by Schaeffer (2009). In the analysis, Corley and Delmonico (2011) found that the FSLA group scored higher than the non-addict group on all three sex addiction/ hypersexual behavior subscales ($p<.001$ for each subscale). This finding indicates that those respondents who self-identified as a sex or love addict met criteria for sexual addiction/hypersexual behavior. Using one or more of these assessments can help you make an informed diagnosis and provide critical information about the impact of the woman's sexual and relationship behavior across a number of domains such as health, work and relationships. Following is a synopsis of a number of the most widely used instruments.

Sexual Addiction Screening Test - Women (W-SAST)

The W-SAST was developed by Patrick Carnes and O'Hara (2000) to adapt Carnes' original Sexual Addiction Screening Test (P. Carnes, 1989) for a female population. This instrument contains 25 *yes-no* items reflecting three components: (a) relationship disturbance, (b) preoccupation and loss of control, and (c) affect disturbance. A score of 13 or more indicates probable sexual addiction.

Sexual Addiction Screening Test - Revised (SAST-R)

Originally a 25-item test developed by Patrick Carnes (1989), the SAST-R was the first attempt at assessment of sex addiction and is widely considered one of the best. There were subsequent efforts to make SAST applicable to specific subgroups (P. Carnes & O'Hara, 2000; P. Carnes & Weiss, 2002) and in 2008 it was revised as the SAST-R 2.0, a 45-item self-administered questionnaire (P. Carnes et al., 2010). The current version consists of 20 core items that are relevant across gender and sexual orientation; an additional 25 items create subscales for heterosexual men, women, and homosexual men. A score of six or more on the first 20 questions indicates the likely presence of sexual addiction.

Sexual Dependency Inventory (SDI)

The SDI is a 179-item scale that is restricted in use to those who are Certified Sex Addiction Therapists (CSATs) by the Institute for Trauma and Addiction Professionals (IITAP) or have received specific training through IITAP. It measures 10 distinct sexual addiction categories: fantasy, seductive role playing, intrusive sex, voyeurism, exhibitionism, paying for sex, trading sex, pain exchange, exploitative sex, and anonymous sex (Delmonico, Bubenzer, & West, 1998), and respondents answer two questions pertaining to each category. Respondents use a Likert scale first to rate how often they engage in behaviors of each category ranging from 0 (*never*) to 5 (*very often*); and second to rate the power of each sexual addiction thought, behavior, feeling, or fantasy ranging from 0 (*no power*) to 5 (*very high power*). The higher the score, the greater the likelihood of a problem. In 2008 the SDI went through a revision (SDI-R 3.0) that changed the existing scales and added new ones. Additionally, it now assesses for attachment styles using the Experiences in Close Relationships Scale (ECS) by Fraley, Waller, and Brennan (2000).

Compulsive Sexual Behavior Inventory (CSBI)

The CSBI is a 25-item assessment designed by Coleman, Miner, Ohlerking, and Raymond (2001) that yields a total score and three subscales. The total scoring can range from 28–140 with higher scores indicating a problem with sexual addiction. The three subscales assess for (a) ability to *control* behavior; (b) *violence* and whether the experience of violence exists; and (c) history of *abuse*. Respondents rate each item on a 5-point Likert scale ranging from 1 (*very frequently*) to 5 (*never*).

Sexual Compulsivity Scale (SCS)

The SCS is a validated 10-item test originally created by Kalichman and Rompa (1995) to research high-risk sexual behavior among homosexual men. It has since been tested with various populations and assesses respondents' thoughts, feelings, and behaviors. Test-takers endorse items on a 4-point Likert scale ranging from 1 (*not at all like me*) to 4 (*very much like me*). The test is scored by totaling the answers for each question and dividing that sum by 10, which is the number of questions. Forty is the highest possible score, and a score above 30 indicates the possible presence of sexual addiction.

Hypersexuality Behavior Inventory (HBI)

Developed by Reid, Garos, and Carpenter (2011), the HBI is a list of 19 items that are scored based on a 5 point Likert scale from 1 (*never*) to 5 (*very often*). Scores range from 19–95 with 53 regarded as the cutoff score. The HBI measures three domains of hypersexual behavior: (a) control over sexual thoughts, urges and behavior; (b) consequences associated with hypersexual behavior; and (c) the extent to which an individual uses sex to cope with uncomfortable or unpleasant affective experiences. A higher score represents greater hypersexuality (Reid, Karim, McCrory, & Carpenter, 2010).

Internet Sexual Screening Tool (ISST-R)

Developed by Delmonico and Miller (2003) the original ISST assessed seven variables of online sexual behavior (OSB): sexual compulsivity, sexual behavior-social, sexual behavior-isolated, sexual spending, interest in online sexual behavior, non-home computer use for online sexual behavior, and accessing illegal sexual material. Delmonico and Miller revised the instrument to 177 *true/false* questions regarding sexual thoughts and behaviors while using the Internet.

Love Addiction Questionnaires

Although not a formal psychometric assessment like those mentioned above, a helpful starting point for FSLAs is a series of questionnaires developed by Schaeffer (2009). A self-administered questionnaire covers each of four areas that Schaffer terms love addiction, romance addiction, sexual addiction, and relationship addiction.

Formal Psychological Assessment

Referral to a clinician who specializes in formal personality, neuropsychology, and ability testing can be extremely valuable in evaluating and understanding the client's individual strengths and weaknesses. A thorough psychological assessment will often include instruments such as the Minnesota Multiphasic Personality Inventory-II, a Millon Clinical Multiaxial Inventory-III, and The Rorschach: The Comprehensive System. If there is concern regarding cognitive slippage or other neurological problems, a thorough neuropsychological evaluation is recommended and can free the client from underlying shame if a neuropsychological issue is noted. For example, the client no longer is "lazy" or "underachieving" when a learning disability is assessed. Instead, she's doing the best she can considering her limitations. Ability testing can be useful for treatment planning, and results can assist the clinician to discern subtle deficits that suggest possible organic changes or atypical processing issues.

Implications of Diagnosing

Duplicitous cultural messages around sexuality escalate shame for women who sexually act out. This behavior in women is seen as degrading and is described by words such as "whore," "slut," "nympho," "freak" and "bitch." Understanding addiction as a disease and not a moral failure enables addicted people to separate their shame from their behavior. However, an addictive label can also be a significant challenge. Calling pleasure driven sexual and relational behaviors an *addiction* is both freeing and constricting for the FSLA. It's freeing because for once there's a name to behaviors she has felt powerless to stop, and for possibly the first time the SLA feels understood by someone. This understanding and compassion gives her hope that she can improve her circumstances and experience healing.

On the other hand, defining and diagnosing an FSLA's condition as an addiction can feel limiting since it brings up shame and elicits negative self-statements. An FSLA often feels judged by friends and loved ones for not being able to stop acting out, and this criticism leads to isolation and self-recrimination. Receiving a "diagnosis" is pathologizing and carries negative connotations. It places the woman in a patriarchal medical system in which she is submissive to the medical authority that includes labels and treatments and judgments. For women who often have childhood trauma, the result is a possible regression to a childlike, voiceless state. An FSLA might try to exert control over the diagnostic process not so much from an unwillingness to admit her powerlessness, but as a means of maintaining voice in an anxiety laden situation. Clinicians need to be aware of the transference issues around childhood trauma and a medical model of disease management. Giving clients choices in decision-making around treatment options is one method of sharing control in the recovery process.

When integrating feminist and addiction theories, the clinician is encouraged to be careful in the use of patriarchal metaphors and how a male-centered perspective might influence the FSLA. If done properly, the use of the term *addiction* can serve as an intervention and raise awareness for the FSLA. By being direct, the therapist can serve as a catalyst for change. You are clarifying and educating about addiction, which challenges the cognitive distortions that have kept the female SLA in denial. The conversation has the potential to facilitate commitment to change through a tone of feminine, maternal, unconditional positive regard. Furthermore, you are speaking to the whole problem, not just parts of it. This approach is integrative and holistic and lacks the reductionist and positivistic approach that is often the norm. Past and current traumas and addiction consequences are taken into consideration. Attentive listening models appropriate care and concern for the FSLA.

DSM Diagnoses and Medical Conditions Related to Sexual Acting Out

Clinicians working with women who engage in sex and love addicted behaviors need to be familiar with possible primary and co-occurring primary disorders that can influence diagnosis and treatment. Following are a number of diagnoses included in the *DSM* that may be associated with a presentation of sex and love addiction, along with medical conditions and medications that may contribute to increased sexual behavior.

Sexual Disorder NOS

Sexual disorder not otherwise specified is characterized by the experience of marked feelings of inadequacy concerning a person's sexual performance or other traits related to self-imposed standards of masculinity or femininity. The person demonstrates distress about a pattern of repeated sexual relationships involving a succession of lovers who are experienced by the individual as things to be used. This is the "objectification" discussed in sexual addiction literature, in which the sexually addicted person uses people as objects for her personal satisfaction. Persistent or marked distress about sexual orientation can also be addressed under this diagnosis and isn't necessarily an indication of a compulsive or addictive disorder.

Paraphilia Disorders

Paraphilias refer to a cluster of behaviors associated with sexually arousing fantasies, behaviors or urges that generally deviate from the cultural norm. Little scientific research is available regarding paraphilias and much of what exists is within the context of sexual offending (Gordon, 2008; Marshall, Marshall, & Serran, 2006). Research regarding females with paraphilias is very limited, which likely reflects a cultural disbelief that women manifest sexually aberrant behaviors.

Paraphilias can be divided into offending and non-offending categories, although this position is not clearly defined as such in the *DSM-IV-TR*. Certain behaviors, although problematic for the client, aren't violent, offensive toward other people, or illegal. Examples include exhibitionism by a female in terms of provocative attire (which is considered socially acceptable) or exhibitionism as part of a female's work in the pornography industry (which is also considered socially acceptable). Another example is sado-masochistic role-play involving consenting partners that doesn't cause distress or impairment of functioning.

Other paraphilias are clearly illegal and violate the rights of others. Sexual exploitation of children, sexual assault ranging from frotteurism to overt rape, and in some states, bestiality are considered paraphilias. These behaviors are rare in women yet do occur.

Clinical judgment is warranted to assess for level of impairment in life functioning; otherwise, the clinician may over diagnose women for paraphilia when none exists. A novel sexual thought, feeling, or behavior that doesn't interfere with the rights of others or cause significant impairment in functioning is most likely not a paraphilia.

Delusional Disorder NOS

Under the area of delusional disorder NOS are two psychotic disorders that can be identified within FSLA individuals. In ***erotomania*** the person presents in a relatively functional psychotic state (Fitzgerald & Seeman, 2002). Often clinicians fail to recognize the psychosis and believe the client's description of a love affair. Her fantasy life has become her reality, and she's convincing in her descriptions and explanations. However, in erotomania the relationship is a delusional fantasy. Collateral information doesn't support the relationship and the object of affection denies any affair.

Examples of erotomania include teachers who have romantic and sexual relationships with children and identify a child as their "soul mate" and believe they'll have a future together. Individuals who stalk television personalities and therapists are also of concern. For example, Margaret Mary Ray believed she had a romantic relationship with talk show host David Letterman that resulted in numerous arrests for driving his car, telling people she was his wife, and breaking into his home. According to public record, she was diagnosed with schizophrenia and was vulnerable to poor reality testing. In fact, erotomania is known to be rather common in women with psychotic disorders. Ray's obsessive fixation with Letterman was delusional in nature and resulted in significant consequences including hospitalization and arrest. Unfortunately, her illness eventually resulted in her suicide.

Because erotomania is a psychotic disorder, the woman possesses a fixed belief about the nature of the relationship and is highly resistant to information that challenges the delusion. Clinicians should be cautious about challenging this delusion due to the risk for violence or further psychological decompensation. Hospitalization with medication stabilization is necessary.

In ***delusional disorder NOS of the jealous type***, the individual maintains a fixed belief that her partner is having a relationship with another person. This fixed belief persists despite all denials by the partner and all evidence to the contrary. Clinicians working with FSLAs need to be aware that some clients may report psychotic fantasies in a manner that initially presents as believable. When you challenge the logic of the delusional jealous fantasy, the client may put up significant resistance to the suggestion that other explanations exist for the partner's behavior. Agitation and outright rage can result. This extreme focus on the supposed infidelity or betrayal by the client's partner can mimic addictive characteristics. When taking a clinical history, be suspicious of delusional disorder if the FSLA maintains a fixed belief about her partner despite your multiple evaluations of that person that indicate otherwise.

Drugs and Medical Conditions Related to Acting Out

Certain drugs and medical conditions are associated with sex and love addiction. The dopamine agonists, Carbidopa/levodopa (Sinemet), Apomorphine (Apokyn, Ixense, Spontane, Uprima), Pramipexole (Mirapex, Mirapexin, Sifrol), and Ropinirole (Requip) are associated with an increase in sexual behaviors as well as compulsive gambling and shopping. Dopamine agonists are primarily prescribed for the treatment of Parkinson's disease, and recently some medications in this class have been approved for the treatment of restless leg syndrome. After the initiation of this medication a change in behavior may indicate that the client's sexual acting out behaviors are not a primary addiction. Further discussions with the client and her physicians would be warranted.

Certain antidepressant medications can influence sexual behavior. Buproprion, Trazadone, and the SSRIs (Selective Serotonin Reuptake Inhibitors), which are normally prescribed for mood and sleep disorders, can precipitate increased sexual behaviors in some individuals. Paradoxically, these same medications can sometimes assist a client with reducing obsessive thoughts, including sexual ones. It's imperative that the therapist consult and remain in contact with the client's physician to differentiate whether or not these medications are helping or hindering the FSLA's ability to utilize cortical top-down controls of her sexual drives.

Similarly, stimulants can also increase sexual behaviors as well as other salient drives. The use of stimulant medications is controversial in clients with an addiction history given their potential for abuse. Frequently prescribed for ADD/ADHD, this group of medications can increase sexual drive in some individuals. Again, caution is warranted and a thorough timeline is necessary to determine the cost-benefit ratio when utilizing stimulant medication in clients who engage in addictive behaviors. Certainly clinicians need to be cognizant of the influence these medications may have on sexual drives and consider the possibility that the medication itself may be the cause for hypersexual behavior. A drug holiday may further assist the clinician in determining the influence the stimulant medication may have on sexually driven behaviors. Again, this is a medical decision and requires consultation with the client's physician.

Androgens are another group of medications that have come into more frequent usage in recent years. Androgens such as testosterone can increase sexual drive and aggression in both men and women and are prescribed to both, especially at midlife or menopause. Women whose partners are using these substances as creams and who are exposed to androgens by body to body contact may notice an increase in their own sexual drive and aggression. Higher peak concentrations of testosterone are noted in people prescribed injectable forms of this hormone, and periods of heightened sexual desire may result.

Benzodiazepines influence sexual acting out behaviors by decreasing cortical controls over limbic drives. Benzodiazepines facilitate disinhibition, which can result in loss of control over sexual drives. Benzodiazepines don't necessarily increase sexual drive, but they facilitate acting out upon existing urges, fantasies, and behaviors by decreasing top-down controls.

Finally, some neuroleptics (Lamotrigine-Lamictal) and antihistamines (Cyproheptadine-Periactin) are associated with increased sexual drive. It's important that clinicians working with clients who are prescribed medications remain in collaboration with the prescribing physician to discuss problematic behaviors and other symptoms such as changes in mood or cognitive processing.

Medical Conditions

Medical conditions that negatively impact cortical control can also disinhibit the FSLA and result in atypical sexual behaviors. One medical condition known to increase sexual acting out includes neuro syphilis (tertiary stage). Syphilis is a spirochete bacterium that destroys brain tissue. When the prefrontal and orbitofrontal cortex is impacted, increased disinhibition occurs and a variety of impulsive and compulsive behaviors result. A type of acquired brain injury, tertiary syphilis can present with diverse symptoms depending upon the areas of brain damage. Similarly, injury to septal nuclei and lesions of the temporal lobes and hypothalamic regions can result in increased sexual behaviors. Frontal lobe lesions associated with traumatic brain injury (TBI) can also result in disinhibition.

TBI is an import issue in addiction given the prevalence of co-morbid drug and alcohol addiction among individuals with TBI. Conversely, a significantly disproportionate number of individuals with addiction have multiple TBI events that impact their ability to obtain and remain sober. Both TBI and addictive behaviors involve brain injuries, and sadly, individuals who return to drug use after TBI have poor brain rehabilitation outcomes, which furthers the cycle of addiction and brain injury. Women aren't immune to this cycle, and addiction makes them vulnerable to assault and other forms of victimization.

Co-occurring Disorders

Many women who struggle with sex and love addiction also suffer from an accompanying psychiatric disorder. It's important to identify any co-occurring disorder (formerly known as a "dual diagnosis") because both conditions often impact and influence each other. For example, a woman who acts out sexually may also be dealing with depression, and she seeks "love" partners to elevate her mood and feelings of self-worth. If the addiction is treated without addressing the underlying mood disorder, she's at high risk to relapse. Some of the more common co-occurring disorders are briefly discussed below.

Depressive Disorders

Addictions, including sexual addiction, are mood altering. Often they can circumvent or make worse underlying mental health concerns like depression or anxiety. Sometimes an Axis I diagnosis underlies and accompanies the FSLA's acting out behavior as a sort of self-medicating attempt to alter the experience of her depression.

A research study by Reid, Carpenter, Spackman, and Willes (2008), indicated that depression, poor stress management, and alexithymia are most closely associated with what Reed terms *hypersexuality*. Though this study has limitations regarding its generalization to FSLAs because only four of the 120 subjects were female, it does demonstrate some preliminary relevance since women tend to have higher rates of depression than men overall. In fact, women are two to three times more likely to develop dysthymia than men (Centers for Disease Control and Prevention, 2011).

Major depressive episodes with atypical features are two to three times more common in women (Halbreich & Kahn, 2007) and include features such as excessive guilt, personal rejection, sensitivity, and feeling as if one's arms and legs are heavy and made of lead. Female addicts are more prone to shame and depression then male addicts, who are more prone to detachment (O'Connor, Berry, Inaba, Weiss, & Morrison, 1994). In a large study of FSLAs using the W-SAST, depression was significantly correlated to sexual addiction (Opitz, Tsytsarev & Froth, 2009).

Dissociative Disorders

All addiction is dissociative in function. Altering mood through addictive behavior removes the FSLA from the reality of the discomfort she's experiencing in the moment. According to Gold and Seifer (2002), dissociation among people with sexual addiction is often a means of re-enacting childhood sexual abuse. Dissociation is a failure to integrate emotional intimacy with sexuality due to insecure or disorganized attachment and association of sexual activity with non-arousing experiences. Dissociative disorders include dissociative amnesia, dissociative fugue, depersonalization, dissociative identity disorder, and dissociative disorder NOS. Although these conditions are rare in the general population at only about 1%, they are seen in 5–20% of trauma survivors and 98% of patients hospitalized for psychiatric reasons (Sidran Traumatic Stress Institute, 2010). Since many FSLAs are trauma survivors and others are admitted to a psychiatric in-patient facility, the prevalence of dissociation about this population requires clinicians to be familiar with this diagnosis.

Loewenstein offers categories that warrant exploration with FSLA clients to identify possible dissociation (Loewenstein, 1994). Ask about blackouts or loss of time; behavior that isn't remembered (such as being told of behavior the client can't recall or awakening after evidence of sexual behavior that she doesn't remember); fugue states (not knowing how she got somewhere or not recognizing her surroundings); unexplained possessions (either acquired, created, or lost without any memory of them); changes in relationships, habits, or skills (significant changes in relationships, tastes, or abilities such as writing with the non-dominant hand); lapses in memory especially of childhood or significant life events; or experiences of depersonalization where the client feels like she's floating outside her body or is able to block out physical pain. If an FSLA identifies with any of these or similar symptoms, she likely is suffering from some level of dissociation that warrants further diagnostic exploration.

Post Traumatic Stress Disorder

Post traumatic stress disorder (PTSD) is a mood/anxiety condition that results from an experience of severe threat to self or other. Normally there is a clear and identifiable situation in which a threat to life is experienced. However, in many cases of complex stress disorders, the triggering event isn't clearly identified. PTSD is characterized by intrusive and avoidant features. Intrusive recollections are evidenced by traumatic nightmares, flashbacks, sympathetic nervous system arousal, and psychological reactions such as rumination, fear, and hypervigilance.

Avoidant and numbing symptoms include efforts to avoid traumatic thoughts, feelings, and activities. The development of addiction can be rooted in the addict's effort to numb out traumatic thoughts and feelings with her drug of choice, including sex and love addiction. In people with PTSD, psychogenic amnesia can occur, which renders the person without clear memory of the traumatic event.

People with PTSD often develop a restricted range of affect and quite possibly anhedonia. This emotional numbing is a means of coping with the constant and intolerable anxiety and an activated sympathetic nervous system. Emotional response to the physiological activation includes a lack of interest in life with feelings of doom, despair, hopelessness, and a sense of foreshortened future. People with PTSD are waiting for the next horrible thing to happen, and often it does, as people with PTSD are at higher risk for secondary traumas.

Disorders of Extreme Stress

Unlike PTSD, in which there is a clear and usually known threat, a type of complex trauma known as disorders of extreme stress (DES) is murkier in identifying critical events. DES is diffuse and cumulative with multiple, less obvious traumatic experiences building upon each other. Prolonged childhood abuse (especially sexual abuse), neglect, chronic illness, and growing up in an addictive family system are examples of diffuse traumas. Intrusive thoughts and hyper vigilance can also occur without a clear sense of the threat. Anxiety levels are elevated and the person often has little understanding of what a relaxed and balanced state feels like. Issues of trust result and people with DES can become avoidant. Sometimes they will overly trust and bond to hurtful or harmful people, thereby repeating traumatic relationships in their lives. In DES chronic fear alters the hippocampus, which results in difficulty integrating the sensory and cognitive nature of threats as well as effects regarding cognitive impairment, impulse control, aggression, and emotional dysregulation. These difficulties leave a woman at higher risk of problematic sexual and relationship behavior.

Substance Abuse or Dependence

Diagnosing protocol for FSLAs must include a basic assessment for chemical addiction. Although little research specifically explores women with co-occurring chemical and SLA disorders, alcohol is a well-known facilitator in sexual acting out because of its ability to disinhibit. Going to a bar, having a few drinks and then leaving with a stranger for anonymous and risky sex is a frequent pattern among FSLAs. Unfortunately, many alcoholic women with SLA go untreated for the behavior addiction because traditional drug and alcohol treatment providers fail to recognize this pattern.

Using crack cocaine and having sex in exchange for drugs is prevalent and society even names such women, "crack whores." Cannabis, opioids, and nicotine all have sexual patterns. Research with marijuana indicates that men are sexually inhibited with cannabis whereas women cannabis users are sexually disinhibited (Gorzalka, Hill, & Chang, 2010). Obviously, then, any woman who admits to using marijuana should be assessed for sex and love addiction. FSLAs who also abuse drugs or alcohol may be at greater risk for sexual violence simply by the co-occurrence of substances as immobilizer agents such as the so-called "date rape" drug.

Rapid assessment instruments such as the CAGE (Ewing, 1984) can be a starting point for evaluating drug abuse issues. It's critical to understand that substance abuse and SLA disorders often interact so strongly that a woman is apt to struggle with obtaining sobriety without significant support. For example, FSLAs with substance disorders are at risk for "13th Stepping" behaviors at Alcoholics Anonymous or Narcotics Anonymous meetings, which is slang for being propositioned by another (supposedly sober) attendee for a sexual or romantic hook up. Cravings and physical complications from drug and alcohol abuse can be deterrents in SLA recovery. A woman may return to mood-altering substances to medicate her anxiety or SLA withdrawal and vice versa.

Eating Disorder

Eating disorders are a significant concern to monitor when working with women with sexual addictions. Although very little research is available examining the relationship between eating disorders and sexual addiction, some studies have emerged examining eating disorders and other addictive behaviors. Wiederman (1996), in a review of multiple research studies regarding women with eating disorders and their sexuality, found some general relationships among anorexic women and bulimic women. Namely, anorexic women tended to have negative views about sexuality and be engaged in less sexual behaviors than a control group. Bulimic women, in contrast, were more likely to engage in more frequent sexual encounters than controls. Both groups had less satisfaction and more overall problems around sexual issues than controls. Numerous studies suggest that food, gender, and sexuality are linked phenomenon.

Many clinicians are familiar with female SLAs who have struggled with a weight problem for years and vacillate between their sexual acting out and disordered eating. When they're controlling their food and maintaining a normal weight, they act out sexually. When the shame from SLA gets overwhelming, they binge eat and gain weight in order to appear less attractive to potential partners, which serves as a protective measure against acting out in their sex and love addiction. This pattern becomes a vicious cycle. Although the disordered eating may not rise to a clinical diagnostic level, it's important to address food issues for women struggling with SLA.

Similarities between chemical addiction and eating disorders are noted in multiple studies. Certainly, a relationship exists. According to Root et al. (2010), the prevalence of drug and alcohol abuse is approximately 50% in individuals with an eating disorder, compared with a prevalence of approximately 9% in the general population. Similarly, among individuals with substance use disorders, over

35% report having an eating disorder compared with a 1–3% prevalence of eating disorders in the general population. Of theoretical importance is that among persons with some form of an eating disorder, substance addictions are more common among those who binge eat.

Clinicians working with FSLAs need to be aware of this significant risk for comorbid and interactive addictive behaviors and screen for them aggressively. Instruments such as the CAGE for alcohol (Ewing, 1984), PATHOS for sex (P. Carnes et al., 2012) and the SCOFF for eating disorders (Morgan, Reid, & Lacey, 1999) can be useful instruments to prioritize the evaluation process. Additional measures include the Body Attitudes Test, Eating Attitudes Test, Body Attitudes Questionnaire, and the Eating Disorder Examination Interview.

Somatic Symptoms

Women with traumatic stress disorders often present with complaints of somatic symptoms. Examples include gastrointestinal distress symptoms such as chronic constipation, increased gastric motility, gastric ulcers, and other stress related gastric conditions. Increased urine catecholamines are present, which reflects exposure to chronic stressors. The immune system is less effective and healing is slower. Corticosteroid levels are elevated while cortical fatigue can occur. Clinicians working with FSLAs need to assess for the presence of traumatic stress related somatic conditions, as medical complications can compound recovery from trauma and sexual addiction.

Personality Disorders

The use of personality disorder diagnoses is also an area of controversy. Many addictions therapists defer on the use of these diagnoses due to the notion of the fixed nature of an Axis II disorder. The use of fixed labels can be damaging to some FSLAs as it re-enforces a sense of defectiveness that they are helpless to overcome. Generally, it's recommended that therapists defer a confirmed diagnosis of Axis II disorder for about two years post sobriety to allow for affect regulation and therefore the personality stabilization that results after enough time has passed for the brain to heal.

Conceptualizing personality traits as an attachment problem can. be helpful in that attachment problems are considered manifestations of affect dysregulation, which lead to disorders of the self. These traits, then, are malleable as the client becomes more regulated through her therapy, and they may diminish or soften as she repairs aspects of herself.

Differential Diagnoses

Understanding differential diagnostic issues is an important aspect of the clinical approach to client care for FSLAs, because sexual acting out behaviors can occur for a variety of reasons. Addiction, mood disorders, and even brain tumors can present with problematic behaviors involving sex and relationships. It's important to differentiate between sex and love addiction and other disorders because effective treatment is based on an accurate diagnosis.

Impulse Control Disorder

Impulse control disordered behaviors are generally harmful behaviors in which the person experiences increased tension and arousal before the behavior is performed. Pleasure, gratification, and relief at the time of the act are also reported. There is a failure to resist the impulse and there may not be regret, reproach, or guilt after the impulsive behavior.

According to Goodman (2001) the *DSM* description of impulse control disorder is a generalized diagnosis. Although it does accurately characterize the sexual syndrome of sexual addiction, it also defines a number of other driven behaviors. Use of this diagnosis isn't appropriate if another more specific diagnosis is available, such as a paraphilic disorder. Some subtle diagnostic concerns arise in utilizing such a generalized diagnosis. For example, the progression seen in addiction isn't inherent in Impulse Control Disorder. Neither is tolerance. While some clinicians may use this diagnosis, it requires a careful explanation to clarify the impulsive behaviors associated with the condition, because the client's behaviors will not be readily identified by another clinician.

Interestingly, pathological gambling is noted under the diagnosis of Impulse Control Disorder, and gambling presents with an addictive clinical course. Conditions also captured by this diagnosis include Intermittent Explosive Disorder, Kleptomania, Pyromania, and Trichotillomania. According to the *DSM*, this diagnosis may not be appropriate if another diagnosis in the *DSM* better describes the person's underlying problems. For example, the paraphilias may best describe some sexual acting out behaviors. Impulse Control Disorder behaviors are interactive with other compulsive and or addictive behaviors. However, this diagnosis may not best describe the complex issues associated with persons who present as sexually addicted.

Obsessive Compulsive Disorder

Obsessive compulsive thoughts and behaviors are highly anxiety driven conditions that are rarely initiated as a pleasurable activity. More often these conditions are a function of negative obsession, followed by a behavior that controls the underlying fear. Counting, checking, hand washing, and organization are examples of OCD behaviors. OCD is a condition of control, and beneath control there is quite often anxiety and fear.

An example is helpful to illustrate the differences between OCD and other addictive or compulsive disorders. A woman presented to an outpatient practice to address a concern her family had about her behavior. She admitted her behaviors were unusual, but without her ritual she felt overwhelmingly anxious. She reported that she was driven to engage in a nightly bedtime ritual. Upon retiring for the evening, she would walk down the stairs of her home, walk past the television and turn down the volume whether the TV was on or not. She would then proceed to the kitchen and turn each of the gas knobs on the stove to be certain they were off. She did this for hours each night and no one could redirect or alter her pattern. In fact, when her family tried, she became increasingly agitated. This ongoing behavior is what prompted her visit.

Unlike addiction, which is rooted in pleasure, OCD entails fear of harm or unpleasant consequences. The compulsion serves to reduce anxiety. The woman described above expressed no pleasure in her compulsion and didn't look forward with anticipation to engaging in the behavior. Her ritual was rooted in anxiety and fear. Her story revealed that when she was a young child, she watched a neighbor family being removed from their home after being asphyxiated from carbon monoxide. Their deaths were highly traumatic and caused significant anxiety. Her compulsions relieved the anxiety, which enabled her to sleep each night.

Obsessive compulsive disorder isn't primarily driven by pleasure. The intent of the ritual is to minimize anxiety (*DSM 3 R*, *DSM IV TR*), and the behavior decreases the tension. Whereas addiction can progress to a condition that appears to be compulsive, the initial pleasure component is crucial to understanding the mood altering aspects of addiction.

Bipolar Disorder

Bipolar disorder can present with sexual acting out behavior that is reflected during periods of increased energy. In some individuals there is increased agitation and even euphoria associated with the condition. The manic experience is described as occurring across all domains of the woman's behavior, not just sexually. It often presents as grandiosity and over confidence. Females with bipolar disorder will report less need for sleep during the manic phase. Sexual acting out in bipolar disorder tends to be a function of the impulsivity and experience of mania. In contrast, sexually addicted people will act out sexually in an effort to alter and medicate depressed and anxious moods. In bipolar disorder, the sexual acting out doesn't necessarily alter mood. Conversely, it is the mood that alters behavior.

Unlike the FSLA, the woman with bipolar disorder is often much less interested in usual activities during the depressed phase and may not engage in sexual behaviors during that time. Appetite and sleep patterns change and can reflect vegetative symptoms. Despair, restlessness, and irritability are often present as well as intrusive thoughts of suicide and death. It's imperative for clinicians to assess for suicide and homicide risk in individuals with mood and addictive disorders as they are at particular risk.

Considerations for Treatment Planning

Information gleaned from the various diagnostic tools can answer important questions that influence treatment planning. These include: What is the preferred problem-solving style of this woman? Is she more likely to use her thoughts and logic or her feelings in her approach to problem solving? Is her problem solving style well developed? Is it flexible or rigid? If she doesn't have a well-developed problem solving style and instead goes back and forth with neither avenue being adequate, what's the best way to help her strengthen one style that will best suit her? For example, if a woman doesn't have a well-developed problem solving style and she's easily overwhelmed with emotion, it's best to move her in the direction of a more logical and reasoned style. Likewise, if she is thought disordered, it may be best to strengthen her intuition based on her feelings for more effective problem solving.

The clinician will need to assess the FSLA's ability to participate in creating the treatment plan. The client needs to always be part of this process no matter how impaired she may be in the beginning of her healing. Clinicians are urged to make the following assessments and re-evaluate periodically:

1. What is the quality of her thinking? Is there cognitive slippage? Does she demonstrate symptoms of borderline personality or psychosis? Does she have a disorganized style of attachment? Is a diagnosis of Delusional Disorder NOS (erotomanic type) appropriate?

2. What is the nature of her ideation? Is she overly global in her thinking or rather too narrowly focused? What is the quality of her focus and concentration? Are there indications of attention deficit/hyperactivity disorder or bipolar disorder? Are there significant cognitive distortions? Is she tangential in her thinking? What is the quality of her reality testing?

3. What is the nature of her interpersonal relationships? Are her relationships "up close and personal" or does she prefer "arm's length" space? Is she interested in

others? If she's isolated, is it by choice? Is she avoidant and/or dependent in her relationships? Does she see others accurately or does she misinterpret social/ interpersonal cues? Does she have an accurate view of herself? Does she or doesn't she expect to collaborate or cooperate with others? Is she narcissistic in her approach with an overly self-centered world-view? Does she demonstrate empathy?

4. In general, what is her attachment style and how does it shape the characterlogical underpinnings of her personality? How do these factors manifest in her relationships?
5. What is the nature of her defenses and what is the best way to help her to utilize higher functioning defenses and relinquish primitive defenses (denial, minimization, projection)?
6. What is her relationship to authority? Is she oppositional or antisocial? Can she manage her emotions, particularly her anger? If she can control her emotions, does she or doesn't she choose to do so? Is she suicidal or homicidal? Is she self-injurious?
7. What is the quality of her judgment and can she adequately anticipate the consequences of her behavior?
8. Does she identify with real people and have opportunities to do so, or is there an abuse of fantasy or imagination?
9. To what degree is she able to introspect? What is her level of insight and intelligence?
10. Does she demonstrate adequate social skills? Does she have a support system?
11. What is her experience of locus of control?
12. What are her characteristic strengths and how can these be mobilized and utilized to motivate her to continue in treatment to a successful conclusion, including ongoing recovery?

Sharing the Diagnostic Results

When the evaluation is complete, time should be set aside to go over the results with the client. Typically, a two-hour session is ideal to deliver the results in a thorough and sensitive manner. It's always best to explain that formal evaluations, which include testing, are never perfect, and the female SLA is welcome to comment and give feedback regarding her perception of the results and their accuracy. It is generally accepted protocol that raw data isn't given directly to the client, but can be shared with other licensed clinicians who are trained to interpret it. However, if resources permit, a report designed specifically for the client can be given to her. You should explain that the results of her evaluation may be used by subsequent therapists in treatment planning, which saves considerable time and energy and will result in more accurate and timely intervention.

Once a body of information regarding the client is obtained, it's recommended that you conceptualize her difficulties into a working hypothesis, which becomes the assigned diagnosis. This diagnosis is best viewed as a living process that's malleable. At this point you can also share with the client a preliminary treatment plan, which has integrated the results of the evaluation to make sure that it's individualized and suitable for her particular circumstances. Treatment considerations, approaches, and specific methodologies are discussed in Part Two.

Contributing Writers

Deborah Corley - Assessment Tools

Alexandra Katehakis - Assessing

Anna Valenti-Anderson - Sex Addiction and the DSM

REFERENCES

American Psychiatric Association. (2000). *Diagnostic and statistical manual of mental disorders* (4th ed.). Washington, DC: Author.

American Society of Addiction Medicine. (2012). DSM criteria for diagnosis. Retrieved from http://www.asam.org/definitionofaddiction-longversion.html

Carnes, P. (1989). *Contrary to love: Helping the sexual addict.* Minneapolis, MN: CompCare.

Carnes, P., Green, B., & Carnes, S. (2010). The same yet different: Refocusing the sexual addiction screening test (SAST) to reflect orientation and gender. *Sexual Addiction & Compulsivity, 17*(1), 7-30. doi:10.1080/10720161003604087

Carnes, P. J., Green, B. A., Merlo, L. J., Polles, A., Carnes, S., & Gold, M.S. (2012). PATHOS: A brief screening application for assessing sexual addiction. *Journal of Addiction Medicine,* 6(1), 29-34.

Carnes, P., & O'Hara, S. (2000). *The Women's Sexual Addiction Screening Test.* Unpublished measure, Wickenburg, AZ.

Carnes, P., & Weiss, R. (2002). *The Sexual Addiction Screening Test for Gay Men.* Unpublished measure, Wickenburg, AZ.

Centers for Disease Control and Prevention. (2011). Retrieved from http://www.cdc.gov/mentalhealth/data_stats/depression.htm

Coleman, E., Miner, M., Ohlerking, F., & Raymond, N. (2001). Compulsive sexual behavior inventory: A preliminary study of reliability and validity. *Journal of Sex and Marital Therapy*, *27*, 325–332.

Corley, M. D., & Delmonico, D. (2011, September). *Closing the gap: Results from the Women's Sexuality Survey on Female Sex and Love Addicts.* Presentation at Society for the Advancement of Sexual Health Conference, La Jolla, CA.

Courtois, C., Ford, J., & Cloitre, M. (2009). Best practices in psychotherapy for adults. In C. Courtois & J. Ford (Eds.),*Treating complex traumatic stress disorders: An evidence-based guide* (pp. 82-103). New York, NY: Guilford Press.

Delmonico, D. L., Bubenzer, D. L., & West, J. D. (1998). Assessing sexual addiction with the sexual dependency inventory-revised. *Sexual Addiction & Compulsivity*, *5*(3), 179.

Delmonico, D. L., & Miller, J. (2003). The Internet Sex Screening Test: A comparison of sexual compulsives versus non-sexual compulsives. *Sexual and Relationship Therapy*, *18*(3),261-276.

Ewing, J. A. (1984). Detecting alcoholism: The CAGE questionnaire. *Journal of Addiction Medicine*,*252*,1905-1907.

Fitzgerald, P., & Seeman, M. (2002). Erotomania in women. In J. Boon & L. Sheridan (Eds.), *Stalking and psychosexual obsession: Psychological perspectives for prevention, policing and treatment* (pp. 165-180). Hoboken, NJ: Wiley & Sons Press.

Fraley, R. C., Waller, N. G., & Brennan, K. A. (2000). An item-response theory analysis of self-report measures of adult attachment. *Journal of Personality and Social Psychology*, *78*, 350-365.

Gold, S., & Seifer, R. (2002). Dissociation and sexual addiction/compulsivity: A contextual approach to conceptualization and treatment. *Journal of Trauma and Dissociation*, *3*(4), 59-82.

Goodman, A. (2001). What's in a name? Terminology for designating a syndrome of driven sexual behavior. *Sexual Addiction & Compulsivity*, *8*(3-4), 191-213.

Gordon, H. (2008). The treatment of paraphilia: A historical perspective. *Criminal Behavior and Mental Health*, *18*, 79-87.

Gorzalka, B. B., Hill, M. N., & Chang, S. C. (2010).Male-female differences in the effects of cannabinoids on sexual behavior and gonadal hormone function. *Hormones and Behavior*, *58*(1), 91-96.

Halbreich, U., & Kahn, L. (2007). Atypical depression, somatic depression and anxious depression in women: Are they gender-preferred phenotypes? *Journal of Affective Disorders, 102*(1), 245-258.

Kalichman, S. C., & Rompa, D. (1995). Sexual sensation seeking and sexual compulsivity scales: Reliability, validity and HIV risk behavior. *Journal of Personality Assessment, 65*, 586–601.

Loewenstein, R. J. (1994). Diagnosis, epidemiology, clinical course, treatment, and cost effectiveness of treatment for dissociative disorders and MPD: Report submitted to the Clinton administrative task force on health care financing reform. *Dissociation*, 3-11.

Marshall, W. L., Marshall, L. E., & Serran, G.A. (2006). Strategies in the treatment of paraphilia: A critical review. *Annual Review of Sex Research,17,* 162-182.

Morgan, J., Reid, F., & Lacey, J. H. (1999). The SCOFF questionnaire: Assessment of a new screening tool for eating disorders. *British Medical Journal, 319*(7223), 1467-1468.

O'Connor, L., Berry, J., Inaba, D., Weiss, J., & Morrison, A. (1994). Shame, guilt and depression in men and women in recovery from addiction. *Journal of Substance Abuse Treatment,11*(6), 503-510.

Opitz, D., Tsytsarev, S., & Froh, J. (2009). Women's sexual addiction and family dynamics, depression, and substance abuse. *Sexual Addiction & Compulsivity,16*(4), 324-340.

Reid, R., Carpenter, B., Spackman, M., & Willes, D. (2008). Alexithymia, emotional instability, and vulnerability to stress proneness in patients seeking help for hypersexual behavior. *Journal of Sex & Marital Therapy, 34*(2), 133-149.

Reid, R., Garos, S., & Carpenter, B. (2011). Reliability, validity, and psychometric development of the hypersexual behavior inventory in an outpatient sample of men. *Sexual Addiction & Compulsivity,18*(1), 30-51.

Reid, R., Karim, R., McCrory, E., & Carpenter, B. (2010) Self-reported differences on measures of executive function and hypersexual behavior in a patient and community sample of men. *International Journal of Neuroscience, 120*(2), 120-127.

Root, T., Poyastro Pinheiro, A., Thornton, L., Strober, M., Fernandez-Aranda, F., Brandt, H., . . . Bulik, C. (2010). Substance use disorders in women. *International Journal of Eating Disorders, 43*(1), 14-21.

Samoon, A. (2010) Suicide and substance abuse. In D. Brizer& R. Castaneda (Eds.), *Clinical addiction psychiatry* (pp. 37-44). Cambridge, UK: Cambridge University Press.

Schaeffer, B. (2009). *Is it love or is it addiction?* (3rd ed.). Minneapolis, MN: Hazelden.

Schneider, J. (1991). How to recognize the signs of sexual addiction: Asking the right questions may uncover serious problems. *Postgraduate Medicine, 90*(6), 171-182.

Sidran Traumatic Stress Institute. (2010). What are dissociative disorders? *Sidran Institute.* Retrieved from www.sidran.org

Wiederman, M. (1996). Substance use among women with eating disorders. *International Journal of Eating Disorders, 20*, 163-168.

Part Two

Treatment Philosophies and Practices for Female Sex and Love Addicts

CHAPTER 4

Therapeutic Considerations and Settings

Marnie Ferree, Alexandra Katehakis, Kelly McDaniel
with contributions by Anna Valenti-Anderson, Jill Vermeire

Clinical training provides therapists with a guideline to cause no harm. Unfortunately, however, harm is broadly defined, and many of the covert ways clinicians cause harm to their clients aren't covered in degree programs. One critical way to cause harm is failing to grasp the importance of the therapeutic relationship and the application of this truth to working with a female population—a wounded, attachment-impaired, shame-based one at that. Since sex and love addiction isn't part of the *DSM*, preparation for treating this population is largely non-existent. Even with more prevalent compulsions such as drug and alcohol addiction, graduate students are rarely trained within the structure of academic institutions to properly understand the nature of the addictive system. Yet the foundation for treatment, like the recovery process itself, is "simple, but not easy" (a recovery slogan) and it rests on the clinician's ability to form a positive therapeutic alliance (Luborsky, McLellan, Woody, O'Brien, & Uerbach, 1985).

Therapeutic Relationship

The APA Presidential Task Force (2006) states unequivocally, "Psychological practice is, at root, an interpersonal relationship between psychologist and patient" (p. 277). This assertion holds true regardless of the type of mental health practitioner. Magnavita (2006) adds, "The process of psychotherapy uses relational factors to stimulate healing and growth. The quality of the therapeutic relationship is probably the most robust aspect of therapeutic outcome" (p. 888). Indeed, today the majority of clinical thought views the therapeutic alliance as a critical, crucial, and even the most important variable in treatment success, regardless of treatment modalities (Cloitre, Stovall-McClough, Miranda, & Chemtob, 2004; Romano, Fitzpatrick, &

Janzen, 2008; Safran & Muran, 2000; Stern, 2008).

If we correctly view sex and love addiction as a problem of disordered regulation due to a fundamental attachment disorder, the importance of the therapeutic relationship becomes even more clear. If early attachment trauma results in later deficits in right brain affect regulation (Schore, 2012), it's not surprising FSLAs suffer with emotional reactions of high intensity and find it difficult (if not impossible) to maintain emotional and psychic stability. According to Schore, the best way to integrate the right and left hemisphere, which is a goal of successful therapy, is by working with the implicit right hemisphere significantly more than the left hemisphere. Therefore, it's vital that clinicians establish a right brain-to-right brain connection with the FSLA and remain attuned to the regulating mechanisms present in the therapeutic relationship. Simply put, good therapy involves good re-parenting. As was explained in chapter 2, the client who is securely attached, in this case to her therapist, can take the risk to explore her behavior patterns and her inner world.

In addition to understanding how an FSLA's impaired attachment impacts her relationship with you, being an effective therapist with this population requires you to understand the way women are wired to prioritize relationships, and women's unique psychological and developmental needs (Covington & Surrey, 2000; Siegel, 1999). Growth for women over the lifespan occurs in connection with others, and various theorists and clinicians have devoted their work to advancing this perspective. Since female SLA research and treatment is in its infancy, much can be gleaned from models that have preceded this field. Trauma, addiction, attachment, and relational-cultural theory are the fields most relevant to treating the female SLA. Relational-cultural psychology asserts that females rely on relationship and connection to form and define a self (McDaniel, 2012; Miller,1986; Miller, Jordan, Stiver, Surrey, & Kaplan, 1991). An awareness and appreciation of this psychology adds necessary clinical sensitivity for understanding the unique pain a woman faces when she examines her potential for sex and love addiction. She wonders, *How can I be addicted to the very thing I need for self-definition? How do I recover from something (or someone) so necessary?*

Research shows that the more a therapist facilitates a client's affective experience and its expression in psychotherapy, the more the client makes positive changes (Diener, Hilsenroth, & Weinberger, 2007). Exactly how this process works and the science behind it is explored in chapter 7. At this point, as you consider what it means to work effectively with FSLAs, you might reflect on your sensitivity to your clients' non-verbal expressions of emotional (attachment) experiences and how you might foster what's known as "corrective emotional experiences."

How Treating Women Differs From Treating Men

Men and women have different brains. Clinicians have long recognized that therapeutic interventions that work with one gender don't necessarily translate to the opposite gender. The same is true when treating sex and love addiction.

Using the Tasks

Many in the sex addiction field recognize Patrick Carnes' Task Model (Carnes, 2006) as part of the standard of care for sex addicts. These 30 tasks are described in resources and workbooks that typically focus on the first days and months of recovery. For addicts, tasks are critical for healing damaged brain chemistry and attaining healthy relational skills. At the same time, the recovery tasks have been designed for a male brain. Like most medical interventions that have been tested and researched using male bodies, sex addiction research is focused on men.

However, men and women approach tasks differently. Remember, women are more hard-wired for relationship, and this brain-based outlook influences how women experience the Task Model, which is largely cognitive-behavioral or left brain. Men may see the task as an opportunity to "get to work," "get something done," and "move on." A woman may view the same task as either a movement away from her therapist ("I just want to talk") or a distancing mechanism ("Can't you handle me?").

A task represents an action step, which is positive and important, but for women is best done in connection with you, her therapist. A female will better respond to the task and have more chance of completing it if she's in the room with you. Left alone or sent home to complete the work represents further isolation for the female SLA. It requires that she move from her right brain, which is busy connecting to you, into her left brain, which is already taxed from taking measures to get help and trying to figure things out. Alone, she may have trouble concentrating or sitting still. With you, she can use both parts of her brain more effectively because she's safe, connected, and therefore, she has more energy. Whereas a male client may appreciate your delegating the tasks as homework, be aware that a female client may see the same gesture as dismissive and find herself unable to complete the task, which is a set-up for more shame.

When used supportively at the right time, the recovery tasks can be helpful for FSLAs. The Task Model has extensive recommendations for specific tasks, and some are more helpful than others for any specific client. Generally speaking, certain tasks such as making a secrets list, romantic timeline, problems list, and understanding the addictive cycle have proven effective in assisting women SLAs. At the same time, these task assignments are best used as opportunities to bond and connect. Be sure to incorporate your understanding of the female brain, her need for attachment, and her sensitivity to shame. *Be with her in the process.*

Avoiding Covert Betrayal of Enmeshment

In the formative years for many SLAs parental abandonment takes the form of enmeshment. As a result, an adult woman may come to therapy unconsciously or consciously expecting to be used, needed, or otherwise taken advantage of. Her vulnerability requires that her defenses are up, which can manifest through behaviors like flirting with you (regardless of gender), challenging you, talking rapidly, keeping secrets, wearing seductive clothing, or bringing small gifts early in the process.

The client needs you to be keenly aware of the abusive nature of enmeshment and filter her defensive strategies as her efforts at self-protection. Understand that her defense mechanisms have been necessary to keep her from being engulfed. Practice good boundaries while fostering a warm relationship that avoids enmeshment. Move slowly and allow the FSLA the time she needs to feel safe. In general, the therapeutic work is paced more slowly with women SLAs than it is with men.

Role of the Therapist

Working in the field of love and sex addiction means you're working in the sophisticated arena of human needs, fears, and the tenacious adaptations that protect women from these emotions. You're working with clients who have experienced a lifetime of attachment injuries, and protection from harm is critical for the treatment of women addicted to love, sex, and relationships. They have no reason to trust, limited ability to bond, and they endure incredible pain within the healing process. As with sexual abuse survivors, this population is watching for and accustomed to betrayal and abandonment from authority figures. Most SLAs don't recognize abuse in its many forms, yet they are uniquely tuned into myriad threats. Their intuitive guide has been distorted by addiction and can mislead them. A woman's addiction serves to insulate her from emotional pain while simultaneously thwarting her innate ability to register "warning" and "danger."

Her first experience with safety may be with you, her therapist. You will set the template for secure, safe attachment. You'll need to keep this responsibility at the forefront of your mind in treatment even though the female SLA may appear invulnerable and/or immune to emotional pain.

In order to facilitate a relationship with your client, you must have an intimate, healthy relationship with yourself. This includes your own time for personal reflection, fun, and self-care. You'll be most effective if you are steady and committed to your own therapy. Be vigilant and tender with the dark places in your psyche that you want no one to see, as this process will help you be reverent and humble in the face of the women you treat. Stay mindful of how difficult it is to trust, bond, and heal your own attachment injuries. Recognize, then, how much more difficult it likely is for the female sex and love addict.

Therapist's Gender

Opinions vary about the appropriateness of a clinician treating an opposite gender client when the issue is sex and love addiction. Many believe the best practice is for the client and therapist to be the same gender, especially early in the client's recovery process. Others believe the therapeutic relationship is more important than the gender match. Clearly, there's no hard and fast rule in this area, and the issue is complicated by the relatively limited number of clinicians trained in treating SLA and the even smaller number of females seeking treatment for the problem. The important factor is to take into account a number of therapeutic considerations in relation to the therapist's gender.

Female clients often perceive authority figures with suspicion, and gender plays a factor. Some women will avoid a female therapist for fear of competition and feelings of inferiority. Because of their maternal and cultural wounds, most FSLAs don't connect well with women. To enter a therapeutic relationship with another female is simply too vulnerable and frightening. At the same time, other FSLAs will avoid a male therapist for fear of being abused, or of acting out with a male. Some female clients, though, may be drawn to working with men based on a tendency to put men on a pedestal, a belief they'll be able to manipulate a male therapist, or perhaps out of a deep distrust of women.

The reality is that male and female clinicians can both work effectively with female sex and love addicted clients. In fact, each gender can provide a healing, corrective experience regarding maternal and paternal wounds. The crucial factor is the personal health and appropriateness of the therapist. The clinician's power within the therapeutic relationship is immense, and it must be safely harnessed. The female SLA may be used to sexualizing all relationships, for example, and she'll continue that practice with her therapist. If the professional hasn't addressed his or her own vulnerabilities around sexuality and the lure of dependent relationships, the so-called helper can easily become an exploitive wounder.

The wise clinician takes prudent therapeutic cautions when working with a straight client of the opposite gender (or a homosexual client of the same gender). Schedule appointments when others are in the building, for example. Have a small window in the door entering your office, and position yourself so that you're visible (and the client's identity is obscured) by anyone who happens to glance in. Be especially careful with self-disclosure and therapeutic touch, which each might be misconstrued. Seek supervision if you're attracted to a client, and report a client's statements of attraction toward you to a supervisor or trusted colleague. As a bottom line, do your own healing work and practice scrupulously appropriate boundaries.

Approach

Whether you are male or female, it's important for the therapist to be both direct and empathic in order to gain the FSLA's trust. This approach is generally standard when working with addicts. Most have tried everything they know to do in their efforts to arrest their acting out behaviors, and SLAs need you to provide a clear roadmap to healing. Remember, addictive behavior is supported by faulty thinking, and therapists and recovering people often remind addicts of the recovery slogan, "Your own best thinking got you here."

At the same time many of your recommendations may be dismissed, or the client may balk at what you propose despite how understanding and responsive you are. In part this reaction is due to her shame at her dependence on the behavior, and her uncertain commitment to change. Remain firm in your direction regarding best practices for arresting addiction (outlined in chapter 6) while offering acceptance and the right to self-determination. Your responsibility is to provide the roadmap; it's the client's responsibility to choose her way.

Role of Setting: Wardrobe, Energy, Touch and Environment

Part of creating successful treatment for women SLAs is very personal. You must be aware of your gender, body, and office as instrument. How you dress, conduct yourself, and arrange your office is a critical part of treatment. Your feelings about your gender also impact the treatment process.

Wardrobe

The clinician treating women addicted to sex, love, and relationships must be aware of the messages conveyed by clothing. We live in a culture that sexualizes most kinds of attire: shoes, pants, skirts, blouses, jackets, ties, and so forth. Tight clothing, low cut blouses, and short skirts typically suggest sexual confidence or interest. When deciding what to wear to work, consider that your body and wardrobe are part of the climate of therapy—a tool that can be helpful or harmful. Diminishing this reality can compromise your successful treatment of sex and love addiction. Ask yourself the following: Are you dressing for work with the intent to create safety? If so, how do you wear clothing that feels good to you and also sends a message of safety to your clients? Do you find yourself dressing for a particular client? If so, why? If your clothes could speak, what would they say about you?

Energy

We each have a personal energy. Brizendine (2006) explains how a little girl, even before her language skills are completely formed, intuits more than she can cognitively identify or express. Brizendine asserts that a client will know if your mind wanders. Since women are wired to read emotions, physical gestures, and facial expressions, successfully working with women requires monumental self-awareness. Be aware of your emotions and how you manage them. If you're angry, aroused, or otherwise altered during sessions, expect that she will know. Most female SLAs won't know what to do with this energy and may internalize it as their own, which, obviously, will complicate successful healing.

Touch

While human touch is a legitimate need, be cautious about your physical interaction with FSLAs. Most find it hard to separate healthy touch from sexualized touch, and may misinterpret what you intend as an innocuous, affirming hug or pat on the back. It's generally more appropriate to offer a warm handshake, especially early in a therapeutic relationship. If you decide to hug a client, it can be helpful to wait for her to ask, which allows the discussion to be part of learning about boundaries. You may want to discuss your feelings about touch as part of the therapy. If you decide that hugging is okay with you and appropriate with your clients, be sure it's a "side" or "tent" hug that doesn't involve close body-to-body contact. It's also best to open your office door so that any physical exchange is in public view.

Environment

Working with sex and relationship addiction necessitates an environment free of sexually charged material. Avoid mainstream magazines in the waiting room, because most contain sexually charged advertising and photos that can be triggering. Safe waiting room material includes information about upcoming workshops, handouts about addiction and associated disorders, general material about healthy living practices, and/or general information about you and your practice. Take care, also, about music that's played in your waiting area. Mainstream music of all genres is full of triggering themes, especially for many FSLAs. Pre-select background music that's instrumental and not identifiable as recognizable songs.

In your treatment space, keep in mind your own comfort with personal boundaries and arrange your chair accordingly. When initially greeting a client, assist her acclimation to the space by explaining where you like to sit and offer her the alternatives. This initial explanation establishes boundaries and illustrates your ability to contain the space to meet your needs. If you are safe, she'll feel your confidence and be able to begin the process of trusting you. You can build on this process by explaining how you work with issues of time, contact outside sessions, and/or time away for vacation.

Transference and Countertransference

When working with individuals with attachment issues like FSLAs, transference inevitably occurs. This process is normal as the client unconsciously transfers earlier experiences, perceptions, feelings, and longings about a significant person onto her therapist. As the therapeutic relationship deepens, the client begins to experience you the same way she experienced people and situations from her past. Therefore, you become the triggering mom of the FSLA's childhood, or the abusive former friend, or the abandoning lover or the absent father—the possibilities are endless. The client expects you to behave toward her the way the prior person did, and she will likely react to you with her personal array of coping mechanisms such as rage, withdrawal, sexualization, or excessive dependence, to name a few. Again, there are endless possibilities.

Transference actually occurs in many of the FSLA's relationships and can be part of her addictive pattern. In the therapy setting, though, transference is beneficial, because when recognized, it provides a window into the client's disowned self-states, internalized abuse, and coping strategies. Valent (1999) explains that transference may be the only way a severely traumatized person can reveal her untold (or unrecognized) story, and therefore transference becomes a valuable tool for processing unresolved experiences. When you're attuned to the client's right brain and body, and you're able to bring projections from the past into the present therapeutic relationship and explore them openly, you have the opportunity to both intervene on unconscious patterns and to create a corrective emotional experience.

The challenge is being able to withstand the sometimes overwhelming nature of an FSLA's transference. Kalsched (2003) writes,

> For our early trauma patients to get well again, they will have to suffer through a retraumatization in their transferences. This repetition in the transference will be the person's way of remembering, and may actually lead to the potential of healing of trauma, provided that the therapist and patient can survive the *furor therapeuticus* that such transformation requires. (p. 157)

Surviving the furor requires that you recognize what's happening, address it openly without defensiveness, and gently invite the FSLA to share what she's experiencing in the moment, and, more importantly, what she's feeling. You must stay connected to her during these stressful ruptures in the therapeutic alliance. As Tutte (2004) expresses, working through transference issues requires a profound commitment by both participants involved in the healing process, and a deep emotional involvement on the part of the therapist. Schore (2003) asserts that you must maintain significant tolerance for the client's affective expressions, which allows her to expand the range and intensity of emotions that she shares as together you process the transference. Certainly, this part of working with FSLAs is taxing and requires that you're self-aware and emotionally strong enough to press on through this challenging, but healing path.

The possibility of countertransference in the therapeutic relationship is equally strong. As therapists, we come to this field with our own sexual feelings, confusion, ignorance, judgments, and trauma. In working with women SLAs, any untreated or uncovered issues around sexuality will emerge. The careful clinician prepares herself or himself by including consultation, supervision, and/or personal therapy as part of healthy business practice. Consultation with similarly trained clinicians is a necessity. Attending educational opportunities offered by professional organizations in the field such as the Society for the Advancement of Sexual Health (SASH), the International Institute for Trauma and Addiction Professionals (IITAP), and the American Association of Sexuality Educators, Counselors and Therapists (AASECT) makes best use of continuing education requirements. Likewise, for most of us, maintaining our own clinical development requires the help of a trusted therapist who can hold the issues we are working through.

The careful clinician takes note of her or his own sexual arousal in session and uses these powerful feelings as another tool for healing. A clinician learns to differentiate between his or her own sexual feelings and those of the client. When disowned sexual feelings are in the room, someone will pick them up. If you find yourself aroused during a session, check in with yourself about why. Is it something your client is saying? Is it the way she's dressed? Take note of your reactions and practice containment. At your earliest convenience, speak with a trusted colleague or your personal therapist to manage your arousal. It's possible you've found a new area for your own treatment and healing. If you can't identify something that feels arousing to you, it's possible you could be picking up your client's feelings. Ask her, "Are you feeling aroused as you speak with me?" If you have a steady connection with your client, she'll be able to explore her feelings and share them with you. If she is aroused, this will be an opportunity to identify her trigger and explore it together. Sometimes, however, she can't experience her own sexual arousal in connection with you because it's too threatening. In this case, acknowledge the sexual energy, make note of the client's wall, identify possible shame, and create the possibility of later exploration.

Therapeutic Enactments

Be aware, though, that your best-laid plans can go awry, especially when your subjective input into the therapeutic relationship is minimized (Friedman & Natterson, 1999). Therapeutic enactments, which are emotionally laden events that can include behaviors, can occur when your countertransference dominates the therapeutic field, or when your unconscious material collides with your client's unconscious material and brings both of your pasts into the present. Enactment is a "jointly created interaction" fueled by the unconscious processes of both the client and therapist (Chused, 1997, p. 265, as cited in Maroda, 1998). No matter how scrupulously you watch the process, you can't know what you don't know.

Enactments are an inevitability that render great opportunities for healing, yet they can "represent the most stressful moments of the treatment" (Schore, 2011, p. 152). In those affectively heightened moments of enactment, the client and the therapist are startled because something happens that throws them both into confusion. There's a mutual sense of being out of control emotionally in a way that feels "mysterious and powerful" (Maroda, 1998; p. 519). At the moment of rupture, the therapeutic alliance is broken, and in those instances where you might not be able to name what's going on, your client might.

It may also seem like this gross misattunement is a grave threat to the therapy. However, keep in mind that this event is bringing forth valuable emotional knowledge that otherwise couldn't have been known (Ginot, 2009). In any case, you must handle these situations with care and sensitivity, because the client's transference will distort reality. She may imagine that you feel toward her in the present the way another family member had felt toward her in the past.

Constructive expressions of these emotions and the mutual working through of the subsequent emotions and behaviors are crucial. Feelings to be on the lookout for within yourself are murderous rage, sexual attraction, anger, overwhelming grief, a desire to physically hold or touch the client, envy, deadness, not caring, and so forth. An enactment can also take a behavioral form such as a heated argument, spontaneous hug, physical gesture, sadomasochistic exchange, shortening or lengthening of session, failure to collect fees, unexpected dissolution into tears, or a withdrawal into silence (Maroda, 1998).

Keep in mind that both you and the client have to control and limit behaviors so the therapy can progress. Remember, the drama of the enactment ultimately belongs to the client. It's her chance to relive the past from an affective standpoint with a new opportunity for awareness and integration. When your client stimulates something real and primitive in you that's split off or disowned, then the two of you can relieve the drama in a real way together.

While the affect-laden enactment is inevitable, your behavior as the therapist should not be in terms of rage, erotic countertransference, or any other inappropriate reaction. You should remain reasonably in control, admit what you're feeling, and take responsibility for it. Avoid extensive processing of your behavior and feelings, keep explanations brief, and return the focus to the impact on your client. Whatever you do, don't blame your client. Instead, accept what you feel, which will give you greater control over your behavior (Maroda, 1998).

Ultimately, more of the client's past should be re-created than yours, and you should make a space for your client to have every opportunity to safely work through the events within the boundary of the therapeutic relationship (Maroda, 1998). Unlike countertransference, which should be worked out in your own therapy or consultation, enactment requires that the event be worked out between you and your client because it's an interpersonal event. The enactment is born of the two of you, and therefore needs to be negotiated and repaired by the two of you.

Therapist Self-Disclosure

Individuals are drawn to the therapeutic career path for a variety of reasons. Many people in the recovering communities find their way into the counseling field due to their own profound experiences in healing their personal addictions. A standard adage is that there are three types of therapists who treat this population: (a) the addict or partner in recovery; (b) the non-addict; or (c) the untreated addict who needs to be in recovery. If you work with FSLAs, it's important you have an accurate perception of which category best describes you.

Cognitive Self-Disclosure

Most literature states that therapist self-disclosure is usually left to the discretion and comfort level of the therapist. It's defined as any behavior or verbal sharing that reveals a clinician's personal information to the client in a way that's either deliberate, accidental, or unavoidable (Pizer,1997). Self-disclosure can be useful if clinically relevant and beneficial to the client's process in healing. In other cases, the disclosure can negatively change the tone and direction of the therapeutic environment if done inappropriately or for the wrong reasons. The disclosure of a therapist's recovery or personal experiences with sex or love addiction can be slightly more complicated due to the more explicit nature of the addiction and associated behaviors.

Consider the client whose acting out behavior has included escorting or prostituting herself. Without divulging too much information, the therapist shares she, too, is an addict in S recovery. The client is left with her imagination and might then be thinking graphically of her therapist in the same types of situations she herself had experienced. If the rapport isn't strong enough and the disclosure is mishandled, the client may feel uncomfortable or awkward, and the progress in therapy can be thwarted, sort of like a teenager's reaction when thinking of her parents having sex.

On the other hand, a love addict client who feels as if she's lost her mind and thinks she's a "crazy person" may benefit from knowing her therapist can relate as she, too, has been through her own process of recovery for love addiction. This self-disclosure could provide a resonance that opens the dialogue to a deeper level of sharing. In many cases the client appreciates knowing she's not alone and is being heard by someone who "gets it." It's not necessary or appropriate to share the "gory details," but disclosing in a general way could be beneficial to the therapeutic process. A possible way to approach this would be for the therapist to ask the client, "Would it be helpful to you if I shared a personal experience I had about this situation?"

Conversely, consider the therapist who has entered the profession without addressing his or her own SLA issues. This could become a very dangerous situation as the disclosure can be motivated by the therapist's own inquiry and "research." This therapist may not consciously disclose her issues, but she'll likely act out unconscious processes in the form of implicit communication. The client will read these non-verbal messages, which could destabilize the therapy. Unfortunately, the untreated SLA therapist often causes more harm than good by disclosing inappropriate or misguided information. It's vital that therapists choosing to engage in the treatment of this population be willing to delve into their own personal therapy and identify possible SLA issues of their own, along with their attitude and values around sex and love. As with any good training program, a therapist learning how to work with a new population should always address and keep an open dialogue about transference and countertransference issues.

Since part of the therapeutic process involves the therapist acting as a role model and sometimes being idealized by her clients, it's important to consider carefully before choosing to self-disclose. Some self-inquiry questions could be:

- Will the self-disclosure reveal or impose my own morals or values?
- Could the information create an unsafe or uncomfortable environment for the client?
- Can the information be disclosed without compromising appropriate therapeutic boundaries?

The best way to approach therapist self-disclosure is to first decide if it's within your own comfort level and personal value system. Then consider if it's clinically appropriate and potentially helpful to your client. Important aspects of the decision include weighing the pros and cons beforehand, playing it through to the possible end results, and then making the decision to disclose or not, how much, and when. If you're unsure or confused about this issue, it's best to seek consultation with a trusted colleague or the legal assistance provided by most licensing boards or associations. Therapist self-disclosure is a grey area in the clinical world and demands that each individual clinician be familiar with his or her own licensing board's ethical guidelines about this issue, as well as knowing personal boundaries and beliefs about revealing personal information to a client. The client's best interest always comes first, and remembering this principle about self-disclosure is considered the best practice.

Affective Self-Disclosure

Your female clients have to feel that you're *feeling* them or understanding them from the *inside,* not just that you have a cognitive understanding of them. When you invite and allow your authentic feelings to show, your sensitivity becomes a crucial building block to the therapeutic alliance because it's an emotional communication. Trust and safety are built upon your emotional availability, and your clients will use the therapeutic bond in order to experience interactive regulation.

When you're aware of your feeling states, prosody, pitch, rhythm, timbre of voice, facial expression, body gestures, and posture, and that you're in a right brain-to-right brain communication, you create a deepened sense of connection with your client. Your responses make your client's implicit experience explicit, thereby decreasing her anxiety about negative affect and leading her to a greater sense of connection and safety both with herself and with you (Quillman, 2011). Let her feel your humanity; she'll respond less to what you say than to how you say it.

Treatment Settings

Women seeking help for sex and love addiction normally enter the therapeutic process because of some crisis related to their behavior or in response to an intervention by concerned loved ones. Sometimes an FSLA seeks help when her awareness about the unmanageability of her life convicts her that "the pain of staying the same is greater than the pain of changing," as Twelve Step language describes it. Regardless of the motivating factor, FSLAs have many avenues for seeking assistance, and determining the one that best meets her immediate needs is a critical task for the clinician who has first contact with her.

The trained clinician may be the first person to recognize and name the FSLA's issue. You must be able to conduct a thorough assessment (described in chapter 3) and consider all the factors that influence the most appropriate treatment setting. The intensity and duration of care for FSLAs depends on various factors, predominantly your client's mental health status, overall functioning, ability to follow through with behavior changes, level of risk for self-harm, and compliance with the treatment plan. Placement is typically made according to the least restrictive intervention and progresses toward a more intensified environment as clinically indicated.

The American Society of Addiction Medicine (2001) adopted guidelines in late 2000 for assessing the severity of clients' problems in order to determine the most appropriate level of care. Co-occurring disorders (sometimes called "dual diagnosis") and suicidality are primary concerns in determining the level of placement. Four levels of care are outlined (ASAM, 2001):

1. Level I is early intervention/outpatient treatment
2. Level II is intensive outpatient treatment/partial hospitalization
3. Level III is supportive housing/residential/inpatient treatment with seven gradations of intensity
4. Level IV is medically managed inpatient treatment

ASAM differentiates "medically managed" care, where medical professionals are in charge of and directing care, and "clinically managed" care, where psychological professionals direct and manage care. Psychotherapy and adjunctive support may be present throughout all levels of care. Below is a chart comparing the different forms of care other than Level I, out-patient treatment.

Differences between Inpatient, Residential and Supportive Housing

Inpatient (usually "medically managed" care)	**Residential** (usually "clinically managed" care)	**Supportive Housing**
• 24-hour structure and support • 24-hour access to medical, psychiatric, or nursing services • Severe, immediate risk and imminent danger	• 24-hour structure and support • Primary medical services unnecessary • Moderate or significant risk and imminent danger	• Structure and support • Primary medical services unnecessary • No immediate risk or imminent danger

American Society of Addiction Medicine

Figure 4

In assessing the best level of care for your FSLA client, consider the myriad dimensions of her readiness for change, her medical and clinical needs, and what she is able or willing to do within her emotional, physical, financial, and social limits. Be aware that different professionals and programs often use some terms and descriptions interchangeably without clear differentiation. Be sure to thoroughly investigate a treatment setting and make an informed decision about its appropriateness for a specific client before making a referral.

Outpatient Treatment

The woman who looks for help with SLA normally first makes an appointment with an individual clinician for out-patient counseling. Even if an FSLA participates in other treatment settings, individual psychotherapy forms the core of most women's healing work. Individual and couple's counseling is often the most lengthy part of a woman's healing course. The best practices described about creating a safe therapeutic environment and the principles and cautions regarding a therapist's self-disclosure are especially pertinent in the outpatient setting.

Individual therapy initially focuses on helping the FSLA de-escalate the areas of unmanageability and crisis in her life. Emphasis is on breaking through denial, increasing her willingness to endure the rigors of the recovery process, engaging her in the tools of recovery, and developing a support system. Initially, you can act as a temporary support for your client in early treatment by having her check in with you via voice mail in between sessions, if necessary. This practice gives her the sense of a lifeline until she gets socialized into a Twelve Step program or group therapy. Your job is to be an active, caring, intervention source. Eventually, the client explores her family of origin and attachment issues, her faulty cognitions, and making decisions about her relationships. Individual or conjoint sessions may occur before and after other treatment settings and provide the backbone of most women's therapeutic process.

Outpatient treatment also includes group therapy, which is covered extensively in the next chapter.

Psychiatric Referral

As described in chapter 3, an FSLA may also be struggling with other co-occurring issues such as an eating disorder, mood disorder, or trauma. A psychiatric referral and possible medications are warranted, and often the outpatient clinician is the first one to recognize this need. It's important to establish a good relationship with a psychiatrist or medical addiction specialist for a collaborative treatment partner in supporting clients.

Intensive Outpatient Treatment

An intensive outpatient program, also called an IOP, is often recommended for a higher level of care. A client who's in crisis and has reached a "bottom" where her sexual or relationship behaviors are concerned is appropriate for an IOP. Often women's lives have come to a halt when their partner has discovered their double life, they've been fired from a job due to the effects of their addiction, or they've just had enough. An IOP helps clients restore their humanity and dignity in a short period of time. Given the up-to-date understanding about the causes and costs of sex and love addiction, an IOP can assist clients in getting sexually sober without a long and costly in-patient treatment program.

An IOP is also appropriate for those who have attempted to stop their behaviors through working a Twelve Step program, but who continue to slip over time. Often these women have "holes" in their program or blind spots that they aren't seeing. The IOP can be very constructive for tightening their definition of sobriety, identifying a mood disorder or some other mental health issue that may be perpetuating their acting out, or healing some unresolved trauma that's causing pain.

Typically, IOP programs are one to two weeks' long, facilitate a comprehensive First Step, and use a relapse prevention model. The overall intention is to assist the client in breaking through the denial structures she's set up over the years that have allowed her to rationalize her destructive sexual behaviors, so that she can begin to see the harm she's caused herself and others. Focusing on her personal addictive cycle and how early relational trauma fostered her behaviors over time, the FSLA begins to have compassion for herself, for the family she grew up in, and empathy for those she's hurt over the years.

An IOP should consist of psychoeducational lectures that pinpoint issues related to sex, love, and relationships, and how the client's past has led her to pathological attachment and distorted thinking patterns. Individual, group, and family therapy are also essential components during the program. Trauma protocols such as eye movement desensitization and reprocessing (EMDR) or art therapy are helpful to get to deeper affective states. Additionally, attendance at Twelve Step meetings should be incorporated into the IOP, so that the client has contact with others in recovery and is learning to use her program in the most effective way.

Finally, a solid aftercare plan is crucial for continuation of care. This plan should specifically outline who her treatment team will be once she's left the IOP. Her primary therapist's and psychiatrist's names and phone numbers should be on that plan along with her commitment to see them on a regular basis. Any ancillary therapies should also be listed such as a nutritionist, exercise trainer, neurofeedback practitioner, and so forth. Relationship boundaries, what the client wants to continue working on in the future, and what her recovery plan will be in the instance of a slip should also be detailed. The point is that the FSLA is making a sound plan for herself while she's "sober" in her thinking, so that if she slips, she has a roadmap to follow that she created and committed to.

Intensives/Workshops

A "first cousin" to a full intensive out-patient program is a clinical intensive or workshop, which is typically about a week in length. Like an IOP, the female SLA is referred to an intensive or workshop (the terms are generally synonymous) for either a jumpstart in her recovery process, or if she has difficulty maintaining sobriety. She may also benefit from a clinical workshop if she wishes to intensify her commitment to recovery. Typically these programs focus on recovery needs, roadblocks, spirituality, and sometimes an introduction to attachment issues and wounds from family of origin. Although often clinical in nature, a workshop typically doesn't make any formal diagnosis or use protocols like EMDR, and normally consists of group work rather than individual counseling. This option, then, is usually less expensive than an IOP, yet it provides a significant acceleration to the recovery process.

It's important to determine the philosophy and staffing of an intensive or workshop program. Some are staffed with at least master's level, licensed clinicians who are trained in treating sex and love addiction. Others use peer-leaders who are personally in recovery instead of licensed therapists. Still others are staffed with a mixture of the two. Unless your client is well down the path of recovery and free from co-morbid conditions, use caution when referring to a non-clinical, non-professional workshop. The editor's bias is that a gender-segregated (women only) intensive or workshop setting is best, especially early in an FSLA's process or if the focus is on achieving sobriety.

Not all clients are appropriate for an IOP or workshop setting, and it's essential to know when to refer to an in-patient program. Clients who are in active chemical addiction in addition to their sexual addiction may need a higher level of care, as well as women who have major mood disorders such as bipolar disorder or post traumatic stress disorder. Those who struggle with personality disorders or who have a history of suicide attempts, eating disorders, problems with cutting, or rage would also be better suited in an in-patient setting.

Inpatient Treatment

What's commonly called "inpatient treatment" has different meanings in different contexts and is often used interchangeably with terms that describe other forms of care. "Inpatient" treatment actually has seven different levels of intensity, and the nuances that differentiate them are largely determined by what entity is ultimately in charge and which medical services are provided and at what level.

Level IV Inpatient Treatment

Medically managed inpatient treatment (Level IV) is the highest, most restrictive level and is best when the FSLA has such a serious biomedical or psychiatric disorder that she needs immediate stabilization in a medical or psychiatric facility that provides 24-hour-a-day treatment. Medically managed treatment is appropriate for FSLAs who require medically-supervised detoxification from substances or to address severe mood disorders or personality disorders. Safety, stabilization, and crisis management are the primary goals of a Level IV facility rather than long-term therapy or addressing underlying issues. Emphasis is on helping the FSLA transfer to a less intense level of care, often to a more typical "inpatient" residential facility, or if she is doing very well, to an outpatient setting with comprehensive clinical and social support. The length of stay in a Level IV in-patient setting is usually quite short—only the amount of time (frequently just a few days) to stabilize the client sufficiently to be appropriate for a lower level of care.

Level III Inpatient Treatment

What's typically referred to as an in-patient treatment environment usually offers *clinically managed and medically monitored care*, which designates a Level III treatment setting. Medically monitored services are provided by an interdisciplinary staff of medical and non-medical personnel such as nurses, psychotherapists, addiction specialists, and other health and technical personnel under the direction of a licensed physician. Many inpatient treatment facilities do have a physician and psychiatrist available during the regular workweek and on-call; however, the primary day-to-day treatment work is facilitated by clinical and adjunctive staff.

If an inpatient referral is indicated, it's important to find the setting that best fits the client's needs. Does she require a segregated treatment setting (women only) or can she tolerate a mixed gender environment? When a gender segregated option is available with clinicians specifically trained in treating FSLAs, that's usually the ideal choice, especially if a client isn't sober when she presents for treatment. Even if males are present on the facility's campus, it's very helpful when women can be sequestered for most of their targeted work. Nevertheless, a mixed gender environment can usually succeed in an inpatient setting because there's sufficient structure to provide safety and time to process the triggers and interactions that surface. However, it's critical that the treatment staff have extensive understanding of the nuances of the patterns and rituals associated with sex and love addiction in women, which are often more subtle than men's. Be certain the treatment center has boundaries and supervision that prevent couples from pairing off.

Inpatient settings typically address the female SLA's family of origin history, trauma history, attachment injuries and dysregulation, distorted thinking, readiness to change, relapse prevention plan, and aftercare options. Many inpatient programs also offer a family weekend or period where the client's partner or family is invited to participate in psychoeducational and experiential work with the client. One of the primary benefits of inpatient treatment is that the FSLA can immerse herself in a setting that focuses on her needs, provides containment, and helps minimize outside distractions.

Many professionals believe clinically managed inpatient treatment, which is normally a minimum of 30 days and may extend to 60 or 90 days, offers recovering women the best chance for long-term sobriety. Obviously, inpatient treatment involves a significant investment of money and time, which puts it out of reach for many FSLAs. You must balance a woman's clinical needs with her resources when you make a treatment recommendation.

Residential Treatment

Residential treatment is also considered a Level III setting where the client is medically stable and doesn't require intensive medical intervention, although some residential facilities do provide access to medical staff as needed. Residential care varies from low-intensity (half-way house or supportive living) to medium-intensity (extended care) to high intensity (therapeutic community).

A residential setting is appropriate when an FSLA is unable to consistently respond to partial hospital or outpatient treatment and therefore benefits from having staff available, if not necessarily on site. Extended care or long-term residential facilities usually provide in-house psychoeducation, individual, and group work each week ranging from 5–20 hours. A residential setting allows the client to live in a safe and stable living environment, complete with community meetings and staffing support, to improve and practice her relapse prevention. The length of stay depends on the client's progress and stability, although 3-to-12 month stays are common.

Supportive Housing Environments

In addiction recovery, "supportive" housing (sometimes called "transitional living") is often recommended after discharge from a residential facility to assist the client in transitioning to life after treatment. Supportive housing prevents an addict from returning to former "playgrounds and playmates" and allows her to reintegrate into life outside a treatment facility with the help of a sober, supportive environment. For some FSLAs, supportive housing is a good alternative to returning to a toxic living environment. A "sober living house" (previously sometimes called a "half-way house") is an arrangement where a client pays to live in a house, apartment, or community with others. Typically a house manager or supervisor, often an individual who is in personal recovery, lives on-site with residents. Supportive housing is focused on providing a safe, sober living space, but beyond that objective, other services vary widely. Residents usually are required to attend Twelve Step meetings and "house" meetings, and either be employed, looking for employment, or in school. The primary focus of this phase of recovery is learning to manage a more complex life in the real world while continuing to keep recovery the first priority.

Stages of Treatment

There are various points where an FSLA may enter or exit the treatment process in general or with a particular therapist or in a specific setting. A woman's focus and her treatment needs and goals depend on the phase of treatment, which, in turn, influences the treatment modalities, setting, and approach. Clients differ in their readiness for change and may present in varying stages of that process. Healing from sex and love addiction will be unique to each woman; however, there are some identifiable touchstones in the progression of recovery. Understand that the stages of treatment are often fluid and overlapping. This discussion is more to provide you with a big-picture roadmap of your work with an FSLA, not necessarily to inform her about her headway.

Beginning Stage

Women come to treatment for various reasons, and it's not often that a client presents as a self-identified sex and love addict. While this scenario is changing as more information about the issue becomes available, it's common that women don't identify their behavior as addictive or tie their current problems to their addictive patterns. A certain event may drive the need for therapy such as a divorce, an affair, or loss of work. As this addiction increasingly affects younger women, you may see women enter treatment because they've been dismissed from school, or are unable to juggle the rigors of education with addictive use of the Internet, time spent working as strippers or escorts, or a secret life of anonymous sexual partners.

The initial stage of treatment is about building a relationship. In order for healing to take place, women must have a healthy therapeutic relationship in which to process and face this addiction. The early stage of treatment typically focuses on crisis management and reducing the FSLA's life chaos. Achieving and maintaining sobriety is a primary goal, which means the primary clinical approach will be cognitive-behavioral as the client arrests her addictive behaviors. (More about this process is described in chapter 6.) The FSLA will endure withdrawal as she identifies her addictive patterns of preoccupation, rituals and acting out, and she'll need extensive support to tolerate the anxiety of this phase. Psychoeducation is also an important part of early stage treatment as you introduce concepts around attachment, dysregulation, and family systems.

Much of your work in the initial stage of treatment will be to help the FSLA stay in reality. Since sex and love addiction involves escape and fantasy as coping skills for unbearable loneliness, the hour she spends with you each week may be the only time she can tolerate moments of truth. Outside your office, her brain races, always on overdrive. As she learns to trust you and feels a connection with you, her brain will slow down enough to take in reality, which is often quite painful during this early stage of treatment.

A thorough assessment, discussed in chapter 3, is part of the beginning work of psychotherapy. A clinician often makes a referral to a medical professional for evaluation for medication during this stage. Some clients require in-patient treatment, which may be identified during this time.

Middle Stage

The core therapeutic work generally happens during the middle stage of treatment, which is usually quite lengthy. During this time the recovering FSLA explores her family of origin in more depth. She addresses her attachment wounds and her other trauma experiences and faces more fully the unhealthy ways she's used to cope. Often, the client goes through a deep grieving process as she lets go of the victim stance that keeps her stuck and moves into a survivor, healing stance. Being part of a group is key during this stage as the client breaks her isolation. Encourage the FSLA to participate in a Twelve Step fellowship for recovery from sex and love addiction, which she has probably resisted until this stage. This is the best time to introduce the Task Model (P. Carnes, 2006) with women after a strong therapeutic relationship has formed.

Recovery isn't a linear process, and it's normal for the FSLA to return to denial at times, or to slip in her sobriety, or even to relapse. Expect these occurrences as a normal part of the healing journey, and help your client maintain perspective when progress seems to be slow or regressions occur. Sometimes, a relapse provides both of you a better understanding of what's fueling the addiction and opens a new door for deeper healing.

The recovering woman is examining every aspect of her life, both former, present, and future, during this stage. She usually is conflicted or ambivalent about her primary relationship, and significant time in therapy is devoted to this issue.

The best practice is to encourage her to postpone any major decision like getting a divorce or deciding to leave a primary relationship for an affair partner until she's maintained at least a year of solid sobriety. Conjoint sessions with the FSLA's partner usually occur during this time as the couple goes through the process of disclosure and explores the future of their relationship. The middle stage is also the time to promote the FSLA's participation in group therapy, which is discussed at length in the following chapter.

Ending Stage

In the later stage of recovery, your client will show clear signs of health and healing. Because her shame has diminished significantly, she has room for greater self-acceptance. With renewed energy that comes from abstaining from addictive behavior, the recovering woman is ready to be the architect of a new life. You'll be instrumental in assisting your client to design and reclaim a life she lost, or perhaps never had in the first place. This is time for celebration and enjoyment, but also for renewed focus. Help your client direct her fresh energy into healthy paths to avoid detouring back into addictive patterns.

During the ending stage of the therapeutic process she'll determine new goals and pursue them. She'll put in place healthy strategies for self-care, relationships, and sexuality. Ideally, she'll begin to experience gratitude for her journey and even find some meaning in her pain. These concepts are explored fully in Part Three.

Contributing Writers

Anna Valenti-Anderson - Levels of Treatment Settings
Jill Vermeire - Cognitive Therapist Self-Disclosure

REFERENCES

APA Presidential Task Force. (2006). Evidence-based practice in psychology. *American Psychologist, 61*(4), 271–285.doi: 10.1037/0003-066X.61.4.271

American Society of Addiction Medicine. (2001). *ASAM patient placement criteria for the treatment of substance-related disorders* (2nd ed., rev.). ASAM PPC-2R.

Brizendine, L. (2006). *The female brain.* New York, NY: Broadway Books.

Carnes, P. (2006). *Facing the shadow.* Carefree, AZ: Gentle Path Press.

Cloitre, M., Stovall-McClough, K., Miranda, R., & Chemtob, C. M. (2004). Therapeutic alliance, negative mood regulation, and treatment outcome in child abuse-related posttraumatic stress disorder. *Journal of Consulting and Clinical Psychology, 72*(3), 411-416.

Covington, S., & Surrey, J. (2000). *The relational model of women's psychological development: Implications for substance abuse.* Boston, MA: Stone Center Working Paper Series #91).

Diener, M. J., Hilsenroth, M. J., & Weinberger, J. (2007).Therapist affect focus and patient outcomes in psychodynamic psychotherapy: A meta-analysis. *American Journal of Psychiatry, 164*,936-941.doi:10.1176/appi.ajp.164.6.936

Friedman, R. J., & Natterson, J. M. (1999). Enactments: An intersubjective perspective. *Psychoanalytic Quarterly, 68*, 220-247.

Ginot, E. (2009). The empathic poser of enactments: The link between neuropsychological processes and an expanded definition of empathy. *Psychoanalytic Psychology, 26*(3), 290-309.

Kalsched, D. E. (2003). Daimonic elements in early trauma. *Journal of Analytical Psychology, 48*, 145–169. doi: 10.1111/1465-5922.t01-2-00003

Luborsky, L., McLellan, A. T., Woody, G. E., O'Brien, C. P., & Uerbach, A. (1985). Therapist success and its determinants. *Archives of General Psychiatry, 42*(6), 602-611.

Magnavita, J. J. (2006). In search of the unifying principles of psychotherapy: Conceptual, empirical, and clinical convergence. *American Psychologist, 61*(8), 882-892.

Maroda, K. J. (1998). Enactment: When the patient's and analyst's pasts converge. *Psychoanalytic Psychology, 15*(4),517-535.

McDaniel, K. (2012). *Ready to heal: Breaking free of addictive relationships* (3rd ed.). Carefree, AZ: Gentle Path Press.

Miller, J. (1986). *Toward a new psychology of women.* New York, NY: Beacon Press.

Miller, J., Jordan, J., Stiver, I., Surrey, J., & Kaplan, A. (1991). *Women's growth in connection: Writings from the Stone Center.* New York, NY: Guilford Press.

Pizer, B. (1997). When the analyst is ill: Dimensions of self-disclosure. *The Psychoanalytic Quarterly, 66*(3), 450-489.

Quillman, T. (2011). Neuroscience and therapist self-disclosure: Deepening right brain to right brain communication between therapist and patient. *Clinical Social Work Journal, 40*(1), 1-9. doi:10.1007/s10615-011-0315-8

Romano, V., Fitzpatrick, M., & Janzen, J. (2008). The secure-base hypothesis: Global attachment, attachment to counselor, and session exploration in psychotherapy. *Journal of Counseling Psychology, 55*(4), 495-504.

Safran, J. D., & Muran, J. C. (2000). *Negotiating the therapeutic alliance: A relational treatment guide.* New York, NY: Guilford Press.

Schore, A. N. (2003). *Affect regulation and the repair of the self.* New York, NY: Norton.

Schore, A. N. (2011). *The science of the art of psychotherapy.* New York, NY: Norton.

Schore, A. N. (2012, February). *Working in the right brain: A regulation model of clinical expertise for treatment of attachment trauma.* Keynote presentation, International Institute of Trauma and Addiction Professionals Symposium, Scottsdale, AZ.

Siegel, D. (1999). *The developing mind: How relationships and the brain interact to shape who we are.* New York, NY: Guilford Press.

Stern, D. (2008). The clinical relevance of infancy: A progress report. *Infant Mental Health Journal, 29,* 177–188.

Tutte, J. C. (2004). The concept of psychical trauma: A bridge in interdisciplinary space. *International Journal of Psychoanalysis, 85,* 897-921.

Valent, P. (1999). *Trauma and fulfillment therapy: A wholist framework.* Philadelphia, PA: Brunner/Mazel.

CHAPTER 5

Best Practices for Group Therapy

Deborah Corley, Marnie Ferree, Linda Hudson, Alexandra Katehakis, Jill Vermeire, Sonnee Weedn

Group psychotherapy is well accepted as an effective and proven modality when treating addictive behaviors (Brooks, 2011; Flores, 2007). Starting with the late 1930s grass roots movement of Alcoholics Anonymous to the development of formalized group therapy, many people across all socioeconomic strata have found help for problems related to addiction within some kind of group setting. For the FSLA, too, the use of group psychotherapy can be an excellent and integral part of her recovery. Group therapy offers an opportunity for establishment of a sense of community (Ormont, 1992), and studies have shown a strong positive correlation between cohesion in group and patient improvement (Bednar & Kaul, 1994; Burlingame, Fuhriman, & Johnson, 2001). If female sex and love addicts struggle with a fundamental attachment disorder, it's only logical that a key way to observe and address the manifestations of attachment injuries is through the crucible of a group setting. Indeed, group psychotherapy offers a perfect arena to learn healthy relating with the assistance of a clinician to ease the process.

Group therapy differs from Twelve Step and other forms of support meetings in several important ways. The primary difference is that a licensed therapist(s) leads group therapy, and the safety of her clinical presence allows cross talk, discussion, and feedback, which enhance dialogue and intimacy among group members. A drop-in group such as a Twelve Step group or support group may provide help and encouragement, but it isn't to be confused with group psychotherapy. The group experience can be offered in any therapeutic setting: in-patient and residential care, a sober living house, private practice settings, mental health clinics, intensive out-patient treatment, and the penal system.

Practical Advantages and Disadvantages of Group

A lengthy in-patient stay or long-term individual therapy is costly and open only to those with exceptionally generous health insurance or abundant resources. Group therapy, however, is typically far less expensive than other alternatives, and therefore offers greater accessibility for women where cost containment is a consideration. If the client is finding value in weekly individual sessions and has limited resources, she may feel she has to choose between individual work and the group option, and she may want help exploring the most beneficial alternative long-term. Some therapists will lower their individual therapy fee in order to accommodate the client, so that she may continue individual work as well as join a group. Some situations may support bi-weekly therapy sessions and/or titration from individual work over the course of several months while the client becomes more cohesive with the group. In some cases, you and the client may feel group is a better option at this point in her process and agree to suspend or terminate individual therapy. Obviously, the most important consideration is the client's best interest.

Although group therapy is usually less expensive, it's also less flexible in terms of scheduling and time commitment. A group is a set time that can't be changed based on a woman's unexpected schedule conflicts. If she misses her group session, the opportunity for that particular experience is lost. Depending on the contract for the group, the client may be charged for the session whether she's present or not. Most groups are also at least one-and-a-half hours to two hours in length (some experiential groups are longer) instead of the shorter 50-minute therapy hour.

Therapeutic Advantages

Yalom (2005) wrote about the "curative factors" that are the primary agents of change in group therapy. They're listed below along with their application to the female sex and love addict population.

1. *Instillation of hope.* The FSLA often feels ashamed and hopeless when she initially enters treatment. As she experiences other women who are further down the recovery path, or observes others working through difficult issues, she feels hope that one day she, too, may be in a different, more positive place.

2. *Universality.* More than anything else FSLAs report feeling alone in their struggles. They rarely meet another woman who admits to addictive sex or relationship behavior, and there are few places where a woman feels safe enough to share her secrets. Through the group setting, an isolated FSLA can begin to break her isolation, and discovers that her feelings and experiences are shared by others.

3. *Information giving.* Psycho-education provides factual information regarding sex and love addiction, its etiology, progression, and effective methods for addressing it. Resources for FSLA are still scarce, and many women find the material written for men only increases their sense of being different.

4. *Altruism.* FSLAs can begin to see that competition can be replaced with kindness, gentleness, and generosity in spirit, word, and deed. Being part of a therapy group is often an FSLA's first experience of this sort of relationship. As a woman grows, she finds she's able to help others, which greatly improves her self-esteem.

5. *Corrective recapitulation of the primary family.* FSLAs typically have grown up in some sort of low-functioning family that didn't provide for the unfolding of healthy psychological developmental stages. The group can be an open system where healthy relationships can be learned and practiced. A functioning authority figure (the group leader) becomes the nurturing parent the FSLA may have lacked, and other group members become siblings with whom to negotiate different kinds of relationships than probably existed in the FSLA's original family. The group provides a corrective experience for problematic family dynamics.

6. *Improved social skills.* FSLAs, for all their facile social adeptness, may not have developed more mainstream, appropriate ways of relating to others as opposed to flirtatiousness and seduction. Group therapy offers the give and take of conversation and reveals the FSLA's sometimes improper social relating. As group members offer feedback about a client's behavior, she learns how to improve her social interactions.

7. *Imitative behavior.* Through observing the group therapist and other flourishing group members, FSLAs can learn how to express themselves verbally, identify feelings, and offer well-intentioned feedback.

8. *Interpersonal learning.* The FSLA is underdeveloped in modes of relating to others such as seeing other women solely as competitors, and seeing men as something to be seduced and conquered. Group therapy develops new ways of seeing others, being seen, and practicing how she wants to be experienced. It's a learning ground for the complexities of relationships.

9. *Group cohesiveness.* Group facilitates learning to ask for help, receiving useful assistance, assisting others, and generally operating as a member of a community that works together for the health and healing of all. This cohesiveness counters the FSLA's isolation and secretiveness and provides a critical place to belong.

10. *Catharsis.* FSLAs have typically had little or no outlet for their feelings or even any awareness or understanding of their feelings. A mainstay of the group process is

members recognizing and experiencing their emotional selves, which is a powerful encounter that usually brings emotional relief. While catharsis can't be forced and doesn't always happen for everyone, a group setting offers an ideal opportunity.

Assessing Readiness and Preparing the FSLA for Group

Issues of timing, availability, and group type are important considerations when deciding to make a referral for group work. Consider the client's readiness to benefit and respond appropriately from this type of psychotherapy. Though there are some exceptions, most clients will need considerable individual therapy before they're ready for a group. An FSLA needs to learn to ground and resource herself, find value in giving and receiving feedback, and perhaps begin trauma resolution work in some form before taking part in a group process. It's important that she's able to stay in the moment and participate, rather than dissociate or disrupt the group.

Some clients may have limited insight into their own problems, feelings, and thoughts, or have never verbalized their own experience to anyone. Therefore, beginning with ample individual therapy and then adding group therapy after the FSLA is more familiar with the therapeutic process provides a continuum of care appropriate to her level of maturation. Building an alliance with the therapist, making a commitment to treatment, and demonstrating emerging self-awareness may be indicators that an FSLA has reached a milestone in her recovery and is ready to move into a group experience.

For the client who is hypersensitive to feedback or struggles with difficult or complex personality issues, it may be best to have her begin with a group focused on dialectical behavioral therapy (DBT) or a short-term psychoeducational group. The structure in these formats is more time-limited and focused on skill building and education, where the FSLA can learn about addiction and acquire basic tools needed to regulate her moods and urges to act out. She can also practice interacting with others in a healthier way. When this process has been completed, she may then be a candidate for a less structured, interactional, open-ended type of group therapy.

If the client is highly reactive, unable to stay on task, or is acting out and unable to stop high risk behavior, she's unlikely to be ready for a group experience in an out-patient setting, especially if the group is a long-term, open format model. Group treatment requires the ability to wait for her turn to speak, attend to the experience of others, tolerate feedback, and be reflective regarding the experience as a whole.

Preparing the FSLA for group

If you and your client determine group therapy is a good fit for her at this stage of her process, it's wise to take some steps to help her prepare for the experience. If she has significant trauma that needs to be addressed, suggest that while this is weighty material for her to deal with eventually, it's also important for her to gain internal and external support before doing this central work. Explain that addressing deep trauma often spawns triggers that might tempt her to return to acting out. Suggest that she put the memories and thoughts surrounding her trauma into a box and shut the lid until she's stronger. You can actually have a shoe box or similar small box available that you offer her to take home. Propose that when any memory arises, she draws a simple picture to represent it and puts the drawing (or perhaps just a notation about the memory if that's more comfortable for her) into the box until later. This containment lets the FSLA know the trauma will be addressed in due time and helps her to stop obsessing over those triggers.

Another helpful step before a client begins group therapy is to train her to create and utilize a safe place and set of internalized resources. This is a practice that's long been used in eye movement desensitization and reprocessing (EMDR). If you're trained in EMDR, use a few sessions to install the FSLA's safe place and internal resources that she can use as a temporary rest during emotional processing, to help when her emotions become extremely distressing in group, or as an aid to closing down the disturbance or to deal with disturbing materials that may arise between group sessions. If you're not trained in this modality, consider referring her for this work.

As an alternative you can use guided imagery to create a safe place and envision help she can call on when needed. Suggest she think about someone she trusts: a person who would have her back should she be in a jam, who would lovingly confront her if she were on the wrong path, and who would be a good cheerleader if that was all she needed. (Be sure to assess if the person she's selected is truly safe and not someone who has also hurt her or is a former acting out partner.) Some women will use characters in books or movies, an angel, Spirit Guide, God, Higher Power, or even a pet, or animal totem. The selection doesn't matter as long as the FSLA believes the resource will help her. Have her specifically visualize the person (or item) she's selected and identify what she sees, hears, and feels when she's near the person. Ask where in her body she feels this person's presence and support, and have her press that area or rub it in a small circle. Then suggest she ask this resource if he or she will be a cheerleader, or guardian angel, or whatever term she chooses. If the resource says *yes*, ask her to look into the resource's eyes and feel that commitment. Suggest she practices accessing her safe place and resource several times before she enters the group process.

Making the referral

If you aren't leading a therapy group that fits for your FSLA client or you don't have space in a current group, you may have to refer her to another therapist for group treatment. It's important to collaborate with the group facilitator (with a release of information, of course) in order to determine if your client is appropriate for this particular group. Most clinicians require an intake and screening interview before a client joins a therapy group. Often a therapist refers her individual clients to her own therapy groups as well as accepts referrals from other therapists. In this case, the therapist will already have a therapeutic alliance established with her own clients that won't exist with the referred clients. Explain this situation so that your client understands this dynamic and isn't unduly disturbed by it. Educate her to expect it may take her a bit longer to feel connected to the group and that this experience is normal.

The Nuts and Bolts of Group Therapy

Group therapy can be structured in different ways and have varying formats. The "best" option depends on the clinician's experience and theoretical orientation, along with who comprises the group and their goals. Following are some effective options for groups in general that are targeted to recovery from sex and love addiction. A later section describes some particular factors that are significant in groups of female sex and love addicts.

Time limited or open-ended

Most outpatient clinical groups are contracted for a specific amount of time ranging from a minimum of three months to six or even 12 months. A definite time commitment is more appealing to most FSLAs, especially for their first forays into group therapy. An open-ended group is usually best for an already established group that has finished its initial commitment, and the members decide to continue meeting indefinitely (usually on a less-frequent basis like once a month). In this case members stay in the group until they believe they've reached their goals, resources force them to stop participating, or some other circumstance requires them to make other decisions about therapeutic care.

Open or closed membership

Almost all outpatient psychotherapy groups are closed, which means members can't join after the group starts (or at least after the first session or two). This policy maintains the safety of the group and is less threatening for many clients. Sometimes a long-term group allows new members to join when attrition opens a space, and the group leader follows the protocols outlined in a later section for integrating someone into the group. Members should be made aware of the group's policy on accepting new members before they decide about joining. In-patient groups have members rotating in and out as they enter and leave treatment, and the leader assists with these transitions.

Focused or general membership

This characteristic is sometimes called a heterogeneous or a homogeneous group. Some therapy groups are open to a broader audience like any woman interested in personal growth, for example (heterogeneous). A group with focused membership would be one that's only for female sex and love addicts (homogeneous). The parameters and recommendations of this section are directed toward a group limited to FSLAs.

Number of participants

Most clinicians find a group of six to eight members is ideal. A psychoeducational format allows for more participants, but in most cases when the membership tops 10 or 12 people, there isn't enough time during the group sessions for members to adequately participate.

Requirements for participation

Some groups for sex addicts require a certain amount of sobriety, usually somewhere between 30 to 90 days, and generally assume (or sometimes require) that the client is participating in a Twelve Step sex addiction fellowship. Other groups may advocate a harm reduction approach where the focus is on limiting destructive behavior and increasing functioning in other areas of the FSLA's life. Some groups require members to be participating in individual therapy while taking part in group therapy.

Contract for group participation

It's imperative to have a group contract regarding specific requirements and expectations for participation that each member signs and dates. Recovery is, in part, about making explicit commitments and keeping them. By having a contract in writing, there's no confusion about what's expected and what the boundaries are. This form of containment also creates safety, because each group member is held to the same standard, therefore if one person violates the contract, all members are aware of the rule that's been broken.

Each time you begin a new group, discuss your group contract as the first group activity after your welcome and housekeeping items. Distribute copies to each member and ask them to take turns reading each point out loud. After each point is read, they're to ask any questions they may have, initial the point, then move on to the next one. After all points have been covered, ask members to sign and date the contracts and return them to you. Explain that you'll sign their contracts, make copies for their files, and give them a copy the following week.

When a new member enters a pre-existing group follow the same protocol, this time passing a single sheet around for existing members to read aloud while the newcomer reviews her own copy. Ultimately, the new group member initials each point, signs and dates the contract, and returns the original to you. This ritual assists in making the new member feel welcome and refreshes the memories of current members.

At a minimum the contract should include the following:

- Confidentiality regarding the anonymity of each person participating in group.
- Length of group commitment (the number of weeks or months or open-ended).
- Fee for group sessions and specifics about payment arrangements. (How you structure fees is up to you. Some groups offer a slightly lower overall fee if all group sessions are paid up-front, while others hold a set fee that's subject to increasing based on the therapist's policies.)
- Dates and times when group meets; policies about being tardy, leaving early, vacations, and holidays; as well as policies for payment when the client is absent.
- Procedure for early termination, including giving a certain amount of notice to the group leader and group, and the method of leaving a group (like attending a final group session to say good-bye and provide closure to other members).
- Agreement to refrain from sexual or romantic contact between group members.
- General comportment in group such as no eating or smoking, no verbal or physical violence, not attending group while under the influence of alcohol or drugs, etc.

Some therapists find it helpful for the client to include in her group contract the particular goals she has for participating in the group. Each woman shares her goals during the discussion about the contract and writes them in a designated space on her contract. These may include the ways she predicts she might sabotage her treatment, and the length of time she believes she'll need to complete the goals she's set if the group is open-ended. This isn't to say she'll automatically terminate from group when her written goals have been reached, but these issues are diagnostic and provide a starting place from which to proceed.

Remember, a contract that's reviewed and signed by each participant is a useful way to make explicit the guidelines of the group and the client's commitment and expectations. A basic sample contract for group is included in the Appendix.

Marketing a therapy group

Most clinicians find it difficult to attract female sex and love addicts to a group for the same reasons described earlier that make a therapy group challenging for FSLAs. Some clinicians find it more appealing to advertise a "healing intimacy issues," or "sexual wholeness" group, or some similar description. Others have success with stating clearly the group's makeup, especially since more attention is being given to the problem of sex and love addiction among women.

If no group specifically designed for FSLAs exists in your geographic location, consider starting one with the women in your practice who fit the FSLA description. If you only see one or two female sex addicts, ask colleagues for referrals. While the ideal number of participants for most therapy groups is six to eight people, don't be afraid to consider forming a group with only three clients in order to involve FSLAs in this therapeutic process. Any beginning point is an opportunity to prime the pump for other women to join.

Types of Therapy Groups

Different types of groups are effective depending on the group's goals. Some groups are intended primarily to educate, others to assist in inter-personal relationships, and still others to address trauma or other individual issues. Each type is valuable for FSLAs and different types may be helpful at different points in her therapeutic process.

Psychoeducational

A psychoeducational group can be extremely beneficial to the FSLA, since education is a crucial component of understanding the causes and influences of her maladaptive patterns, which helps reduce shame and elevate self-compassion. Additionally, a psychoeducation group is a more comfortable way for the FSLA to experience group therapy because this format slowly introduces her to the idea of healing in community. This type of group is ideal in early recovery because it's structured, supportive, and directive, and the group leader's focus is on facilitating group member's emotional attachment to one another (Flores, 2001).

Generally, a psychoeducational group covers specific topics which might include understanding addiction, the process of recovery, social and interpersonal issues in recovery, healthy self-help group and support systems, managing feelings in recovery, relapse prevention, and long term maintenance (Daley, Mercer, & Carpenter, 1998; Ormont, 2001). Topics specific to women are endless, but might specifically include sexual health and safety, attachment styles and how to earn secure attachment, love and loneliness, the emotionally absent mother, mother hunger (see McDaniel, 2012), financial management of slim resources, or being a good-enough parent, to name a few.

A psychoeducational format often includes reading or other assignments that are completed and brought to group. For example, some clinicians utilize a standardized treatment model such as a particular workbook or other curriculum-based format. Homework is assigned and then shared in the group session. Examples of curricula specifically written for FSLAs are included in the Suggested Reading section of the Appendix.

Process

A process group functions as the name describes: a place for members to process issues and events in their lives. It's less structured than a psychoeducational group and normally doesn't involve outside assignments. Members typically volunteer to "work" during a particular group session, which means that person (or more, depending on the session length) is the focus. All members, though, benefit from that person's experience and the feedback within the group. Process groups also are more concerned with the interactions between group members, and frequently use some group issue as the focus for part of a session. As such, they offer a rich training ground for developing relationship skills.

Experiential

An experiential or psychodrama group is usually the most advanced in terms of the intensity, and is recommended for women who are in the later stages of recovery. Qualifications to participate might include remaining sexually sober on a plan, participating in consistent individual therapy for six months to a year, working a Twelve Step program, and making use of a sponsor or making consistent program calls. Similar to a process group, the members volunteer to work during a session, which means they delve into their affective process through experiential or psychodrama activities instead of simply talking. These types of groups are particularly helpful for dealing with core issues like attachment injuries and other forms of trauma. They're also well suited to mixed genders and provide a safe way to develop understanding, empathy, and non-sexual intimacy with the opposite sex.

Because this format is potentially quite powerful for group members, it's vital that a clinician has specific training before attempting to lead an experiential or psychodrama group. Witnessing an experiential process such as psychodrama or personally taking part in a experiential group doesn't qualify you to direct this powerful process. It's critical that you have in-depth training in experiential and psychodrama methods so that you create a safe and effective container for all.

Format of Group Sessions

The specifics of what happens during a group session obviously depend on the type of group. A psychoeducational group is structured closely, and a process or experiential group is more client-directed. Some general practices, though, are helpful regardless of the particular type of group.

Opening and check-in

Begin with a standard procedure that's repeated each group session. We recommend starting with a moment of silence to ask a Higher Power for guidance and to summon forth for the meeting the presence of the strong recovering woman inside. As the group leader, use a soothing, tempered voice to lead members into some slower breathing. This consistent opening lets the FSLA regulate her heart and nervous system for the group process so that she can be prepared for the important work ahead. Next, the group shares a check-in by each member where participants take a brief turn to "get current" and report on various aspects of recovery since the previous group session. It's useful to provide a laminated sheet outlining the check-in procedure that members pass around to keep everyone on point during the check-in process. Possible things to cover in a check-in include:

- Feelings check (perhaps also sharing how she's feeling physically, mentally, and spiritually, as well as emotionally).
- Sobriety report (any slips, relapses, or close calls).
- Program report (the number and kind of Twelve Step meetings she's attended since the last group, Step work she's completed, etc.).
- Positive report (healthy, positive behaviors she's engaged in like self-care, connection with others, etc.).
- Request for time (for a process or experiential group a member may offer a brief description of the issue she wants to work on that session and an estimate of how much time she needs).

If the group is directed toward women early in SLA recovery, the sobriety and program reports are critical. If it's a process or late-stage recovery group, the feelings check and request for time are important. In either case, it's best to limit the check-in process to approximately five minutes per person to keep it from consuming the entire session. If you find this opening taking too much time, be firm in limiting the check-in to a few words or brief sentences. The check-in procedure is one thing that differentiates a sex addiction *treatment* group from a generic therapy group, because it creates a forum for assertion and accountability from the moment group begins.

Working portion

After the check-in, a teaching segment usually follows in a psychoeducational group. Next, members are encouraged to share their reaction to the material, or their homework or assignment from the last session. Normally, every member has a chance to share.

If the group is process oriented or experiential, a determination is made after the check-in regarding who will work during that session. Ideally, the group members make this selection based on the interest in the topics or issues described during the check-in. Members will typically agree on a topic with ease, and someone steps forward to work during that session. This protocol means that not everyone works during each group session. Instead, one or two people are the focus, and the other members provide feedback and support. Even if a member isn't the main focus of the session's work, she still benefits from the process and learns vicariously by the experiences of others.

The leader monitors who works in group and should encourage those who usually pass to step up to the center and claim some time. This situation, too, is appropriate for a group conversation. When one person rarely or never works, or conversely, when one person dominates the group time, it's healthy for the group to discuss the impact of these dynamics on the group environment.

Ending

Typically, each group meeting runs anywhere from an hour and a half to three hours depending on the number of clients and the nature of the group. A psychoeducational group usually requires two hours to allow time for teaching as well as discussion of any homework. Weekly process and experiential groups also need up to two hours in order to accommodate everyone's need, though one-and-a-half hours may be sufficient if only four people are in the group. Some experiential or psychodrama groups run two to three hours if they meet less frequently such as every other week or once a month.

As the time draws to a close, check in with those group members who didn't share. Ask them to take initiative to get their needs met by going for coffee with another member after the group, making program calls, or going to a meeting. Whatever the member decides should be stated as a commitment to the group, which provides accountability. To close the session many therapists find it's meaningful to create an ending ritual such as a statement of affirmation everyone says together. One example is "We are strong, beautiful, healing women, and we value ourselves and this group." The most common way to close a group session is for the group members to stand, hold hands, and say the Serenity Prayer.

Providing feedback about group session

Drawing from a comprehensive review of 40 years of outcome studies, Duncan, Wampold, Miller, and Hubble (2009) point out that by applying a simple, valid, and reliable method for assessing and enhancing alliance at the end of a session, you can increase your retention in group therapy and positive therapeutic outcomes. You can do this with a session rating scale handout that asks about the therapeutic relationship, goals or topics, approach or method of delivery, overall rating, and ideas for improving the session. Using a five-point Likert scale, the client rates if she felt heard, understood, and respected by the therapist. A separate question asks the same thing regarding the other group members. Regarding goals, the rating handout asks if the group worked on or talked about what the client wanted to address. It asks if the therapist's approach was a good fit for her. And finally the rating handout asks if there was something missing, or if the session was right for her on that day. There's also room for the client to submit comments or suggestions. Ask group members to complete the handout and turn them in (a pretty basket is nice for this purpose) just prior to whatever closure activity in which the group engages. This practice becomes an objective measure for how you're doing and what you could do to enhance the group experience. There's nothing more powerful for an FSLA than to be asked her opinion and to have it valued. For most, this didn't happen in her family of origin or in the circles in which she's been socialized.

Graduation

One of the most gratifying and important parts of group therapy is when a group member is genuinely ready to leave and is celebrated in her departure. A conscious send-off is modeled in ways that are intimate, touching, and moving. For many women, this is the first time they've ever said good-bye to someone they've attached to, or had the experience of leaving without some dramatic event that left both parties with hurt feelings and resentment. More importantly, this may also be the first time for some to have constructed a safe, loving relationship with another woman or women to whom they can say good-bye and continue to stay connected as friends over time.

As a group leader, you'll have a sense of when you think a woman is getting ready to leave the nest. It's imperative that you, like a good-enough mother, make a space in your own consciousness for women to graduate from your group. If you're holding them there unnecessarily, such as worrying about not having enough group members, or for financial reasons, you should seek consultation. Differentiating and going out into the world with what she's internalized from you and the group is an important part of her development and growth. When a woman mentions leaving group, ask her to talk about her thoughts and feelings in detail, and as always, process it with the group. If you determine that her reasons are sound and you feel she's met her goals and the criteria of the group, then ask her to set a date for the following month so that the group can prepare a graduation ceremony with her. A specific send-off ritual is suggested in the last section of this chapter.

Guidelines for a Healthy Group

All members need to be present consistently for the group to be vital and healthy. A client becomes an intrinsic part of the group by agreeing to be present at a specific place and time and by being held accountable for this commitment. Help each woman understand that her very presence in the group, whether she says a lot or very little, contributes to the overall tenor of the group. All members are treated equally, and are equally important to the process of the group. It often takes a new member some time (perhaps many weeks) to become a part of the functioning group and to feel a sense of belonging and the support that comes with it. Newcomers are frequently anxious until they feel more comfortable with the routine and come to know the names and stories of other members.

Role of the group leader

In the early stages of a group, the leader must be fairly directive and interactive with the clients and keep structure and support in place. Your responsibilities include starting and ending group on time, collecting money, taking process notes, reviewing completion of individual assignments, and attending to feelings and somatic cues in group members, between group members, and within yourself. Be clear about boundaries such as when payment is due, turning off cell phones, not eating or chewing gum during group, and so forth. These activities and processes create containment and demonstrate that you're the most consistent and reliable member of the group.

Begin group on time and let group members know that if they're going to be late or miss group that they must contact you directly via voicemail or email, as opposed to sending a message through another group member. If a group member doesn't call or show up, call her immediately after group to let her know of your concerns. Remind group members to check in with that client, too, in case she's in distress and needs help. End group on time, as well, unless there's a significant crisis.

Many FSLAs have financial difficulties in their lives, and many therapists are challenged when it comes to talking about money. Now's the time to get clear about any lingering issues you may have with money. Likewise, make your policy clear about what you expect regarding group payment and stick to it. It's imperative that all group members pay the same fee for group, without exception. Differing fees will only create problems and unbalanced feelings. If a client is having financial challenges, lower her individual therapy fee, not her group fee, so as to maintain consistency.

There's always room for the occasional mishap (a forgotten checkbook, a paycheck that's been issued late due to circumstances out of her control, a stolen credit card, etc.) and for making exceptions. However, pay attention to chronic difficulties with money and address them immediately. It's best to ask the group member who's struggling with her financial obligation to stay after group so you can find out what's going on. If she has financial messes, she needs to talk about them in the group and put her attention on them. In any event, don't let clients run balances. Be clear and explicit.

It's important to offer clear direction about what constitutes an emergency that warrants a call to you rather than simply seeking support from other group members. Female sex and love addicts' attachment issues may cause them to want to connect with you outside group meetings about every little issue and minor crisis in their lives. It's your role to help them develop internal and external resources and to avoid fostering an unhealthy dependence on you. Suggest practical exercises like completing the "12's List," which is 12 things the client will do to take care of herself before calling you. Provide a handout of specific resources of Twelve Step meetings that are female-friendly and any other information you feel would benefit the clients. At the same time, remind them that certain situations such as feeling suicidal warrant quickly asking for help.

Where process notes are concerned, every state and licensing board has different rules and guidelines, so make sure you understand and abide by the rules that govern your license. Taking brief process notes during the group check-in is typically acceptable. Consider making a print out that you use from week-to-week that lets you make notes based on the check-in sheet you've created (see *Format for Group*

Session). You can then file this form in a folder you keep for each group you facilitate.

Once the group has checked in and you've completed your note taking, attend to the most serious matters first, then proceed from there according to how you've structured your group. As the group moves into the process phase, assist group members in connecting emotionally with one another so that they can, eventually, attach to one another. This is no easy feat given that FSLAs have attachment disorders that make it difficult for them to read non-verbal cues. They're also challenged with limited capacities to identify their thoughts and feelings, or to accurately read another. Over time you'll assist them in finding words for feelings by identifying sensations in the body and naming them, understanding their motives, beliefs, and desires, and the emotions and thoughts of others. Using your own somatic cues and tracking those of your clients will help them with their capacity for self-reflection and empathy (Cohen, 2011). Group therapy can be a powerful place to experience interactive regulation, which leads insecurely attached clients into a process of self-regulation, and therefore, a more secure way of attaching to others.

As a therapist it's important to recognize when you've found yourself off balance, and take action to return to a more calm and centered place. The Buddhist practice of *tonglen*, which means transformation, is a practice of creating space so people can breathe freely and relax (Chodron, 1997). Whenever you encounter pain, you breathe it in and wish that the world could be free of pain. When you breathe out, you send positive feelings of hope and trust. Visualize your client's pain as a black storm cloud, encompass it, and feel it as it enters your system. Then transform the cloud into a ball of white light that holds your client, the group, and yourself. Do this at least three times and feel the energy shift in the room.

Transitions for members entering or leaving group

At the inception of a therapy group or when a new member arrives or another member leaves, remind group members that one of the most stressful times in any family is when a new member is added to the family (birth of a child, addition of an elder, etc.) or when someone leaves the family (death, divorce, departure of young adult, etc.). Similar stress occurs in the life of a therapy group. The members can expect that times of transition will affect each person differently, and often in a variety of ways that provide good process material for the group as a whole.

When a new member arrives in a pre-existing group, it's good practice to have a current group member tell her story. Choose a woman to share who has the same or similar story to the newcomer, so that she can immediately relate to someone. Ask the newcomer to then share her story with the group, so as to begin her process of shame reduction. The sharing between these women will facilitate the newcomer's feeling welcomed and relieved that she belongs in the group.

In addition, boost the new FSLA's connection to the group by identifying and asking someone in the group if she's able to be a temporary cheerleader. That means she'll say hello first, sit next to the new FSLA, share contact information, check in daily until the next group meeting, and ask the new group member to go to coffee and to at least one Twelve Step meeting together before the next group session. The cheerleader also explains the group norms such as how to introduce self, check-in, ask for time, and provide feedback. The cheerleader defines certain terms the group uses such as "carefrontations," which are gentle ways to confront a member. Building rapport and support among the group is part of the power of group work, so having a cheerleader is helpful to increase retention and cohesion in the group. This practice also provides members a way to offer service, which increases their self-esteem and offers important validation for their hard work in recovery.

It's important for group members who've volunteered to be temporary cheerleaders to have guidelines about what to do if the new FSLA is depressed or in relapse. During an occasional group session process what it's like to be a cheerleader and what that role brings up for the recovering woman. Challenge any caretaking or codependent issues you observe.

Early termination from group is another transition that must be handled with equal intention. While leaving group prematurely is an option for all group members, it should be discouraged, because it's often unfortunate for the group member who's leaving and disruptive to the group. When a client does decide to leave group early, have her process her thoughts, feelings, and rationalizations. Leave plenty of time for the group to comment on what they're hearing, thinking, feeling, and relating to. Ideally, she'll agree to come back for a final termination session or, better yet, give the group a date by which she'll be leaving. This is always the best-case scenario and gives everyone time to express feelings, concerns, and well wishes about her departure.

If a group member leaves unceremoniously, the group is usually upset and has a tendency to want to talk about the departed member in disparaging ways. The group leader must contain her own transference issues about the member who's left so as not to allow inappropriate conversations or slip personally into talking about the absent member in a negative way. Group members should have the time and space to process the event in terms of how the departure leaves them feeling, what it reminds them of, how it makes them feel about the stability of the group, and so forth. Gossiping, bad mouthing, and general disrespect should not be allowed.

What happens in group, stays in group

Traditional group therapy insists on a therapeutic frame that doesn't allow for contact among group members in between group meetings. Clients are highly discouraged from "contaminating" the therapy by socializing with each other in any other context. Conversely, clients in group therapy who are also in recovery from sex and love addiction are *encouraged* to make contact out of group. Group members will often attend Twelve Step meetings together, attend fellowship afterward, call each other, and celebrate birthdays, anniversaries, and holidays with each other. The group can become a tight-knit family of choice that socializes its members and keeps them out of isolation. While these activities are crucial for the group members' growth and change, they can create pitfalls which can ultimately destroy the group if boundaries and rules aren't made explicit and adhered to.

To that point, one of the most important principles of group therapy is "what happens in group, stays in group." That means anything that is said or done during group therapy must not be discussed until the next group meeting. It's not acceptable to form cliques (sometimes called *sub-grouping*), which is the practice of gathering with a group member or small number of members outside the group session to gossip or register a complaint against the group therapist or another group member.

Because FSLAs often have difficulty with and confusion about boundaries, the leader should offer specific examples of what constitutes these sorts of violations, as well as reasons why these behaviors could be destructive to the function of the group. For example, a discussion by several members outside the group regarding their dissatisfaction with the group process can lead to an underlying feeling of dissatisfaction, distrust, and general uneasiness within the group. By not bringing the issue to the group, the dissatisfied members won't have the experience of assertive, honest communication with those they're disgruntled with, which is likely repeating previous dysfunctional communication styles. Additionally, other group members are robbed of the chance to discuss their concerns and to offer input and possible solutions for the issues at hand.

It's important to realize that this sort of explanation is often necessary to connect the dots for FSLAs, who frequently don't understand the implications of their own behaviors for themselves and others. Explain that if a member brings an issue to you, your response will be to steer her back into the group. Be clear that you'll invite her to share her concern with the group if she fails to bring it up, because failure to do so undermines the group as a whole. Remind the group that the principle of keeping group issues within the group is a critical tenet of group therapy. Emphasize that recovery requires rigorous honesty, and without it, the integrity of the group will be affected. Any infractions must be discussed in the group session and resolved in favor of the well-being of the group.

Group safety

Helping women to feel safe in a group requires intentional consideration of their fears. Because many women distrust other women, and because few women entering a group have experience with the deeply intimate sharing that takes place in a therapy group, particular care must be taken to build a container of safety where each woman can emerge in her own way without undue fears concerning shaming, gossip, or exclusion. The therapist can speak directly to the issue of trust and how to know when it's wise and safe to trust others, and what sort of signals or evidence would indicate a lack of trustworthiness or safety. These are important lessons in discernment.

At the first group session you should be prepared with a list of your group rules and boundaries, but initially let the group members collaborate to create their own guidelines and rules. This practice gives everyone a buy-in and eases the members into the kind of listening, sharing, and give-and-take that's part of group participation. Once they feel comfortable with their rules and boundaries, check them against yours to see if anything is missing, and if so, suggest any additions for their discussion. Once a consensus is reached, post the group "norms" where all can see them during sessions. When a group is working well together, they'll develop trust and respectful bonds with each other and incorporate these norms into a way of life.

Be sure to emphasize the importance of confidentiality, which has unique applications to the group setting. Sometimes a client shares another group member's story outside the group and believes she hasn't violated confidentiality because she didn't use the member's name (or at least not her last name). Invite the group members to share how they feel about this practice. Ideally, the group will establish for itself a boundary about this breech. Help group members understand that the group process is sacred, and it's unacceptable for a member to share anyone's process except her own. Especially when it comes to a population of FSLAs, the numbers are usually small in a given community, and it's too easy for someone to be identified by her story even if a name is withheld.

In addition, make sure that no group member reveals too much too soon and becomes over-exposed and too vulnerable. This objective can be achieved through simple guidance and explanation of the process that's taking place. Introducing subjects for discussion such as betrayal, competition, and verbal violence can give group members an opportunity to raise fears they experience in the present. Review the group guidelines from time to time and ask how the group believes it's doing at providing safety for all members.

Gender Make-up of Group

Recent research has shown gender differences in all phases of substance addiction, including patterns and levels of use, progression of the addictive process, relapse rates (Evans & Foltin, 2006; Franklin, Napier, & Ehrman, 2004; Lynch 2006), and treatment needs (Center for Substance Abuse Treatment, 2005). In studies of women-only groups for substance use disorders and other co-occurring conditions as compared with mixed gender groups, the researchers found that those in women-only groups had greater problem severity (partner violence, risky sexual behavior, PTSD, and other mood disorders) but also had the best outcomes (Center for Substance Abuse Treatment, 2005; Niv & Hser, 2007). Whereas to date no known research has studied women-only groups for recovery from sex and love addiction, it makes sense that similar benefits would likely apply. Zweben (2009) speculates that gender specific groups create a type of synergy that combine many factors that make it hard to measure what specific piece is most effective. Part of that synergy is about the alliance between group members (Lambert & Barley, 2001).

McClellan, Grisson, and Zanis (1997) have shown that it's the goodness of fit between the individual woman's problem profile and the actual services received that make gender-only groups relevant. For example, women who have been sexually or physically abused have a host of problems including PTSD and attachment issues. Early in recovery, women are less apt to discuss trauma related issues in a mixed gender group, since males can be less relational and nurturing than females. To add a further complication, women who have been perpetrated by males can have a more difficult time trusting men with these tender secrets. These considerations make it complicated for women to participate in a therapy group with men, especially early in a woman's recovery or group process.

Women-only group

Treating female sex and love addicts in a gender specific group is often the best practice for women in early recovery. When both the woman and her sobriety are fragile, she's better able to focus without the distraction of men. A forum for breaking the isolation of her addiction and connecting with others independent of intrigue and romantic or sexual entanglements is likely a new experience for her, and one that will bring her a sense of community and relief. Without the presence of men, a gender-specific group offers a more level playing field in which to practice the difficult relationship skills she needs to learn. Regardless of how much work an FSLA has done in individual therapy, there's no substitute for interacting with a group of peers. According to Gottman (2011, p. 138), "Loneliness has been shown to be enormously stressful and does not get better just on its own with the passage of time." A cohesive women's group will create an invitation for her to delve into the unexplored regions of raw pain, much of it experienced at the hands of men whom she either objectified or felt victimized by.

There are several challenges to be overcome, however, regarding a female-segregated group for recovery from sex and love addiction. A fundamental problem is that a gender-specific group for FSLAs often isn't locally available. Women simply aren't yet equally represented in recovery from sex and love addiction, and the pool is smaller for forming groups. In addition, some women may find it challenging to attend group meetings consistently. Females often act as primary caretakers for others, especially children and elderly parents, which may make it more difficult for them to give to themselves appropriately. They'll almost always put the needs of their loved ones before themselves. When females don't have a career position that allows for flexibility and latitude, it's hard to take time off for attending therapy. Beyond those practicalities, other complications make gender specific groups challenging for women, and those issues are outlined in a following section.

Mixed gender group

Despite the challenges of being in a mixed-gender group with men who also struggle with sex and love addiction, this situation can be very beneficial. It provides a chance for the FSLA to see men as simply other hurting human beings who battle with similar issues. Further, a mixed group allows her to practice boundaries where males and females are together for a common reason. The structure of the group provides safety as she unravels aspects of herself that she was previously unable to do without sexualizing the situation.

The group therapist must be aware of how women's voices can be silenced more easily as they navigate an environment where cultural norms regarding men can dominate. You need greater sensitivity and willingness to intervene when gender biases occur in the group. At the same time women have a unique voice, and feedback within the group is different when both sexes have the benefit of another perspective. As boys develop they typically play only with each other from around the age of seven until as teenagers they become interested in girls again. As a result boys develop a communication short-hand, and they frequently haven't cultivated the emotional intelligence that girls do by the nature of their more interactive and relational play (Gottman, 2011). Often the feedback women give their male peers comes from the empathic position of relating to their spouse or partner. Conversely, when men can be empathic, affirming, and encouraging without any sexual agenda, feedback can be embraced in a way that most FSLAs haven't encountered. Using their intuition and empowered by the group, they can take risks they otherwise wouldn't have had the courage to take.

That's not to say that things are always smooth in mixed groups. When an FSLA gets stuck in a victim stance and is unwilling to take responsibility for her behavior, men in groups begin to tune out. They're frequently dealing with women in their personal lives who have blamed them for much of what's gone wrong in their relationships, and the male addict's system has learned to throw the circuit breaker and dissociate from the conversation. If, on the other hand, an FSLA becomes critical or judgmental, she may find she has a fight on her hands, because her male peers are more likely to be confrontational. A strong group leader can assist by helping the entire group look at what's familiar in the process. Where have they found themselves in this situation in the past, and what was the outcome of the stance they took? What can they learn from each other about how to approach interactions differently? Perhaps they would benefit from using a softer startup rather than a harsh one, making effective repair attempts, and de-escalating the use of negativity by acknowledging the other's point of view in a way that can be heard rather than feeling resentful or disempowered (Gottman, 2011).

Ideally, an FSLA participates in a mixed gender group after she's been involved in a women-only group and has an established period of strong sobriety. Many therapists, though, have found the benefits of a mixed gender group outweigh the risks even for an FSLA who is newer in recovery. The best practice is to insist that an FSLA who is fresh in her healing process remains in concurrent individual therapy to have a place to process the challenges of being with men in such a vulnerable setting. By carefully choosing the participants, a co-ed group can provide the perfect opportunity to practice appropriate boundary setting and to learn to bond with men in a safe and supervised way.

Female sex addicts who have avoidant attachment styles seem to do better in mixed groups than women who are primarily love addicts and may have more ambivalent or disorganized styles. The detached and sometimes aggressive interactions of women who are seeking power through conquest often feel compatible with the men's interactions in a mixed-gender group. These women feel they can hold their own and don't overtly look to men for the approval many love addicts seek. Ways that these women use seduction in dress, mannerism, and innuendo are more likely to surface in a co-ed group rather than a gender-specific group, and the ability of the therapist to gently confront this behavior in either gender helps both see the addictive thinking.

Love and relationship addicts have a different task in mixed-gender groups. Love addicts create fantasy partners when they minimize their voice in deference to their male counterparts. As these women participate in group with men who are attracted to the same fantasy that the "perfect partner will save me," the addictive spell is broken for both.

Therapist's gender

As was described in the previous chapter, the gender of the therapist is an important consideration, which also applies to group therapy. Again, some controversy exists in the clinical community, and no known published research is available as a guide. The conventional wisdom is that a gender-specific group is best led by the same-gender therapist. Although that practice might lessen the clinical challenges of leading the group, it's still somewhat impractical given the limited number of therapists who are skilled at both group therapy and working with a sexually addicted population.

Clinical expertise and personal health are more important than the therapist's gender. It may be harder for a male therapist initially to join with a group of female SLAs and to manage the transference issues that may quickly emerge, but it's definitely possible. A male therapist may provide a corrective experience for female members if he enters the group process with his affective self while maintaining skilled boundaries.

Specific Challenges FSLAs Bring to the Group Setting

It must be stressed that managing FSLAs whether in a gender-specific or mixed gender group is quite challenging. Most women in this population are adept at seduction and manipulation as coping strategies, which have served significant survival purposes in their lives. Some of these strategies are conscious, while others remain unconscious. When unconscious, the client doesn't initially identify or understand her behaviors as dysfunctional. Unhealthy maneuvers may include a wide range of behaviors such as jealousy toward other group members that masquerades as criticism or hostility, competition for the attention of the therapist or "floor time" during group, attention-seeking behaviors (histrionics, self-dramatizing, etc.), seductive behaviors toward others, manipulation through money or gifts, talking about group matters or members outside the group setting, and so forth.

Often, detrimental, regressive behaviors that have been extinguished in individual therapy will re-emerge in group therapy or come into play for the first time due to the demands of the group setting. (Developmentally, think about the toddler who regresses into earlier behaviors when there's family stress.) This stage may come as a surprise to the therapist, who must be prepared to confront the client's process in a straightforward but supportive manner, which demonstrates to the group the expectations of how group will operate and what it has to offer. The clinician can emphasize to all members that group therapy often surfaces long-buried coping mechanisms, and that the group offers a place to learn healthier ways of behaving and communicating.

Dynamics among women

The most predominant challenge to the group process is the dynamics among the women themselves. As described in an earlier chapter, women often have a deep dislike and distrust toward other women. Females are seen as the enemy—the competition for men or adversaries to women. This stance toward other women may play out consciously or unconsciously, is deeply rooted in attachment injuries, and is defined by what McDaniel (2012) calls "mother hunger." Females have an innate longing for their mothers, but unfortunately many mothers have been wounded themselves, and are thus ill equipped to meet their children's needs. Women may idolize other women who seem nurturing, like some women in a therapy group, and then may blame and turn on them when the women fail to meet the FSLA's every need. This dynamic is played out repeatedly among women in various settings such as work, social settings, school, church, or synagogue.

Women who have had cold and distant relationships with their mothers aren't likely to trust easily. While drawn to a nurturing therapist, they are quick to see you as siding against them at the slightest hint of disapproval. Being too direct, especially too quickly, can result in deflection of any feedback. Karpman's Triangle (Karpman, 1968) is an especially dangerous trap where the therapist can get caught bouncing between either persecuting or rescuing while the client is firmly in possession of the victim spot. (More details about the Karpman's Triangle are in chapter 7.)

Clients who have had overly enmeshed mothers will find that they're being seduced into a trap of always offering encouragement or affirmation and struggling to keep solid boundaries. These FSLAs don't know where they stop and others start, and they can be seductive as you approach them with approval. Remember they need to learn differentiation, and setting healthy boundaries is an important task for them. Help them be gentle with themselves and understand that it's okay for them to set limits for themselves, and it's okay for them to assist others at times. These decisions aren't right or wrong, and the point is for these FSLAs to learn from whatever decisions they make, as each one potentially increases their self-understanding.

Competition among themselves is another challenge women sex and love addicts encounter in group therapy. Culturally, in a still largely patriarchal society, women compete for recognition and jobs with other women as well as with men. Women learn they must be smarter, faster, and tougher than men (and each other) if they want to get ahead. The "glass ceiling" has thick double panes, and only a limited number of women are allowed to touch it, much less push through it. Further, women are bombarded from birth with images of the perfect woman, and women judge themselves and other women harshly against this false, unattainable model. Women frequently report feeling the stinging judgment of other women, and the group clinician must be sensitive to this dynamic, both as a perception and as a reality.

Poor communication skills

In addition, women in group therapy often have little or no experience with honest, direct, and assertive communication. Again, a male-dominated culture, where direct communication is accepted, is still often uncomfortable with women who communicate in that way. Women who master healthy, assertive communication are often labeled "bitches" instead of good communicators. Women, therefore, learn to temper their views and lower their voices. Unless the skill of direct, assertive interaction is taught and modeled with ample opportunity for practice, FSLAs will revert to hinting, subterfuge, gossip, and criticism.

The acute codependency of the FSLA makes it very difficult for her to present a subject or concern if she fears her opinion won't be met with universal approval. Although she may have been able to track the therapist's affect and responses in an individual setting and moderate what she presented to please the therapist, this type of hypervigilance becomes impossible within a group audience. The FSLA won't be able to observe the reactions of all the participants to make sure she's pleasing all of them. This circumstance may cause her such extreme discomfort that it becomes a serious obstacle to her participation, and she may want to terminate group therapy prematurely. The leader and the group members can help her identify this challenge, validate its difficulty, and encourage her to continue.

Further, the FSLA may misinterpret differences of opinion in very black and white terms; that is, a difference of opinion must mean that one of us is wrong. This mindset, coupled with indirect and ineffective communication skills, makes a group ripe for division and sub-grouping. Watch for the woman who gravitates toward other group members she perceives as viewing things similarly for the purpose of banding together to indirectly attack those who are on the "other" side.

Group dynamics and communication challenges should be specifically addressed in the group sessions on a regular basis. The facilitator may have to initiate conversation about group dynamics she or he observes but that haven't been previously talked about. Learning to tolerate differences of opinion and negative feedback is part of the healing process. In the case of negative feedback, learning to determine what aspects of this feedback ring true and seem valid, as well as what doesn't seem accurate, is again part of the healing. Most FSLAs are highly sensitive to any sort of feedback, and hearing feedback that's perceived as negative can be quite triggering. It's important for the therapist to understand the deep fears of abandonment, profound shame, and betrayal that plague the FSLA. Gently guide her into vulnerable sharing while also coaching the other group members on acceptance, honesty, and supportive disagreement.

Codependency

The term codependency was originally coined in substance abuse treatment to describe the characteristics of the wives of men who abused alcohol. The term was intended to describe some of the reactions that regularly occur as a result of the distorted reality that comes from being in a relationship with an addict. The concept of codependency has evolved to describe a dysfunctional style of relating (Irwin, 1995). And to take it a step further, this type of relating also reflects similar behaviors common to someone with an anxious attachment style (Wallin, 2007). These clients are filled with self-doubt and are fearful about being too independent. Fosha (2003) observes they can feel, but they can't deal (with their fear of abandonment). At times these clients can seem almost borderline, drawing attention by being overwhelmed and helpless, or angry and chaotic, while also being superficially cooperative and seductive with attempts to help. Being an intruding and compulsive caretaker, there is constant need for confirmation and attention. They have incredible fear of abandonment and are hypervigilant for any sign of displeasure from the group leader or members. Because some attention is never enough to quench their longing for love and acceptance, they exhibit poor boundaries and frequently put themselves in harm's way (Corley & Hook, 2012).

Higher propensity to drop out

It's not uncommon for FSLAs to complain that they feel worse when they leave a group session than when they came in. Frequently these women witness someone in the group experiencing a high level of emotional feelings, which can be overwhelming for someone new to therapy. The FSLA may realize she might have to feel her own feelings rather than medicate them. This reaction can be the reason women give for their desire to terminate group therapy almost immediately upon entering.

Other reasons for leaving group that have been cited in research with other addictions (Daley, Douaihy, Weiss, & Mercer, 2009) include scheduling difficulties, relapse or desire to use, not finding group helpful, wanting a different type of therapy (wanting more individual time), unwillingness to participate, and need for higher level of care. Research reflects that women with the highest level of burden tend to be at greatest risk for early termination and poor outcomes (Brown, Huba, & Melchoir, 1995).

Influencing Motivation to Change Through Group

Motivation is viewed as an important component throughout the process of change. Research has found the stages of change to be significant in a client's success in maintaining consistent and sustained recovery (DiClemente, Schlundt, & Gemmell, 2004; Miller & Rollnick, 2002; Prochaska & DiClemente,1983) either in group or individual therapy. Like other addicts, most FSLAs enter therapy with some ambivalence about the changes they want to make and report being in the contemplation stage of change (Moyers & Rollnick, 2002; Reid, 2007). Generally the greater the attendance and compliance with treatment directions, the better a client does (DiClemente, Schlundt, & Gemmell, 2004), so it's important to assess readiness and stage of change and address both in individual work and group if possible.

The stages of change as defined by Prochaska and DiClemente (1984) are pre-contemplation, contemplation, preparation, action, and maintenance. A widely used instrument for assessing the stage of change is the Stage of Change Scale (McConnaughy, DiClemente, Prochaska, & Velicer, 1989; McConnaughy, Prochaska, & Velicer, 1983), but we've found it's just as easy to give the client a handout with the stages and a brief explanation about each, and let her tell you which stage she thinks best describes her. Each stage is explained below with the implications for an FSLA's participation in group therapy and how to address where she is in her process.

Pre-contemplation stage

When an FSLA comes into treatment at the insistence of another person, she often enters in the pre-contemplation stage. This point means that she'll likely use any excuse to leave group and say it's not right for her. She isn't convinced that the negative aspects of her behavior outweigh the positive. These clients are either reluctant, rebellious, or resigned, and they can rationalize their way out of almost anything. A reluctant FSLA often fears the discomfort of changing or has tried and failed before, and she just can't see herself as being able to cope without acting out. Often these women combine their sexual or romantic behaviors with the use of alcohol or other drugs, so they're also resistant to giving up the substance. The thought of not using is overwhelming.

To manage a reluctant pre-contemplator, listen carefully, provide feedback with empathy, and summarize what you hear. Ask another member of the group to talk about what it was like for her early in the process, or to share how the group member dealt with similar issues. Affirm the pre-contemplating FSLA with some insight she's already gleaned about herself or empathize with the level of burden with which she's trying to cope. Help her reduce her anxiety by learning to breathe deeply while exhaling very slowly, which allows her muscles to relax. In fact, ask the whole group to demonstrate with you while everyone does it. The group somatic calmness will help regulate her (and you).

If the pre-contemplator is rebellious, she'll have researched the problem, knows more than anyone else about the problem, and doesn't want to be told what to do or be pushed around. Ask a group member to provide a menu of choices to think about as a possible solution to an issue. Start with small changes and even think about harm reduction in the beginning, such as wondering if she might consider more self-care by engaging in some less risky behavior rather than stopping cold turkey. Again this is a place that a group member or several group members can offer suggestions about what behavior might be less risky for her health. Since FSLAs are more likely to put themselves in harm's way more often than non-FSLAs (Corley & Delmonico, 2011), this is a great area to get the group to support each other in valuing safety first.

A few of the pre-contemplators have made many attempts to stop their addictive behaviors, but they haven't had any success in long-term sobriety and have given up. This is a time to ask another group member to review a relapse biopsy/autopsy, which offers detailed work about how her sobriety got sick or died with a relapse, emotional and situational triggers, thinking errors, or excuses she employed. Then ask the FSLA what she learned about her own recent relapse from the other group member. Ask her to do her own biopsy/autopsy, but make sure you ask her what will stand in the way of her completing this assignment. Request volunteers from the group to be accountability cheerleaders for her and to make a commitment to check in with her during the week to help her get at least some of the assignment done. Transform any insights she might have to motivational self-talk.

For the rationalizer who has all the answers and doesn't want to change because of the personal risk or cost involved, ask the FSLA to help you understand how the sexual or romantic behavior helps her. What problems does it solve for her? After she realizes you're not going to argue with her, she may be more willing to complete a decision making matrix, or you can ask the whole group to make a decision matrix about a similar behavior as an example. Examine the pros and cons of the behavior and summarize what you hear the client saying. It's important to go slowly and not move to confrontation. Remember, the rationalizer has already been confronted by her spouse, parents, and friends, and she's sick of the war of words. Encourage, inform, and summarize, reframe the behavioral change desired, then leave the door open for her to return.

The "perfect" recovering FSLA will fly into health, appearing as if she's in the action stage and taking to recovery like a duck to water. Beware. This woman will enter treatment because she's been in tremendous pain and knows she can't stop her behaviors. She'll exhibit a strong intellect and quickly be able to use the language and tools of the program, which will appear to create cohesion in the group. Often she becomes a beacon of recovery to newcomers on "how to do it." However, after she's made it through withdrawal and stabilized, she'll decide that she's "better enough." Ask the group members to intervene before she decides to leave the group by having them talk about the effect her easy recovery has had on them, and how she's managed to get it together so quickly. The group can give her feedback on what her perfectionism sounds and feels like to them, and they can inquire about the details of her personal life such as whether she's starting to groom a new guy. If you're seduced by her façade, she'll begin to miss group with the excuse that she's busy at work, working on a new project, or has family matters to attend to. You may find yourself calling her and beginning the chase, trying to get her back into group. Don't be surprised when you learn that she's had a breast enlargement to make herself feel better, that she's met a "great new guy," and that she won't be coming back to group.

Contemplation stage

The second stage of change is contemplation. This FSLA knows there's a serious need for change, but she goes back and forth between considering change and then rejecting it. Your role is to help tip the balance in favor of change. What sets the contemplator apart from the pre-contemplator is that she can see how little good her addictive behavior is doing to solve her problems now. At the same time she has difficulty determining the amount of work it will actually take to obtain recovery, and she has no idea the impact that the loss of her addiction will have on her, so sometimes she seems overly confident that she'll be able to change. It's important for her to have accountability partners/cheerleaders who check in with her daily, and agree to have coffee, or go to Twelve Step meetings together. Very promising research from the drug addiction arena indicates this supportive behavior fosters success in terms of longer periods of sobriety and wellbeing (Kaskutas, Bond, & Humphreys, 2002).

Determination stage

The FSLAs in the determination stage have made some small efforts to change, but they haven't fully embraced everything necessary to really change. These are the group members who're excited to do assignments, but don't always follow through, or who volunteer to be helpful to others as part of their service, but sometimes take this step because they want to feel wanted. Rather than trying to cheerlead this person into trying harder, your task is to help her find a change strategy that is acceptable, accessible, appropriate, and effective. Using solution-focused language is very important. For example, ask, "What's worked thus far when you find that you're fixated on someone in a restaurant, but you want to focus on the person you're having lunch with instead?" Again, this is a great time to utilize the group to bring up examples where members have noticed the FSLA hasn't come through, and then to support her in trying another strategy.

Action stage

In the action stage the FSLA is consistently engaging in particular actions intended to bring about the desired change. It's difficult to avoid relying on these group members to supply great examples for new members, but be cautious. When someone is in the action stage, she often wants to look good to the others and doesn't ask for help when she really should. Always ask the FSLA group member who's in the action stage to identify one area where she lied (by omission or commission) or engaged in behaviors that didn't help her recovery. Her responses help her formulate assignments or discussions in group regarding the next stage—the maintenance stage.

Maintenance stage

This final stage is when the FSLA is really working to identify high-risk situations and coming up with action plans for those troublesome areas. A fun group activity is to discuss the "perfect relapse," and then prepare a relapse prevention plan for the situation described. Have part of the group come up with a list of the excuses they would use to engage in perfect relapse, while the other half of the group formulates effective rebuttals for any excuses. These types of activities lighten the group, help the clients foster teamwork, and highlight the reality of how easy it is to relapse.

"Magical" Themes and Activities to Use in Group

When a women's group is functioning well, it can be a magical force for growth. The synergy, carefrontation, and genuine affection among the group members creates a compelling energy that propels women forward. While this occurrence is partially due to unidentifiable reasons such as the chemistry among the group members (including you as the leader), there are avenues a group therapist can follow that foster these "magical" moments. Some of these paths involve your exploration of clinical themes, and others have to do with more concrete activities. The possibilities are limited only by your clinical intuition, imagination, and expertise. Following are some specific examples of using both themes and activities in group therapy.

Archetypes

Folklore, myths, and literature have used archetypes for thousands of years, and some of these images can be employed to add depth to group members' self-understanding. Caroline Myss outlines four archetypal figures that are especially pertinent to many FSLAs. Called the "Survival Archetypes," Myss identifies four primary symbols that illustrate our major life challenges and how we choose to survive: the Child, the Victim, the Prostitute, and the Saboteur (Myss, 2004). She describes how these voices work together to show us how we handle fear, insecurities, and vulnerabilities. The Child represents our guardian of innocence, the Victim the guardian of self-esteem, the Prostitute the guardian of faith, and the Saboteur is our guardian of choice. As we learn to identify these voices we can bring them into alignment with our spiritual selves, and they'll become voices of strength, guidance, wisdom, and faith.

In group settings you can help your FSLAs identify which voice they are embracing and whether they are coming from a shadow or fear-based place, or a light or healed perspective. If the Child is demanding all the attention in the room and pouts if she doesn't get her way, explore how the FSLA can lovingly embrace the Child and calm her fears by reassuring her there's no need to dominate the group to get attention. She doesn't need to fall into the Victim and accuse the group of not valuing her or her experience about some situation, and therefore expecting the group to rescue her by constantly reassuring her that her viewpoint is right. The Prostitute archetype will tell the FSLA that her voice doesn't really matter, and that to get the love and attention the group has to offer, she must sell her soul and agree with whatever the others say, even if she doesn't concur. The Saboteur is the voice that causes self-doubt and interrupts the process of change. The FSLA will need the courage to trust her intuitive guidance and move forward, even if it doesn't always seem logical to do so.

This theme of survival offers rich fodder for group process and activities. If you're familiar with experiential therapy or have training in psychodrama, you can have group members select an object that represents their Survival Archetype or act out these symbolic voices. If a group member is unable to see herself as operating from one of these survival places, others can invite her to stand beside the figure with whom she most identifies, and the group can offer her feedback regarding how they experience her. Another idea is to ask each client to create a collage or picture of her primary Survival Voice and share it with the group.

Miscellaneous activities

An almost unlimited number of exercises and activities can enrich the group experience. Indeed, most of the power found in group therapy comes from the guided interaction among members that the therapist orchestrates. Regardless of the activities you choose, keep in mind the critical objectives of this work: to create safety and to foster connection within the group and to a Higher Power. A few specific ideas for eloquent group activities follow.

The Well

As a closing group exercise, invite the women to stand and form a tight ring by turning slightly to the side so that their left shoulders are pointed into the circle and their left arms are extended forward, then hooking their left thumbs in front of them (with their right arms remaining free on the outside of the circle). Explain that the space in the middle represents a deep and magical well that holds many wonderful treasures. It also provide a bottomless receptacle for anything that's discarded into its depths. Invite the women to take turns dropping something imaginary into the well and pulling something imaginary out. Explain they're to put something into the well that they know they need to leave behind or get rid of, and they're to draw out of the well a treasure they would like to receive. Here's how it works: A woman "throws" something into the well by stretching her right hand behind her head and pretending to toss something into the abyss. As she makes a slow throwing motion, she says, "I put into the well . . ." and as she brings her arm back over her head she says, "and I take out of the well . . ." She completes each sentence with only a word or two; for example, "I put into the well my shame, and I take out of the well comfort." After each woman has participated, the group says together the final words over the well, "And let it be so."

She's My Sister

This exercise is particularly powerful for offering comfort to a hurting group member. If someone is flooded with her internal negative voices or messages, or for any other reason seems in need of extra encouragement, invite her to sit in a chair in the middle of the group. Ask her to imagine what she'd like to hear if each woman could say something to her. Give her a moment to collect her thoughts and then ask her to share two or three statements that have come to mind. If she's comfortable with being touched, invite the members one by one to move slowly to her chair and place a hand on her arm or back, and then say, "I am with you." Each group member remains touching the seated woman as other group members join the circle, each time repeating the phrase, "I am with you." When all are in the circle, encourage the seated woman to breathe in their support, and help her to stay grounded, if necessary. After the group has stood in silence for a moment, invite them to close with the Serenity Prayer or another meaningful saying.

Voice of an Angel

From Dayton's work (2005), this angel exercise illustrates the gift of resilience and offers sweet affirmations. Ask group members to think of someone who was significant in their childhood, someone who reached out to them or saw their potential: an angel in their lives. Place an empty chair in the middle of the circle and ask a volunteer to start the process. She stands behind the empty chair, imagines the angel sitting in the chair, and introduces the angel to the rest of the group and describes the angel's place in her life. Next, the client reverses roles with the angel, which means the client speaks as if she were the angel, and the empty chair now represents the client. The angel stands behind the empty chair and tells the group about the client. For example, the angel says, "Kathy [the client] was creative and found ways to entertain herself when no one was taking care of her. She had a sweet spirit and was quick to go to someone else's rescue," and so forth. Each person gets an opportunity to hear from her angel, and the group shares about the experience.

Graduation ceremony

A graduation ceremony is a powerful and affirming way to mark the end of a woman's participation in group therapy, and it offers a chance for members to use their sensuality and creativity to fashion a meaningful send-off. Women will often go the extra mile for partners they're addicted to, but will rarely take the same time and care for other women they've befriended. Creating a graduation ceremony for a sister in recovery alters that pattern. You can set some parameters so that the group time is used effectively and the graduate gets what she needs, but leave the rest up to the remaining group members.

Time and ritual are key to saying a healthy good-bye. One example of a graduation ceremony requires a good bit of advance preparation, but it's also powerful in its symbolism and impact. Instruct group members to come prepared for the graduation session by bringing a note for the graduate that describes the positive recovery they've seen in her, as well as any concerns for her future. Ask members to also bring in a small gift for her that symbolizes recovery. Remind them not to spend money on lavish gifts but to make it a gift from the heart. Appropriate items might be a small candle, affirmation stone, or personal item the member wants to pass on. Also ask the graduate to choose two women as stewards for her graduation ceremony, and invite them to bring simple flowers, a candle, and a small cake or goodies for the event. The graduating woman also prepares a card and brings a token for each group member as described above.

At the group meeting that includes the graduation, divide the time so that half is spent on group business as usual, and the other half on the graduation ceremony. Ask the stewards of the ceremony to set the mood by lighting candles, placing flowers, creating an altar, or whatever else they've designed for the ritual. Arrange the chairs in a semi-circle with two chairs in the center so that the graduate can sit in one and other group members can take turns sitting in the other. When you're ready, ask for a volunteer to start the process. The first group member reads her card regarding the recovery she sees in the graduate and the concerns she has for her recovery. She then shares her token and its meaning. When she's finished, the graduate reciprocates in the same manner. This process continues until the entire group has had a turn with the graduate. In addition to affirming her, it provides affirmation and encouragement for each member present.

As the group leader you can choose to participate or not. If you do, you may read a letter that tracks the graduate's progress from the time you met her to the present day, give her a card, a token, or not. It's up to you and what you deem appropriate given the tenor of the group, the make-up of personalities in the group, and your therapeutic style. Whatever you choose, do it consistently for every graduation so that you continue to model good boundaries.

Finally, end the group by placing the graduate in the middle of the circle. If she's comfortable with the practice, have group members place an affirming hand on her and say the Serenity Prayer or another Twelve Step prayer in unison, or read a passage or poem that has meaning to them as recovering women. When that moment is complete, share the refreshments the stewards have brought. Leave a few minutes for everyone to mingle and laugh before they say their final good-byes.

Conclusion

Group therapy offers a potent avenue of healing for the FSLA and near limitless opportunities for therapeutic work. To return to the concepts of Yalom (2005) that opened this chapter, group therapy contains the curative factors the recovering woman desperately needs: a boost of hope, a sense of safety and belonging, a place to practice new behaviors, an opportunity to learn, and perhaps most important, a place of connection with other women on a similar healing journey.

REFERENCES

Bednar, R., & Kaul, T. (1994). Experiential group research: Can the canon fire? In A. E. Bergin & S. L. Garfield (Eds.), *Handbook of psychotherapy and behavior change* (4th ed., pp. 631-663). New York, NY: Wiley.

Brooks, D. M. (2011). Group therapy. In M. Galanter & H. D. Kleber (Eds.), *Psychotherapy for the treatment of substance abuse* (pp. 277-298). Washington, DC: American Psychiatric Publishing.

Brown, V. B., Huba, G. J., & Melchoir, L. A. (1995). Level of burden: Women with more than one co-occurring disorder. *Journal of Psychoactive Drugs, 27*(4), 321-325.

Burlingame, G. M., Fuhriman, A., & Johnson, J. E. (2001). Cohesion in group psychotherapy. *Psychotherapy, 38*, 373-384.

Center for Substance Abuse Treatment. (2005). Substance abuse treatment: Group therapy. Rockville, MD: Substance Abuse and Mental Health Services Administration (US); (Treatment Improvement Protocol (TIP) Series, No. 41.) Three Criteria for the Placement of Clients in Groups. Retrieved from http://www.ncbi.nlm.nih.gov/books/NBK64215/

Chodron, P. (1997). *When things fall apart: Heart advice for difficult times*. Boston, MA: Shambhala.

Cohen, S. L. (2011). Coming to our senses: The application of somatic psychology to group psychotherapy. *The International Journal of Group Psychotherapy, 63*(3), 397-413.

Corley, M. D., & Delmonico, D. (2011, September). *Closing the gap: Results from the Women's Sexuality Survey on Female Sex and Love Addicts*. Presentation at the Society for the Advancement of Sexual Health Conference, LaJolla, CA.

Corley, M. D., & Hook, J. (2012). Women, female sex and love addicts, and use of the Internet. *Sexual Addiction & Compulsivity, 19*(1-2), 53-76.

Daley, D., Douaihy, A., Weiss, R., & Mercer, D. (2009). Group therapies. In R. Ries, D. Fiellin, S. Miller, & R. Saitz (Eds.), *Principles of addiction medicine* (4th ed., pp. 757-768). Philadelphia, PA: Lippincott Williams & Wilkins.

Daley, D., Mercer, D., & Carpenter, G. (1998). *Group drug counseling participant recovery workbook*. Holmes Beach, FL: Learning Publications.

Dayton, T. (2005). *The living stage: A step-by-step guide to psychodrama, sociometry, and experiential group therapy*. Deerfield Beach, FL: Health Communications.

DiClemente, C., Schlundt, B., & Gemmell, B. (2004). Readiness and stages of change in addiction treatment. *The American Journal on Addictions, 13*, 103-119.

Ducan, B., Wampold, B., Miller, S., & Hubble, A. (2009). *The heart and soul of change: What works in therapy.* Washington, DC: APA Press.

Evans, S. M., & Foltin, R. W. (2006). Exogenous progesterone attenuates the subjective effects of cocaine in women but not men. *Neuropsychopharmacology, 31*, 659-674.

Flores, P. J. (2001). Addiction as an attachment disorder: Implications for group therapy. *International Journal of Group Psychotherapy, 51*(1), 63-81.

Flores, P. J. (2007). *Group psychotherapy with group populations: An integration of 12 Step and psychodynamic theory* (3rd ed.). Binghamton, NY: Haworth Medical Press.

Fosha, D. (2003). Dyadic regulation and experiential work with emotion and relatedness in trauma and disorganized attachment. In M. L. Solomon & D. J. Siegel (Eds.), *Healing trauma: Attachment, mind, body, and brain* (pp. 221-281). New York, NY: Norton.

Franklin, T. R., Napier, K., & Ehrman, R. (2004). Retrospective study: Influence of menstrual cycle on cue-induced cigarette craving. *Nicotine Tobacco Research, 1*, 171-175.

Gottman, J. M. (2011). *The science of trust: Emotional attunement for couples.* New York, NY: Norton.

Irwin, H. J. (1995). Codependency, narcissism, and childhood trauma. *Journal of Clinical Psychology, 51*(5), 658-665.

Karpman, S. B. (1968). Fairy tales and script drama analysis. *Transactional Analysis Bulletin, 7*(26). Retrieved from http://en.wikipedia.org/wiki/Karpman_drama_triangle

Kaskutas, L. A., Bond, J., & Humphreys, K. (2002). Social networks as mediators of the effect of Alcoholics Anonymous. *Addiction, 97*(7), 891-900.

Lambert, M. J., & Barley, D. E. (2001). Research summary on the therapeutic relationship and psychotherapy outcome. *Psychotherapy, 38*, 357-364.

Lynch, W. J. (2006). Sex differences in vulnerability to drug self-administration. *Experimental & Clinical Psychopharmacology, 1*, 34-41.

McClellan, A. T., Grisson, G. R., & Zanis, D. (1997). Problem-service matching in addiction treatment. *Archives of General Psychiatry,54*, 730-735.

McConnaughy, E. A., DiClemente, C. C., Prochaska, J. O., & Velicer, W. F. (1989). Stages of change in psychotherapy: A follow-up report. *Psychotherapy, 26*, 494–503.

McConnaughy, E. A., Prochaska, J. O., & Velicer, W. F. (1983). Stages of change in psychotherapy: Measurement and sample profiles. *Psychotherapy: Theory, Research, and Practice, 20*, 368–375.

McDaniel, K. (2012. *Ready to heal: Breaking free of addictive relationships.* (3rd ed.). Carefree, AZ: Gentle Path Press.

Miller, W. R., & Rollnick, S. (2002). *Motivational interviewing: Preparing people for change.* New York, NY: Guilford Press.

Moyers, T. B., & Rollnick, S. (2002). A motivational interviewing perspective on resistance in psychotherapy. *Psychotherapy in Practice, 58*(2), 185-193.

Myss, C. (2004). *Sacred contracts: Awakening your divine potential.* Carlsbad, CA: Hay House.

Niv, H., & Hser, Y. I. (2007). Women-only and mixed-gender drug abuse treatment programs: Service needs, utilization and outcomes. *Drug & Alcohol Dependency, 87*(2-3), 194-201.

Ormont, L. (1992). *The group therapy experience.* New York, NY: St. Martin's Press.

Ormont, L. (2001). Meeting maturational needs in the group setting. *International Journal of Group Psychotherapy, 51*, 343-360.

Prochaska, J. O., & DiClemente, C. C. (1983). Stages and processes of self-change of smoking: Toward an integrative model of change. *Journal of Consulting and Clinical Psychology, 51*, 390-395.

Prochaska, J. O., & DiClemente, C. C. (1984). *The transtheoretical approach: Crossing traditional boundaries of therapy.* Homewood, IL: Dow Jones-Irwin.

Reid, R. (2007). Assessing readiness to change among clients seeking help for hypersexual behavior. *Sexual Addiction & Compulsivity,14*(3), 167-186.

Wallin, D. (2007). *Attachment in psychotherapy.* New York, NY: Guilford Press.

Yalom, I. (2005). *Theory and practice of group psychotherapy* (5th ed.). New York, NY: Basic Books.

Zweben, J. E. (2009). Special issues in treatment: Women. In R. Ries, D. Fiellin, S. Miller, & R. Saitz (Eds.),*Principles of addiction medicine* (4th ed., pp. 465-478). Philadelphia, PA: Lippincott Williams & Wilkins.

CHAPTER 6

Best Practices for Arresting Acting Out

Susan Campling, Deborah Corley, Marnie Ferree, Linda Hudson

Stepping into a therapist's office is a courageous and terrifying choice for the woman who struggles with sex and love addiction. If she's at all psychologically minded, some part of her may recognize the importance of this step, and that if she follows it with myriad subsequent steps, this process will change her life profoundly. At the same time, the FSLA usually can't imagine living without her primary coping mechanism, much less entertain the process required to do so. She suffers perhaps the quintessential double bind: She can't envision life without her addiction, yet this "life" is undoubtedly killing her, at least internally. Your role as her clinician is to employ the therapeutic considerations discussed in chapter 4 along with the best clinical practices as outlined by experience and research. It's no easy task and requires both sensitivity and stamina.

Complete a Comprehensive Life History

The need for a full life history is paramount for the therapist to begin work with a sex and love addict. It's both a method of assessment and treatment planning as well as a model of treatment. Often the therapist is the first caring and supportive person who has entered the life of an FSLA and offered her enough safety to tell her story.

However, before she can take this step, the FSLA must challenge her denial, which often requires gentle therapeutic intervention. Denial is to be expected with any addict's story. It isn't easy for the FSLA to let go of the illusion that her behavior is working for her, or that she's unique, or that no one is injured by her actions. She has employed countless rationalizations to normalize her behaviors and grant herself permission to act out. These mechanisms enable the FSLA to develop ego-syntonic cognitions to behaviors that would normally be abhorrent for her. Shame makes it extremely difficult for the FSLA to be honest about her behavior and even her family history. The maladaptive narrative must be deconstructed to enable the recovering FSLA to create a new and healing self-story. Denial disrupts the rewriting of the story and serves as a "writer's block" to recovery. Be patient and understand this process is often frightening and upsetting to your client.

Genogram

There are a number of effective ways to obtain a comprehensive life history. A genogram or family map (McGoldrick, Gerson, & Petry, 2008) is helpful as the FSLA begins to name the players in her life that have formed attachments, nurtured, dismissed, encouraged, provided approval or acceptance, criticized, demeaned, abused, or abandoned her. Even though many women have given thought and often assigned great value to the ways they interact with family members, literally putting the family tree on paper is one of the most powerful techniques available.

The genogram provides a format for drawing a family map that outlines family relationships. Ideally this map includes at least three generations. It provides a visual outline for information rich with context and historical data. Although taking a written clinical history is certainly important, it easily becomes part of the file that may be quickly buried in the midst of other client information. Using a genogram provides a way to update the clinical picture as it emerges. It offers clients a visual diagram of intergenerational family relationships, illnesses, occupations, and behavioral patterns, and it provides clinicians a large amount of information quickly that can be added to or corrected in each session.

Genograms offer a way to join with an FSLA often from the first session. Using this tool to gather information helps clients see their own history in a new way, through a different lens, and from a systemic perspective. Clinicians can reframe, detoxify, and normalize emotion-laden issues, and often diffuse shame in the process of seeing the family currently and through time from previous generations.

In discussions around each generation you can learn what part ethnicity, nationality, sexuality, religious beliefs, culture, and addictions have played in the belief systems a client has developed. Identifying the rules that operated in her family frequently brings to light reasons for the unconscious ways the FSLA has been interacting with relationships. For example, if her father was dismissive or emotionally unavailable to the client, her need to have a partner "pay attention" to her might explain why she continues to pursue a fantasy object, despite all indications that he isn't interested in a reciprocal relationship.

Genograms are simple to use. Men are identified as squares and women as circles. A line connecting the two indicates marriage or significant relationship, and a double line through the connecting lines indicates divorce or separation. An X across the circle or square indicates a death; a triangle indicates a current pregnancy. Drawing double lines between two people indicates a close relationship, and triple lines indicate an enmeshed relationship. A jagged line between people indicates conflict in the relationship (McGoldrick et al., 2008). Genogram software programs can also be useful for clinicians who want to use this method.

The following illustration shows the basics of constructing a genogram. The subject of the genogram (your client) is identified by coloring in his or her symbol.

Sample Genogram

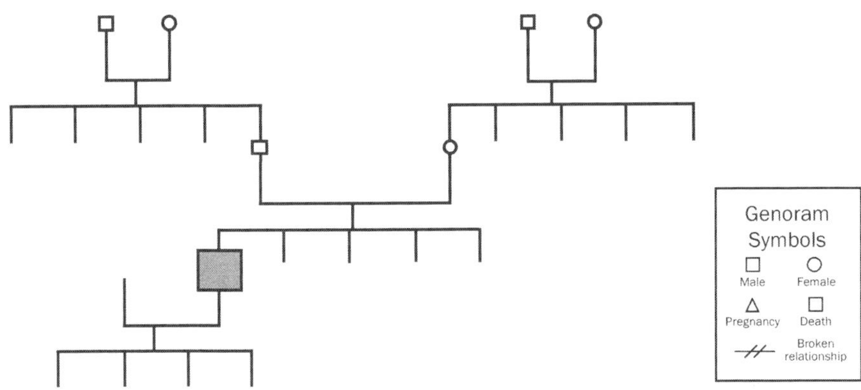

Source: *Genograms: Assessment and Interventions*
Retrieved from http://www.genopro.com/genogram/templates/Template.jpg

Figure 5

Enormous history can be found even when a client believes she knows fairly little about her extended family. Saying out loud that grandmother Mary was devoutly religious and very submissive to grandfather Bill may take on new meaning when put in the context of Mary's experience of being a first generation immigrant whose own parents didn't speak English. Perhaps Mary's parents were abusive, or maybe she heard some whispered story about her brother that was never openly discussed. As this process unfolds, the client frequently begins to see that her own story has context and more meaning than she's given it. Looking at the covert rules that emerge from generation to generation may help put her story into a new perspective. Most female sex addicts are in great pain by the time they begin treatment, and their self-perception is often as distorted as their own family history. Telling the story of her family can be a starting point for telling her own personal narrative.

Trauma Egg

For most FSLAs "telling the story" is much more difficult than it sounds. Denial, shame, and self-hatred compromise her ability to admit the truth of her history internally, much less out loud to another person. A number of helpful therapeutic techniques can ease a woman into her story and allow her the emotional distance to begin recounting her experiences. One of the most powerful is the Trauma Egg drawing, which was originally conceived by Murray (1991) and refined by Patrick Carnes (1997).

Using a large sheet of paper like one from a flip chart pad, the client writes family roles, rules, and descriptions of father and mother in the respective four corners of the paper. Then she draws a large oval (an "egg") with a dotted line across it near the top. Using pictures, she illustrates key traumatic or impactful events, starting at the bottom with her earliest traumatic memory. The client "grows herself up" by using pictures to describe significant events in her life, especially experiences of abuse or abandonment. Each picture is separated from the others with a circle or oval. It's important to include all sexual experiences and all romantic relationships. (It's acceptable to use one picture that represents a number of events, like drawing a string of stick figures to represent a time of promiscuity that involved a number of sexual partners.) By the time the FSLA reaches the dotted line toward the top of her egg, she's progressed to her current age. Some people find it helpful to number the pictures and create a cheat sheet on separate paper that identifies the event represented.

When the drawing is complete, which is usually a lengthy process, the FSLA shares it with you as her "fair witness." The role of the therapist is to help her identify patterns or themes. These patterns can help her to identify her "mission statement," which is written above the dotted line inside the egg. Examples include, "I must be perfect," or "I'm worthless," or "I have to take care of everyone else."

The template for a Trauma Egg drawing as outlined by Patrick Carnes (1997) follows:

Trauma Egg

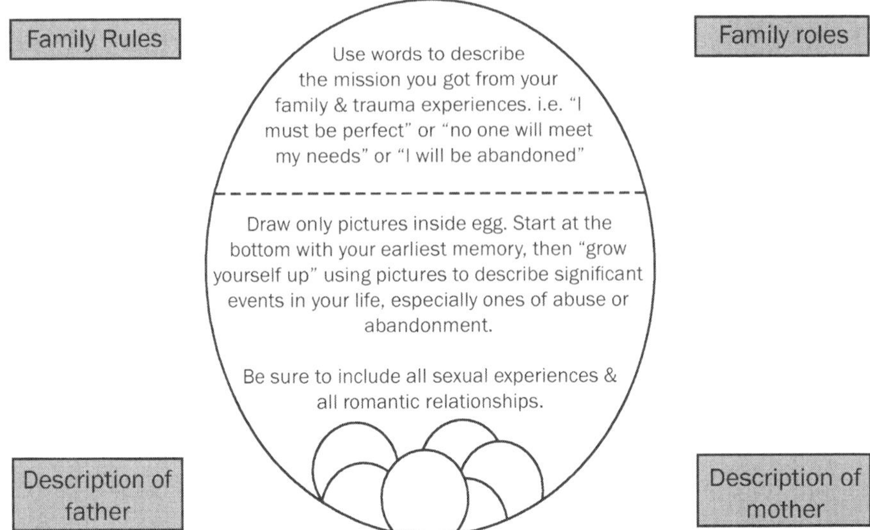

Reprinted with permission from *The Betrayal Bond* by Patrick Carnes (Deerfield Beach, HCI Publications, p. 195).

Figure 6

The Trauma Egg exercise is extremely powerful. Drawing pictures and symbols instead of writing words assists in accessing emotions. Visualizing the completed artwork is enlightening, and for many clients, often overwhelming. The patterns are usually clear and credible. The (unhealthy) messages flow convincingly from the drawings, which the client created herself and thus is more able to accept. The exercise normally reduces shame, promotes self-forgiveness, and provides rich therapeutic fodder for exploration and healing.

Other methods

Creative approaches to accessing therapeutic content such as art, collage, dance, music, poetry, and journaling are additional methods for the FSLA to tell her story. Narrative approaches to therapy view telling the client's story as an essential component of healing. Experiential approaches such as psychodrama and art therapy work toward reconstructing the personal story of the recovering person. Both methods are important for the client attempting to change a self-story full of trauma, shame, and pain into one of transformation, self-love, and joy.

Another approach offered by Pinkola Estes (1992) is creating the *descansos*. The descansos refers to the white crosses that mark the roadside places where a death has occurred. The descansos identify a sacred space physically, as well as emotionally, spiritually, and relationally where an individual's life has changed. The descansos exercise is an opportunity to map out on a long piece of butcher paper the small and large "deaths" that have taken place in the FSLA's life. The descansos can richly tell the story of roads not taken, hopes that never came to fruition, and the dark times of the client's life. They become love notes to the traumas that can sometimes mistakenly define the FSLA's life. The exercise of drawing the descansos enables the client to see that her life isn't only a collection of grief stricken crosses, but also the journey of the larger road. This exercise fosters a greater expansion of being that allows the recovering FSLA a broader self-perception.

Impact of telling the story

The technique you employ to facilitate a client telling her story is less important than the process and experience itself. For the FSLA, telling the story becomes a vehicle for change. By rewriting the story, processing her feelings, and creating the new narrative, she has an opportunity for empowerment, increased self-worth, and integration of the trauma story that created her original pain. With each telling of the story and each new affective experience that you both implicitly and explicitly co-regulate, the FSLA's shame is reduced. She connects both to herself and to another, which are crucial intimacy-building encounters.

As her denial begins to fade and the reality of the story unfolds, the sadness surfaces. Losing the addictive and fantasy-infused self-story results in a profound process of grief, which unfolds in stages rather than as a single event. What hasn't been felt because of the addictive high now begins to hit the FSLA hard. All the head or heart knowledge in the world doesn't prepare her for seeing the pieces of her life shatter at her feet. Packed suitcases by the door, tearful scenes with a partner who is reeling from disclosure, children who hide in fear or confusion, or waiting quietly in unemployment lines bring to life the consequences of her choices made during her active addiction. Allowing the sadness to surface is necessary to healing, but it is definitely painful.

Often the sadness is deeper than the immediate impact of disclosing secrets and experiencing withdrawal. Wounds and unresolved feelings that have been buried from childhood begin to surface. Most FSLAs carry around a barrel of unresolved feelings. Painful conversations or experiences get stuffed in the barrel, because she doesn't know how to resolve them. What might have started as a small annoyance has now grown into a major resentment. She believes herself a helpless victim of circumstances, and fuels her eroticized rage with resentments and pain. Because most clients have been medicating feelings for many years, they tend to have either suppressed negative feelings, or have gotten stuck in them. After all the years, the emotional power of these experiences has become a fermented vat of undifferentiated thoughts, feelings, and experiences. The FSLA can no longer tell the difference between the feelings that happened five minutes ago from the feelings she had 15 years ago. As this barrel gets full, it begins to leak. Toxic waste seeps out around the edges and can be the catalyst for an eruption of anger or sadness when it's exposed to the light and air of day.

The intensity of the emerging feelings can seem unbearable, and the FSLA may react accordingly. Emotions continually left unprocessed and unexpressed become like thunderstorms, which escalate into tornadoes or hurricanes. She often exhibits a type of character defect in which the slightest trigger shifts her reality and fear-based reactions. Over-utilized personality disorder diagnoses add additional shaming messages to an already fragile ego. Don't label a wounded, grieving, reactive woman as personality disordered until she is sober and has the chance to develop adaptive coping skills. Some diagnostic labels are premature, at best, and damaging at worst. The clinical picture often changes with a period of sobriety and the stability it brings.

Using metaphors can help an FSLA gain a different, transformative perspective on her painful story. You can reframe her volatile, overwhelming feelings as currents of energy that are simply passing through. Compare her feelings to a thunderstorm that builds as cooler air meets warmer air. The difference between a gentle rain and a violent thunderstorm can be significant, but both eventually pass and the sun shines again. Helping clients become more conscious of what they're feeling and engaging their bodily-based feelings, long before the lightning flashes and the thunder roars, empowers them to recognize they have more control over their emotions than they often believe.

Metaphors and other narratives of transformation can add richness to the developing conversion of the recovering FSLA's narrative from a story of damaged sickness into a non-pathological story. Other transformative approaches and tools include meditation, music, prayer, and any sober approach that the FSLA embraces to add color to her artistic pallet. Artwork can be a tangible symbol of recovery to replace addictive treasures, and can also be presented to a therapeutic group as an illustration of the recovery story. The use of metaphor and art activate the right hemisphere and feelings states in the body, which insures that deeper affective states will be engaged which assists in long-term change.

Importance of the listener

The therapist is an important component to the FSLA's rewriting process and essential for her to sort out feelings and reframe experiences. Within the context of Narrative Therapy (White & Epston,1990) the witness plays an important role for the client. When a supportive listener hears and affirms her story, the FSLA obtains a reality consistent with her experience, which contributes to a greater integration of self.

After revealing her story to a therapist, sharing with a support or therapy group is a helpful step for most clients. (Most FSLAs need the safety of an individual therapeutic setting for first telling their story before they're willing to risk sharing before a group.) Within the context of the group, the FSLA has an opportunity for group members to witness, identify with, express empathy, and perhaps offer feedback regarding their shared feelings and similar situations. An FSLA is empowered by the process. This affirmation shatters the isolation of living with the shame of trauma and sex and love addiction and validates the survivor's pain.

In highly functional groups, members offer not only identification but sometimes a different perspective, as well. Group witnesses can challenge the FSLA's self-effacing comments and offer her an alternate group reality. Such interconnectedness is an imperative for the recovering FSLA, especially given the relational context of women's lives. Story-telling in communal contexts fosters connection and support for the journey.

Endure Withdrawal and Achieve Abstinence

For most women sobriety begins with a period of abstinence. Although the FSLA may recognize she's created chaos in her life and she's now facing the consequences, the high that comes with acting out is still very intoxicating. If the addiction is advanced far enough, abstinence can be painful, and acting out allows the FSLA to feel "normal." Achieving and maintaining abstinence is often more difficult and distressing than the FSLA expects. As the neurochemical high subsides, addicts experience withdrawal symptoms, which can be both physical and emotional. An addict often has changes in vital signs such as pulse and blood pressure, and experiences sweating. Irritability, depression, despair, anxiety, changes in eating, sleep difficulties, and other somatic manifestations of trauma can occur. The FSLA discovers her acting out was necessary to prevent withdrawal and the resultant feelings of reality. Some women will switch to other medicating behaviors such as eating, shopping, or excessive alcohol to avoid the pain of withdrawal.

Many women find it harder to be abstinent from a relationship partner than from other kinds of sexual behaviors such as masturbation or anonymous sex. It's vital for the clinician to reinforce the task of achieving abstinence by encouraging a *total* timeout from erotic relationships. That means no contact of any kind with an affair partner and not engaging in courtship behaviors with anyone else for a period of time. If the FSLA is single and in a romantic relationship, the best practice is to include that person, too, in her timeout boundary for a period of time (ideally, at least 90 days). It's highly unlikely this relationship is very healthy, and the FSLA needs time alone to discover and differentiate herself. This abstinence period will have to be negotiated with some FSLAs as "one day at a time."

For some recovering women relationship withdrawal is described as an experience of death. One FSLA described the end of her relationship as "more than a broken heart. It felt like someone sliced open my heart and all that mattered drained out of me. The pain was unbearable and I wanted to die, until I met my next affair partner." FSLAs struggle to remember how damaging addictive relationships are, and they search for methods to medicate this pain. Once they replace the loneliness and pain with another partner, they avoid the experience of being "unhooked." A period of abstinence with no sexual contact, no fantasy, objectification, seduction, flirtation, or intrigue is an enlightening—and enormously painful—journey. It brings to light just how often the FSLA's thought process returns to the partner that was causing such turmoil.

Shame spirals are normal during this time as the FSLA begins to see how her behaviors have violated her non-addicted self-image. This awakening is a sobering experience (pun intended). The FSLA must inevitably feel the pain, fear, shame, and despair that are at the core of her addiction, and come out on the other side. This is an empowering experience that again changes her self-narrative. The FSLA begins to switch from helplessness to empowerment, from victim to a person of authentic free will.

The abstinence period, however, is often one of multiple starts and stops. Few women attempt an abstinence period and never again engage in some form of acting out. FSLAs use rationalization and minimization to grant themselves permission to engage in their acting out behaviors. Overwhelming feelings of anger, loneliness, and fatigue can trigger a strong desire to re-engage with an acting out partner. Some FSLAs will fantasize or participate in online sexual behaviors. During this time the clinician provides a new framework for experiencing the craving as another manifestation of grief that will pass. If the FSLA hangs on and rides the wave, the craving eventually subsides. Without sufficient tools and supports, she can be seduced back into her distorted thinking, and ignore what she knows is healthy. Writing out bottom line behaviors, reading good-bye letters to her addictive partners and behaviors, and talking with her sponsor provide a reminder of the pain and consequences of her addiction.

When the FSLA experiences a breach of her abstinence plan, it's important to remind her that no one ever completely starts over. No matter how much shame or discouragement she feels, she has taken important steps down the road of recovery. A key task for the clinician is to provide a safe place that the FSLA can trust and an open invitation for her to ask for help. It's imperative that the FSLA has an outside support system including friends, a sponsor, and others with whom she can talk through her triggers and find support for her withdrawal symptoms. Letting her know what's normal and what needs follow-up is an important strategy.

This early period is a good time to give the FSLA self-care assignments such as undergoing a complete physical examination, including a gynecological exam. Sometimes an FSLA may need assistance finding a doctor if she's never practiced empowered health management. Shame or a history of sexual abuse or rape can prevent or interfere with seeking appropriate care. One helpful approach is to role-play the medical appointment with the FSLA, so that she practices talking with her health care provider. Role-play can assist in preventing shame spirals and noncompliance with medical procedures. Remind her that her physician must know the full extent of her acting out behaviors in order to develop an appropriate plan of care. Encourage the FSLA to write down her current medications, allergies, surgeries, and questions prior to the appointment, so that anxiety doesn't interfere with her ability to recall this information. She can ask if the doctor's office will send forms prior to the appointment, so that she can complete the medical history without feeling pressured.

It's also important that the FSLA follows through with any recommended tests and procedures, not only to determine her physical well-being, but also to make the reality of her addiction concrete if any results indicate health consequences from her acting out. Completing the entire process is very important. Without this reality, she probably will project worst-case scenarios and may become overwhelmed by her anxieties to the point of relapse. Suggest the FSLA takes a friend or sponsor to the follow-up appointment for support. Receiving accurate knowledge about her physical health will usually decrease the FSLA's anxiety.

Identify Sobriety, Triggers, and Rituals

As women more fully enter recovery, they can typically identify the primary behaviors that have created enormous physical and emotional damage in their lives. Avoiding these behaviors is the FSLA's simplest definition of sobriety. It's important for her to specifically articulate these "bottom line" behaviors. Encourage her to write down the acts in which she'll no longer engage. The initial pressing concern for most FSLAs is to stop the pain. Identifying and outlining "bottom line" behaviors stops the metaphoric bleeding and introduces a starting point for change. The FSLA takes the first of the Twelve Steps, which means she admits her powerlessness around these behaviors and surrenders to a power greater than herself to return her to sanity.

Triggers

Triggers can be many things such as thoughts, emotions, or events that can begin the addictive cycle. A trigger can be something in the here and now, or a reaction to a perceived threat that the body identifies is similar to an earlier event. Most of the time clients are aware of the major triggers that occur, for example, receiving a sexual invitation, seeing a sexually suggestive image, or hearing about a friend's sexual exploits. Any of these things prompt fantasy or preoccupation. Once the FSLA experiences the trigger and thinks about acting out, the process of mood alteration has begun.

Elusive triggers can be more challenging, as their name suggests. These triggers can be emotionally based or might occur beyond conscious awareness. Walking through a store's fragrance department and smelling an affair partner's cologne may not initially register consciously; however, the cued recognition can begin a cascade of addictive associations, fantasies, sensations, impulses, and obsessions. Pheromones may also have an influence, although the impact of pheromones in humans needs further research. Nonetheless, the possibility of social behavior being influenced by subcortical activation of reproductive hormones has merit (Adolphs, 2003). Recovery wisdom regarding awareness about "people, places, and things" speaks to the impact of memories in cueing euphoric recall and subsequent addictive behavior, especially if the FSLA isn't consciously prepared.

Emotional dissociation also plays a role as a trigger. Anhedonia in early recovery can feel endless, and the thrill of addiction will often win out over the "boredom" of recovery. If the FSLA remains detached from her personal needs and keeps her focus on others, then feelings of loneliness become experiences of abandonment when others don't meet her needs. Entitlement often ensues, and the thought of going into a chat room for company becomes a possible solution, or lying in bed fantasizing about an affair partner may be enough to alter her mood. Eventually the FSLA can slip into an addictive cycle.

According to cognitive behavioral models, identifying the feelings that come before the behavior is critical to stopping forward motion from obsession into action. For example, Beck (1975) described depressed individuals with a negative worldview or schemata. Negative views of the self (shame), the world (anxiety), and the future (despair) are common among FSLAs. This cognitive triad is an interplay of a negative worldview and cognitive bias. Clinicians experienced in working with sex and love addiction are familiar with cognitive bias statements of self-abasement: "*I'm a horrible person*;" over-generalization: "*I'm never going to be sober*;" minimization: "*What's the big deal? Some people are just too sexually repressed*;" or arbitrary and personal inference of the self: "*It's all about me*" (Beck, 1975). Remaining trapped in this three step dance of pain is intolerable, and the FSLA finds relief through acting out unless she's offered another way. Recovery is that different solution.

A helpful acronym that's frequently used in the Twelve Step programs identifies typical triggers for most addicts. "HALT" suggests that FSLAs need to avoid circumstances in which they are Hungry, Angry, Lonely, or Tired. It's important to emphasize basic care skills such as eating several healthy meals a day, talking about feelings, avoiding isolation by attending meetings, and getting adequate rest. These healthy practices can contribute significantly to the addicted woman's capacity to choose sobriety. Helping the FSLA identify triggers is an important and ongoing component of the therapeutic process.

Rituals

When left to their own best thinking, most FSLAs try to stop their acting out behaviors through willpower—and sooner or later most fail. Intending to intervene at the acting out stage is not enough for an effective recovery plan. Understanding the specifics of her addictive process, especially about her rituals, is critical to an FSLA's recovery success. Identifying her rituals can also help her recognize and validate her internal feeling states as they awaken through her recovery process. Clients frequently don't know how or when their acting out starts. The FSLA will say she's "fine" when asked how she feels, and the next thing she knows, she wakes up in the bed of an affair partner. FSLAs are baffled at how quickly (and unconsciously) they fall back into acting out. A large part of the reason is unidentified alchemy ("magic") rituals. The alchemy ritual is the process that moves an addict from the preoccupation stage to acting out. She thinks she's in control, when she's already gone off track.

Surprisingly, most FSLAs appear consciously unaware of the "seemingly unimportant decisions" that lead them down this path. One of the clinician's most important tasks in addressing an FSLA's acting out is to help her identify her unhealthy rituals, which allows her the chance to intervene on them before it's too late. It's also important to challenge her denial regarding the level of awareness she possessed in her attempts to control her acting out and avoid surrender. Calling her affair partner, "forgetting" medications, or not going to meetings aren't passive actions. At this point in her journey these behaviors are probably part of her rituals. Don't let her deny responsibility and accountability for these choices.

Assisting an FSLA to recognize her power may seem like it takes magical powers on the part of the clinician. However, *your* willing people to change doesn't work either, despite your best efforts. Being curious can help. Ask your client to start with the point she recognized she was acting out, and to back up her actions and thoughts. What happened right before she acted out? What happened before that? And before that? She may have to retrace her steps minutes, hours, or even days to recognize the distortions that set the questionable behavior into motion. This progression is illustrated in the diagram below.

Breaking Down the Cycle

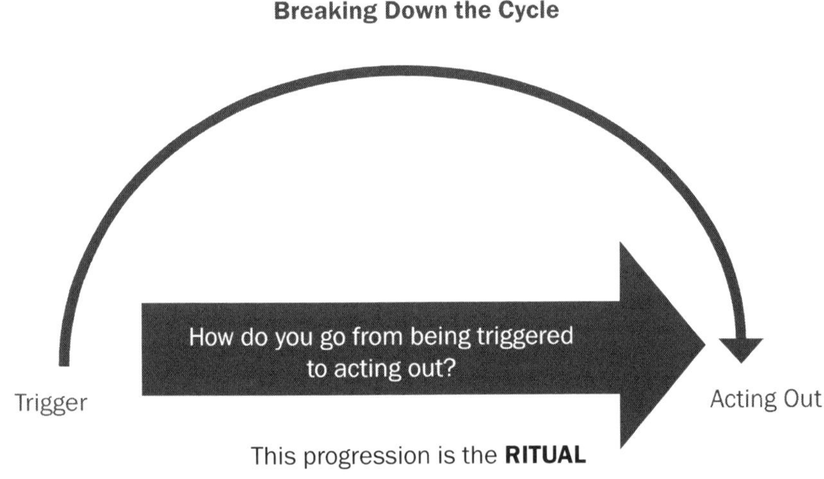

Figure 7

Guide the FSLA as she explores her rituals. With the love or relationship addict, explore her "innocent" behaviors like choosing particular clothes or style of makeup, initiating casual touch, making intense eye contact, consuming alcohol, dancing provocatively, exchanging emails or texts, behaving either aggressively or helplessly, or myriad other ways she sends "rain checks" that she's available if the partner is interested. For the woman whose acting out is more overtly sexual, her rituals are usually shorter and simpler. Cybersex addicts only have to obtain an Internet connection and sufficient privacy. Women seeking anonymous or quick sexual encounters may use rituals like sexual humor or innuendos, sexual touch, or overt sexual invitations.

Clinicians can help the FSLA identify the cognitive behavioral link between her rituals and her underlying feelings, and then the thoughts the feelings fuel. What emotions are most likely to prompt her to act out? What thoughts foster these feelings? Without engaging in this exercise, the FSLA isn't fully empowered to facilitate change in her life. She's more likely to fall back into a victim stance that fuels her entitlement to act out.

Teasing out the client's rituals can take weeks or months. However, once rituals are identified, denial is more difficult for the FSLA. This clear recognition of triggers and rituals allows her to use the tools of recovery, especially establishing boundaries, at a time when they're more likely to work.

Establish Boundaries to Safeguard Sobriety

As the definitions of abstinence, sobriety, triggers, and rituals are more clearly defined, the boundaries required for sustained recovery become easier to identify and more important to maintain. It's fairly easy to see that if there's been an inappropriate sexual partner in a client's life, eliminating contact with that person, no matter how difficult, is essential for recovery. However, what's much harder for the FSLA to figure out is *how* to eliminate all contact. There's always a reason to make contact in the FSLA's mind. And sometimes the partner is another addict who is also unable or unwilling to change his or her behavior, so he or she may intrude past the FSLA's boundaries.

The beauty of boundaries is that they make the theoretical ("I won't have any contact with Fred") into the practical ("I'll put Fred's email address and phone number on a blocked list so I'm not tempted to answer if he contacts me"). It's one thing to have a firm intention to eliminate contact with an acting out partner when the FSLA is in the throes of a relationship that's careening out of control. It's quite another experience to actually resist the urge and keep that intention when the opportunity to connect with that partner presents itself. This is especially difficult if some time has passed, and the acute pain has dissipated. If a firm boundary is already in place and the FSLA has tools and supports to help her through the rough times, she has a hedge of protection to help her stay sober.

It's helpful to teach the FSLA practical ways to prepare in times of strength for the future times of weakness. She can create a list of anniversaries, holidays, and birthdays that are emotionally charged, which identifies potential high-risk times she's likely to reach out to a former partner. Being proactive through this type of exercise is a stretch for most addicts early in recovery. Learning prospective planning and rehearsing the necessary boundaries is enlightening to the recovering FSLA. Without preparation, she may not have sufficient tools to choose a sober route.

Fostering choice is a key component of recovery, and preparation is key to relapse prevention.

Boundaries can be fairly broad and protect against acting out behaviors. The following are examples of behaviors and typical boundaries that can assist in avoiding them.

Bottom Line Behaviors	**Boundaries**
Masturbating after visiting my family	"I will not be in contact with my brother for more than one hour and will bookend all family visits."
Having phone sex with an affair partner	"I will throw away my partner's sweatshirt. I will keep my phones out of the bedroom."
Chatting online to find sexual partners	"I will not use the Internet in private places or alone at night."
Acting out in casinos	"I will not go to Las Vegas or Atlantic City or enter any casino until my sponsor and therapist say that I'm ready."
Drinking and picking up strangers for sex	"I will abstain from alcohol for the next year, then re-evaluate with my sponsor."
Being in relationships with abusive men	"I will not date or have any sexual contact with another person until my therapist, sponsor, and I agree that I'm ready. For now, I won't date until I'm one year sober from my bottom line behaviors."

Figure 8

Several tools are useful in assisting clients in identifying their particular boundaries needed to guard against acting out. Some Twelve Step communities encourage FSLAs to set what they call "bottom lines," "middle lines," and "top lines" that clearly outline behaviors. Sex Addicts Anonymous (SAA) uses the "Three Circle" exercise (inner, middle, and outer) to describe the FSLA's boundaries, sexual values, and self-care activities (International Service Organization of SAA, 2010):

The Three Circles of Sex Addicts Anonymous

OUTER CIRCLE
INNER CIRCLE
MIDDLE CIRCLE

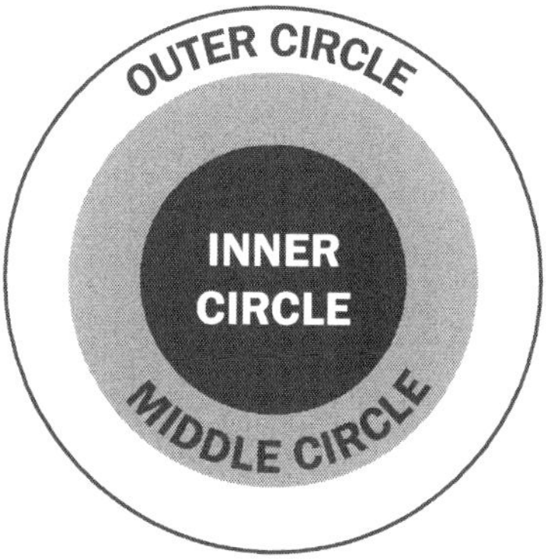

Retrieved from http://saa-recovery.org/SAALiterature/English/GreenBook
Used by permission of Sex Addicts Anonymous

Figure 9

Bottom line or inner circle behaviors are things that need to be eliminated from the addict's options. Setting bottom lines means more than just eliminating sex outside a committed relationship. Bottom line behaviors also include identified rituals that lead to acting out. For example, wearing sexually provocative clothing that's part of the FSLA's addiction must be off limits, even though she may have spent a great deal of time, energy, and financial resources acquiring that type of wardrobe. If a client has had cosmetic surgery to enhance her image, she must be gently confronted about the message she's sending when she flaunts her enhancements.

One approach to outlining and identifying bottom line behavior is to define them as either *Okay/Not Okay* or *Questionable*. The Okay/Not Okay groups are easier to identify. Obviously, Not Okay behaviors are any that violate the FSLA's personal sobriety definition. Concrete examples might include participating in a sexual chat room or being sexual with someone outside her primary relationship.

Questionable behaviors, which are thought of as "middle lines" or "middle circle" behaviors, are more gray areas. Depending on the primary acting out pattern, Questionable behaviors might include:

- Being in a part of town where the acting out occurred
- Participating in social networks or chat rooms where there's a possibility of "spying" on the love object or flirting with other participants
- Being flirtatious or seductive
- Masturbating
- Going to a bar

Any of these actions might be innocent in and of themselves. But if the addict finds that one of these behaviors triggers her, she needs to reevaluate and move it into the Not Okay category. She may need to adjust her bottom lines accordingly.

On the other hand, some things on the Questionable list may initially be of concern, but are found through experimentation to be less of a problem than anticipated. Examples of those sorts of behaviors might include:

- Using a computer or smart phone
- Having comrade relationships with men/women in recovery
- Drinking alcohol after the FSLA has sustained recovery from sexual bottom line behaviors
- Having massages, facials, or other cosmetic procedures

Many times these kinds of behaviors will start in one category and shift to another category as time in recovery increases. It's not always clear which of these behaviors will be safe or ultimately prove to be unsafe. A key recovery principle is to "avoid old playgrounds and playmates," and recognizing these situations and people may take some detective work to fully identify.

Often the more subtle interactions are the ones that prove to be the most elusive when establishing boundaries, and they may often reflect more significant dysfunction. Perhaps the object of the FSLA's fantasy is someone who lives in her building or works in her office. That person may not even be aware he or she is a love interest. The fantasy develops in the addict's mind and she may never disclose it to anyone, including the fantasy object. Nevertheless, the fantasy is highly seductive, and an addict can spend hours developing a history and a future for a partner who has no awareness about that process. Establishing boundaries about her thoughts is usually quite hard for the woman early in recovery. Suggest mind distraction techniques or substituting positive behaviors when she realizes she's lost in fantasy.

For some people, a psychotic process can develop that's difficult to challenge, since the fantasy has evolved into a delusion. Clinicians may need to refer the FSLA to a psychiatrist if she's stalking or crossing other serious boundaries and is unable to recognize the dangers. Conditions such as erotomania and pathological jealousy (discussed in chapter 3) are beyond the "normal" range of addictive behaviors and require careful monitoring.

A recovering woman also needs boundaries that protect her inner world as well as her outward behavior. Some women find it helpful to avoid certain music and media that disturb their serenity in a variety of ways. Media often contain strong triggers about past trauma, idealized romance, or highly sexualized content. Toxic people or environments are best avoided lest the FSLA becomes immersed in shame that might lead to acting out.

It's vital that the FSLA practice what the Twelve Step programs call "rigorous honesty" with herself and those in her support system. She's probably spent years rationalizing and even lying to herself about her inappropriate behavior, and real change requires that she closely examine every part of her life. Any method that helps the FSLA identify bottom line or Not Okay behaviors and establish effective boundaries about them provides healthy empowerment. It's imperative that she has a clear vision of herself as a sober woman to inspire and encourage her.

Recognize Slips and Relapse

For almost all sex addicts "slips" are a part of recovery. Slips are feelings, thoughts, or behaviors that the FSLA may or may not recognize as "prodromal" (early symptom) acting out. A slip involves a step onto the edge of a slippery slope that may begin the descent into a relapse. The FSLA may return to people, places, or things that were part of her addictive process. Perhaps she flirts, or carelessly surfs online, or intentionally dresses seductively. Establishing the belief systems an FSLA brought with her to treatment is important in helping her define what sobriety means to her, and what behaviors might result in slips or relapses.

Part of the process of recovery after a slip is to let go of the secret and immediately get honest. These steps can prevent denial from taking hold and miring the FSLA in a sustained relapse. Honesty about a slip breaks the cycle of secrecy and shame that drives acting out. If the FSLA is in a committed relationship, she and her partner will need to discuss how they want to address slips. Some couples agree a slip must be disclosed within 24 hours; others agree the FSLA must tell her sponsor about a slip, but the partner doesn't want to know unless the slip has crossed one of the partner's bottom line boundaries.

As a therapist, you can help reduce the shame of a slip by framing it as thoughts or behaviors of which the FSLA may not be consciously aware. Most addicted women have a number of rituals, and she may have unwittingly participated in one that hasn't yet been uncovered. Slips can help the woman become conscious of her rituals and recognize when she's headed down a dangerous path. This kind of cognitive behavioral approach fosters critical thinking, which increases the FSLA's ability to maintain sobriety.

The difference between a slip and a relapse may be a matter of degree and underlying intent. Most recovering people and clinicians who work with them view a slip as a "Short Lapse in Progress"—that is, a slip is an isolated, time-limited behavior or event that interrupts the FSLA's forward movement. If she recognizes the occurrence as a slip, admits it, and recommits to her healing journey, it's over. She picks herself up and starts again.

A slip escalates into a relapse when the FSLA doesn't address the infraction of her boundaries or sobriety. If she ignores the occurrence, and especially if she continues in similar behavior, she has abandoned her recovery and is considered to be in full relapse.

Participate in a Twelve Step S Fellowship

One of the single best tools for achieving and maintaining sexual and emotional sobriety is participating in a Twelve Step fellowship for sex and love addiction. Ironically, this best practice is also one of the hardest for female SLAs to embrace. As women who have experienced attachment injuries and struggle with an intimacy disorder, being part of a group is usually terrifying. Community, though, is vital for sobriety and long-term recovery. Almost no one can recover alone, even with the help of an experienced therapist. Certainly it's impossible to learn how to have healthy attachments and practice healthy intimacy without connecting with other people.

The Twelve Step programs for any addiction are based on the Principals and Traditions of Alcoholics Anonymous (Alcoholics Anonymous World Services, Inc., 1976), which was started by two "drunks," Bill W. and Dr. Bob, in 1935. Because sexual addiction was so shame based, sex addicts weren't comfortable identifying their existence in the early days. As a result four different S programs were independently established in different parts of the country without the groups being aware of each other for some time. The main S groups are Sexaholics Anonymous (SA), Sex Addicts Anonymous (SAA), Sexual Compulsives Anonymous (SCA), and Sex and Love Addicts Anonymous (SLAA). The two groups for partners of sex addicts are S-Anon, the companion group of SA, and COSA, which partners with SAA. There is also a group for couples in recovery from sex and love addiction called Recovering Couples Anonymous (RCA). See the Appendix for contact information about the various fellowships.

The only requirement for membership in any of the S fellowships is a personal desire to stop sexual acting out behavior. SA differs from the other S fellowships in that this program dictates what it means to be "sober," whereas the others allow each member to set his or her own sobriety definition. SA defines sobriety as no sex with self, including masturbation, or with anyone else outside a marriage relationship. Most SA groups are attended by men only, and many women don't feel comfortable in that setting. However, for those who follow strict (usually religiously based) guidelines about sexual behavior, the sobriety definition of SA is familiar and helpful.

For many years clients were fortunate to find one S meeting in their state, let alone one in their city, and it was most unusual to find multiple meetings of all the fellowships in one area. Today, as a result of increased awareness and treatment for sexual addiction, S meetings are more available in many communities. The challenge for female SLAs, though, is the lack of meetings that are for women-only, or at least have a good percentage of women in attendance. Most FSLAs find it hard or even impossible to be in a "mixed" meeting where both men and women attend, especially in the early stages of recovery. In many communities there are women-only SAA or SLAA meetings, which are the two groups most open to women. SCA originated in the gay and lesbian community, so many women feel comfortable in that fellowship.

As a clinician, be prepared to suggest alternatives if a woman isn't sober enough or open to trying a mixed S meeting. One solution is to participate in a phone or online meeting, which are offered by many Twelve Step fellowships. Many recovering FSLAs feel more comfortable in these meeting forums because there are often groups for women-only. Even if the phone or online meeting is mixed, it usually feels safer to FSLAs because it's not a face-to-face environment. Either option is a great resource for addicts who aren't fortunate enough to have S meetings available in their communities. However, it's still critical that an FSLA regularly attends a face-to-face S meeting, even if it's only once or twice a month. There simply isn't a substitute for in-person fellowship. Encourage your client to "go to any lengths" to attend a Twelve Step group.

The FSLA can also obtain support from other Twelve Step fellowships by attending meetings of other groups that are designated as "open," which means that anyone is welcome to attend. You don't have to personally struggle with the issue the meeting addresses (alcohol or gambling or whatever) in order to attend. Alcoholics Anonymous, Adult Children of Alcoholics (ACOA), and Codependents Anonymous (CODA) are good options to supplement an S meeting.

Clinicians are encouraged to check in with a client about her experience attending an S meeting. Not only is a woman likely to be in the gender minority, which is unsettling enough, but simply the environment and norms feel foreign at first. Meetings are conducted in a structured format where people introduce themselves a certain way ("Hi, I'm Mary, and I'm a sex and love addict") and interactions are governed by procedural guidelines. Direct feedback, known as "cross talk," isn't allowed, which often feels odd at first. It takes time to understand the language and references and get comfortable in a Twelve Step environment.

Encourage your clients to attend at least 8 to 10 S meetings before deciding the fellowship isn't for them. If she's uncomfortable at the first group she tries, nudge her to go back another time or two, and then visit a different meeting if necessary. Each group is unique, and the people who regularly attend help determine how comfortable the meeting will be for its attendees. Remind the FSLA of the Twelve

Step saying to focus on "principles, not personalities." This motto means that even if an FSLA doesn't care for some of the individuals who may populate a meeting, she can still learn helpful recovery principles in that setting.

Finding a healthy meeting is important. The FSLA should look for a group that focuses on the solution rather than the problem. Members avoid sexually graphic descriptions and sexually abusive language, and instead, they share their "experience, strength and hope" about their walk in recovery.

It's also important to attend as many meetings as possible. The ideal practice is to attend 90 meetings in 90 days, which is a common prescription from Alcoholics Anonymous. Many FSLAs go to one or two meetings a week and believe that's sufficient. In reality, it's not nearly enough. An FSLA needs as much support and fellowship as she can possibly get, especially early in her recovery process. Attending a minimum of three meetings a week is considered best practice, and attending a daily meeting early in recovery gives the FSLA the best support for sobriety.

Prepare a woman to observe good boundaries around her participation in a Twelve Step program. She needs first to pay attention to how she dresses when she goes to a meeting. Conservative or modest attire is important. If in doubt, she should err on the side of caution. An FSLA must also be careful about her interactions with other attendees. Unfortunately, sometimes newcomers are propositioned at a meeting (a practice called 13th Stepping), which makes it even harder for the FSLA to return, or even to try another meeting or fellowship. If she attends mixed meetings, she shouldn't contact a male for support or go out socially with a man alone. Again, it's best that she connect primarily with women, especially in the first months. Identifying safe people may be a therapeutic issue if her acting out pattern has involved both men and women. In this situation, she may need to process triggering people versus a specific gender as a marker for safety.

Eventually, after she's developed more traction in her recovery, an FSLA can experience many benefits from attending mixed meetings if she's solely participated in women-only groups previously. A Twelve Step S meeting is a great place to get to know men as simply other hurting, healing people rather than as lust objects. Meetings are also good environments to practice healthy boundaries in her interactions with men.

Work the Program

Many people across the spectrum of the various Twelve Step fellowships talk about "working the program." Therapists who aren't familiar with the Twelve Step process may assume that a client who's going to meetings is working her program, but that assumption isn't necessarily true. Although it's critical for a recovering addict to attend meetings, it's possible to attend a Twelve Step group regularly and still not genuinely be in "recovery," much less "working the program."

What, then, constitutes "working the program?" The concept can be most easily understood as engaging with living resources to develop and maintain a different kind of life. Working a program involves using the tools of recovery—doing things—that transform an FSLA's life and relationships—her *being*.

Complete the Twelve Steps

Perhaps the most important aspect of working a program is to actually work through the Twelve Steps. Many addicts think this will be an easy, or at least a short process. After all, there are only 12 of them, right? The reality is that doing justice to "working" the Steps requires a minimum of a year, if not longer. It's not enough for a woman to simply read through the Steps and associated material, and think about them privately. It's crucial to actually write out the inventories and assignments of the Steps, and share them with another woman in recovery.

Each Step is designed to assist in repairing relationships. Steps One–Three first repair the addict's relationship with the "God of her understanding." These Steps are crucial because they help her identify her Higher Power, admit her powerlessness to change without a Higher Power's help, and make a decision to turn her life over to the care of that Higher Power. Without a foundation that is as deep as the structure is tall, a building will fall over. So, too, with recovery, and the first Three Steps provide that foundation. If a client attempts to stop acting out through exerting her willpower, she's simply trying harder rather than doing something different. Recovery is paradoxical for the FSLA. *Willing* change is alchemic and remains an addictive process that inevitably fails. Magic can't put the FSLA's life in right order; only turning over her will and accepting the miracle of recovery can accomplish that transformation (Ketcham & Kurtz, 2002).

Steps Four–Seven are about repairing the relationship with the addict—with herself. Most addicts haven't learned how to love and nurture themselves, establish healthy boundaries, and understand how their defects of character sabotage their relationships. Before she can repair relationships with others, the FSLA must learn the concepts of compassion and forgiveness for herself.

Steps Eight and Nine are about repairing relationships with others who may have been harmed by the addict's sexual and emotional acting out. Many clients come into recovery because someone else has discovered their behavior and has confronted them. Addicts want to say a quick "I'm sorry" and move on as a way to reduce their shame. Unfortunately, unless an FSLA has done the work to repair her relationship with herself, she won't recognize the real damage she's caused others. Repair that's motivated from a base of shame will only leave both the addict and the offended person feeling unresolved. Steps Eight and Nine offer specific guidelines for repairing relationships through making amends.

The last three Steps (Ten–Twelve) are called maintenance steps. They address the ongoing process of living a healthier life by continually practicing self-observation, taking personal responsibility, and being of service. Addicts practice self-monitoring and quickly address the wrongs they commit. They maintain "constant contact" with a Higher Power and live according to the will of the God of their understanding. They discover the best way to keep the gifts experienced through working the Steps is to give them away. That means addicts practice helping others in need of the message of hope and healing that recovery offers. This practice keeps the "miracles" fresh and uppermost in mind. These Steps assure that recovery becomes a daily practice and not just a task that's considered finished and put aside.

Utilize a sponsor

A sponsor is a woman's guide in recovery. She should be further down the road in her healing process and have at least six months of sobriety. She should have gone through the Steps at least once and completed each one. A sponsor guides the newly recovering FSLA in working the Steps and provides accountability and a sounding board for recovery. It's important that a heterosexual FSLA select a female sponsor. A lesbian SLA should work with her therapist to determine if a male or female is the best choice.

Connect daily

Sex and love addiction is a disease of isolation and impairment of intimacy, and both issues inhibit a woman's desire and ability to connect with and use others for co-regulation. It's ironic that FSLAs deeply resist the very thing they've been longing for: intimate connection with others. Encourage your clients to connect with another woman in recovery every day, so that she can begin to have the experience of getting her needs met from reliable others. Emailing or texting isn't enough; it's important to at least talk voice-to-voice if the FSLA doesn't connect in person. These contacts are about building fellowship and relationships that are comforting and regulatory in nature, as much as creating an accountability system for her. The FSLA can share the feelings she's experienced through the day, her triggers, and how she's doing with her struggles around sobriety. Connecting daily is much harder for FSLAs than you might expect. Be patient with her failures to follow through, and keep inviting her to give herself the gift of daily connection. Staying current helps prevent the shame spirals that are the bane of early recovery.

Read recovery literature

By now the sex addiction field has advanced enough to offer a variety of excellent books, workbooks, and other forms of media. The S fellowships each have a version of a *Big Book*, which is a manual that describes how the Twelve Steps apply to that particular program and shares members' stories of recovery. Many other resources are available within the recovery community, and a number of them are even specifically written for women struggling with sex and love addiction. It's encouraging for a woman to read about others' experiences and glean tips on navigating this difficult journey. Recovery literature is often called a "portable meeting," and reading can help a woman return to serenity when she's overwhelmed or triggered. The Appendix contains a list of suggested books.

Practice self-care

Healthy living (which involves "outer circle" or "top line" behaviors) is discussed at length in chapter 12, but the basics of self-care are important from the beginning. The FSLA needs to get adequate sleep, nutrition, and exercise, because all help her endure withdrawal, rebalance herself neurochemically, and modulate her emotions. Eventually, she'll learn to practice other "outer circle" behaviors of nurturing herself, enjoying recreation or learning new things, and repairing relationships.

As a clinician, be aware that an FSLA in early recovery is often a fragile creature. Her world has fallen apart, she's facing difficult consequences, and she's trying to let go of unhealthy coping techniques without the benefit yet of easy replacements. Remember the recovery principle of "putting first things first." Gently push your client to ground herself through using these tools of working a program. Going to meetings daily, participating in intensive therapy, completing assignments that exercise the frontal lobes of the brain, and learning stress management techniques all add tools to the FSLA's toolbox.

Disclose Acting Out

Disclosure is one of the most difficult tasks for all addicts, and especially for women SLAs. It's very difficult for any FSLA to remain in recovery if she's holding onto a secret that is full of fear and shame. Disclosure to the therapist and/or a sponsor or group members is often the first step in being set free of the shame that binds the SLA to her pain. Disclosing to a partner or family member is much more difficult. Honesty and disclosure help facilitate the healing process, but a complete disclosure requires incredible trust—in the therapist, the recovery process, and her support system.

Why do clients disclose or resist it?

Frequently, an FSLA feels so guilty or shamed by some behavior that she feels compelled to disclose. Some FSLAs tell their secrets because someone they view as an authority figure says they have to tell. This type of disclosure is often guarded and partial, a form of damage control—telling only what they think the other person has heard, has found out, or will hear from someone else. Rarely is it the whole story. Unfortunately, this partial telling tends to lead to more problems.

Other FSLAs tell because they've been living a painful lie for so long, and disclosing seems like a way to stop the lying. Deep down, despite their past behavior, they value honesty over lying, and by disclosing they're trying to be congruent with their true values. This is especially true of women who are newly in recovery or starting a new relationship after a period of abstinence or recovery. In other cases where the partner's health has been put at risk, if there's an unintended pregnancy, or if huge consequences for acting out are looming, the FSLA feels the other person has a right to know.

Some FSLAs resist doing any disclosure by citing the Ninth Step of the traditional Twelve Steps of Alcoholics Anonymous (Alcoholics Anonymous World Services, 1976). While the preparatory work for a complete disclosure includes some of the same work as Steps Eight and Nine, it's not the same. The Eighth Step states, "We made a list of all persons we have harmed, and became willing to make amends to them all." The purpose of the Eighth Step is to identify individuals who have been harmed by the FSLA's behavior as well as to take full responsibility for her behavior. By preparing to make amends, the FSLA begins the process of releasing guilt and shame in order to make a fresh start. Step Nine states, "We made amends to such people [the ones identified in Step Eight] wherever possible, except when doing so would injure them or others." This is the action Step that builds on the preparation and good intention of Step Eight. This Step offers good advice about not injuring others through making amends, but this principle involves a different concept than disclosure. As an example, an FSLA would identify the wife of an affair partner as someone she's willing to offer an amends. However, the FSLA wouldn't initiate making that amends if the wife isn't already aware of the mate's unfaithfulness. The disclosure about the acting out comes from the unfaithful husband, not from the FSLA who's making amends for her part in the relationship. Too often addicts use Step Nine as an excuse not to reveal the truth to someone who deserves disclosure, because they believe it would hurt the recipient too much.

Help your client see the flaw in the belief that disclosure is to be avoided because it's painful for the betrayed person. Corley describes being a witness to almost 2,000 disclosures between sex addicts and their spouses or significant others, and she asserts that *all* of them were painful for the recipient of the disclosure and the addict alike (Corley & Schneider, 2012). There is no getting around the pain, which is part of the process. Experiencing the pain of betrayal, the loss of esteem, the anger, shame, and fears that accompany the honesty are extremely difficult. At the same time, this process is required for addicts to remain sober and for relationships to heal enough to start new journeys based on honesty and shared goals. The FSLA who insists that to tell would hurt too much or harm the recipient wants to avoid that pain.

Other reasons for an FSLA's resistance about disclosure include fear of loss of the relationship with a partner or children, out of loyalty to someone with whom she's been acting out, or fear and shame of others finding out what she's done. Sometimes a job is at risk or the FSLA fears being shunned by her faith community, or worries that her children will be ostracized by neighbors. This fear supports the FSLA's decision to do a partial disclosure, especially early on, when she wants to "test the waters" to verify that if she tells, she won't be punished or abandoned.

Despite the fears, research and experience confirm that full disclosure is almost always best (Corley & Schneider, 2012). Disclosure is one of the hardest things the client will do in therapy, and the consequences can be both wonderful and awful. However, when a client gets honest, she feels some relief like a burden has been lifted. Corley and Schneider's research verifies that most sex and love addicts are glad they disclosed.

Although it's appropriate to advocate for disclosure with the client, to share your bias about the need for a full disclosure, and to review the research about outcomes of disclosure (see Corley & Schneider, 2012), it is the client's right to decide if, when, to whom, and how much she will reveal. (Legal obligations regarding cases in which a partner's life is in danger are covered elsewhere in chapter 8 about working with couples.)

Disclosure is a process

Remind women who are new in recovery that disclosure is a process, because early on circumstances exist that make complete disclosure difficult. These might include:

- She has acted out in so many different ways or with so many different people or has told so many lies that she genuinely doesn't recall some of the events until a later time.
- She was in an altered state (due to alcohol or other drugs, cutting, or engaging in self-harm as part of a ritual) during some episodes of acting out, and she doesn't remember clearly specific events.

- She hasn't thought certain events or behaviors were significant enough to bother disclosing. With increased recovery, she realizes the need for disclosing that additional history.
- The person to whom the FSLA is considering disclosure has certain circumstances that dictate postponing the disclosure until that person gets therapy for himself or herself. This is also true when the person to whom complete disclosure is needed has recently had serious surgery, is critically ill, or doesn't have enough emotional strength due to his or her own mental health or a significant, unrelated crisis such as a recent death of someone close. Relationships in which domestic violence has occurred require prudence and additional preparation before disclosure, if it's done at all. (Chapter 9 outlines this situation.)

Where do you start, especially if the SLA is a single woman?

As the therapist, it's your job to help the FSLA to sort out in what ways disclosure is right for her. She must determine if, when, and how much to disclose. Help her identify what values she has that will guide and support her to disclose with integrity, instead of disclosing from a place of fear, anger, or disgrace. It's also helpful to determine what information is private and how to set and maintain boundaries about sharing information until you and she determine it's time to do a full, formal disclosure.

Start by having the FSLA speak about the impact the addiction has had on her relationship with herself and others. What did the addiction solve, or in what way did it help—even for a little while? (This exercise would be part of her initial work in examining how her life has become unmanageable, so it would be utilizing and adding to her earlier work in therapy.) What kind of lies has she told (to herself to justify acting out, or to others to cover her tracks) in order to try to make herself feel better? How may she have used acting out to resolve a more fundamental problem (like using sex or a relationship to prove she's worthy, or in an attempt to resolve something related to her own sexual abuse)?

Make a distinction between the emotional secrets an FSLA has about her childhood versus the excuses she uses to engage in addictive or other destructive behaviors. Be curious about the ways in which secret-keeping or lying continue to work for her, or how lying or secret-keeping are now causing more problems than they solve. From this exploration, you begin to formulate ideas about how the FSLA has compromised the important values that represent the person she strives to be—her authentic self. Throughout therapy you can refer to this "authentic self" and the behaviors that support her development. It's useful to give the authentic self a title, and one suggestion is "a strong, independent woman in recovery."

Who to tell

Next, ask the FSLA to list the most important people in her life. Explore ways the client's behavior has impacted her relationship with each person on the list. Then ask her to identify who among those important people has a need or right to know information about her addiction. Rank the people in order by importance in her life, the ones most difficult to tell and why, and those most urgent to tell. This process can be given as homework. For example, an assignment might be to complete a decision-making matrix in which the FSLA identifies the positive and negative aspects associated with telling the person on her list most likely to be supportive about her addiction, and to list the lies she's told this person. Additionally, have her complete a matrix reflecting the pros and cons associated with continuing to keep secrets from this person. In session, process what she understands after doing the homework. By starting this disclosure process with someone whom the FSLA believes will be accepting of her, she can begin looking at a process for preparing for a formal disclosure with her partner. Following is a diagram (Corley & Schneider, 2012) that may be useful.

Disclosure Decision Making Matrix

	Benefits /Positive Consequences	**Costs /Negative Consequences**
Disclose Everything		
Partial Disclosure		
Tell Nothing		

Source: *Disclosing Secrets* by Corley and Schneider
Used by permission

Figure 10

If the FSLA believes the consequences of disclosing to a specific person are too dangerous, she may be too fearful to disclose information about some aspect of her behavior. It's important to explore the risk for physical harm if an FSLA's partner has a history of violence, or if her partner is at risk to harm himself or herself in response to finding out about the FSLA's addiction and betrayal. You can still have her complete a decision-making matrix identifying the pros and cons for telling or keeping the secret or telling some portion, which helps break through her denial and allows her to experience uncomfortable feelings. Caution the FSLA to keep these written exercises in a safe place, so that they're not inadvertently discovered and therefore create a disclosure crisis.

Although some of the reasons not to tell or postpone disclosure are legitimate, stress that it's very important to a client's recovery that she discloses to someone in addition to you as her therapist. Help her define criteria for someone she could trust enough to be a "fair witness" to her disclosure work, so that she can experience the lessening of shame and reduction of fear that comes with telling these secrets. Generally, the most important disclosure the FSLA makes is to her partner, and chapter 8 offers detailed guidelines about that process.

This is an excellent time to inquire about her thoughts and feelings about spirituality and her experiences with organized religion. Depending on her feelings about spirituality, you might speak about the power in the biblical scripture (John 8:32) that says "the truth will set you free." Encourage her to talk about how the secrets and lies have kept her bound to her shame, her pain, her fear, and her past. Homework might include drawing a picture of herself bound to her shame and pain, or writing a series of letters: (a) one to the God of her understanding outlining what she has held onto all these years, what she has shame about, and what she seeks guidance and forgiveness for; (b) one to herself about how life would be if a miracle happened and she no longer needed to lie; and (c) a letter to someone on her "important people list" who has a right to know or a need to know.

Again, review the importance of keeping this early work private during this information clarification phase. Point out that a poorly timed disclosure without appropriate planning and safeguards in place for all involved can be a disaster. Help her identify a safe place to keep her written thoughts private, such as a small safe or locked drawer. Some FSLAs in early recovery subconsciously continue risk-taking behaviors, and leave material available for others to read as a way of chancing high drama situations with partners. Unfortunately, everyone loses with this wager.

When to tell

The context of the FSLA's life and the information to be shared dictate the urgency with which a formal disclosure is encouraged. Often the luxury of time can be compromised if the situation is one where a partner has been exposed to a health condition like Hepatitis C, HIV, or another sexually transmitted disease; if a pregnancy has occurred; if legal action is pending; or some other crisis situation is making disclosure urgent. Unless there are legitimate health or safety reasons to postpone or modify a disclosure, it should happen as soon as possible. Help the FSLA understand the disclosure process honors the other person, even though it's painful and has many consequences. To really honor another person, telling him or her the truth allows decisions about the future to be based on honesty, not partial or false information.

What to tell

Again, the context of the FSLA's life and how her addiction has manifested itself inform and guide the content of disclosure. Disclosure to a spouse is different than to children, to parents, to friends, or to co-workers. Initial disclosure is different than disclosure after a slip or relapse. Have the FSLA think about what her goal is for disclosing, what she thinks the recipient will want to know, and what the recipient should know for future decision making. The answers may be very different depending on the recipient of the disclosure, what he or she already knows, and what the relationship is like. (Specific areas usually addressed in disclosure to a partner and children are listed in chapter 8.)

Information disclosed might also reflect what stage the FSLA is in the addictive process— early, middle, or late stage disease. What personal and relational values have been compromised? How have those betrayals of values been acted out as part of the addictive behavior? As she progresses in recovery, her understanding of these issues will deepen.

What to keep private

Secrets sometimes become private information when they're shared with the appropriate people. So it's important for the client to decide who else needs to know information about her past behavior. It isn't appropriate for the FSLA to tell everyone she works with the details of her First Step, even though she's relieved to finally get honest. This information can be misused in hurtful ways; therefore, it's important to have a specific discussion about boundaries in relation to whom and what she chooses to tell.

Although it's useful for the partner to have certain specific information, the FSLA should determine if she wants her partner or the recipient of the disclosure to keep the information private. If she does want the information to remain private, even if the reason is to give her time to prepare the next formal disclosure, help her practice setting boundaries regarding keeping information private. Remind her, though, that once she shares information, she's powerless over what the recipient does with that knowledge. As discussed in chapter 8, partners need a support system, too, and it's unrealistic and unhealthy to expect a partner to not tell anyone about this painful betrayal.

Disclosure after an arrest or loss of job

In some cases FSLAs are arrested, some aspect of the situation is made public via the media, or there is job loss related to her acting out. Frequently these types of situations impact the FSLA's family, neighbors, friends, and members of her spiritual community. Usually, a "no comment" rule is the best approach. Too often the FSLA wants to defend herself with the "truth," only to have the media or friends misuse the information, and the situation just gets worse. Planning for such instances is useful. Help the FSLA determine who has the right or need to know. What will she tell those in her immediate circle of family and best friends? What about others with whom she or her children and spouse interact on a regular basis? As in all cases, the context of the situation dictates what information is appropriate to share and what to keep private. In general, the FSLA should develop a statement about her acting out behavior that tells the truth without too many details, what she's doing to manage the situation, what she's willing to talk about, and what she needs from the person (that is, prayers, privacy, a safe place for her kids to go play when she's at Twelve Step meetings, support for partner, and so forth).

Postpone Major Decisions

The best practice is to encourage a female sex and love addict to postpone making any major decisions (other than ones that affect sobriety) until she has established solid sobriety and built a strong support system. Usually, it's best for an FSLA to wait a minimum of a year before she decides to divorce, run off with an affair partner, move, change jobs, or make any similar major decision. In the beginning of her healing journey, all her mental and emotional resources are best devoted to recovery efforts. Until she's maintained a substantial period of sobriety and dealt with some of her trauma, an FSLA normally isn't thinking clearly enough to make a healthy decision.

This dictum doesn't mean she stays in an abusive marriage or relationship. She may choose to separate from her partner for a variety of reasons (or the partner may choose to leave). At the same time, she doesn't leave one significant relationship for the sake of another. Instead, she devotes a healthy focus on herself and her own healing and observes the recovery slogan to take "first things first." Clearly, achieving and maintaining sobriety around her sex and love addicted behaviors is a crucial "first" task.

REFERENCES

Adolphs, R. (2003). Cognitive neuroscience of human social behavior. *Nature Reviews Neuroscience,4,* 165-178.

Alcoholics Anonymous World Services, Inc. (1976). *Alcoholics anonymous* (3rd ed.). New York, NY: Author.

Beck, A. T. (1975). *Cognitive therapy and the emotional disorders*. New York, NY: International Universities Press.

Carnes, P. (1997). *The betrayal bond: Breaking free of exploitive relationships*. Deerfield Beach, FL: Health Communications.

Corley, M. D., & Schneider, J. P. (2012). *Disclosing secrets: An addict's guide to when, to whom, and how much to reveal*. Tucson, AZ: Recovery Resources Press.

Genograms. (n.d.). Retrieved from http://www.genopro.com/genogram/templates/Template.jpg

International Service Organization of SAA. (2010). *Hope and recovery: A Twelve Step guide for healing from compulsive sexual behavior* (2nd ed., 3rd printing). Minneapolis, MN: CompCare.

Ketchum, K., & Kurtz, E. (2002). *The spirituality of imperfection* (reissue). New York, NY: Bantam Books.

McGoldrick, M., Gerson, R., & Petry, S. (2008). *Genograms: Assessment and interventions* (3rd ed.). New York, NY: W. W. Norton.

Murray, M. (1991). *Prisoner of another war: A remarkable journey of healing from childhood trauma*. Palo Alto, CA: PageMill Press.

Pinkola Estes, C. (1992). *Women who run with wolves: Myths and stories of the wild woman archetype*. New York, NY: Ballantine Books.

White, M., & Epston, D. (1990). *Narrative means to a therapeutic end*. New York, NY: W. W. Norton.

CHAPTER 7

Best Practices for Addressing Attachment Injuries

Alexandra Katehakis

As outlined in chapter 2, affective neuroscience shows how attachment patterns learned in infancy mold our emotional, cognitive, and behavioral brain functions; that without therapeutic intervention those traits last a lifetime; and that their stunting favors the development of female sex and love addiction. How? Early caregiver attunement shapes the infant's attachment system and includes the co-regulation that, in turn, supports eventual self-regulation. That is, pre-verbal, pre-logical infant-caregiver attachment actually grows the child's neuronal pathways, as interactive co-regulation with the caregiver nourishes the child's own developing affect-regulation abilities of self-awareness and self-soothing. Her good affect-regulation habits will permit later flowering of the mature executive functions of impulse control, focus, planning, self-monitoring, and understanding others.

But without secure attachment to the primary caregiver imprinting her affect-regulating capacities, a child can't self-regulate enough to develop these higher powers. Instead, she becomes neurobiologically programmed to *auto-regulate* (regulate in isolation) dysfunctionally via paralyzing panic or dissociation. A dysregulated system, meaning a chronically depressed, anxious, or numb state, leaves her seeking regulation through any means possible. Like drugs or alcohol, sex and love can provide the FSLA with a temporary, dysfunctional way of regulating her nervous system. This process explains why female SLAs, usually early auto-regulators, use isolated self-soothing strategies like sexual fantasy and masturbation, act impulsively, lack insight, and display flagrantly poor judgment. Female SLAs, then, can be best understood and treated as *regulation-impaired due to a fundamental attachment disorder*.

This piece of the puzzle has radically changed the dated protocol of first stopping the destructive sexual behaviors and only later addressing underlying issues. To treat female SLAs, it's certainly necessary to establish sexual sobriety quickly through cognitive-behavioral therapy and usually a Twelve Step program focused on sex and love addiction. But restructuring ideas and reining in behavior won't be enough for sex and love addicted women. *Only healing deficits in their affective development and doing so right from the start lets you help them achieve lasting, deep change.* This approach creates a dynamic therapeutic process within the context of your genuine, caring relationship—exactly the sort of relationship FSLAs are least practiced in but desperately need. Without altering the dysregulation imbedded in their autonomic nervous system, clients remain chronically panicked, or worse yet, dissociated and can't complete even initial tasks.

Relational Implications of Affect Dysregulation

We saw that when a child suffers any type of trauma, her brain systems get twisted toward offensive or defensive purposes instead of their proper ones. Social synapses no longer seek exciting discoveries about the world, but focus on predicting when others will become dangerous. Her gifts of mimicry are employed to defend herself from others instead of to play, cooperate, and learn. Emotional expression is recruited for battles or truces instead of connectedness (Cozzilino, 2010). Her disturbed regulatory system becomes biased toward arousal and fear, priming her body to sacrifice healthful rest in order to stay on full alert at all times. Finally, the reward systems in her brain, designed to make her feel good through contact with loved ones, are manipulated instead with drugs, alcohol, self-harm, and compulsive sexual and other behaviors.

Changing Attachment Patterns in FSLA Clients

Clearly, for long-term change to occur in FSLAs, regulation of affect must be achieved from the start, along with the cognitive and behavioral interventions needed to contain harmful acting out. And in addition to the neuroaffective element, your awareness of women's physiological, evolutionary, and sociocultural programming helps you help them even more, for you are fighting an addiction with a distinctly feminine face. Most important, just being who you are—a connecting, sensitive, consistent, mature human being—will allow your FSLA clients finally to grow into women capable of genuine relating, self-understanding, and self-regulation.

You can begin the process of healing attachment deficits in FSLAs right away by providing the first underpinning of secure attachment, which is co-regulation of affect, so they can begin to deal with painful feelings instead of resorting automatically to panic or dissociation. At the start of therapy, their dysregulated autonomic nervous system (ANS) is always either over- or under-activated. But once regulated, their ANS will work flexibly, maintain good heart rate variability, and shift easily between arousal states and relaxation. In effect, as the following graphic illustrates, you'll be targeting essential trauma intervention goals immediately by regulating and processing uncomfortable feelings without reactivating trauma.

Goals of Trauma Intervention

1. Regulate her autonomic nervous system (ANS) through co-regulation.
2. Increase her ability to recognize bodily clues to her emotions.
3. Desensitize her to her habitual traumatic triggers.
4. Reduce activation of her fight/flight/freeze response.
5. Activate growth of the emotional regulation centers of her brain.

As the client's ANS begins to become regulated (a habit requiring practice to perfect), you can teach the FSLA simple bodily-based mindfulness and practice it in your office. (Specific exercises are given in the following paragraphs.) This basic mindfulness gradually builds her ability to recognize bodily clues to her feelings, since physical sensations and feelings are the best entry into buried emotions.

When you take your client through these easy activities, your own capacities for auto regulation—to track your physical and emotional state, to regulate yourself, and to convey empathy through your voice and facial expressions—will play central roles in the co-regulatory process. Co-regulation is the *interactive regulation between two people.* This means that your capability to allow your emotions to be touched by your client (without destroying you in the process) will assist her when she becomes overwhelmed by painful material. Over time, she'll adopt your regulatory strengths, which will implant an earned, secure attachment to herself and the skills of self-regulation.

Using Your Own Feelings to Assist FSLAs

As an emotionally healthy person, you can perceive your physical and emotional feelings consciously, describe them to yourself, and figure out their cause. These talents give you powerful hints about what your clients genuinely feel or felt at the time of a trauma, even if those sensations are now denied or dramatized. Using this insight, your delicate but directed questioning will model the very skills they lack.

Since co-regulation is an interactive process between you and the FSLA, you will feel and can therapeutically use sensations your client may not yet be aware of. Such *somatic countertransference* (Orbach & Carroll, 2006; see also Stone, 2006; Vulcan, 2009) includes your own bodily reactions to session material (sleepiness, pain, nausea, muscle tension, feelings of suffocation) and ideas it brings up (erotic images and impulses, fear, rage, shame). These reactions all provide central clues to your client's buried experiences—ones she probably trivializes or displays without genuine affect—and how your unconscious material is meeting hers.

Since female SLAs usually hide their feelings from themselves and others, at the start you'll have to depend on your own gut reactions as well as on your observations of your client. That is, you'll be acting like the attuned caregiver she never had in her earliest years. That good attachment would have given her, as a child, the experience of emotional co-regulation that would have matured into independent self-regulation, which would in turn have nourished all her affective, cognitive, and behavioral abilities. But you can help her catch up!

Of course you'll continue to support sexual sobriety through Twelve Step meetings and group therapy, and you'll apply the simple somatic interventions described below to teach clients to "read" *embodied* (bodily-based or "gut") self-knowledge. As therapy progresses, it will be this new, secure, interactive attachment that will help your client finally attain real human connection, insight, integration of rejected parts of herself, and independent self-regulation of affect.

Understanding the needs of FSLAs with each attachment style from the outset will help you tailor your immediate therapeutic interventions. (See chapter 2 for a quick review of attachment theory.)

General Strategies for Clients With an Avoidant/Dismissing Attachment Style

When working with a client displaying this type of attachment, recall that her regulatory system has designed a strategy for preventing the pain she associates with connection: warding off all thoughts, feelings, or behaviors of real relationship. Her attachment style propels her toward sex addiction. In session, avoidant-dismissing clients will need you to highlight their buried affective states and bodily-based reactions.

Start by taking a brief history. Since the FSLA is likely to deny any good qualities in her family members, have her sit quietly and write down what she got from them—good or bad—that has served her positively, and how she might have benefited if her parents had been attuned to her needs and helped regulate her upsets. If she's in a relationship now, have her list how her own behaviors might have led her to avoid and dismiss her partner (and children).

As you continue talking about current issues, utilize the emotional competence she does possess by helping her identify what she's feeling in a given situation. Encourage her to talk about how she thinks she handled the situation by asking questions like, "How did it go? What did you do well? How might you have made the situation better? Did you make matters worse? Did you under- or overreact to the situation? Looking back, do you notice any thinking errors?" Then move into exploring her emotional state during the situation by asking, "What were you feeling? Do you remember noticing the feeling in your body? If so, where?" Drawing on what she says, suggest that the two of you create a future plan of action for similar situations. Another exercise that will help her develop insight is to instruct her to keep a daily "Thinking/Feeling Journal" to capture her on-the-spot reactions to everyday events.

The avoidant/dismissing woman needs to understand ultimately that the only way out of her pain is by confronting it, but that she can't do it alone. Help her create the friendship skills she never had: asking for and accepting help, seeking positive traits in others, practicing empathy for them, and, ultimately, befriending herself. At the same time she needs to strengthen her judgment by having safer bonding experiences and giving to others without exploiting herself. Clearly, sponsorship and fellowship in a Twelve Step S program or group therapy is invaluable to this population.

General Strategies for Clients With a Preoccupied Attachment Style

The FSLA with a preoccupied attachment style works hard to look like she's got it all together. Her strategy for processing attachment-related thoughts and feelings is to exaggerate them as she always had to do to reach her detached caregiver. She may be able to connect to others in a superficial, theatrical way, but she doesn't know how to be genuinely intimate. She needs, first, simply to acknowledge that her current behaviors guarantee that she won't get her needs met—a project she'll initially resist by becoming defensive or offensive, which are her usual strategies to avoid feeling vulnerable. In session, the preoccupied client may need to be calmed by your right brain regulatory capacities.

You can best assist her by helping her focus on her real emotional needs and on the possibility and value of getting help from others. Teaching her to practice mindfulness will let her locate feelings accurately in her body, eventually discern what she truly wants, and finally state it. She may have difficulty at first recognizing her authentic self and asking for what she desires in a softer, less critical way. Having her keep a "Thinking/Feeling Journal" will show her how to track her ideas and affect closely. These experiences in real feeling will help her control her tendency to react superficially based on what she thinks others expect. You can further help her change these reactive patterns by designing plans to reduce drama in her life and practicing them in session. Have her identify people who can be her coaches and cheerleaders.

General Strategies for Clients With an Avoidant/Fearful Attachment Style

This client probably had a caregiver who was simultaneously scary, controlling, narcissistic, and neglectful. The person who should have been a safe haven presented a threat. So the avoidant/fearful (disorganized) client desires and doubts relationships at the same time. As a result, she avoids all true intimacy and instead tends toward the love addiction end of the SLA spectrum, obsessing about (and perhaps even stalking) a love object without actual connection. Socially anxious and longing for closeness, this client is so afraid she won't get what she needs that she defends against intimacy by alternately clinging or distancing herself. You'll need to remind her often to proceed slowly in romantic relationships.

She will certainly be slow to warm up to you, as she typically takes a victim stance and will reject your attempts to soothe her, since caring relationships have always been a double-edged sword for her. She will usually use inconsistent coping strategies such as seeking negative attention or shifting without notice from dead silence to unstoppable chatter.

Working with the anxious-fearful or disorganized type takes particular time and patience. If your client can't attach to you, can't follow treatment recommendations, and continues to act out sexually, she may need inpatient care to resolve trauma before she can achieve sexual sobriety and benefit from outpatient individual therapy.

When initiating therapy with this client, focus on strengthening her coping skills rather than on her trauma history. Take seriously any past or present suicidal ideation and design strong emergency coping plans with her. Remind her that when she's in distress, her family of origin wounds may make her want you to do everything her parents didn't do for her, but they may also make her feel that whatever you do isn't enough. Carefully note moments of dissociation, which may be difficult to distinguish from her chronic hyper-aroused state.

For your own sake and to stay useful to her, it's essential to maintain "impeccable professional boundaries" (Larson, 2006) with a client who has an avoidant/fearful attachment style. It's not uncommon for therapists to be pulled or bullied into giving this type of client consideration well above and beyond the call of duty: late-night "emergency" sessions, frequent and long phone calls, endless emails. Don't do everything she asks in an effort to calm her extremes of dependency and hostility, and don't take those emotional storms personally. See them instead as her intrapsychic chaos. Most of all, be willing to tolerate "failed" sessions that end without closure

(Larson, 2006). Actively seek consultation and consider referral for medication or trauma resolution therapy such as Dialectical Behavioral Therapy (described at the end of this chapter under "Other Modalities").

Attachment Styles and Interventions

AVOIDANT/DISSMISSIVE ATTACHMENT STYLE:

- **Characteristics**
  - Presents an incoherent narrative
  - Describes experiences superficially (gives just the plot)
  - Lacks awareness of her emotional style
  - Lacks empathy
  - Is comfortable without close relationships
  - Dismisses the value of intimacy
  - Presents as fiercely independent and confident
  - Is rigid in her thinking and responses
  - Expects to be rejected
  - Dismisses attachment to the therapist
  - Dismisses attachment thoughts, feelings, and behaviors
  - Has a high stress load in the body
  - Is always on the look-out for danger
- **Interventions**
  - Give her a clear therapeutic structure and review the goal of each session.
  - Direct her to track her physical feelings to stay grounded.
  - Use your tone of voice, facial expression, and body stance to attune to her.
  - Empathize with her distress.
  - Help her with friendship skills and practicing safe bonding.
  - Help her take accountability for her own behaviors rather than defending them.
  - Talk about your relationship with her, and predict that she will fear it as it grows. Make a relationship management plan with her.

PREOCCUPIED ATTACHMENT STYLE:

- **Characteristics**
  - May be verbal but in ways that are vague and irrelevant
  - May overwhelm therapist with emotional material
  - Under-regulates emotion (tends to be hyper-aroused)
  - ANS is primed to distress
  - Needs external regulation from another to calm down
  - Not discriminating about what she says and does
  - May have little capacity for self-soothing
  - Experiences anxiety, anger, and fear
  - Exaggerates attachment thoughts, feelings, and behaviors
  - Preoccupied with past attachment relationships
  - Maintains connection through negative affect
  - Is likely to stay in relationship via anger
  - Fears intimacy

- **Interventions**
  - Encourage client to reflect on her own concerns and experiences.
  - Permit client to learn from experience, don't disrupt exploratory behaviors unless they are unsafe.
  - Recommend her keeping a journal of thoughts and feelings.
  - Pay attention to your gestures, facial expressions, prosody, and body language so as to increase interactive co-regulatory processes.
  - Direct her to track her physical feelings to stay grounded.
  - Work through changes or disruptions in treatment (therapist travel, new appointment time) well in advance.
  - Identify patterns that increase drama in her life and push others away.

AVOIDANT/FEARFUL (DISORGANIZED) ATTACHMENT STYLE:

- **Characteristics**
  - May appear both dismissing and preoccupied
  - Suffered extreme childhood abuse
  - Needs resolution of childhood trauma
  - Has biphasic characteristics of Borderline Personality Disorder: fear of engulfment and abandonment
  - Uses prolonged silence or monologue
  - Gets attention negatively
  - Has intense transference and difficulty resolving it
- **Interventions**
  - Focus on containing destructive sexual behaviors and attachment issues before addressing trauma resolution.
  - Use cognitive restructuring or Dialectical Behavior Therapy for containment (see "Other Modalities" at the end of this chapter).
  - Address early childhood trauma resolution only once sexually compulsive behaviors have been contained.

  - Avoid eliciting potentially disorganizing affect early in treatment.
  - If needed, provide an additional session per week or arrange in-patient treatment.
  - Direct her to track her physical feelings to stay grounded.
  - Be alert to potential dissociation and combat it with grounding techniques such as breathing and concentrating on the "here and now."
  - Hold unwavering professional boundaries.
  - Stick to the treatment plan.
  - Take careful notes.

Figure 11

Initial Treatment Tasks: Specific Interventions

Given the tremendous importance of the therapist-client relationship in healing your client's attachment wounds and allowing her emotions, thinking, and behaviors to mature, how can you build that crucial connection? As with any client, your first step is allowing, recognizing, and validating her feelings. But since female SLAs often hide their feelings from themselves as well as from others, you know you must learn from your own physical and emotional reactions in sessions, especially early on.

Clearly, then, *your relationship with your client is the most powerful force for healing her damaged attachment.* Your holistic therapeutic alliance—the space you build for her transference, your countertransference, and your collaborative work—is where healing happens. Her use of your healthy regulatory abilities is a necessary first stage and an on-going process. Only through your initial and consistent understanding and expression of her feelings, as well as your expression of your own feelings and experiences in relation to her, will she ever be able to experience her bodily sensations, uncover her feelings, and finally learn to trust and regulate them.

To give affect its proper center-stage position in your sessions, avoid analyzing the words she speaks (a verbal, left brain activity) and instead focus on deepening your connection through both of your right brain emotional systems. In fact, your prosody (tone of voice), facial expressions, gestures, body language, and physical proximity weigh far more than do words at this stage. But be aware that only your genuine concern and attunement will succeed, because an FSLA's spectacularly sensitized nervous system expertly detects any whiff of falsehood.

As noted, body sensation exercises and mindfulness practices are crucial for increasing FSLAs' consciousness of how they feel physically. More important, *they alone provide entry into their emotional states.* But how can you get them to do these practices? Avoidant clients deny their feelings; clients with a preoccupied attachment style exaggerate them wildly; and those with anxious/fearful attachment may be so dissociative that they need inpatient care before they can benefit from outpatient therapy.

Fortunately, your first and most effective technique is also the simplest *somatic* (body-based) intervention: track your own physical and emotional self-state, be willing to tell her what you're feeling, and pose gentle questions to guide your client in tracking her own. Gauging your own sensations and affect as well as your client's will help you attune better to her, letting you uncover what's denied and calm what's overdramatized. Certainly, disclosing your affective states to your client carries risks. But it puts you in direct relationship with her. You're out of the realm of the cognitive where you feel safe and are traversing the inner world of the body where you must be willing to "not know" what happens next. Like the highly attuned mother, you will have misattunements and repairs, which will build trust and safety, as well as profoundly intimate meetings, and times when your client denies your reality. All these experiences must be processed in the most emotionally honest way possible in order to unlock the FSLA's compartments. By validating what was invalidated or ignored in her childhood, the disowned parts of her can come forward, be seen, and accepted to create a more coherent, integrated self.

Note that each therapeutic element detailed below, although presented roughly in its likeliest order, doesn't get "finished" before moving to the next. While every aspect of your treatment is put in place when appropriate, it always stays in play even after others are added.

Observe yourself and your client

First, notice your client's tendency to avert her gaze. It's a way to regulate herself and to distance herself from you, just as her habit of sexual or romantic objectification is an attempt to self-regulate by preventing genuine relationship. So to start establishing a connection that can help her, use your powers of emotional observation to note her somatic signs of anxiety: muscle tension in the arms and legs, fidgeting, shaking in extremities, or sighing heavily as she attempts to regulate. These symptoms reveal part of her *procedural memory system*—unconscious actions, thoughts, and sensations learned in her neural network that are now habitual, automatic defenses against painful sensations. Examples of positive procedural memories are riding a bike or tying shoelaces. But you can imagine her growing up in a family with a rageful parent. Her early somatic response to the parent's fury became habituated in her neural networks and ANS through repeated activation, and soon turned into an automatic response elicited whenever the situation seems similar enough to her brain and body to retrigger the trauma, even if the responses are objectively irrelevant at present.

Guide her through a mental body scan

Now you can introduce a simple somatic exercise. Begin this one (and all bodily-based activities) by having her ground her feet on the floor and feel her back body against the surface she's sitting on. Invite her to close her eyes (but don't insist) so you can verbally guide her through a mental body scan. (Your scanning will always proceed from her feet upward, since feet are usually the least emotionally charged area of the body.) Instruct her simply to "notice and breathe." Ask her to sit comfortably and to notice the way her feet feel on the floor and in her shoes. Ask whether she is aware of any pain, tension, tightness, or any other sensation in these areas, without stopping to judge or explain it. If there is, ask her to breathe and to let the sensation go. Sequentially, ask these same questions about her ankles, shins, knees, and thighs.

Proceed up the body by having her notice her seat on the surface she's sitting on, her belly, solar plexus, and chest, reminding her all the while to notice any physical sensations in these areas and to breathe into the feelings. Continue by having her attend to her back. Ask if there is lower-back, mid-back, or upper-back tension. If so, instruct her to breathe into it. Then have her check her shoulders, neck, and face. Invite her to relax any tension in the jaw and around or above the eyes, and then to notice the top of her head. When you've completed the body scan, sit quietly and remind her to notice if there's any lingering tension and, if so, to let it go by breathing into it gently.

If at any point she feels anxious, have her stop, ground her feet on the floor, and connect to her back body on the surface she's sitting on. Advise her to place her hand on her belly and take three deep breaths into her belly as a way to settle down her nervous system. If she's feeling depressed and lethargic, have her place her hand on her chest and take three deep breaths into her chest to activate her system. (If you're trained in EMDR, you can teach her how to tap as a way to self-soothe.)

As you observe her and ask her about her feelings, you can say very simply that her bodily movements and feelings are trying to defend her against emotions. By your simply taking note of her bodily tension and asking her if her body "wants to move in a particular way," your client will begin to notice her sensations herself, which will relax her defenses and eventually allow affective states to come forward.

If, on the other hand, there is no visual evidence of anxiety in the extremities and your client reports she feels "nothing" or "numbness" in her body, instruct her to close her eyes and take a deep breath into her chest. Ask her where in her body she feels the "nothing" or "numbness." Often clients locate this deadness in the center of the body around the heart or solar plexus. Once she can give you a clear idea of where this non-feeling (often described by the client as a "hole") resides, ask her to describe the hole. "Does it have a size, shape, or color? Does it have a weight to it? Are the boundaries smooth or jagged? If the hole could speak, what would it say?" Remind her not to think about it too much but to speak from the hole, as the hole. You can coach her by suggesting it may want to say, "I feel . . .; I need . . .; I want . . ." The simple act of investigating this self-state, without judgment, begins to activate her brain to make a connection with her body and vice versa. This investigative act can also shift into an affective state. Note whatever happens as interesting data without judging it as "good" or "bad." This is especially important for the FSLA who is primed for self-criticism. At this juncture, it's important that you, too, track the impulses in your own body. Where are you feeling anxious, tense, or numb? What bodily-based shifts are occurring in you? Share this data with your client so that she knows you are with her and she can feel you "feeling" her.

A dissociated client will find closing her eyes and investigating her body too much to bear, and she'll quickly open her eyes. Note it, and remember this is a process of gradually expanding her ability to tolerate small doses of emotional novelty into her system. As always, notice your own somatic clues and use them as data for yourself, and for your client when appropriate. For example, if your client can't tolerate being in her body due to extreme discomfort, commend her for being willing to try. If your own anxiety shoots up because you're worried that "it's not working" or "I don't know what I'm doing," take note of that, and recognize that you're in a deeply empathic state with your client who is likely feeling the same way. You may share with her that you're aware of tightness in your chest that tells you that fear is arising, and ask her if she notices any fear in her that may be associated with your process together. By doing so you're allowing and using your somatic countertransference, and are applying affective disclosure with her to create a high level of attunement. If she responds, "no" to your question about her fear, ask her what it's like for her to see you feeling for her, then stay in an honest dialogue with her about her reality and yours. Your patient, painstaking interpersonal engagement allows increased and flexible negotiation, and lets a mutual, inter-subjective truth emerge.

In sum, your main aims are to keep her directed into her body, stay in your own body, use data about what's arising in you in relation to her, disclose your affective truth with her, and process it together. This modality illustrates the co-regulatory process. In other words, it's through the relationship that you are affecting and changing one other. As you experience and validate her impulses, nuances, and emotions, she perhaps for the first time will begin to feel, invite in, and finally integrate those parts of herself.

CASE STUDY

A week prior, I'd had an EMDR session with "Jane," a 19-year-old SLA, recovering cocaine addict, and alcoholic, during which we targeted the moment in her childhood when her parents announced they were divorcing. Throughout the reprocessing phase of the work, there was no discernable affect but plenty of discharge in the body.

Today, we sit knee to knee, with me to her left side as she sits on the sofa, which is the "ships passing in the night" position as the EMDR protocol terms it. I sit to her left so as to engage her left visual field and auditory canal, allowing me to make contact with the right hemisphere of her brain.

This position also lets me make contact with her from the left side of my face and body, so there's right brain-to-right brain communication taking place, regardless of our words.

In a typically flat affect that telegraphs her chronic dissociation, Jane tells me that she touched a deep loneliness inside herself last night which made her cry and experience compassion for herself for being so lonely. She tells me that this loneliness is present with her today. I feel my anxiety arise as I glimpse into the abyss she lives in. Worried that I can't help her out of it and feeling a bit helpless, I take a breath to regulate my own system.

I ask her to take a moment and put both feet on the floor and close her eyes. I instruct her to dive into the deep loneliness, and to let me know where she most feels it in her body. Right away, she tells me she feels something in her stomach. I ask her if she can speak from her stomach and let me know what it's saying. Jane reports that her stomach would make a "blood-curdling scream." She then notices a feeling in her chest. I ask her to check in with her chest and report what her chest wants to express. She tells me it's a feeling of disgust.

Disgust typically resides in the gut, buried deep in the body. But Jane's sense of self-loathing is close to the surface, as evidenced by her report of feeling disgust in her chest. Her rage and anxiety, however, are chronically dissociated, so I become more interested in what's happening in her stomach. I go back to that because I'm noticing a constriction in my own throat, and I ask Jane what the "blood-curdling scream" would sound like. After a moment of silence, she tells me her throat won't let her scream. She reports being in a battle between her stomach, which wants to make a "blood-curdling scream," her chest where the "disgust" resides, and her throat, which will not allow her to scream. She can't hold these states for too long and fairly quickly dissociates.

Jane looks at me and I take a deep breath while holding gentle eye contact with her. Modulating my voice, I ask her to breathe into her chest in hopes of activating her ANS. I notice she's in a "stilling" state, which is a good sign that she's not moving deeper into dissociation but is instead idling.

As I breathe normally, I stay in contact with her and notice her breathing change, signaling that she's back to a more regulated state. I recognize this as a sequence for introducing novelty into her system. First, she contacts her bodily feelings, notices them, gives them a voice, and then moves into dissociation. Then, through a co-regulatory process of breathing, eye contact, and prosody, her ANS rhythmically synchronizes with mine, increasing her window of tolerance for novel stimuli (namely her internal feeling states and my capacity for empathy). Thus she has slightly strengthened her capacity for self-regulation.

The conversation turns to how her body clenches and how she's not enjoying sex any more because she doesn't feel she deserves the pleasure. She states that she doesn't make eye contact while being sexual with her boyfriend and doesn't allow for pleasure in her body. I ask her if she's willing to pay attention to these matters the next time she has sex with him and she agrees. Her body imperceptibly tenses and her breathing becomes shallow as we talk, and I begin to realize I'm talking too much. I ask her what she's feeling in the moment, and she reports feeling tenser at the memory of what happened in her childhood household. In a slightly more connected but quiet voice, she tells me she knows it was "pretty bad," but can't remember.

We sit in silence and I begin to notice my body temperature rising as my eyes well up with tears. I'm in a state of reverie where there's a melding of my own childhood loneliness with visions of her mother and father constantly arguing in her presence. I feel how terrifying the household she grew up in must have been. I look at Jane with tears in my eyes and I tell her that I understand why she can't feel those feelings, and that I'm feeling them now. Jane looks at me without much change. I ask her what it's like to see me feeling for her. She says she doesn't know what she's feeling but that she is feeling something. I ask her if what she's feeling is safe or scary. Jane looks at me and slightly turns her head more toward the left, then cocks her chin in an upward motion, her amygdala clearly checking me out. With eyes surveying me from above, she says she isn't sure. Knowing we're in a resonant moment, I instinctively change my language to match parlance and ask, "Is the feeling okay or weird?" She answers by saying, "It's kinda weird and unsafe, but I feel seen by you, but I don't like it so much." I offer that this must feel a bit like pulling the covers off her head, kind of like in hide-and-seek, then pulling them back up again. She smiles and laughs and says, "Yeah" and we laugh together in a natural play state. My fear and tears have disappeared. I feel my heart open and I amplify this moment by allowing our smiles and giggles to reach a natural crescendo. There's a distinct bodily shift in the space between us. It's closer and more intimate and we're both more alive, she with a slight sparkle in her eyes.

Check her comfort level

Don't forget to ask about bodily functions—chronic headaches, stomachaches, or irritable bowel syndrome—which signal higher levels of anxiety and deeper somatization of feelings. Gently point out how deeply embedded in her body her trauma has become. Accustom her to notice these physical manifestations as her defense against emotions. By simply directing her attention to her bodily conditions as valuable keys to her feelings, she will begin to know where her emotions reside in her body. For example, if she has constant gastric distress, ask her what her bowels would say if they could speak by wondering, "What are they irritated about?" If she has chronic headaches ask, "Where are they most pronounced—in your eyes or behind your eyes? What do your eyes want to express?" If other tensions arise in her body during this investigation or if specific images come forth, process whatever comes to the fore through calm questioning.

Finally, consistently check with your client while working with deeper affective states to see if she is experiencing perceptual disturbances such as ringing in the ears or tunnel vision. If these symptoms arise, call a halt to dismantling her defenses and stabilize her. Bring her into the here and now by having her ground her feet on the floor and feel her body on the surface she's sitting on. Slow down and consider seeking consultation when necessary.

Teach healthy self-soothing

Another easy way you can begin to help your client regulate her nervous system is by teaching her about healthy auto-regulatory behaviors. Because FSLAs are dysregulated, they need to acquire new habits of wholesome self-soothing behaviors. Teach her that non-sexual self-touch such as giving herself a hand, foot, or scalp massage is an effective way for her to calm herself. Remind her of other forms of comforting self-care she's already learned in her recovery: going for a walk, singing a favorite song, hugging a pet, taking a warm bath, doing yoga, journaling, reading, or meditating. Physical activities like skiing, surfing, and hiking, as well as creative activities such as composing music, writing, and making art also encourage a flow state in the brain. Recalling and practicing this set of healthy skills bolsters her powers of self-regulation.

Although these suggestions sound obvious, your client's relational trauma probably included an almost unimaginable degree of neglect (few if any visits to dentists or doctors, no concern with hygiene, nutrition, cleanliness at home, schoolwork, or friendships) or, conversely, with superficial spoiling (showy presents and vacations, pricey schools) masking real deprivations of basic safety, honest communication, love, and plain everyday childhood fun. Don't underestimate her inability to provide self-care and healthy self-soothing. She can't use behaviors that she hasn't observed or experienced, and the FSLA will likely need you to teach her practices you may find natural, even automatic.

Track affect and match it

You already know that when tracking affect you'll note both the client's and your own emotional and somatic reactions. But remember not to assume you know what her sad facial expression or tears are about. Even though you want to avoid verbal analysis of words, you'll need to ask her directly what her reactions mean to her. By checking for accuracy instead of guessing, you'll deepen your affective attunement to your client.

When it comes to yourself, attend closely to your own eye contact, prosody, expressions, and gestures as well as tension and emotions in your own body, and check your own internal state changes nonverbally at all times. Especially now, matching your voice, facial expressions, gestures, and physical stance to hers is more powerful than your (or her) words.

Intermediate Treatment Tasks: Specific Interventions

As the therapeutic relationship solidifies and becomes safer, the co-regulation between you and the recovering FSLA allows her defense to continue dropping so that she can explore her trauma more deeply. With you as a support and guide, she learns to tolerate the normal ups and downs of a healthy relationship, including the one with you. She also increases her tolerance for delving further into core wounds that may underlie her addictive behavior, in large part because she's come to experience you as emotionally reliable.

Recognize and repair misattunements

No matter how careful you are, accept that you will inevitably be occasionally misattuned to your client. More important, know that therapy can actually benefit from this opportunity. Ruptures between therapist and client usually occur when disturbing material in session elicits your reaction of disgust, shock, or disconnection, which the client receives with shame. So be aware of what happens in your own body, voice, and face when material becomes uncomfortable for you, and use your reactions therapeutically by briefly sharing your honest, non-judgmental experience. The act of repairing a breach in attunement through openness about your process—probably totally novel to her—is essential for therapy to progress and for her to grow.

Deal with complex trauma

If we define trauma as any experience that terrorizes the child so much that she can't integrate affective material from it, you understand that early relational deficits are trauma, indeed. You also know that repeated traumatic disruptions in the child's sense of security that aren't responded to or regulated lead her to block future attachments and to replay these same patterns. If her life should include later trauma (physical, emotional, or sexual abuse; neglect; receiving or witnessing violence; illness with invasive treatment; bullying; or sexual harassment), you can expect that this insecurely attached person, with her hobbled regulatory capacities, will be even less able to manage the fallout. She may then suffer from disorders of extreme stress not otherwise specified (van der Kolk, McFarlane, & Weisaeth, 1996), and you'll need to address each of its factors.

Specific information about treating issues like recovering from childhood sexual abuse, physical violence, and other forms of trauma are beyond the scope of this book. Nevertheless, the writers of this text posit that the best practices outlined in this and the preceding chapter provide helpful beginning points for treating complex trauma. The foundation for treatment is an attachment-based, strong therapeutic relationship as outlined here. (See the Suggested Reading section of the Appendix for resources that delineate effective interventions for these issues.)

Advanced Treatment Tasks: Specific Interventions

In addition to suffering attachment deficits, female SLAs tend to be disconnected from their emotional realities because they grew up in families where it was unsafe to express feelings. Living in a dysfunctional family created profound shame and low self-esteem, both of which led them toward isolation and addiction. In many instances, they have sexualized themselves in order to get their need for intimacy met, and they confuse sex with love. As a result they may define intimacy as purely sexual. You'll need to both educate and demonstrate that this basic need for intimacy can be (and should have been) met by any two people who are honest with each other.

Following are suggestions for dialogues about the deprivation of your client's basic needs:

- Remind the FSLA about the basic human needs for safety, health, nutrition, and social connection, and ask her if she believes she got these basic needs met as a child.
- If not, ask her how was she neglected and by whom? What feelings does this reality bring up and where in her body does she locate the feeling?
- Ask her if her basic needs are currently being met, and if so, who's meeting them? What's it like to receive from someone? Can she take in the care, or does it make her uncomfortable and want to push it away?
- Because she likely grew up in a toxic family, she may need to be told that family is the primary location that meets our most basic needs. In her denial or codependency, she may tell you that her family was "fine." Without your guiding her to examine her experiences and check her perceptions, she'll continue to protect her fantasy of her "fine" family. One way to check this out with her is to track what she's experiencing in her body as she talks about her family. As always, notice your own internal cues as well as her gestures, facial expressions, skin tone changes, and muscle tension and process both of your affective states with her.

Accepting that her needs weren't met by her family and experiencing the death of her fantasy that they will be met by them one day are very painful, but essential steps in her recovery. Expect this to be a lengthy and often challenging part of your client's journey. Her grieving process about her attachment injuries and other core wounds will require your tender, consistent care.

Explore abuse and neglect and how to end the cycle

Not surprisingly, an adult victim usually struggles with feelings of helplessness, self-pity, low self-esteem, shame, hopelessness, and an internal sense of unworthiness. These emotions stem from her dissociated self-states that have yet to be expressed, regulated, and integrated. Why? Her ANS is primed for defense and disconnection from the self, and she's been programmed to believe that everything that happened, happens, or will happen to her depends on events outside of her control.

The worst cost of being a victim may be the tendency victims have to become victimizers in turn, or to fear that they will. Your client may feel deep shame when forced to reflect on the possibility that she herself may be or become abusive. Remind her that you will work through her shame together, and that looking honestly at herself and taking responsibility for her actions are strengths she can be proud of. Begin by reviewing basic information about family systems and descriptions of abuse and neglect (as outlined in chapter 2 in the Environmental Factors section). Now that she has a healthy attachment to a positive figure, the FSLA is better able to look at these painful issues, including how she may be perpetuating the cycle through her own behavior. Dialogue about the effects of your client's experience of invalidation:

- Ask her, "Being subject to dominating behavior can make you lose your self-respect. Was there a time in your childhood when you were denied your reality or had your feelings invalidated? If so, by whom, and what did the person do?"
- "What effect do you think this has had on you over time? What feelings arise in you as you talk about these incidents?"
- "Addicts in particular are likely to demonstrate unpredictable emotional states and responses. Have others behaved in that way to you? Do you feel you have ever behaved in that way?"
- "How has that impacted you? How does it make you feel about yourself now?"
- "If so, what can you begin to do differently? What do you need to let go of? What do you need to receive? What help do you need in doing things differently?"

Explain to your client that the pain and anger from the abuse may be turned inward toward herself or may be directed outward onto another person. Keep in mind that she has also likely cut off parts of herself or compartmentalized them so completely that she can't feel anything, meaning she tends toward dissociation. Watch for dissociation during these conversations and begin to explore it in your sessions. First, notice your own tendency to dissociate and times that you ignore or shy away from moving closer to her when the material gets disturbing or challenging. If you find that you did avoid her emotionally at such a moment, you will likely have disappointed her. As you recall, to recognize and repair this misattunement you'll need to own your part in her disappointment as honestly as possible, thereby once again validating her experience with you in the "here and now."

Clarify that victims of childhood abuse may become victims again, victimizers, rescuers, or all three. Tell her that when the victim of childhood abuse turns the anger and pain she feels inward, she may practice self-destructive behaviors such as addictions, self-mutilation, or suicidality. Victims may also project their pain outward by "persecuting" others through blame, rage, passive-aggressive behaviors, or martyrdom. Victims too may be "rescuers" by focusing on controlling, "helping," or manipulating others, which many victims see as positive behaviors. The Karpman's Triangle illustration is quite helpful in addressing trauma (Karpman, 1968) and is easily understood. Ask the FSLA, "Do you see yourself in this victim-persecutor-rescuer cycle? If so, where? Can you think of examples? Are there times when you've changed positions on the cycle?"

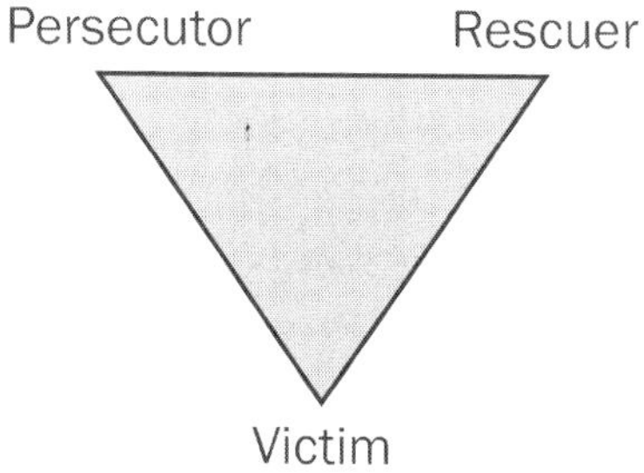

Karpman's Triangle - Stephen B. Karpman, M.D.
Used by permission.

Figure 12

Explain that regardless of the "starting point" where she enters the unhealthy triangle, each position is rooted in trauma, and each position is actually a victim-driven stance. With your help and the support she gets from her Twelve Step program, friends, and others, the female SLA can heal and become internally resilient enough to stop this cycle of hurting and being hurt.

Other Therapeutic Modalities

You've seen that modern attachment theory is essentially regulation theory. By expanding Bowlby's (1969) contribution to include bodily-based processes and interactive regulation (co-regulation), new therapeutic modalities focus squarely on the interaction between therapist and client—the dyadic(two-person) system—as the key to creating profound, long-lasting change in attachment-disordered clients (Schore & Schore, 2007).

As you've also seen, practicing with a regulation theory perspective requires no formal training. But it does demand an understanding of regulation theory, affective honesty, and mature clinical skills. To increase your techniques for working in the affective realm, you may wish to pursue certification in the modality you prefer. This section presents a sampling of cutting-edge protocols that blend the insights of attachment theory with those of affective neuroscience.

Post Induction Therapy

Post Induction Therapy for Developmental Immaturity Treatment (PIT) was founded by Mellody in the 1970s and further developed in 1986 (Mellody, 2003). This modality is used to treat the effects of early developmental trauma and the resulting issues of developmental immaturity, also called codependence. The core of PIT includes specific protocols drawn from a variety of theoretical models that take place in individual, group, and couple therapy.

PIT is a multi-part process whereby the therapist works initially to re-parent the client through cognitive restructuring of specific core issues related to developmental immaturity. Emphasis is placed on self-esteem, boundaries, reality issues, dependency issues, and issues related to moderation and containment of affect and behaviors. Ultimately, the client re-parents her early childhood wounding through inner child work, shame reduction, and integration of dissociated self-states. These processes are facilitated by a therapist and include visualization, gestalt work (use of the empty chair), and affect regulation.

Emotional Freedom Technique

Developed by Craig, Emotional Freedom Techniques (EFT) derive from the premise that negative emotions such as those accompanying traumas directly result from a blockage of the body's energy system (Craig, 2010). Through repeating positive affirmations and tapping on acupressure points, EFT practitioners believe this "emotional acupuncture" frees the body's energy to resolve phobias, anxiety, abandonment feelings, stress, and chronic pain, as well as improve energy levels.

The simple process doesn't require the presence of a professional, and the EFT website offers do-it-yourself manuals for beginners. The "Basic Recipe" begins by defining a given problem, rating the client's associated level of distress on a scale of 1 to 10, preparing for change through repeating affirmations of self-acceptance, then tapping specific acupressure points about seven times, and reassessing the client's stress level. This sequence is repeated until the measure of distress falls to zero or one.

Certification is available through the EFT Universe website, but many facilities offer certification programs for similar therapies utilizing a combination of positive affirmations and pressure-point tapping.

Somatic Experiencing

Based on over 40 years of research and clinical experience with trauma clients, Levine formulated the Somatic Experiencing (SE) therapeutic modality. Levine (1997) noted that animals in the wild experience frequent threats to their safety yet don't seem traumatized by them as do human beings. Attributing this resiliency to biological processes within animals' autonomic nervous systems, Levine theorized that people, like animals, have the ability to recover after trauma, but the act of freezing prevents this self-regulation. In freezing, a person appears calm while her nervous system becomes highly activated, which produces a surplus of undischarged energy which remains trapped inside the body. According to SE, traumas are thereby carried in the body indefinitely until the autonomic nervous system can discharge its pent-up energy. Believing that "the key to healing traumatic symptoms in humans lies in our being able to mirror the fluid adaption of wild animals" (Levine, 1997, pp. 17-18), the SE practitioner guides clients to discharge "stuck" energy by using their current sensory experience to develop awareness of tension and other physical symptoms which manifest their trauma.

SE treats both single-event traumas such as rape or natural disasters and long-term or ongoing developmental traumas. Certified Somatic Experiencing practitioners have participated in a credential program of training, consultation, personal SE sessions, and participate in continuing education.

Sensorimotor Psychotherapy

In her practice with trauma clients, Ogden noticed that although cognitive and emotional processing provided some relief, somatic symptoms often persisted. To address these as well, Ogden developed Sensorimotor Psychotherapy as a protocol integrating the three different modes by which we process experience: cognitive, emotional, and sensorimotor (Ogden & Minton, 2000). Ogden asserted that bodily-based awareness is essential for treating trauma, which is stored in the body as procedural memory (Ogden, Minton, & Pain, 2006). Therefore, treating the client's trauma via the body (instead of treating it cognitively or emotionally) allows the trauma to be successfully processed, which then leads to a shift in affect regulation that ultimately impacts cognition. A wide variety of techniques are used including sound, mirroring, movement, and breath. Like Somatic Experiencing, Sensorimotor Psychotherapy relies on increased consciousness of sensory experiences such as breath, heart rate, and muscle tension. But in SE, sensory awareness and the discharge of stored energy themselves are said to resolve trauma, while in Sensorimotor Psychotherapy these are only the first steps.

Ogden theorized that heightened physical arousal at a moment of perceived threat leads to both excessive emotional arousal and distorted cognitive processes. By first focusing on the body, then finding ways to reduce physical arousal, and finally learning to differentiate between physical and emotional arousal, clients can calm their cognitive and emotional disturbances and at last begin to reexamine them. So in Sensorimotor Psychotherapy, recovery derives from the deeper exploration of the emotional and cognitive processes associated with trauma, facilitated by reducing their original intensity (Ogden et al., 2006).

Somatic therapy may include actual physical contact with the client when the practitioner is certified in a modality, which qualifies him or her to do so appropriately. Touching clients without proper training is typically out of most therapists' scope of practice and is usually against psychotherapeutic licensing regulations. Touch can, however, be used adjunctively with other modalities in most treatment settings. Certification in Sensorimotor Psychotherapy requires completing a three-year training course (with consultation) as well as continuing education.

Neurofeedback

Neurofeedback is based on the discovery that different brainwaves accompany and can create various levels of relaxation, concentration, and other cognitive and emotional processes (Lubar, 1995). Utilizing our innate ability to maintain mental homeostasis, neurofeedback relies on electrical feedback to assist clients in increasing self-regulation. Electrodes placed on the scalp measure the activity of different brainwaves, which is immediately displayed on a screen. By observing their own brain patterns, clients can effectively use relaxation techniques to influence and ultimately change them. This "physical therapy for the brain" retrains its electrical currents as they are electronically mirrored back to the client.

Neurofeedback has been found effective in treating ADHD, learning disabilities, epilepsy, brain injuries, PTSD, anxiety, and drug and alcohol addiction. Certification for Neurofeedback practice is available through the Natural Therapies Certification Board.

Brainspotting

Dr. David Grand, a specialist in healing trauma, developed Brainspotting (Grand, n.d.). As a client shares her trauma or emotionally disturbing memory, the therapist guides her to find a "Brainspot," a focal eye position in which the sensory response to the trauma is most activated. Physical cues such as the client's eye twitches, body shifts, and facial tics indicate the location of a Brainspot. Theorizing that the trauma, most likely stored in the amygdala, the hippocampus, or the orbitofrontal cortex of the limbic system, is made accessible by holding this Brainspot, the therapist has the client maintain this eye position while focusing on her sensory and somatic experiences.

Brainspotting is believed to allow a deep level of healing for unconscious physical symptoms of trauma. Like EMDR, Brainspotting is considered most effective when paired with bilateral sound, or sounds alternately transmitted to the left and right hemispheres.

Eye Movement Desensitization and Reprocessing (EMDR)

Developed by Shapiro (1995), EMDR is a psychotherapeutic modality that stimulates both hemispheres of the brain with bilateral eye movements, tones, taps, or vibrations while processing maladaptive thoughts or beliefs. EMDR posits that maladaptive thoughts are often associated with minor or major traumas, as information processing during a trauma or the storage of memory about the trauma is incomplete, which results in a disconnect between the mind and body. Through the EMDR protocol, traumatic memories are said to be reprocessed in the mind and body, and information is reintegrated more holistically, which ultimately reduces emotional distress and cognitive disturbance (Shapiro, 1995).

The eight-phase process of EMDR begins with obtaining a comprehensive history of traumatic events and ensuring that basic coping and self-soothing mechanisms are in place. Then the client identifies a traumatic event, along with associated physical sensations or imagery, and notes negative thoughts and images as bilateral stimulation is provided. The therapist guides the client to conduct mental body scans for significant sense memories, which continues the integration of mind and body. Subjective levels of disturbance regarding the targeted event are rated, and the process is repeated until the client has significantly reduced emotional distress and improved overall functioning.

The American Psychiatric Association (2004) and the Departments of Defense and Veterans Affairs (Department of Veterans Affairs, & Department of Defense, 2004) recommend EMDR for trauma treatment, and the International Society for Traumatic Stress Studies finds it effective in treating PTSD (Foa, Keane, Friedman, & Cohen, 2009). To be certified, EMDR therapists must have two years of experience in their field, participate in an EMDR Institute of America (EMDRIA) approved training course, conduct at least 50 EMDR sessions with 20 hours of consultation, and complete 12 hours of continuing education every two years.

Dialectical Behavior Therapy

Designed to surpass the efficacy of Cognitive Behavioral Therapy (CBT) with chronically suicidal clients, Dialectical Behavior Therapy (DBT) was developed by Linehan (1987). She found DBT particularly effective in treating individuals suffering from Borderline Personality Disorder (BPD) as it targeted their characteristically poor affect regulation and distress tolerance. The term "dialectical" refers to the therapy's focus on balancing multiple coexisting tensions, particularly those between validating and accepting a client while simultaneously helping the client change (Dimeff & Linehan, 2001). By combining awareness practices, mindfulness, and self-soothing with skills training, group therapy, and problem-solving techniques, DBT helps such clients become more adaptable to change and better able to regulate their emotions.

Additionally, DBT was formulated to help therapists work with difficult countertransference issues often provoked by work with BPD clients. Linehan saw that therapists' encouragement of change was often experienced by BPD clients as invalidating and provoked severe backlash from the clients (Linehan, 1993). In addition to punishing the therapist for suggesting change by exhibiting very difficult behavior, clients rewarded the therapist for avoiding discomfort-inducing topics by exhibiting agreeable behavior. This manipulation hamstrung any therapist without iron-clad boundaries and extremely high levels of differentiation. In DBT, such mechanisms are kept to a minimum as the client must participate in group therapy and group skills training in addition to individual therapy. The therapist also utilizes a consultation team to maintain focus in the treatment.

Conclusion

Teaching female SLAs to feel their bodies and emotions is hard. They don't have access to their bodily-based feelings or practice sharing feelings (and may have gotten punished for trying to). Their nervous systems are so programmed to seek a dopamine high from sex and love, they literally can't imagine deeper goals. And now you want them to stop acting out and even fantasizing—their primary survival strategies!

But affective neuroscience teaches that providing emotional regulation allows FSLAs finally to experience secure attachment. Now you know that her brand-new experience of co-regulation depends on her attachment to you, and that it lets her achieve emotional self-regulation and develop the cognitive and behavioral abilities that were hobbled in her infancy. More important, you can now create lasting healing for her and expand your treatment aims from basic sexual sobriety to include genuine human connection, insight, and, ultimately, independent self-regulation of affect.

REFERENCES

American Psychiatric Association. (2004). *Practice guideline for the treatment of patients with acute stress disorder and posttraumatic stress disorder.* Arlington, VA: Author.

Bowlby, J. (1969). *Attachment and loss: Vol. 1. Attachment.* New York, NY: Basic Books.

Cozzilino, L. (2010). *The neuroscience of psychotherapy: Healing the social brain* (2nd ed.). New York, NY: W. W. Norton.

Craig, G. (2010). *The EFT Mini-Manual.* Fulton, CA: Energy Psychology Press. Retrieved from http://www.eftuniverse.com/images/pdf_files/EFTMiniManual.pdf

Department of Veterans Affairs & Department of Defense. (2004). *VA/DoD Clinical Practice Guideline for the Management of Post-Traumatic Stress.* Washington, DC: Veterans Health Administration, Department of Veterans Affairs and Health Affairs, Department of Defense. Office of Quality and Performance. 10Q-CPG/PTSD-04

Dimeff, L., & Linehan, M. M. (2001). Dialectical behavior therapy in a nutshell. *The California Psychologist, 34*, 10-13.

Foa, E. B., Keane, T. M., Friedman, M. J., & Cohen, J. A. (2009). *Effective treatments for PTSD: Practice guidelines of the International Society for Traumatic Stress Studies.* New York, NY: Guilford Press.

Grand, D. (n.d.). Retrieved from http://lisaschwarz.com/wp-content/uploads/2011/03/Brainspotting-for-German-Trauma-Journal.pdf

Karpman, S. B. (1968). *Fairy tales and script drama analysis.* Transactional Analysis Bulletin, 7(26).

Larson, N. (2006). Treating Borderlines: A neuroscience update. An unpublished paper based on a presentation at Randers Hospital Psychiatric Department, Denmark.

Levine, P. A. (1997). *Waking the tiger: Healing trauma: The innate capacity to transform overwhelming experiences.* Berkeley, CA: North Atlantic Books.

Linehan, M. (1987). Dialectical behavior therapy: A cognitive behavioral approach to parasuicide. *Journal of Personality Disorders,1*, 328-333.

Linehan, M. M. (1993). *Skills training manual for treating borderline personality disorder.* New York, NY: Guilford Press.

Lubar, J. F. (1995). Neurofeedback for the management of attention deficit hyperactivity disorders. In M. S. Schwartz (Ed.), *Biofeedback: A practitioner's guide* (pp. 493-522). New York, NY: Guilford Press.

Mellody, P. (2003). *Post induction therapy workshop for developmental immaturity treatment* (5th ed.). Wickenburg, AZ: Unpublished manual.

Ogden, P., & Minton, K. (2000). Sensorimotor psychotherapy: One method for processing traumatic memory. *Traumatology,* 6(3), Article 3.

Ogden, P., Minton, K., & Pain, C. (2006). *Trauma and the body: A sensorimotor approach to psychotherapy.* New York, NY: W. W. Norton.

Orbach, S., & Carroll, R. (2006). Contemporary approaches to body in psychotherapy: Two psychotherapists in dialogue. In J. Corrigall, H. Payne, & H. Wilkinson (Eds.), *About a body: Working with the embodied mind in psychotherapy* (pp. 63-82). London: Routledge.

Schore, J. R., & Schore, A. N. (2007). Modern attachment theory: The central role of affect regulation in development and treatment. *Clinical Social Work Journal.* doi: 10.1007/s10615-007-0111-7

Shapiro, F. (1995). *Eye Movement Desensitization and Reprocessing: Basic principles, protocols and procedures* (1st ed.). New York, NY: Guilford Press.

Stone, M. (2006). The analyst's body as tuning fork: Embodied resonance in countertransference. *Journal of Analytical Psychology, 51,*109–124.

van der Kolk, B., McFarlane, A. C., & Weisaeth, L. (Eds.). (1996). *Traumatic stress: The effects of overwhelming experience on mind, body, and society.* New York, NY: Guilford Press.

Vulcan, M. (2009). Is there any body out there?: A survey of literature on somatic countertransference and its significance for DMT. *The Arts in Psychotherapy, 36,* 275.

CHAPTER 8

Systemic Issues in Treating Female Sex and Love Addicts

Deborah Corley, Marnie Ferree
with contribution by Kelly McDaniel

Females who struggle with sex and love addiction aren't the only ones affected by their behavior, of course. Addiction is a distressing, powerful force for everyone involved with the addict, especially those who share the closest relationships. Husbands or partners and children of FSLAs are especially impacted when a woman is acting out with sex or relationships. Their lives, too, are usually plagued by confusion and chaos. They also need therapeutic support, attention, and intervention. For convenience, the discussion focuses on men as partners of FSLAs, and masculine pronouns are used to identify these individuals. In general, similar dynamics and issues exist within a lesbian relationship. (See chapter 9 for information about sex and love addiction in the lesbian population.)

Addiction and Systems Theory

Addiction is best viewed through a systemic lens instead of a perspective focused solely on the individual. According to Satir (1983) systems theory maintains that groups operate according to a complex interplay of individuals and relationships. A system, whether it's an organization or a family, is best understood by looking at the relationships and interactions among all the members. Each person plays a part in the system, yet the whole is greater than the sum of its parts. Each person brings her individual thoughts, feelings, behavior, and wounds to the system, and those intermingle in a complicated dance with the thoughts, feelings, behavior, and wounds of all the other members of the system. The whole constellation also adds its own rules, roles, and boundaries to the mix, which further confounds the system's complexity and potential issues. Within psychotherapy the system that's been studied most closely and is best understood is the social group of the family.

A female sex addict and her partner form a family group, and this system (with or without children) interacts like a mobile that hangs over an infant's crib: Any movement or disturbance to one element automatically affects the system as a whole.

Within this conceptualization, sexual addiction is clearly a family affair. When sex and love addiction is present, it becomes the organizing principle for the family. The partner and the FSLA become consumed with the addiction in differing ways, and the addiction both influences the family and vice versa. Addiction affects the family's beliefs, behavior, feelings, communication, boundaries, roles, and rules. Simply put, addiction has a chilling effect on the family's identity, structure, and operations. In turn, the way family members respond to and interact with the addicted person influences not just the family member, but the addiction's impact on the system as a whole.

Alcoholism treatment has influenced this understanding of addiction as a systems issue. Rather than focusing solely on the alcoholic, treatment efforts (focused on men, of course) including Alcoholics Anonymous found the addict had a greater chance of long-term sobriety if his wife was also involved in recovery work. The first edition of the *Big Book of Alcoholics Anonymous* (1939) included a chapter "To Wives," though ironically, recovering alcoholic Bill Wilson reportedly wrote it instead of asking his wife Lois to do so. Current addiction treatment is solidly based on systems theory and specifically includes partners of addicts and families in treatment when they're willing—and strongly encourages them to be involved in the process when they're not.

The editor's strong bias is that the systems approach is a crucial theoretical concept for the discussion about an FSLA's partner and children. To miss this idea is to quickly stray off-track in working with partners and families and to operate from false assumptions about the FSLA and the healing process. As work with alcoholic family systems evolved (again, with a focus on men as the problem drinker) clinicians observed a consistent pattern that the couple's problems weren't automatically solved when the alcoholic got sober. In fact, many times the family situation got worse as the now-sober husband tried to insert himself into the family's structure, especially as an authority figure. The delicate, though deadly balance the couple had created during active alcoholism no longer worked, and both spouses had difficulty adapting to a new status quo. The wife was equally off-kilter when the coping mechanisms she'd established to deal with her mate's addiction were no longer needed. She often discovered they had been ineffectual and even harmful all along for both her own well-being and her husband's. The alcoholic family system had to incorporate a new model if it was to thrive, and the same is true for a relationship plagued with sex and love addiction.

MODELS FOR WORKING WITH PARTNERS

Within the last couple of years a great deal of clinical discussion has focused on two main approaches for working with partners of those who struggle with sexual addiction. The primary schools of thought are outlined below.

Co-Addiction Model

The traditional model for working with partners is based on the systems theory outlined above. It views partners as integral components of the addictive system, and as such, partners are also in need of personal recovery whether or not the addict gets or stays sober. In this model those in a significant relationship to a sex addict are referred to as "co-sex addicts" or simply "co-addicts." This description isn't pejorative and it doesn't blame the co-addict for the addiction. It simply depicts the relationship between the two parties. In general, *co-addict* identifies the partner of any kind of addict, not just an FSLA, though the term is most closely associated with sexual addiction. This approach best aligns with the familiar codependency model and the principles of Al-Anon and other groups for loved ones of addicts.

The co-addiction model is based on the "trauma model" of addiction as it's outlined in this book, which recognizes attachment injuries and other forms of family of origin trauma as critical roots of current behavior. As applied to co-addicts, this model believes that the partner is as equally impacted as the addict by early attachment and other wounds. The partner also experiences dysregulation as a result of those childhood injuries and similarly develops coping skills to ameliorate his painful experiences. Indeed, the dysregulation and unproductive coping methods resulting from his family of origin experiences are present in the co-addict throughout his history, and as such, they pre-date his relationship with the FSLA.

Viewed from this lens, the co-addict is "set up" to chose an addicted mate just as much as the addict is "set up" to act out through sex and love addiction. Based on largely unidentified attachment patterns and unconscious coping skills, the co-addict finds a familiar dynamic (or a reactive opposite dynamic) in the dance he enacts with the FSLA. Without awareness or intention, the co-addict joins a habitual system that re-enacts or seeks to remake the rules, roles, and boundaries he learned in his original family system. Neither the addict or the co-addict is at fault for this reality nor caused this foundation that drives their unconscious behavior. In Twelve Step language, "it is what it is." Both partners are wounded people simply trying to survive.

More than being a victim of the FSLA's behavior, the partner brings his own troubled music to the dysfunctional dance. Based on his attachment styles and coping mechanisms, the partner is prone to becoming consumed with the addict and her behavior, which is the foundation for the description of co-addiction: The addict is addicted to her acting out behaviors, and the partner is addicted to a compulsive preoccupation with the addict. Other attachment styles lead the co-addict to disengage from the relationship and be out of touch with his body and emotions. This scenario often results in a partner who protests, "But I didn't know anything about her acting out! I don't have anything to do with this. How could I be a co-addict?" The answer is that this partner is relationally and intimacy impaired as Ferree terms it (2010). He tolerates or doesn't recognize the lack of intimacy in the relationship because his family of origin failed to model the practice of emotional intimacy and authenticity. He doesn't miss what he doesn't have because he's never experienced it in the first place. This situation, too, is illustrative of the partner's wounds and need for personal healing.

Common coping behaviors among co-sex addicts include denial, minimization, rationalization, playing detective, controlling, raging, adjusting sexually (becoming either more sexual or less sexual with the addict), threatening, pleading, focusing on appearance, eating, exercising, working, manipulating, and focusing on the addict, children, or anything else that provides distraction from pain. Often these behaviors spin in an out-of-control cycle that's frequently termed codependency. Eventually, most partners settle on one or two primary coping tactics that seem best to meet their needs or to soothe their distress.

According to the systems roots of the co-addiction model, if a partner hadn't picked this particular sex or love addicted woman, he would have unconsciously chosen another equally impaired mate. The female sex and love addict and her partner are "heat seeking missiles" (Laaser, 2004) who find each other and connect from their cores of unhealed trauma. Early research confirmed this belief as P. Carnes' (1991) initial study of almost a thousand sex addicts and their partners found that both suffered from various forms of abuse at almost identical rates, as indicated in the following table.

Type of Abuse	Sex Addicts	Co-Sex Addicts
Physical abuse	81%	81%
Sexual abuse	72%	71%
Emotional abuse	97%	91%

Consequently, the co-addiction model views both the FSLA and her partner as equally impaired. Both suffer from an intimacy disorder (Ferree, 2010), and although they may appear different and practice different coping mechanisms, the addict and co-addict are really flip sides of the same coin. They both maintain similar levels of differentiation of self, and thus they play out the old adage that "water seeks its own level." The co-addict, then, needs his own personal healing just as much as the addict, and in fact, he needs and deserves healing regardless of whether or not the addict chooses recovery.

The co-addiction model believes that neither party is solely responsible for the difficulties in their painful relationship, and to assign blame is to miss the point of the systemic interaction between them. It validates the recovery principle that "It's about me, not about you," which means the addict would have acted out regardless of the person with whom she was in relationship, and the partner would have chosen another addict or wounded person if he wasn't in relationship with this particular one. Many partners of addicts report a pattern of relationship after relationship with an addict of some kind, and with each new connection they believe they've found the right one.

The co-addiction/codependency model holds each partner—the FSLA and the mate—personally responsible for her and his individual health or lack thereof. Each one requires attention and healing for personal attachment injuries, trauma, dysregulation, and unhealthy coping mechanisms. Together, then, they are both responsible for the health or dis-ease in their relationship.

Trauma Model

The co-addiction or codependency model has been challenged in recent years by the trauma model, which employs a partner sensitive emphasis (Steffens & Means, 2009) in the treatment of sex and love addiction. The trauma model seeks to honor the partner's pain from what's called sexual addiction-induced trauma. It's important to clarify that "trauma model" as it relates to partners of sex addicts isn't to be confused with the so-called *trauma model of addiction* that views addictive behavior as dysregulation due to early attachment injuries. In this section, trauma model describes a treatment approach based on the traumatic nature of being in a significant relationship with an FSLA.

The trauma model highlights the partner as a focus of treatment and advocates that the partner receive equal clinical attention by someone with proper training to work with this underserved population (S. Carnes, 2011). It rejects the co-addiction stance that the partner is impaired with the process addiction called codependency. It stresses the partner's devastation and views his so-called codependent responses as natural reactions to the pain of betrayal (Steffens & Means, 2009). Recent research by Schneider and Corley (2012) indicates that 77% of a small study of partners (cohort of 92) identified themselves as a victim of relational trauma.

The trauma model avoids using terms like *co addict* or *codependency* and believes these descriptions are demeaning to the partner and a way of shifting blame away from the addict. This approach honors the partner's frequent distaste with being labeled, especially as anything other than a traumatized person who's in significant pain that's not of his own doing. In a recent study approximately equal numbers identified with the two prevailing conceptualizations for partners: 41.3% identified self as *co-addict* and 40% said *not*, whereas 18.5% said *somewhat* (Corley & Schneider, 2012).

The trauma model places specific emphasis on the traumatic nature of discovery or disclosure of a loved one's addiction. Research based on this model indicates that 70% of partners met the clinical qualifications for post-traumatic stress disorder from the trauma of learning sex addiction was present in their relationship (Steffens & Means, 2009). Partners frequently describe experiencing sexual or emotional betrayal as being worse than having a mate who was using alcohol or drugs or gambling compulsively or engaging in any other kind of addictive behavior. Sexual or emotional betrayal is so *personal*. Coupled with the repeated lying that's part of an addict's modus operandi, the trauma is pervasive and protracted.

Minwalla (2011), one of the key proponents of the trauma model for treating partners of sex addicts, reports that partners can be compared to rape victims in their symptomology and complex PTSD. Partners suffer from re-experiencing the trauma of discovery or disclosure, constant triggering and reactivity, hypervigilance, panic, anxiety, and somatic symptoms, which are the normal, predictable responses of people who have been deeply betrayed. Further, partners deal with social embarrassment, shame, and isolation as friends and family often withdraw, or, worse, blame them for the addict's problem. Partners worry about their children's safety and fear potential sexual molestation by the addict (Minwalla, n.d.). Indeed, partners clearly have been traumatized within the addiction-laden relationship.

The primary work for the partner involves attending to the multiple kinds of traumas he's experienced in relationship with an FSLA such as relational betrayal, deception, emotional abuse, marginalization, manipulation, and compartmentalization (Minwalla, n.d.). Of particular impact on the partner is the addict's practice of gaslighting, (Jason & Graves, 2011; S. Carnes, Lee, & Rodriguez, 2012b) which refers to an insidious form of emotional abuse that challenges a partner's perception of reality. The FSLA diverts any questions about her behavior back onto the partner and accuses him of being insecure, too sensitive, lacking a sense of humor, pathologically jealous, or any variety of similar manipulations that challenge his reality. The gaslighter creates a reaction in the partner and then blames him for having the reaction. It's crazy-making and chips away at the partner's definition of reality and even sense of self. Eventually, the once-confident partner becomes less assured of his discernment, and if he wasn't very confident to start with, his negative self-image is doubly enforced. Ferree (2010) calls gaslighting the red grass syndrome, which uses the metaphor of the color of grass to describe the addict's manipulation. If a partner is told long enough or loudly enough that the grass is red, eventually he'll come to doubt his perception of green. The trauma model identifies this dynamic as one reason a partner continues to tolerate unacceptable behavior and even makes excuses for the addict: He's no longer certain about reality and thus isn't able to recognize when something is clearly off. A partner slowly loses his voice in the relationship and even within his own mind.

The trauma model operates from an empowerment focus that's designed to provide the partner validation, support, empathy, and resiliency. Minwalla (n.d.) uses the word *impacted* as an operational principle. He likens the partner's trauma to a major vehicle accident that causes significant psychological destabilization and crushes the partner's sense of safety and identity. He terms "harmful" and "inadequate" any treatment that fails to address the partner's trauma. In fact, Steffens and Means (2009) refer to treatment-induced trauma that partners experience when their pain isn't compassionately acknowledged and they're pushed, especially too early in the clinical process, to look at their "own stuff."

Effective Treatment Approaches

Which model, then, is the most effective in working with partners of female sex and love addicts? Like most principles of recovery from FSLA and for treating it, the answer isn't black and white; it's *both/and*. Best practice combines both approaches into a seamless paradigm that supports the partner through the continuum of his healing journey. Effective treatment covers all the needed aspects: honors the partner's pain, makes sense of his "crazy" situation, encourages positive steps that deal with the many crises at hand and fosters his psychological well-being, identifies the formative factors that may have influenced his thinking and choices, and addresses his wounds of attachment and trauma.

Both models have advantages and disadvantages, of course. The co-addiction model can certainly feel blaming to a partner early in his recovery process. He needs help *now* in navigating the challenges of disclosure, talking with his children, family, and friends, and enduring the addict's consequences that involve him in collateral damage. He especially needs validation and support for the crushing losses he's experienced and the painful grieving process he must endure. The trauma model provides a needed course correction to the sometimes hard-line approach of the co-addiction model that leap-frogs over a partner's anguish.

At the same time, eventually the partner deserves to look beyond his painful, current circumstance and examine himself more thoroughly as an avenue for positive growth. This process requires exploring his attachment and family of origin wounds and identifying the coping mechanisms that may no longer be serving him productively. He benefits from reviewing his core beliefs and somatic experiences so that he can make adjustments that foster psychological health and allow him to be fully present with himself and in all his relationships.

To be fair, most proponents of the trauma model believe a partner's family of origin or other personal wounds can benefit from clinical attention in due time. And most seasoned practitioners who use a co-addiction model have long realized the importance of validating a betrayed partner's pain and supporting him through a grieving process related to his betrayals. In the editor's view, both models have merit and are best when used conjunctively.

As emphasized earlier in this book, the therapeutic relationship and appropriately-timed interventions are core components of effective clinical work. A key tenet of building a therapeutic relationship is joining with the client, and obviously, you can't join with a client who feels you're blaming him for the mess he's in. As one male partner pleaded, "Just let me lick my wounds and save a little face for a while, okay?" No one likes to be labeled. Female sex and love addicts usually recoil from that label just as much as partners dislike a co-addict label. Don't wrestle with your clients around these terms. Sidestep those battles and meet your client in his or her own space. Attend to the client's immediate needs and trust the process, both of the therapy and the individual's growth track.

Jason (2009) developed a helpful model that shows the integration of the two approaches. It begins by performing psychological triage to identify the most pressing source of the partner's pain, which is usually the devastation caused by discovery or disclosure of the betrayals. After attending to those traumas, employ a process of Trauma Resolution Therapy (TRT) to address the dual nature of trauma: (a) the damage from the original trauma-inducing event; and (b) the damage from the survival responses or symptoms the individual develops.

Dual Track Protocol

As implied in earlier paragraphs, the starting point for effective work with an FSLA's partner is to provide an honoring, supportive environment for him to grieve the pain and losses he's suffered in his relationship with an addict. Until the partner feels heard, understood, and supported, he'll likely be unable to take positive steps of self-care and self-protection.

In addition to a grieving tier, the editor's bias favors a dual-prong approach for working with partners of FSLAs, which is best illustrated with an image of train tracks.

One track represents a focus on the partner's current unproductive or distressing coping reactions, arresting them, and installing more useful thinking patterns and behaviors. The parallel track represents attending to the partner's underlying trauma and attachment injuries that likely stem from his family of origin. If you recall, this protocol is similar to the treatment trajectory recommended for the sex and love addict herself that's proposed in this book: chapter 6 outlines the best practices for arresting sex and love addictive behavior, and chapter 7 describes best practices for addressing underlying attachment styles.

The Partner's System

Because the principles for treating core attachment and trauma injuries as outlined in the previous chapter are the same for both FSLAs and their partners, we'll concentrate here on the other track of clinical focus: addressing the partner's current reactions to the addict, his unproductive coping mechanisms regarding the addict and in other situations and relationships, and establishing boundaries for his safety and well-being. Helping the partner identify these reactions and coping strategies is the first step.

Similar to the FSLA's cycle of beliefs and addiction, partners also follow a predictable cycle (S. Carnes, 2008), and many in relationship with sex and love addicts find this diagram helpful in making overt their often unconscious patterns. This cycle is usually called the "Co-Addictive System" by those who subscribe to that model, and the "Partner's System" by those who favor the trauma model. The name of the cycle isn't nearly as important as the process it describes. Clinicians who use both approaches generally employ these concepts and the associated clinical interventions. The Partner's System and Cycle is shown on the right.

The Partner's System

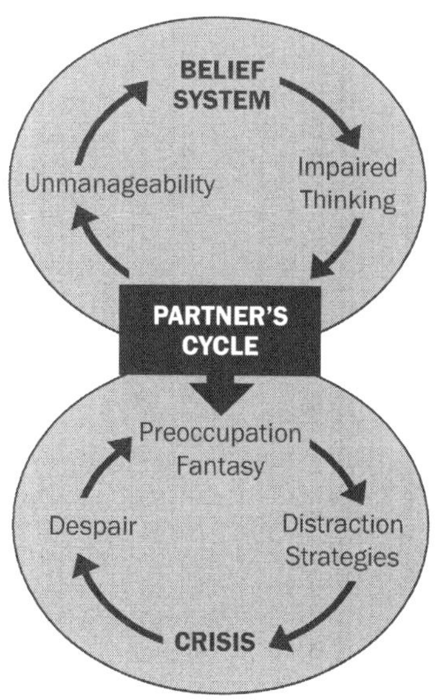

Published in *Mending a Shattered Heart*, 1st edition (2008).
Used by permission of Gentle Path Press.

Figure 13

Belief system

Similar to sex and love addicts, partners of FSLAs entertain a number of core beliefs that influence their feelings and behaviors. While Patrick Carnes outlined the four standard beliefs for sex addicts (Carnes, 1991), Stefanie Carnes adapted them for partners (Carnes, 2008). Typically, partners believe:

1. I am a bad, unworthy person.
2. No one will love me as I am.
3. No one will meet my needs.
4. Romance, a relationship, or sex is my most important sign of love.

These core beliefs fuel a partner's interactions and reactions with the FSLA. Many of the beliefs were formed in the crucible of the partner's family of origin as he experienced breaches in attachment or wounds of abuse. They are often reinforced in subsequent relationships, including with a female sex and love addict. Other core beliefs contribute to a partner's poor sense of self and include thoughts such as "I'm unlovable," "I'm not worthy," or "I'm not desirable." These beliefs may play a role in a partner's choice to stay in a relationship with an unfaithful person because the partner fears no one else will choose him for an intimate relationship.

Impaired thinking

Faulty core beliefs influence cognitions, and those who are partnered with an FSLA often think they must be attractive in order to keep the addict's attention, or they must withhold any complaints because the addict will leave, or everything will be okay if they are giving or selfless enough. This kind of impaired thinking leads to self-blame instead of holding the addict properly accountable for her behavior.

Preoccupation and obsession

Some kind of trigger—a stimulus from the environment or within the partner's own impaired thinking—often spurs the partner's descent into his particular form of unproductive behavior. He begins to preoccupy about the FSLA and her behavior, thoughts, or feelings. He may fantasize (imagine) that she's with another person or once again acting out online. Without intervention, the partner becomes obsessed with an outward focus on the FSLA. He wonders, "what if . . .?" or "if only . . ." or "is she . . .?"

Distraction strategies

The pain of these thoughts and obsessions is terrific, and the partner attempts to distract himself in a variety of ways. Perhaps he works excessively, or abuses alcohol, or engages in other unproductive behaviors such as gambling or over-eating. His distraction strategies may be socially acceptable and even applauded. For example, he may take over all the financial matters or pour himself into sports or a hobby. Often a partner turns his focus toward his children or other family members. Frequently, he plays detective and checks up on the FSLA by tracking her movements or checking her cell phone or email. Some partners join the FSLA in her sexual activities as a way to control her behavior, or they may engage in sexual acting out independent of the FSLA.

Crisis

Eventually, the situation reaches a crisis point. The partner discovers the FSLA's betrayals beyond any doubt or he receives disclosure from the addict (usually without benefit of clinical support or planning). In any case his distraction strategies are no longer working, and a crisis is at hand. S. Carnes (2008) describes two paths a partner frequently takes during a crisis: externalizing and internalizing. Externalizing involves overt behaviors to deal with the crisis such as controlling, manipulating, raging, or even resorting to physical violence. Internalizing entails more covert responses such as shutting down, withdrawing, avoiding, or even denying the problem altogether.

Despair

Regardless of what form the partner's reaction takes, the result is rarely a positive outcome, at least long-term. This on-going disappointment leads to a state of despair, where the partner feels hopeless to effect positive change. He may engage in self-defeating behaviors, over-function to make up for the addict's deficits, or even experience suicidal thoughts or attempts.

Unmanageability

The painful feelings and behaviors associated with despair led to a sense of unmanageability. Despite the partner's best efforts, life remains chaotic, even tumultuous. Perhaps the couple is considering divorce or experiencing some other negative consequence. The partner may realize he's losing his own identity as he pursues a solution to his difficult circumstances. Often he becomes increasingly isolated because he's reluctant to disclose his betrayal, especially as a man who's being defrauded by a female. When his situation doesn't resolve and the FSLA continues to act out, his core beliefs are again reinforced and the cycle begins anew.

Effective Interventions

Similar to the best practices described in chapter 6 for arresting an FSLA's acting out behavior, a partner also benefits from constructive interventions to prevent his own unhealthy cycle. Although it may be surprising to therapists who aren't experienced in working with partners, the best practices for partners are almost identical to those used with FSLAs. A partner needs to tell his story to help him identify his patterns, and he, too, profits from having a fair witness. He then must understand his coping system and identify his ineffective strategies of distraction and crisis management. A partner benefits from working a personal program of recovery, which includes attending his own Twelve Step meetings for partners of sex and love addicts, working the Twelve Steps, using a sponsor to guide his process, and connecting with others to provide encouragement and support.

Boundaries

These processes establish the foundation for his ability to set and maintain appropriate boundaries both for himself and ones that provide safeguards regarding the FSLA's behavior. The best practice is first to address the partner's unhealthy coping strategies and replace them with more beneficial alternatives. A partner must arrest any enabling behaviors that have allowed him to collude with the FSLA. Examples include denying or minimizing her infractions, joining the addict in sexual activities he finds demeaning or incongruent with his value system, or threatening to leave the relationship without following through. When a partner finds himself engaging in any of his own unhelpful strategies identified in his cycle, he can call a supportive friend or put stop-gaps into place that provide him enough emotional space to allow his better thinking to take charge. Simply put, a partner also uses the tools of recovery to extricate himself from old, ineffective patterns. He learns to "trust his gut" and pay attention to his affective experiences that alert him something is awry.

A partner's healing also includes establishing healthy boundaries to safeguard his well-being regarding the addict's behavior. This is a critical point that many partners need help understanding. A boundary is created to protect, not to control. For example, when a partner declares, "You can't have cybersex with online partners" (certainly a reasonable component of a committed relationship), he's trying to dictate the addict's behavior, which he's powerless to do. Instead, he can insist, "I'm not willing to stay in relationship with someone who has anonymous sex online, and if you continue to act out that way, I'm no longer going to live with you." The difference may sound like semantics, but it's much more than just words. Healthy boundaries keep a partner from being a victim of the addict's behavior. They put him in charge of his well-being and hold the FSLA accountable for hers.

A partner can also identify his bottom lines, which are those behaviors he'll no longer tolerate on the part of the FSLA. That bottom line is different for each partner, but it's critical that he determines the limit that's too much for him and establishes the consequences he'll enforce if that line is crossed. Again, participating in a Twelve Step or other support group for partners is crucial to assist in developing these protective boundaries. The pattern of accepting unacceptable behavior is well engrained in many partners, and it's quite difficult to imagine another way of relating, or to have the courage to refute his core beliefs and hold firm the boundaries he's established. A partner benefits from the wisdom of others more experienced in setting boundaries with an addict who doesn't react well to them. The best practice is to include this strong recommendation in a partner's treatment plan.

MALE PARTNERS OF FEMALE SEX AND LOVE ADDICTS

If females are the forgotten sex addicts who've received little notice until recent years, men in relationship with FSLAs are the invisible ones, the totally unrecognized parties in this dis-ease. It simply has rarely occurred to most clinicians, even those who work in the area of sex addiction treatment, that men are anything but sex addicts themselves. Cultural stereotypes persist for men as much as for women, and being sexually betrayed by a female partner definitely doesn't fit the image of the typical modern male. A man is still expected to be the virulent one, the partner in charge, and the only one who might possibly go outside the relationship for sex.

Characteristics of Male Partners

Again, research is just beginning to explore the experience of women in relationship to a sexually addicted male. To date, no known research has specifically examined men who are partners of female sex and love addicts, and clearly more research is needed about each gender as well as about partners of sex addicts in general. Clinical and anecdotal experience inform this section, and although these thoughts aren't yet verified by research, those of us who have long treated FSLAs and are now treating their male partners have observed common characteristics and unique issues among these men. Male partners usually fall into one of the three A's, as described below.

The first characteristic is that many of them are ***also addicted***, usually sexually. This is the only characteristic with any research base, as one prescient study of those in relationship with sex addicts (Schneider, 2005) did include male partners, and findings revealed that 71% of these men also personally struggled with sexual addiction. Clinical experience shows that male partners also sometimes abuse substances or are chemically dependent. Male partners who are also addicts are actually often the easiest to treat because they understand the compelling nature of addiction. If they're willing to address their own addictive behaviors, that foothold in recovery assists them in looking at their role as a partner.

Generally speaking, men in relationship with FSLAs who themselves aren't addicts of some kind fall into two distinct camps. A first group is extremely ***angry***. Obviously, female partners of male SAs are also justifiably angry, but male partners seem to be excessively so and to remain stuck in their anger. They're prone to rage and inter-personal violence, and special cautions must be in place about disclosure and other areas of the FSLA's recovery process. If the male is also sexually addicted, he's likely to act out in ways of eroticized rage toward his wife or girlfriend. It's not unusual for this male to wake his FSLA in the middle of the night, berate her for betraying him, and then insist on having sex with her.

This type of partner is usually controlling in the relationship. He may scrutinize or restrict the FSLA's activities and friends. He maintains strict control of the couple's finances and may withhold financial information. He dictates how the FSLA dresses or behaves, and he may alternately encourage and then punish provocative attire and interactions. Far from the typical jokes on late night TV about how fun it would be for a guy to be involved with a female sex addict, these relationships are painfully volatile. The angry men rarely seek help, as they're more likely to divorce the FSLA than to work on themselves and the relationship (Schneider, 2005).

The third category of partners is ***avoidant***. These are the "nice guys" who are passive, steady, and undemanding. They often over-function in the relationship and take up the slack in a practical sense by managing the household or providing primary care for the children. Clinically, they could be considered on a continuum of dependent personality. From an affective standpoint, they're shut down—out of touch with their feelings and bodies. They may dissociate, and they likely exhibit an anxious-avoidant attachment style. They definitely tolerate behavior most would find totally unacceptable. They don't confront the issues and focus elsewhere in a socially acceptable manner. These partners often believe that their kindness, patience, or love will ultimately influence their addicts to stop acting out.

While these men are easier to live with than their angry brothers, from a treatment standpoint, they're often the hardest to engage in their own process. They're more entrenched in the belief that if the FSLA would only stop acting out, everything would be fine. They are less likely to participate in a support group and suffer from extreme isolation as they rarely let anyone glimpse their pain.

Unique Issues for Male Partners

By now you're familiar with the challenges women face as they deal with sex and love addiction in a male-dominated milieu. Male partners of FSLAs struggle with similar hardships in reverse. As the minority population among those who deal with a loved one's sex and love addiction, a male is often overlooked, misunderstood, under-diagnosed, and mis-treated. The scant literature directed toward partners is focused on women, and as mentioned, no known research is yet published that explores male partners' experiences. To mirror the FSLA's phenomenon as often the only woman in an S meeting, the male partner is usually the only man in a room full of female partners. The males who do attend a partners' group are often involved in a gay relationship with a male sex addict, and the heterosexual men report they don't connect fully with that situation.

Culturally, a male partner frequently finds himself the brunt of jokes instead of compassion. His situation historically was described in pejorative terms like "cuckold," which was a medieval term of scorn for a man with an adulterous wife. Though that term has largely fallen out of use in modern English, the derision remains. Alternatively, a male partner may receive a wink or chest-thump from another man who says, "I wish my wife was a sex addict!" Neither response is affirming and both add to a partner's shame and isolation.

COUPLES STRUGGLING WITH FSLA

Research with alcoholic women who were in a significant relationship indicates that behavior couples therapy combined with individual treatment for the alcoholic results in greater reductions in drinking, higher levels of relationship satisfaction, and reduced instances of domestic violence than therapy directed only to the alcoholic individually (Fals-Stewart, Birchler, & Kelley, 2006). While no known research has explored this correlation with FSLAs, it's reasonable to assume similar results. Clearly, the best practice is to include an FSLA's partner in the treatment, and this approach improves her therapeutic outcome.

Clinical approaches vary about the best practice for working with couples. Most individually oriented therapeutic models suggest each person has an individual therapist and the couple sees a third practitioner, whereas systemic models often encourage one therapist to see both parties plus work with the coupleship and the family. Although this systemic method is convenient in many ways, it also has its pitfalls and requires advanced therapeutic skills to avoid becoming triangulated into the couple's dysfunction. Often the best approach is a combination of the two, where a single therapist does the core clinical work and refers one or both parties to another therapist for individual focus such as around a co-occurring disorder or for a specific modality like EMDR, brainspotting, and so forth. As you make decisions about treating just one or both partners and whether to see them as a couple, take care to consider who first presented as your client, the relationship you developed with him or her, and how much time has elapsed before the other party enters treatment.

Therapist as Secret-keeper

If you treat both the SLA and her partner individually as well as in couple's sessions, it's important to declare your policy about keeping secrets at the outset. Including it in the consent information is one good way to make sure both parties are aware of the policy, but it's also important to talk about it in session so everyone understands the guiding principle and why it exists.

Some therapists state up-front that they don't keep secrets between the parties in the coupleship, which means that if something is shared in an individual session and the therapist believes it should be disclosed to the partner, the client has the choice to either disclose it in a couple's session, share the information outside of session, or accept that the therapist will terminate the therapy with the couple and refer them to another counselor. Other therapists will work with the client to understand why it's important to disclose the information and give the person time to discuss the issue with his or her support system and weigh the possible positive and negative consequences for disclosing. The crucial factor is that both parties are aware of the therapist's policy, whatever that may be.

Remember that laws and ethical guidelines sometimes vary state to state and according to specific licensures. In most cases, if the couple is the client, both parties must sign a release of information before anything is disclosed to an outside party about either one of them. According to some state laws, the individual sessions are confidential and thus protected. Ultimately, it's the individual's right to determine what is disclosed, which is one of the difficulties of doing both the individual and couple's work. Unless your boundaries are firm, it's easy to get triangled into the couple's stress and blamed either for keeping the secret or for insisting on disclosure.

Follow your individual state statutes and licensure guidelines regarding cases in which the secret information is related to HIV, suicide or homicide, or abuse or severe neglect of a minor, elderly, or incapacitated person. Declarations about mandatory reporting and duty to warn issues should be included in consent to treat forms as well.

Disclosure Process with a Couple

Disclosing the personal, painful secrets about acting out is one of the hardest choices any addict can make. The stakes are high; the anguish and fear are enormous. Understandably, many addicts resist this process, and unfortunately, some therapists collude with them in keeping secrets. If sexual addiction is best understood as an attachment and intimacy disorder, help your client explore what this means in terms of maintaining deceit. How can the couple develop legitimate, non-sexual intimacy within the relationship if one person is hiding potentially devastating secrets? The structural foundation for the coupleship is fundamentally flawed. Although the FSLA has the right to decide for herself whether she'll go through with disclosure to her husband or partner, share your bias that this path is the best, though rocky, road to providing the true connection she so desperately wants.

As a therapist, facilitating a disclosure session is one of the hardest clinical tasks you may encounter. Don't be caught off-guard by the emotional drain of these sessions. The hours leading up to and going through disclosure require your healthiest, most differentiated self. Disclosure isn't for cowards, including the clinician. At the same time, those of us who've participated in these sessions find that we've entered a sacred space. It's an experience of being on "holy ground," and while it's immensely painful for everyone involved (including the therapist), it's a unique privilege to guide a couple through this potentially healing process.

Initial Couple's Work Before Disclosure

When an FSLA presents for therapy and she's in a significant relationship, her partner may or may not suspect something or have actually discovered some evidence of her acting out. If the discovery or a partial disclosure of her acting out has already been made, inviting the partner to a relational therapy session will seem normal in the context of the FSLA's process. The addict may explain that her therapy is on-going and within the next few weeks she'll be asking her partner to attend a couple's session so she can share what she's learned and to give the partner a chance to ask any questions. Generally the partner is so angry and/or fearful that he's open to coming to at least one therapy session. (As a reminder, masculine pronouns are being used to refer to the FSLA's partner for the sake of stylistic simplicity. The principles, however, apply to a lesbian couple where the FSLA's partner is female.)

If the partner has no idea about the woman's acting out, the initial couple's session is much more challenging. It's important that you be compassionate, confident, and in control of the meeting. Explain that the FSLA has asked her partner to attend a therapy appointment because she has some important and painful information to share with him. Ask if he's willing to receive this information his partner believes he has a right to know. If he is, set the stage that although the information he's about to hear will likely be upsetting, this process actually honors his right to self-determination and gives him the chance to make informed choices about the relationship. Explain that "we're as sick as our secrets," which is a core tenet from Alcoholics Anonymous, and alert him that the FSLA is choosing to tell him some truths about herself that he may or may not already know.

Then invite the addict to share the big picture regarding her problematic behaviors. She should include the general nature of her acting out such as viewing pornography, or engaging in online sexual activity, or having an affair, or engaging in anonymous sex with strangers. She should also disclose any health-related consequences that may put his physical well-being in danger. Take care to support the partner as he hears this information, which is understandably devastating. Expect him to be shocked, confused, and distressed. It's vital for the partner to engage in his own therapeutic process, and you should outline the benefits he'll receive from this process. Be prepared with a list of referrals (including complete contact information) of trained clinicians who are normally able to see a new client on short notice. Depending on your theoretical framework and your agreement with the FSLA, offer to meet with him once more individually if he has to wait for an appointment with another therapist.

After this big picture disclosure, explain that the FSLA will be continuing her therapy to address her acting out and the underlying causes that drive it, and to repair the damage she's caused to him and others. Explain that if the partner is willing to receive full disclosure about the FSLA's acting out behaviors, you will schedule a formal disclosure session with both of them in the near future. Make clear that during that meeting the partner can ask any questions, and you'll be there to provide support, help clarify feelings, and assist both parties in determining their next steps. Encourage the partner to keep a list of his questions and concerns so that everything important to him can be covered in the couple's disclosure session.

Whether the partner is aware or unaware of the FSLA's acting out, an important objective is to instill hope during an initial couple session. Share your observation that the couples who have the courage to walk through this difficult gulch in their relationship and come out on the other side are generally stronger and enjoy a deeper bond than those who don't choose to face this challenge. Offer some basic information about addiction and the recovery process to normalize their situation. Outline the practical actions the FSLA is starting such as going to Twelve Step or support group meetings and talking with a sponsor on a regular basis. You or the FSLA can describe the rules about protecting the anonymity of group members and reassure the partner that the addict's adherence to this principle is out of a desire to be a trustworthy group member rather than wanting to keep secrets from him.

If the FSLA and partner are both willing to take part in a subsequent formal disclosure session, help them establish boundaries around disclosure until that meeting. Urge the partner not to pressure the FSLA for this information out of session. Explain that while it may be tempting to leave this appointment and demand the FSLA tells him everything, your experience with other couples is that it's better to wait until you're together again to have this discussion. Make plain that the FSLA is just beginning to get honest with herself and clear about how her behaviors have directly impacted him, and until she's finished with her assignments about these issues, it's wise to do this work within therapy for now.

Next, while both parties are still present, equip the FSLA in how to respond if the partner asks for more information about her behavior out of session. Suggest she remind him that they've both agreed to wait until the disclosure appointment to discuss this painful material and request that he works with her in maintaining this plan. Ask the partner what he could do to get back on track if he loses patience with waiting. Define the point where he might need to call you for help. As the therapist, you outline the boundary for both parties, predict the waiting will be difficult, and set guidelines for when it's appropriate to call you, a sponsor, or someone else in their support system for help.

Partner's Preparation to Receive Disclosure

Without question, the best practice is be sure the partner has personal therapeutic support before a formal disclosure session. If he's seeing another clinician, obtain a release of information from your FSLA client so that you can discuss the disclosure process with the partner's therapist. If you're seeing him personally, get to know the partner as a person, perhaps by completing a quick genogram. Inquire about his experiences in his family of origin and how he perceives they may influence his relationship with the FSLA. Ask how her behavior has impacted his life and what goals he'd like to accomplish in couple's therapy with her. A partner is usually grateful to have you listen and validate his experience. Offering your undivided attention, empathizing with his fears and uncertainty, and preparing him for disclosure provide an affirming launch into the partner's difficult healing process.

As he thinks about the upcoming disclosure session, ask if there's any information he doesn't want to hear. If so, help him process his reasons and what might change if he were to learn this distressing news. Be sure to provide resources he can access as he prepares for and receives disclosure. Encourage him to participate in a support group for addicts' partners and suggest helpful material he can read. If necessary, offer to meet with him for additional individual sessions or to refer him to another therapist if he's more comfortable with that option.

Teach the partner about the power of journaling, and specifically, ask him to write a letter to the FSLA about the impact her behavior has had on him. Suggest he includes in the letter what he needs in order to be willing to work on the relationship and explain he'll have a chance to share his letter during the disclosure meeting.

Encourage him to prepare a list of questions he has about the FSLA's behavior that he'll ask during the formal disclosure session. Discuss his normal belief that he wants to know all the gory details about his addict's behaviors, and explain that this graphic information isn't helpful to his healing process, and in fact, is usually harmful. Once he has this kind of explicit detail, it's almost impossible for him to erase it. Process his desire for these details and connect it to his damaged self-esteem or faulty core beliefs. Assure him that he'll receive specific information about the addict's behavior, and that it's appropriate for him to fill in the blanks about the inconsistencies he's observed in the relationship. One way to identify some of the unknowns is to complete a timeline of his history with the FSLA and notice any gaps that don't make sense for him. Suggest he ask about situations that made him feel crazy, and validate his reality by teaching him about the gaslighting process in which many addicts engage with their partners.

Be sure to help him think through how to prepare for the formal disclosure in practical ways such as planning who he'll turn to in case he needs support or who can take care of the kids if he wants some time away from the house. Talk with him about keeping realistic expectations for the disclosure session. Alert him that at this early point in the addict's therapy, she's unlikely to fully grasp how much her betrayals have hurt him, and she may not express the empathy and remorse he deserves. Explain that the main point of the disclosure session is to bring the FSLA's behaviors into the light and allow him to become fully informed so that he can make educated decisions about his next steps.

Addict's Preparation for Disclosure

As outlined in chapter 6, the SLA will have identified the excuses she's used to give herself permission to act out, lies she has told, and the behaviors associated with her sex and love addiction that have been betrayals to her partner. She also will have reflected about the impact her addiction has had on him. As she returns to this embarrassing material, remind her to use her sponsor and support system for encouragement.

At this stage the FSLA is ready to complete her Disclosure/Amends Letter, which is the preferred mode of sharing this charged information. Writing a letter allows her to get your feedback as well as responses from her peers in group and her sponsor. It also helps her be complete in sharing her acting out history and avoid a lapse in courage about revealing certain information when the time comes. During the disclosure session, a partner is more likely to listen to the entire letter without interruption rather than stopping to discuss every bit of the disclosure, and the session can stay on track. Because the partner's anxiety is usually very high during the disclosure session, it's often helpful for him to review the letter with you in a later session to get clarity about what was said. Be cautious about giving him a copy of the disclosure letter, and discuss that plan first with the FSLA. On occasion, the contents of a disclosure letter have been shared indiscriminately or used against the FSLA in court.

Some therapists insist this is just a disclosure document and caution that calling it a Disclosure/*Amends* Letter makes it seem like it's Ninth Step work, which was described in chapter 6 in the section on the general principles of disclosure. Although there are definite differences between making a full disclosure and offering a Ninth Step amends, the FSLA does need to accept accountability for her behaviors, clearly state she was wrong, and offer an apology during the disclosure. Most who practice the tenets of a recovery program end up making amends many times—sometimes on a daily basis. It never hurts to say *I am sorry* for a hurtful behavior.

As the FSLA begins to work on her disclosure letter, suggest she consider these issues (Corley & Schneider, 2012):

- What personal and relational values have been compromised?
- How have those betrayals of values been acted out as part of her addictive behavior? (What specific acting out behaviors has she done?)
- Have her encounters been in person, on-line, or in fantasy?
- Have the behaviors been recent or on-going for a long period of time? Have they escalated over time?
- If the FSLA had an emotional or sexual relationship, when did it start? Has it ended, and if so, how and by whom?
- Does the partner know anyone with whom the FSLA has been involved? How would disclosure about the acting out impact that other person involved?
- In what ways did she fail to treat her partner like a best friend?
- In what ways was the health of her partner compromised? (For example, through oral, vaginal, or anal intercourse; protected or unprotected sex with strangers or friends; or other high-risk behavior of either the FSLA or her sexual partner such as sharing syringes or using drugs with others.)
- Has she been tested for STDs and HIV? What were the results? Were any follow-up tests recommended?
- If the FSLA has children, were they aware of or asked to keep a secret about her acting out?

- Were other pregnancies created as a result of the FSLA's acting out? If so, what was the outcome of those pregnancies (an abortion, a miscarriage, an adoption, or a birth)?
- What financial resources were used and for what? Did the FSLA buy gifts or use relational or family finances to develop or maintain the acting out relationship or purchase pornography or sexual services?
- Is there any chance of legal consequences? Any chance of job loss? More financial consequences? Media interest or involvement?
- Did the FSLA talk about her partner to the person with whom she acted out? Did she profess to love the person with whom she acted out? What other emotional betrayals did she make to her partner?
- Did other friends and family members know or collude about the betrayal?
- What were the forms of contact with acting out partners: Internet, phone, in person, in hotels, at her work, or her home, or the home she shares with her partner? Did she act out in the bed she shares with her partner?
- Is there anything the FSLA isn't willing to disclose?

Caution the FSLA against including explicit sexual details in her disclosure letter. While partners indicate that they want the whole truth, research shows it's better to speak in general terms (Corley & Schneider, 2012). When a partner demands specific, salacious details about acting out episodes, he's usually prompted by unhealthy motives. Partners tend to compare themselves to images or acting out partners, and they go "pain shopping" by imagining explicitly what the addict may have done sexually in different situations. Help the FSLA see this reaction as yet another way she's betrayed and harmed her partner.

Names of acting out partners should be omitted unless the addict's mate knows the person and also has occasion to see the other person. If, however, an FSLA has acted out with someone the partner knows, he gets to decide whether he wants to stay in contact or relationship with that betrayer; the addict doesn't get to decide for him by withholding that information. For example, the FSLA should disclose if she's had an affair with a neighbor because the partner is still acquainted with the neighbor and that relationship has changed because of the betrayal. Remind your client that a name given by a stranger she met on-line probably isn't accurate, anyway.

After the FSLA has completed the disclosure letter, it's important for her to review it with you, her sponsor, and trusted members of her support group. She should be open to feedback regarding the level of accountability she takes, the need for removal of inappropriate material such as explicit details or blaming the spouse for causing the behaviors, or if the letter contains information her partner has said he didn't want to know. Once you and the addict's sponsor or peers have approved the letter, the FSLA is ready for the formal disclosure session. A sample disclosure/amends letter is included in the appendix.

Just as you did with the partner, help the addict prepare in practical ways for the disclosure meeting. She should make arrangements to stay at a friend's or relative's home for a few days so that she's prepared if the partner asks her to leave for a time. Help the FSLA come up with an explanation for a support person that doesn't further betray the partner. For example, she can say that she and her spouse are having a therapy session that will address difficult issues and he may insist on some alone time, so she's trying to make advance plans for somewhere to stay for a short time. She should also arrange child care and make any other needed preparations to relieve as much stress as possible for the partner. It's best if the couple drives separately to the disclosure appointment.

Disclosure Session

Schedule at least two hours for the disclosure session. Be sure to prepare the setting thoughtfully with tissues in easy reach of each person (including yourself). Get centered through some deep breathing before you invite the couple into the space. Normalize the emotions that are usually palpable in the room, and commend the courage it takes for each of them to engage in this process. Frame the disclosure session as a crucial first step in building a bridge toward a new kind of relationship.

Next, set clear and firm guidelines for the meeting such as no verbal or physical violence. Explain they each will listen to the other without interruption, and you'll guide the process and help them if they get off track. Remind them you'll also provide a safe forum for asking and answering questions when the time comes.

Briefly outline the session's format, which is structured as follows:

- The betrayed partner will read his letter to the FSLA outlining the impact her behavior has had on him. The addict may take notes if she hears anything she wants to add to the accountability section of her disclosure letter. You'll ask the FSLA to recap what she's heard from her partner and help her summarize if necessary.
- Next, the FSLA will read her disclosure/amends letter to the partner, and he'll listen without interruption. He's encouraged to take notes if he has questions about any of the information.

- After listening to the letter, the partner will have the opportunity to respond with his thoughts and feelings and to ask any questions to clarify the information in the disclosure letter.
- The couple will dialogue about the information in terms of asking and answering questions.
- With your help, the couple will develop a plan for where they go from here, at least in the short-term.

Before the process starts, ask the partner if he's ready to hear the FSLA's disclosure. If he says no, inquire what he needs to be able to proceed, and attend to it as much as possible. Remember, this is sacred ground, and each person deserves the dignity of choice and support. Suggest they begin with a brief period of silence and deep breathing to center themselves before starting the process. As the session unfolds, take care to attend to both parties. Be present with them, and allow yourself to connect with their pain at an affective level. If one or both gets very emotional (which is to be expected) suggest a brief pause to feel their feelings, then invite everyone to take a couple of deep breaths. Remain calm, gentle, and focused; this is a brutal encounter, and they need you to model containment.

After the addict has finished reading her letter, invite the partner to respond. Help each person listen reflectively and recap what they hear as they go back and forth. Assist them if they get stuck. As you bring the session to a close, ask each person what he or she needs in the next few days. Specifically, help them discuss the possible need for a time apart if that seems warranted, and review the arrangements that have been made. In cases where they're going back home together, acknowledge how emotionally difficult this session has been, and ask the partner what he needs *today* to be able to move forward.

If you judge the couple is in a space appropriate for the discussion, ask each person to state a goal that reflects hope for the future and aligns the couple on the same team to fight against the addiction. If the partner is so angry that he says he's no longer willing to work on the relationship, validate his feelings and ask if he can identify a personal goal that offers hope that he can embrace.

Review any boundaries you think are appropriate such as not rehashing the information at home and returning for another appointment if the partner has more questions. Suggest that the best wisdom is to postpone making any permanent decisions about the relationship until each person has had a lengthy period of time to focus on his or her individual recovery. Remind them of the importance of using a support system and of simple ways to focus on self-repair when they feel overwhelmed or out of control. Encourage each partner to return soon for an individual session to process all that's taken place.

Disclosure of Slips and Relapses

After the initial disclosure is completed, the partner is often so angry and hurt that it takes a while to get clear about what to do regarding the future. However, it's best if the FSLA and her partner can proactively determine what information the partner wants on an on-going basis. As part of the "where-to-go-from-here" discussion, talk candidly with the couple about the reality that sex and love addiction is a chronic illness that has to be managed daily for a lifetime. Slips and relapses are usually part of the first several years of recovery for most people. One way to better manage the anxiety associated with that fact is to make a plan for what to do if a slip or relapse happens, including a plan for disclosure. Early in recovery, partners often want every little detail of a slip or relapse. As behavioral evidence of the FSLA's improvement grows, partners usually want less information over time. Reaction to slips and relapse also is influenced by whether or not the partner has other support and is working a program of recovery.

Some partners want to know when the FSLA has had a slip, its nature, and what she's doing to get recovery back on track (such as increasing therapy or Twelve Step involvement, talking more openly about what emotional stress is triggering the addiction, or making the environment safer). Sometimes therapists will ask the FSLA to do a "relapse autopsy," and the partner will want to review that. Other partners prefer the FSLA take this information to her sponsor or therapist, and they only want to know if the FSLA has relapsed in ways that will directly harm them in terms of health or similar matters—or if the addict has given up on her pursuit of recovery altogether.

The best practice is to advise FSLAs and their partners to do disclosures of any slips or relapses in a therapeutic environment during the early stage of recovery. Then as sobriety is strengthened and trust is rebuilt, disclosures can be with a sponsor or another couple in Recovering Couples Anonymous or a similar support system for couples.

Sexual Abstinence Period

If the couple decides they want to attempt to salvage their relationship, an important practice is to go through a period of sexual abstinence. This is a step beyond an addict's sobriety, which means she's not engaging in any of her bottom line behaviors. A period of sexual abstinence within the coupleship is an intentional, agreed on, structured time-out from all sexual activity in the relationship (and for each person individually, as well).

A couple's sexual abstinence agreement is important for a number of reasons. First, it offers the FSLA a neurochemical cleansing to detoxify her brain from the constant bath of sex-related stimulation. Within the coupleship, the benefits are more relational. Regardless of the couple's report of their sexual pleasure together, sex is almost always tainted between them when sex and love addiction is present. Addicts are rarely emotionally engaged during sex with their partners and instead use fantasy or dissociate. Partners, too, often use sex manipulatively as a way to keep the addict in check or to prove to themselves the relationship is okay or the partner is loved. Partners also dissociate or fantasize during sex. None of these realities describe healthy sexuality (discussed in depth in chapter 11).

Explore with the couple the benefits of a time-limited sexual abstinence period. Explain the point is to take the sexual pressure off the relationship and instead, to work on building non-sexual intimacy. Point out that the couple hasn't had a therapeutic sexual abstinence period just because they haven't had sex in weeks, months, or years. That situation, especially before full disclosure, is part of the addict's binge/purge cycle of sexually acting *in* within the primary relationship and acting *out* with self or others outside the relationship. A sexual time-out that results in healing happens when both partners are fully aware of the addiction and its impact, and both agree to make this short-term sacrifice in favor of a long-term goal. Let each person talk about his or her reactions to an abstinence contract, both positively and negatively. Be aware that many partners are especially resistant to the idea, which opens the door to examining their attachment style and beliefs about sex and relationships.

Help the couple specifically detail what their sexual time-out will look like. Will they sleep in separate bedrooms? If they sleep together, how will they deal with sexual arousal? Are they okay with seeing each other naked or does one or both need more privacy to keep the sexual abstinence boundary? Remind them the goal isn't simply to avoid orgasm; the aim is to avoid purposely firing up the sex-related neurochemistry while they focus on building other bonds. Suggest they contract for a minimum of 30 days of abstinence. Many therapists recommend a 90-day period for the greatest benefits, and some couples find they want to continue in abstinence beyond even 90 days as one or both completes therapeutic work around core sexual issues. Together they can decide with your assistance the amount of time that's right for them.

Predict the couple will experience challenges during this time-out. Both parties usually have skewed beliefs about sex and automatically equate being sexual with being attractive or being in a relationship or being loved. Abstaining from sex brings up core beliefs and insecurities. Schedule periodic couple's sessions during this time to process what's surfacing for each of them and what they're learning about themselves, each other, and their relationship. Most couples find that when they again resume being sexual, it's a whole new and fulfilling experience.

Rebuilding Trust

The topic of trust is one of the most concerning for FSLAs and partners alike. Addicts worry *Will he or she ever trust me again?* and partners despair that the addict will never be trustworthy. Encourage the couple that rebuilding trust is a process that unfolds over time. Most partners have naively extended trust when it wasn't yet earned, and addicts categorically betray trust as part of their addiction. Both individuals must learn what constitutes authentic trust.

The primary work of trust-building obviously lies with the addict. She must demonstrate changed behavior over time in both large and small ways. This process isn't rocket science; it's actually quite simple, but like most developments in recovery, it isn't easy. The FSLA must practice common sense behaviors like being where she says she'll be, and doing what she says she'll be doing. She should notify her partner if her plans change and she expects to be late. She should avoid circumstances that appear suspicious and invite her partner to question her anytime he feels concern. The recovering FSLA can offer her electronic devices for his periodic review and accept that accountability without defensiveness. In short, she should "walk the walk" of recovery, not just "talk the talk."

The FSLA should also be willing to modify specific things that may have enabled her acting out. For example, she might change her cell phone number or her email address or block certain people from contacting her. If an acting out partner is someone with whom she works or socializes, the FSLA will need to eliminate contact except for clearly required work-related matters. Even then, if the partner was a close work associate with whom the FSLA must have frequent contact, she may need to alter her work situation in order to maintain her sobriety and to rebuild trust within her relationship.

Beyond these practical steps, rebuilding trust requires vulnerability and humility. Remind the FSLA that her behaviors were extremely hurtful to her partner, and caution her against displaying any whiff of defensiveness or impatience with his reluctance to extend trust. She shouldn't expect to be trusted just because she's been sober for a few weeks or months. Especially if she was good at lying and hiding her behavior, she'll have to accept that establishing trust will take longer than she probably hopes. Strongly advise her to avoid pressuring her partner about trusting her.

It's best, too, if she refrains from making declarations about her commitment to recovery, because these speeches are usually meant to keep her partner from feeling his feelings or holding her accountable. Instead, the FSLA must consistently continue working a program of recovery; over time, her actions will speak louder than her words. Her responsibility is to be trustworthy; the outcome she must leave to her Higher Power.

Addict's Partner Must Also Rebuild Trust

Though at first consideration the idea may be surprising, an FSLA's partner also bears responsibility to rebuild trust. He, too, has usually engaged in behaviors that have damaged the relationship, and he must also demonstrate personal change. Gently suggest the partner reviews the coping mechanisms he identified in his own cycle and takes steps to replace them with healthier alternatives. If he's abused alcohol or drugs, for example, or over-spent, or escaped through working long hours, or raged, he'll have to show he, too, is changing. This necessity is best supported through his own participation in therapy and a Twelve Step community.

Assist the partner in exploring his wounds, especially his experiences of betrayal that pre-date his relationship with the FSLA, as this history impacts his ability to extend trust to her. While she clearly must be accountable for the ways she's betrayed him, often a partner unconsciously places onto the addict the burden of making up for the infractions of all who have ever hurt him. He'll need help to sort out how much of his pain comes from the addict's betrayals and what part is more accurately assigned to others who have similarly violated him.

Validate the partner's insistence on seeing demonstrated behavior change over a significant period of time before he extends trust to the FSLA. Normalize his experiences of being triggered and help him understand that his trigger doesn't necessarily mean the FSLA isn't sober. Teach him to share his concerns with the FSLA rather than ignoring them. Remind him to stay in touch with his body and his emotions; as he progresses in his own healing, they'll become a reliable guide.

Assure the couple that healing happens when they both embrace the process. Trust can, indeed, be rebuilt—or more accurately, created for the first time as an authentic construct. Based on disclosure and reinforced by non-sexual intimacy, which is described next, trust blossoms.

Building Non-Sexual Intimacy

Because many couples struggle with disordered courtship (P. Carnes, 2003), they often leap-frog emotional intimacy early in the relationship in favor of escalating sexual activity. This practices robs them of a strong foundation for their coupleship, which at this point they have the chance to create. Cultivating non-sexual intimacy forges deep bonds that can sustain them through the rigors of recovery and beyond.

As described earlier, this goal is a primary focus of a sexual abstinence period.

First, remind the couple that emotional bonds are built through affective connection. Help them use their bodies to link their minds, hearts, and spirits. Teach them to make eye contact, share their bodily states and sensations, and match their breathing as they navigate meaningful interactions. Encourage them to share frequent non-sexual touch such as a hand squeeze, pat on the arm, or affirming hug. Suggest simple practices like having meals together at the table without distraction and sitting close to each other as they watch TV.

Healthy Conversation Contract

One way to build intimacy is to stop engaging in the behaviors that destroy it. In addition to maintaining sobriety, of course, a core practice is to improve the couple's communication patterns. Suggest they create a healthy conversation contract that spells out what each person needs for a safe discussion. It should include boundaries about verbal violence and a plan for when and where conversations are conducted (for example, such limits like not talking about serious matters in front of the children, not talking after 9:00 pm, and so forth). The contract can also designate the topics that are best left for a couple therapy session for now and outline what the couple will do if either one becomes flooded or they get stuck in a downward spiral.

Daily check-in

A next step is to specifically engage in intimacy-building behaviors, and a daily check-in is a simple and quick practice that many couples find essential. On a daily basis the couple sits together and takes a moment to breathe, then each partner checks in according to this formula:

- Feelings—A list of the primary feelings he or she has experienced that day and where they reside in the body.
- Affirmation—A statement of affirmation for the other partner, such as "I affirm your willingness to talk about our finances," or "I affirm you for picking up the slack when I didn't feel well today."
- Needs—A statement of need that can be either practical or more weighty. Examples include, "I have to work late tomorrow so I need you to pick up the kids and handle dinner," or "I need us to make an appointment with our therapist to talk through the fight we had last night."

The partners simply receive each other's check-in without comments or questions. The objective is to assist each person in stating his or her truth and in listening without judgment to the partner's truth. It offers an easy and quick way to stay current with each other and may surface issues that can be addressed later between the couple or with the therapist's help.

Meditation or spiritual practice

A couple benefits from an intentional practice of meditation or some form of spiritual exercise. Many guides are available that offer a structured way for couples to introduce this activity into their relationship, and some are listed in the appendix. What's most important is that the practice involves material or an activity the couple can agree on instead of something that's divisive if the partners have different beliefs. In that case, a recovery-oriented guide is best.

Recreation

Infusing positive energy into the relationship goes a long way toward building intimacy. Addiction robs a couple of their interest or ability to play, and reclaiming that former part of their relationship is encouraging. The kind of recreation isn't as important as the simple *doing* of it. Ideally, the activity should be something both partners enjoy—or at least, don't actively dislike. Each partner can take turns suggesting an activity, and including the children sometimes is fine. If the couple is stymied about what to do, ask them to create a collage of things they enjoyed when they were dating. Chances are that some of those activities are still appealing. Encourage the couple to focus on inexpensive activities that foster interaction, not expensive ventures where they're passively entertained.

Benefits of Recovery

Despite the wrenching pain and the challenges of facing sex and love addiction within a coupleship, the good news is that partners who courageously trek through this valley and persist in climbing out of its depths emerge stronger and happier than couples who choose to sidestep this journey. Healing happens, including within a relationship, and most couples report the ultimate benefits outweigh the struggle. Paradoxically, the devastation of sex and love addiction includes the potential gift of discovering vulnerability, intimacy, and shared joy.

ASSISTING THE CHILDREN AND FAMILY

When an FSLA and her partner begin a program of recovery, each starts to recognize the many ways in which their children have been harmed. Often, both mates realize they haven't been present with their children while absorbed in their own trauma of the addiction. Children witness their parent's inability to manage emotional distress, and children are often the recipients of misplaced anger or witness parental violence or rage. It isn't uncommon for a child to be asked to lie or keep a secret for a parent, to witness calls or the actual behavior of the FSLA involved in an affair, to be exposed to pornography, or to observe a parent engaged in masturbation or other sexual behavior. Some children have overheard or been the object of sexualized conversations, and others are sexually abused as part of the sexual acting out, or as a result of the couple's neglect that leaves the children ripe for an abuser's grooming. Some children are used as confidants; others become a barrier between the couple in bed—leaving the child to absorb the parents' emotional distress.

As the addiction's impact on the children becomes clear, most FSLAs and partners can agree they want to do a better job of parenting in the future and make amends for past behaviors. This resolve presents a great opportunity for the therapist to encourage the couple to work together toward healthier parenting. They have a chance to re-parent themselves through the process of learning how to be better parents, and a chance to stop the generational transmission of addictive behavior by being proactive in creating a healthier family system.

Regardless of the configuration of the family unit—a heterosexual married couple, a single mother, or a lesbian couple—the family system needs assistance when an FSLA enters recovery. Each person has been wounded, and as individuals and a collective body, the family deserves healing.

Components of Healthy Families

There's no mystery about what constitutes a healthy family; it's simply the opposite of the attachment-impaired, trauma-ridden, shame-based system that birthed most female sex and love addicts. Identifying a healthy family requires merely substituting the antonym of the various elements of dysfunctional families discussed in chapter 2.

In a good-enough family, members talk about issues instead of ignoring or denying them. Each person is encouraged to feel and express emotions and to recognize others' emotions. People accept responsibility instead of blaming. Parents are the adults in charge, not children, and parents take care of the children's needs and find solutions to family problems. Boundaries are healthy, not rigid, loose, disengaged, or enmeshed. Children's attachment needs are met, and abuse is absent. If a child is victimized by someone outside the family, he or she feels free to tell a parent, and the parents take immediate action to protect and support the child. As children develop, they're encouraged to think and explore for themselves, and as they become young adults, parents foster healthy differentiation.

Remind the FSLA and her partner that the best thing they can do to help their children is to continue their own healing journeys. This path provides a positive role model for effective ways of dealing with difficult situations and impaired relationships. It allows children to embrace their imperfection without shame and to pick themselves up and start over when they fail.

Parental Responsibilities

The extensive pain of early recovery creates a self-absorption for addicts and partners alike. Both adults may be struggling simply to function, and it's easy for children to get lost in the shuffle. When the parents are adversarial, which is common in the face of such enormous betrayal, their children may suffer collateral damage as the parents react to each other in anger, hurt, and fear. Remind the parents of their responsibility to be selfless when it comes to their children and to prioritize the children's needs over their own. Be strong in your admonishment that parents avoid asking the children to take sides in this messy situation or to otherwise pull them into the middle of the adults' problems. Children young enough to be living at home desperately need stability and nurturance, and parents have the responsibility to provide it.

Benefit of Group Therapy for Parents

To develop the maturity and perspective to be effective parents in the middle of their own distress, parents need an extensive community of support. In the best of circumstances, couples in early recovery benefit from participating in a couple's group that offers an avenue for psychoeducation, group process, and mutual support. A 12-week minimum timeframe allows for instruction and group activities related to communication skills, improving emotional competency, values clarification, friendship skills, parenting, and other skill-based learning. After the 12 weeks, encourage the group to continue on their own using the same format for an additional nine months. At that point, the group members can determine if they want to continue as a support group, as a social/dinner group, or to disband.

Be sure to create ample opportunities for couples to mingle and form connections during the group process so that they have other couples for support. Devote some of the time together to psychoeducational lectures, and if there isn't sufficient time to cover the material couples need at this stage, arrange for a two-to-three-hour lecture on a weekend every few weeks. Provide a resource list of videos or books by family and couple experts, and assign specific ones for couples to review and discuss at different group sessions. Group therapy has the best outcome, because groups create long-term support for the members and provide a level of accountability that improves therapeutic results.

Importance of Values Clarification

As parents move toward creating a healthier family, they benefit by completing a values-clarification exercise related to general and specific sexual topics. Ideally, the couple (or FSLA if she's a single parent) goes through this activity before they disclose to their children, because it assists in that process. You can help the parents by exploring where their values originated and how the FSLA's and her partner's opinions influenced their core beliefs about themselves and the rules under which they operated in the past.

General values most couples share regarding parenting usually include treating people with dignity, respecting boundaries, providing accurate and age appropriate information about relationships and healthy sexuality, and the importance of creating secure attachments. The FSLA and partner need to discuss the values each has about being a parent and spouse, and how they were compromised during active addiction. Have the couple re-create a set of values based on recovery principles such as being accountable, having a relationship with a Higher Power, making amends, and giving back through service. Suggest the couple generates a values list about behavior based on the Twelve Steps, which is a wonderful way to reinforce the principles of the program while creating their own values list. Hot topics that are often part of values-based discussions may include nudity, sexualized or romanticized conversations, masturbation, infidelity, pre-marital sex, cybersex or other Internet-based sexual activities, lying and honesty, emotional connections, sexual orientation, pornography, objectification, sadistic/masochism, and other sexual behaviors.

Once values are clarified, the parents are better able to determine their goals and create a planned message to share with their children about sexuality, disclosure, or any other value-based topic. Obtain clarity from the FSLA and partner about what they want to disclose to their children now and what is best left for later. Parents need to agree about what to say and who will say what. The following section provides direction for this important, but sensitive, process.

Disclosure to Children

Often the early therapy with the FSLA and partner is focused on stabilization, and disclosure to children is postponed or limited to dealing with what will directly impact the children such as a period of separation, parents sleeping in different rooms, or going to therapy and meetings. Any disclosure to children needs to be well thought out, age appropriate, and reviewed with the therapist (Corley & Schneider,

2012). The values clarification process that leads up to disclosure to children generally increases the partner's level of trust with the addict, because the FSLA is being accountable, and the couple begins to see where they agree on values.

In general, children younger than pre-adolescent (around age 10) or children who are very immature don't need any specific information about sex and love addiction. Sex and love addiction is complex enough for adult abstract thinkers, so for a concrete-thinking youngster, the information shared has to be about concepts they can understand. Therefore, an initial disclosure about violating values rather than details about sexual behavior is more appropriate. As the child ages and becomes more mature, discussions about addictions of all kinds need to occur as part of good parenting. Older teens and adult children often know more about addiction in general and are aware of some of what has happened between the couple. The therapist can help the couple determine when and what information about the FSLA's past behavior needs to be disclosed (see Corley & Schneider, 2012).

Addicts and partners benefit from examples of how someone else has handled this challenging process. Following is an example of a disclosure to an early-to-middle elementary school-aged child about the reason the FSLA is moving out of the house for a period of time.

> I bet you can tell Daddy is feeling very angry and sad right now. That's because I told big lies and broke big promises I made to him. He trusted me, but I lied to him—that was wrong of me and it's normal for him to be disappointed and mad at me. He isn't mad at you; he's mad at me. I'm sorry that I hurt Daddy, because he's supposed to be my best friend. But I didn't treat him like a best friend. Best friends don't lie or break promises.
>
> I'm going to take a grown-up's time-out and spend some time staying with Aunt Ginny for a while. I'm also going to see a special teacher to help me learn to be a better wife, friend and Mommy. Daddy's also going to see a special teacher to help him feel better. None of what's happening between your Daddy and me is your fault and we both love you very much. You didn't do anything wrong, and there isn't anything you need to do to fix it.
>
> I won't be far away and I'll call every morning at 7:30 for a kiss on the phone before you go to school, and I'll call every night at 6:00 to check on you and Daddy. I'll be here on Wednesday night and all day on Sunday. On Wednesdays, I'll make dinner or take you out to eat, and then we'll do homework together, decide what we'll do on Sunday, and I'll tuck you into bed before I leave. If we need to, Daddy and I will also figure out how I can see you more often.

> I'm sorry this might be hard for you while I'm gone. You can write me letters or draw me pictures about how you feel or about what you're thinking or about what happened in your day. You can call my cell phone anytime. I'm going to start my time-out tonight, but I'll call you tomorrow morning at 7:30. It's okay to be upset. Daddy and I will be okay, and you'll be okay, too. Do you have any questions or want to say anything now?

The value that was violated was one of honesty (lying) and how best friends act reliably (broken promises). The next day the FSLA needs to ask how the child is feeling and offer structure, guidance, protection, and nurturance. Encourage the parents to give the child an avenue to communicate even if he or she is in too much shock or shame to talk at the point of the disclosure. Drawing pictures, keeping a journal, writing an anger letter or daily letters to one or both parents, or talking to a trusted friend or therapist can help a child process feelings.

After the disclosure, both parents should take responsibility for talking with the children and responding to "teachable moments." The FSLA should be prepared to offer amends about how she also broke promises to the child, which sometimes opens the door for further disclosure. With practice, the message becomes easier, and family values emerge as a strength for families in recovery.

Parents' Containment During Disclosure to Children

Discussion of difficult topics related to the disclosure with children often brings up emotional feelings for the partner and is sometimes triggering for the FSLA. Predict this emotional distress and remind the couple of their goal for better parenting and accountability as the foundation of the disclosure. Help the couple make plans or coach them about what to do if one or both becomes emotionally distraught. Sometimes the partner is so angry that he or she doesn't want to be a part of the disclosure process. It's important for the partner to separate his emotional distress from his responsibility as a parent. Work with the partner on increasing his self-soothing skills, or if the couple has made progress, to ask the FSLA for what he needs to co-regulate the distress (such as holding hands, closing eyes, and breathing slowly). Children are dealing with their own distress, and it's actually healing for them to witness both parents having feelings and tolerating the emotional distress of a difficult discussion. Children need parents to be emotionally supportive during the disclosure.

Ask the parents to practice their disclosure to children with you in session before they carry out the plan. Even with these suggested interventions, sometimes a partner is unable to deal with the distress of talking with children about these sensitive issues. If an emotional outburst happens in the practice disclosure session, the partner should ask for permission to leave to do some emotional self-repair. You can work with him prior to disclosure to determine other ways he can be supportive of the children before and after the disclosure if he decides he won't take part in the discussion itself. Encourage the FSLA to practice her own emotional competency by being emotionally present for her partner, by verifying that his feelings are valid given her past behavior, and by asking what she can do today to help him. The same process can be done for children who have an emotionally difficult time during or after a disclosure.

Disclosure to children remains one of the most anxiety-provoking tasks for the FSLA and her partner. However, like many elements of recovery, this challenging stage offers rich opportunities for healing—this time for an entire family. Disclosure to children is the first step toward breaking the cycle of family dysfunction and creating a new environment of repaired attachment, improved relationships, and healthier family dynamics.

Family Healing

A family affected by sex and love addiction benefits from family therapy, which is best offered by a licensed marriage and family therapist specifically trained in working with the entire family. The more people in the room, especially with widely varying ages and in the middle of complicated circumstances such as those experienced in an addictive environment, the more challenging the therapeutic task. Children too young for talk therapy or experiential exercises can participate in play therapy, which offers them a supportive venue. Remind the FSLA that her pain has opened the door to healing for a wider circle.

A first priority for family therapy is to develop a "press release" of what family members will say about the FSLA's situation. If public or offending behavior has occurred, the children may be asked or even harassed about their mom's actions, and having a plan and practicing it reduces everyone's anxiety. Children and adolescents will also need help dealing with other family members such as grandparents, or aunts, uncles, and cousins, who likely will be asking questions. These situations provide an excellent time to learn healthy boundaries and the difference between private and secret information.

Talk with the family about the rules and roles (see chapter 2 for a reminder) that characterize many dysfunctional families. Each person can make a collage that describes his or her perceived role in the family and share it during a session. Frequently, even young children take on the role of peacekeeper or "little mom" or a doer that manages practical chores in the family. If the therapist is trained in psychodrama, sculpting the family is a powerful exercise. As homework, ask family members to write a letter of resignation from their unhealthy roles and invite them to share it at the next session.

A structural framework helps parents see their proper place as the adults in charge and strengthens their position as a unified entity. Experiential techniques and psychodrama are particularly well-suited to family therapy. For example, if the family has a pet, ask someone to speak from that pet's perspective to describe the family. The possibilities for this kind of therapeutic work are vast and offer a less threatening way for family members to share.

Adolescents and adult children can join their parents in creating a family genogram. Devote a session to each parent, and invite input as the parent describes his or her own parents and grandparents. This kind of exercise helps family members recognize the generational nature of addiction and dysfunction and often generates more compassion for the FSLA and the partner. Teenagers present special challenges in family therapy as they're in a developmental period of differentiation, less comfortable in talking with parents in general, and particularly uncomfortable discussing sexual issues with their parents. Encourage teens and young adults to participate in individual sessions as an adjunct to family therapy. Some Twelve Step S fellowships have a program for teens. A good alternative is Alateen, which is designed for substance abuse issues, yet also offers principles that are applicable to any addiction.

Even adult children profit from family therapy. Encourage the FSLA to embrace the time and expense required to engage adult children in the healing process. Making amends is a crucial part of the movement to a healthier relationship, and many FSLAs and their adult children need help in talking through their difficult history. Initiating family counseling helps prevent estrangement and emotional cut-offs.

Parenting

Female sex and love addicts may be at risk for abandoning their children, surrendering their role and rights as mothers, unwittingly using their children as surrogate spouses or best friends, and/or exposing their children to a series of lovers. In recovery, some mothers are highly motivated for the sake of their children to learn healthy parenting skills, while others are not and may need more direct intervention when it comes to parenting. During their own childhoods FSLAs often experienced dysfunctional modeling and boundary violations when a parent placed his or her wishes, emotional needs, or goals ahead of the child's. While every well-meaning parent can make this mistake occasionally, abusive parents have the attitude of righteousness and entitlement when making mistakes and don't offer apology or repair. Recovering women usually have a large amount of repairing to do; yet they often lack the tools for healthy parenting even when they have the desire.

For FSLAs, being responsible for children is an often unconscious, but powerful and overwhelming trigger. A woman is faced with a horrible contradiction: The child she adores is terrifying and/or suffocating her. The task to bond with a child stirs unconscious attachment fears that sets in motion a cascade of potentially destructive behaviors which can include fits of rage, periods of disassociation, feelings of helplessness, and the desire to flee. Some mothers have no awareness of the attachment risks for their children. Others are profoundly pained by the powerlessness they feel as mothers and the pain they inflict on their vulnerable children.

To support your client, it's helpful to name the challenges she faces as a mother. Your ability to identify and name her struggle will assist her recognition of parenting issues, reduce the shame involved, and move her toward healthy behavior. Remind her that she can only provide her children what she has available within herself. When she experiences shame about the level of care she has or hasn't been providing, remind her that her most important job is first to heal herself, and assure her that her children will benefit from her process.

Childless FSLAs

Sex and love addiction robs many women of the choice to be mothers. If your client's story includes aborted children or the lost opportunity for having children, it's important to help her understand her choices. Gently suggest that choosing abortion or feeling unable to mother a child can both be acts of sacrifice. Women intuitively know their wounds may transfer to their babies, and in an attempt to protect, some women avoid giving birth to keep their children safe from either themselves or their dangerous lovers. Affirm this choice. Help her see her heart's desire to love. The awareness of lost opportunity for giving birth and nurturing can be overwhelming, even to a woman who says she never wanted children. To midwife her through this difficult grief is a wonderful gift of grace for her unique pain.

Writers

Deborah Corley – Disclosure to Partners, Disclosure to Children

Marnie Ferree – Systems Theory, Models for Treating Partners,
Male Partners, Couples and Family Recovery

Kelly McDaniel – Parenting

REFERENCES

Alcoholics Anonymous. (1939). *Alcoholics anonymous* (1st ed.). New York, NY: AA World Services.

Carnes, P. (1991). *Don't call it love: Recovering from sexual addiction.* Minneapolis, MN: Compcare Publishers.

Carnes, P. (2003). Anatomy of arousal: Three Internet portals. *Sexual and Relationship Therapy, 18*(3), 309-328. doi: 10.1080/14681990310153937

Carnes, S. (Ed.). (2008). *Mending a shattered heart: A guide for partners of sex addicts* (1st ed.). Carefree, AZ: Gentle Path Press.

Carnes, S. (Ed.). (2011). *Mending a shattered heart: A guide for partners of sex addicts* (2nd ed.). Carefree, AZ: Gentle Path Press.

Carnes, S., Lee, M. A., & Rodriguez, A. (2012a, February). *Partner's recovery workshop: Using exercises, materials, tasks and actual client case examples,* Presentation at the International Institute for Trauma and Addiction Professionals symposium. Scottsdale, AZ.

Carnes, S., Lee, M. A., & Rodriguez, A. (2012b). *Facing heartbreak - Steps to recovery for partners of sex addicts.* Carefree, AZ: Gentle Path Press.

Fals-Stewart, W., Birchler, G. R., & Kelley, M. L. (2006). Learning sobriety together: A randomized clinical trial examining behavioral couples therapy with alcoholic female patients. *Journal of Consulting and Clinical Psychology,74*(3), 579-591. doi: 10.1037/0022-006X.74.3.579

Ferree, M. C. (2010). *No stones—Women redeemed from sexual addiction* (2nd ed.). Downers Grove, IL: InterVarsity Press.

Jason, S. (2009, September). *Treating trauma first.* Presentation at the Society for the Advancement of Sexual Health conference, San Diego, CA.

Jason, S. V., & Graves, J. (2011, September). *Gaslighting and trauma: The experiences of partners of sex addicts.* Presentation at the Society for the Advancement of Sexual Health conference, La Jolla, CA.

Laaser, M. (2004). *Healing the wounds of sexual addiction.* Grand Rapids, MI: Zondervan.

Minwalla, O. (2011). What about me and my sexuality? In S. Carnes (Ed.), *Mending a shattered heart: A guide for partners of sex addicts* (2nd ed.). (pp. 93-112). Carefree, AZ: Gentle Path Press.

Minwalla, O. (n.d.). A call for professional action—Recognizing the psychological treatment needs of partners of sex addicts, Institute for Sexual Health website. Retrieved from http://www.theinstituteforsexualhealth.com/ish-articles/a-call-for-professional-action-and-awareness-recognizing-the-psychological-treatment-needs-of-partners-of-sex-addicts/

Satir, V. (1983). *Conjoint family therapy*. (3rd ed.). Palo Alto, CA: Science and Behavior Books.

Schneider, J. (2005) *Back from betrayal: Recovering from his affairs.* (3rd ed.). Tucson, AZ: Recovery Resources Press.

Schneider, J. P., & Corley, M.D. (2012). *Surviving disclosure: A partner's guide for healing the betrayal of intimate trust.* Tucson, AZ: Recovery Resources Press

Steffens, B., & Means, M. (2009). *Your sexually addicted spouse: How partners can cope and heal.* Far Hills, NJ: New Horizons Press.

CHAPTER 9

Special Populations and Treatment Issues

Susan Campling, Jill Vermeire
with contribution by Robin Cato

Treating the female sex and love addict is challenging, at best. Employing best practices, the clinician uses a dual-track approach to arrest acting out behaviors and address underlying issues regarding attachment and trauma. Supporting and guiding a woman through this recovery journey requires advanced, informed clinical skills. The FSLA's treatment is complicated when she's dealing with special treatment considerations in addition to her primary challenge of SLA itself. This chapter explores four issues that provide special considerations for a woman's treatment.

LESBIAN ISSUES

Although treatment of the lesbian SLA is fundamentally the same as the heterosexual female SLA, there are a few considerations to keep in mind. As discussed in chapter 4 about therapeutic considerations, the therapist's gender is one factor. Similar to the issues that can present for men treating women, the same can be true for female clinicians treating gay women. The possibility of erotic transference exists in the same way. It's important to pay attention to the energy, body language, and countertransference during sessions. As with any client, if the FSLA expresses romantic fantasies or feelings for you as her therapist, the best course of action is first to acknowledge the courage it takes to express these feelings and the vulnerability that follows. Then process in an ongoing dialogue the characteristics of sex and love addiction and the intrigue of unavailable people (in this case, the therapist). Also explore the aspect of intimacy in the therapeutic relationship, which is the experience of being seen, heard, and known. This concept of intimacy is often replayed or transmitted in the client's interactions, and for the attachment-wounded FSLA, it's quite understandable that she would romanticize or sexualize the feelings of warmth, caring, and closeness she's experiencing in therapy.

As with any population, diversity issues can include shame about one's own gender and sexuality, and this is true for lesbians. Kasl (1990, p. 208) points out,

> People at the extreme ends of the spectrum may have little inner conflict about their sexual preference. They don't feel they have a choice; they simply feel they were born lesbian or heterosexual. However people who are somewhere between the two poles may experience more discomfort or have doubts in the recesses of their minds.

Ascertain the client's sexual history and her process of "coming out" if that has happened. If she was traumatized with shame or rejection about this disclosure, she may be carrying that shame, which would fuel her acting out behaviors. Shame reduction work and/or trauma work around this experience would be necessary in this situation, as well as work about any other carried or unprocessed feelings around her sexuality.

One example of shame reduction work is to have her write out in narrative form what her coming out process was like for her. How did she come to a decision to tell her family? When did she tell her family? How old was she? What was their response? What were the repercussions? Did she have a community of support or was she isolated and alone? After she's written about the process in detail, have her read it aloud to you or in group therapy when appropriate so that she can have the experience of feeling her feelings and getting validation and support for her process.

Some lesbian clients will have a history of seducing and having sex with men even though they aren't aroused or attracted to males. This experience is indicative of the power and control issues in FSLA, as well as the propensity to seek unavailable partners. When this behavior presents you may assume this client is perhaps actually heterosexual or bisexual. Both positions are possible examples of the therapist's values and/or countertransference impeding the therapy, and this reaction highlights a time when seeking consultation is imperative. If the client feels she's being judged or misunderstood, it's possible she will feel re-traumatized or terminate the therapy altogether. It's important to accept the client's experience and stay away from labels. Be mindful of jumping to conclusions or labeling the client.

Seducing straight women is closely related to the issue of seducing men for the lesbian SLA, which is another behavior that illustrates the attraction to unavailable partners. When a lesbian successfully seduces and becomes sexual with a heterosexual woman, she experiences the high she seeks. However, when this process occurs unconsciously, it's likely a therapeutic enactment may be bringing to life her faulty attachment pattern with her mother. In either case, be careful not to jump to any conclusions. Remain objective, open minded, and curious. Upon further exploration of a lesbian's pattern of seducing and engaging straight women, either consciously or unconsciously, you'll often find family of origin and trauma issues around the mother or female caregiver. Processing these mother wounds can access some very deep grief for the SLA. Acknowledge and address her mother hunger (McDaniel, 2012) and move into the grief work.

Another presentation of FSLA is the woman who identifies as a heterosexual female but who has acted out with women, usually lesbian women. Again, exploring this behavior with an open mind and sense of curiosity is the best course of action in order to avoid possibly shaming the client or further adding to her likely confusion around this behavior. Often this type of acting out is an example of tolerance and the escalation of her addiction, as well as a drive fueled by mother hunger. It's important for the clinician to remain open to all possibilities and focus on the task at hand: aiding the client in understanding her addiction, identifying her patterns, and increasing her awareness of underlying issues. Who she is, what her sexual orientation is, and what constitutes healthy sexual behaviors versus addictive sexual behaviors will be revealed as the therapeutic work unfolds.

It might also be tempting for the client or the therapist to minimize this same-sex behavior since there's a wider acceptance of women being more sensual and fewer stigmas about experimenting with other women. This mindset is very different than the overall, quick-to-judge, societal beliefs about heterosexual men who act out with other men. Likewise, at some point this client will need to look at consequences accrued as a result of this kind of acting out. She'll need to take ownership for causing hurt feelings or confusion by leading a lesbian woman on (that is, letting the lesbian woman believe that she was desired by the FSLA when, in actuality, she was only part of the client's sex addiction and never really a viable candidate for a relationship). These types of partners will most likely be included in the FSLA amends process.

Homophobia is another frequent issue that needs attention while working with a lesbian SLA. It's not uncommon for a gay person to be homophobic. This means she doesn't embrace her culture (homosexuality) and might actively avoid social circles, situations, or environments that promote the gay or lesbian lifestyle. It's really about the client devaluing or rejecting a significant part of who she is. This situation isn't to be confused with someone who is still exploring her sexual identity. A homophobic lesbian will downplay her sexuality, avoid anything that has to do with being a lesbian, and reject the homosexual culture completely, sometimes even criticizing or mocking lesbians and/or the same-sex lifestyle. This mindset is closely related to the issue of shame and will cross over with the lesbian women who seduce men. An essential part of this woman's therapy is to deconstruct her critical and negative beliefs about her homosexuality so that she can learn ways to embrace and integrate her sexuality as a valuable part of who she is.

Choosing a sponsor

Clients who actively participate in an S recovery program will need to find a sponsor. The recommendation for the heterosexual female is that she finds another heterosexual female to work with as a sponsor. However, the choice about the best gender for a sponsor is somewhat more complicated for the lesbian SLA. Unfortunately, finding a sponsor in an S program can be a bit more challenging than in other, larger Twelve Step fellowships. For the lesbian FSLA the ideal sponsor would be someone she can't intrigue, flirt, or act out with, and can ultimately form a safe and non-sexual bond with—in other words, a gay male. Since finding a gay male as a sponsor might not be feasible, the lesbian FSLA will need to seek out someone she deems as healthy, works a strong program, and has little to no chance of becoming the focus of fantasy or intrigue by the FSLA. Help her look objectively at all the possible scenarios, the pros and cons of each sponsor candidate, and stay focused on the goal: finding a sponsor who is safe and can help her work the Steps and build a life of grace and integrity in recovery. It might turn out that the best person will be a heterosexual female or male, or another gay woman. As long as the sponsor and the sponsee (your client) have an open and honest discussion about their individual needs, boundaries, and expectations, it can be a mutually beneficial relationship regardless of gender or sexual orientation. Affirm that selecting a sponsor can be daunting for anyone no matter what sexual orientation or gender she is, and it's always okay for the FSLA to change her mind if, at some point, it seems the relationship isn't working. The mere act of considering, discussing, and choosing a sponsor shows that she's making progress and is participating in her recovery.

FEMALE SEX OFFENDERS

Many clinicians who work with individuals who demonstrate sexually addictive behaviors feel confident working with Level I addicts, who are those individuals engaged in socially neutral and legal behaviors (P. Carnes, 1983). However, the Level II and III sex addict is a greater enigma to many therapists. Learning about this subgroup of compulsive individuals is important to clinicians open to working with sexually offending sexual addicts (SOSA). Special knowledge is required to perform appropriate assessment and adequate treatment that meets a standard of care accepted within the clinical and legal community. It's important for therapists who work with FSLAs to have, at minimum, a basic understanding of offending behaviors in women and especially in those who struggle with sex and love addiction so that an appropriate referral can be made if necessary.

Certainly not all sexual offenders are sexual addicts and not all sexual addicts are sexual offenders. A review of the literature found no studies examining the correlation between being a female sex and love addict and female sex offender. Preliminary data from the Women's Sexuality Survey reveals that FSLAs acknowledge sexual contact with minors, but these numbers are small and further research is needed to examine the topic more closely (Corley & Delmonico, 2011). Nevertheless, overlap exists. For the non-addicted sexual offender, multiple other issues can be part of the offending behavior, including severe personality disorders and medical/organic disorders. These conditions are beyond the scope of this section.

The term *sex offender* is problematic in mental health treatment and research because it isn't a diagnostic term, the scope is broad, and the term carries considerable negative connotation. Because sex offender isn't a psychological condition, research conducted with offenders doesn't always assess for compulsive or addictive behavior other than *DSM* criteria. This research also tends to view sexual offenders as a homogenous group even though it's well known that they are not. Therefore, there are limitations in discussing sexual offenders and particularly the female sexual offender (FSO) due to problems with generalizing the research. Be aware that sexual offenses occur for a variety of reasons, and psychopathology isn't always causal to the crime.

Female sex offenders pose their own set of research and clinical issues. Few large-scale studies have been done with this population. Even among incarcerated sex offenders, women make up only about 1-2% of the population, and only approximately 1,500 women are convicted of sexual offenses each year in the United States (US Department of Justice, 2007). Finding a large pool of subjects is also problematic due to the diversity of these crimes. And, despite the drive for equality among men and women in our culture, viewing women as sexual offenders remains somewhat blinded by definition. Until January 2012, men weren't recognized as rape victims by the US Department of Justice (Russo, 2012). The definition of exhibitionism requires the exposure of genitals but not breasts to unsuspecting persons, and far more women might meet criteria if breasts were included in the definition. Certainly the underlying intent is the same when a woman exposes her breasts to an unsuspecting person. Discrepancies in definition can alter statistics and impact our understanding of the scope of sexual offending in women, funding for treatment, and further research.

Data suggest that the number of adult FSOs has declined in recent years, although the number of adolescent FSOs has increased (Sickmund, 2006). Despite this reality, the Federal Bureau of Investigation data indicate that less than 10% of adults and adolescents who come to the attention of authorities for sexual offenses are female (FBI, 2006; Mathews, 1989). Women make up less than 1% of arrests for rape and less than 6% for other sexual offenses. Data for adolescents indicate that minor females account for 3% of forcible rapes and 5% of other violent sex offenses (Sickmund, 2006). According to Lawson, women are more likely than men to offend with an accomplice, and those who offended with a male were frequently involved in abusive relationships with their co-offenders. Women who molested children independently were more likely to have been severely molested themselves prior to the age of 10 than women who molested with an accomplice (Lawson, 2008).

If research on FSOs is in its infancy, then studies with FSLAs who sexually offend are still in the womb. Little research with FSOs addresses the addictive nature of offending behavior outside of co-occurring chemical addictions. Preliminary data from the Women's Sexuality Survey indicates that some FSLAs engage in sexual behaviors with minors, but interestingly, when asked about offending behaviors, these same FSLAs denied them (Corley & Delmonico, 2011). Mathews (1989) found that among female sex offenders in the teacher/lover typography, women perceived themselves as having romantic or sexual mentoring relationships with children and didn't consider their acts to be criminal in nature. This perception among FSOs may explain this discrepancy in the Women's Sexuality Survey between women's report of sex with minors and their disavowal of offending behaviors.

Whereas most research regarding reoffending rates among sex offenders examines only male perpetrators, a few studies have examined female sex offenders. Despite the perception that most child sex offenders will re-offend, the data don't support this belief. A meta-analysis of 10 studies involving almost 2,500 offenders showed that female sexual offenders have extremely low rates of sexual recidivism (less than 3%) when measured six and a half years after adjudication (US Department of Justice, 2003). The recidivism rates for violent (including sexual) offenses and for any type of crime were predictably higher than the recidivism rates for sexual offenses, but still lower than the recidivism rates of male sexual offenders (Cortoni, 2010). Another large study from New York State examining FSOs (n=1466) found that recidivism rates for all criminal offenses were low in comparison to male sexual offenders (Sandler & Freman, 2009).

The following chart delineates the typographies of female sexual offenders as outlined by Mathews (1989).

Typographies of Female Sexual Offenders

Typography	Characteristics
Male Coerced	Male-coerced women fear abandonment and allow their children to be abused by a male who pressures them into permitting the abuse.
Predisposed	Predisposed women are vulnerable to sexually offending due to histories of incest, presence of deviant sexual fantasies, and significant psychological problems.
Teacher/Lover	Teacher/lovers are women who believe they are in a romantic relationship with a minor child and don't consider their behavior as deviant. These women often have relationship difficulties with adults.

Figure 14

Another study by Vandiver (2006) found differences between women who offend with a male partner (FSO/P) and those who offend alone. FSO/Ps tended to have multiple young victims that included females as well as males. FSO/Ps also victimize their own children more and are more frequently charged with multiple other offenses at the same time they're charged with the sex offense. Mothers who offer their children for sex via the Internet are a possible new subgroup of women who offend. Although no formal studies exist, reports from these women and their partners suggest that they barter their children for the opportunity to find a partner for themselves. Offering their children for sex may also be part of a vicarious sexual experience for these women. Whatever the motive, this behavior is legally considered a sexual offense. Further research is needed to evaluate the nature and motivation in this subgroup of women.

In a study by Wijkman female sexual offenders were studied for victim, victimizer, and offense characteristics in a cohort of 111 women known to the criminal justice system in the Netherlands between 1915 and 2005 (Wijkman, 2010). In 77% of the cases, the female sex offenders had abused children; almost two thirds of the women had perpetrated with a male co-offender. The women mostly abused their own children in conjunction with their intimate partner, whereas women who raped normally did so alone. A number of the offenders had themselves previously been victims with 31% of the female offenders reporting sexual abuse, whereas 59% exhibited mental disorders. Young offenders tended to act single-handedly; women who were psychologically disturbed and women who allowed their children to be sexually abused were usually older offenders.

In comparison to the general population, female sexual offenders demonstrate higher levels of psychiatric hospitalization and diagnoses of psychosis and substance abuse (Fazel, Sjöstedt, Grann, & Långström (1971). However in comparison to other female violent offenders, there are no differences in substance abuse, personality disorders, emotional neediness, and cognitive distortions (Strickland, 2008). Nevertheless, childhood abuse history is different between these two groups with female sexual offenders demonstrating more significant trauma. Miller, Turner, and Henderson (2009) found consistency with other research that female sex offenders, in particular, are more likely than their male counterparts to exhibit symptoms of a personality disorder and levels of depression and anxiety.

A history of substance abuse raises the possibility that FSOs may also have SLA issues due to the interactive nature of addiction. This poly-addiction is certainly seen among male addicts. Although substance abuse doesn't exonerate these women for responsibility for their offending behaviors, alcohol or drugs may act as a facilitator or disinhibitor for repressed desires. Again, these questions can't be answered until further research examines the issue of sex and love addiction in female sex offenders.

Women are believed to primarily sexually offend against children, rather than against adult males. However, this data might also reflect social bias given that few men report sexual assault by women. Recent discussions have emerged regarding the revision of prejudicial definitions of certain sex crimes that would encourage the inclusion of men as victims of sex crimes, including rape (Stemple, 2009). The Department of Justice reports that 92,700 adult men were forcibly raped each year, and that 2.78 million men experienced an attempted or completed rape in their lifetime (US Department of Justice, 2008), though much of this sexual violence is thought to be male on male.

Male sexual assault includes the bias that men can't be sexually assaulted the same ways that women can and therefore can't be raped by women (McGee, 2011). This belief may be disputed as our understanding of rape increases and the definition is broadened. In January 2012, the U.S. Department of Justice changed the definition of rape to include, "The penetration, no matter how slight, of the vagina or anus with any body part or object, or oral penetration by a sex organ of another person, without the consent of the victim" (Russo, 2012). This is a significant change in definition from 1927, when women were the only defined victims. A significant number of sexual offenses committed against men occur in a prison setting. A Department of Justice study estimated 10,400 inmates reported that they had unwilling sex with staff, and nearly 62% of reported incidents of staff sexual misconduct involved female staff with male inmates (US Department of Justice, 2008). Clearly, in some cases of male sexual victimization, women are the perpetrators.

In addition to prisoners, detainees of armed conflicts are another group vulnerable to sexual assault and rape. Research focused on wartime sexual assault often fails to recognize the role of female war supporters and combatants and the victim-abuser issue of wartime aggressor roles (Ibanez, 2001). Women are known to participate in the sexual humiliation and degradation of males in prisoner of war camps as illustrated by the reports regarding Lynndie England and the Abu Ghraib tortures. Female soldiers forced their Muslim prisoners to masturbate, rub against other men, and simulate sex acts, which are all degrading behaviors to devout Muslim males. The use of sex as a weapon isn't new to war, yet until the Abu Ghraib pictures emerged, men were thought to be the only culprits. Interestingly, the belief that sexually offending women are somehow less culpable than men was noted in the England case. Jeffreys opined that Lynndie England was a victim of masculine aggression and that her womanhood and sexuality were used by her comrades (Jeffreys, 2007). Holding women less responsible and professing that men are the only sexual aggressors and never victims promotes harmful perceptions about gender stereotypes (Stemple, 2009).

Finally, minor-age males are also victims of FSOs. Based on client accounts, women may offend against young males more frequently than the statistics capture. Some male victims report that they feared telling an authority figure about the abuse because their mother was their primary caretaker as well as their perpetrator. Other males feared abandonment by their families. Some abused men feared they wouldn't be believed if they reported the abuse because of the perception that since boys are physically stronger than girls, they could ward off abuse if they chose. Society also re-enforces the stereotype that teenage males sexually desire the women who abuse them, and therefore the males aren't really victims. If the males don't desire the sexual contact with the female perpetrator, it means the victim is somehow less than a man.

The perception of FSOs as women who are sexually desired was recently demonstrated in the popular press. In May 2011, the *Houston Press* released its list of the "10 Hottest Female Sex Offenders" (Connelly, 2011), which was met with controversy in part because the child victims of these women ranged in age from 2 to 14 years old. According to one un-cited commentator in an article written in response to the *Houston Press* piece,

> Since its publication the article has generated almost 700 comments, most of which criticize Connelly for sugarcoating the crimes of female rapists. Calling these women 'hot' seems to condone their actions, as it perpetuates the idea that female rapists are only fulfilling a fantasy shared by every teenage male that these women are seductresses, not criminals. (Ngo, 2011)

Connelly later issued a written apology saying that he offered the list to challenge popular belief that sex offenders were unattractive men. Such a view of female sexual offending as comical and sexy likely further inhibits males from coming forward about their victimization at the hands of women. Paradoxically, such failure to hold FSOs accountable disempowers women in the larger society.

Media reports of teachers who engaged in sexual relationships with male students may have changed our view of FSOs. As an example, the case of Mary Kay Letourneau involves a 34-year-old married teacher who "fell in love" with one of her sixth grade students. Ms. Letourneau, who was already the mother of four, gave birth to two children fathered by her 13-year-old student. After she served time in jail for assaulting her student, they married in 2005. This case, despite or possibly because of its outcome, increased awareness regarding the criminal nature of sexual relationships by adult females with boys. Public perception began to change and re-enforced that all sexual relationships with children by adults are criminal (Wormer, 2010). Viewing the sexual abuse of boys as a crime versus a coming-of-age experience reflects the authentic experience of boys thrust into sexual relationships before they are emotionally ready.

According to Mathews, the boys victimized in these situations are often emotionally troubled, vulnerable, and responsive to the emotional attention provided by the adult female (Mathews, 1989). As boys, they react disruptively and are prone to school related behavioral problems, which puts them at risk for further exploitation, criminal behaviors, and drug abuse. As adults they experience posttraumatic stress disorder, addiction, and other life coping problems (Nelson, 2009). Sexual offending behavior is abusive and not an experience of being in love as many female sexual perpetrators avow. Nonetheless, despite increased awareness of female offenders, rape, exhibitionism, and child molestation by women often go unreported.

> Feminist author Val Young offers an important perspective on sexual abuse: What is needed is a clear message to abusers. What we, as feminists, could be doing is accepting that equal rights means equal responsibility and using whatever means possible to put pressure on society to inform abusers that they should stop, and of the harmful effects of abuse on their victims' lives. (Young, 1994, p. 100)

This strong message is necessary whether the offender is male or female.

FEMALE SEX WORKERS

The term *sex worker* refers to women, men, and transgendered individuals who engage in a variety of sexual behaviors for compensation, which can take the form of money, goods, or other services. The activities of sex workers include (but aren't limited to) prostitution, erotic massage, exotic dancing, stripping, acting in pornography, and engaging in phone sex chat and other paid-for phone services.

As discussed in the previous section regarding women who sexually offend, women who exchange sexual services for payment may or may not be sex and love addicts. Little data is available regarding FSLA and sex workers. The Women's Sexuality Survey revealed that 8.4% of self-identified sex and love addicts had traded sex for money compared to 2.2% of non-sex addicts; 26.3% of FSLAs had provided sex for gifts as compared to 5.7% of non-FSLAs; and 7.8% of FSLAs identified themselves as sex workers compared to 4.4% of non-FSLAs (Corley & Delmonico, 2011). Despite women's understandable reluctance to identify as a sex worker, those who admit to being sexually or relationally addicted clearly are exchanging sex for gifts. This discrepancy between practice and self-perception illustrates the importance of asking the right questions in the right way.

Other than the Women's Sexuality Survey, little research is available that explores this correlation between female sex addicts and female sex workers. Most information indicates a complicated matrix of the etiology and confounding factors of women who are involved in the sex trade. At best, women who are sexually addicted and engaging in selling their bodies as part of that addiction present significant treatment challenges if they seek clinical help. At worst, women in the sex industry are victims of horrendous crimes, including their initial conscription into this work, and their path to freedom and healing is strewn with obstacles of unusual proportion.

Inherent in these activities is the exchange of money, goods, or services for sexual activity. The suspension of reality and the selling of a fantasy are interwoven in all forms of money-sex transactions. This fantasy can range from the Girl Friend Experience (GFE) currently common among high priced escorts to the fantasy of "consensual" sex with women who are actually sex slaves. A common belief (especially among those who use the services of sex workers) is that offering sex for sale to willing buyers is a victimless crime that actually benefits both the seller and the buyer. Statistics, however, reveal otherwise. Because of the dangers and challenges of prostitution, the financial gain doesn't always benefit the sex worker or prostitute. Customers or "Johns" seeking sexual services will often utilize the Internet, which generates considerable profit to Internet advertising businesses. For example, Kristoff (2012) reported that research conducted by Advanced Interactive Media Group LLC (AIM Group) indicated that since Craigslist stopped actively advertising prostitution on its website, Backpage.com has become the industry leader with 70% of Internet sex advertisements in the United States. Further, Backpage.com alone had income in one month of over one million dollars and yearly revenue of over \$20 million (Zollman, Frederick, Townsend, & Werth 2011). According to a sex crimes police officer in Louisiana, a pimp can make \$200,000 a year off the work of one woman

(Lee, 2011). And shockingly, street gangs such as the MS-13 in Washington, DC operate child prostitution rings with girls as young as 12 performing sex acts with men for $40 to $100 (Wilber, 2011). Clearly, others are profiting financially much more than the sex workers themselves.

The spectrum of sex workers can include individuals with various levels of consent ranging from voluntary engagement in sex acts to enslavement and sex trafficking. This diverse continuum ranges from high priced solo escorts who offer the illusion of intimacy to girls and women tricked or sold into human slavery. Women and girls are often deceived or manipulated into prostitution or sold by impoverished families (Lever & Dolnick, 2000). Romantic fantasy and the hope for financial stability is often part of the manipulation. In Mexico, young women are romanced by pimps and enticed to come to the United States for marriage. Once in the U.S. they are forced to work in traveling brothels and don't stay at one site long enough to establish ties or find resources for escape. Others are kidnapped by Mexican-run prostitution rings (Pearson, 2012).

It's difficult to imagine that human trafficking for prostitution exists in the United States, especially when children are involved. Yet, Texas Attorney General Gregg Abbott noted, "The Super Bowl is the greatest show on Earth, but it also has an ugly underbelly. It's commonly known as the single largest human trafficking incident in the United States" (Jervis, 2011) as sex traffickers and pimps take advantage of the testosterone-driven demand that's concentrated in a single location. According to UNICEF, 1.2 million children are being trafficked every year (UNICEF.org, n.d.), primarily from Third World countries and South America. At the same time, children in the United States are also at risk, according to U.S. Deputy Attorney General James Cole, who says: "Some of our most vulnerable children also face the threat of being victimized by commercial sexual exploitation. Runaways, throwaways, sexual assault victims, and neglected children can be recruited into a violent life of forced prostitution" Cole, 2011). The average age of girls who enter street prostitution is between 12 and 14, and it's unreasonable to assume they do so at their own initiation. Indeed, human sex trafficking is the fastest growing business of organized crime and third largest criminal enterprise worldwide (Walker-Rodriquez & Hill, 2011).

Certainly women this vulnerable—the women who are victims of sex trafficking—aren't the only face of sex workers in the U.S. However, according to the Federal Bureau of Investigation (2006), the idea of women and girls consensually and voluntarily engaged in the business of prostitution without complaint is extremely inaccurate and fictional. It's true that some female sex workers report they engage in the behavior as a means of earning an income for school or other items or services they need, and these women don't report significant mental health issues (Romans,

2001). For most women, however, participating in the sex industry is extremely dangerous in every way. According to WomensLaw.org, female prostitutes and other sex workers experience rape, physical assault and intimate partner violence, verbal and emotional abuse, financial control or manipulation, isolation, threats, and intimidation. About 80% of women prostitutes have been victims of rape, and on average, a female prostitute is raped eight to 10 times a year. Fifty-eight percent of American prostitutes reported violent assault at the hands of clients, and 85% of prostitutes are raped by their own pimps. Many prostitutes don't report their abuse for fear of being judged or arrested. Further, women in prostitution have a death rate 40 times higher than women not involved in prostitution (WomensLaw.org, n.d.).

According to Laws.com, the average female prostitute enters her job when she is only 16 or 17 years of age. Female prostitutes leave the sex industry less frequently than their male counterparts, which is mainly because a smaller proportion of males work for pimps and therefore enjoy more independence. Due to the high incidence of physical violence perpetrated against them, female prostitutes are more likely to get murdered. In a period of five years in Newark, New Jersey, 14 homicide victims were known prostitutes, which is an incredibly high figure in a city of 280,000 residents with an average annual murder rate of 7 homicides per 100,000 persons. In terms of the emotional toll and the impact on children, 90% of New York City prostitutes had to surrender at least one child to child-protective services (Laws.com, n.d.).

For some women selling sex can be a method of medicating and feeling power over men. Strippers and exotic dancers wield significant power as customers are allowed to look but not touch, which puts the sex worker in control of the exchange. Stripping and dancing is a form of self-objectification for these women and numbs the psyche and soul (Farley, 2004).

Prostitution is illegal in all states except Nevada, where prostitution is permitted within designated brothels. When Nevada legalized prostitution, provisions were made to regulate the practice and test prostitutes for STDs. However, addiction statistics weren't readily available, and there were no regulations noted in Nevada law regarding testing women or men for drugs. Chemical addiction is a definite accompanying factor, as a study of street prostitutes revealed a high prevalence of alcohol and drug abuse in their families of origin during the drift into prostitution and as part of prostitution (McClanahan, 1999; Silbet, 1982). It's likely that the majority of women who participate in the sex industry do so to feed a drug habit. Unfortunately, accurate statistics are difficult to obtain due to the illegal nature of the behavior and the secretive nature of prostitutes (Farley, 2006; Weitzer, 2006). However, Laws.com reports that roughly 26% of New York City prostitutes were homeless and addicted to illicit drugs and resorted to prostitution to serve their addiction to drugs like crack, cocaine, and heroin (Laws.com, n.d.).

Street prostitutes suffer much greater marginalization than the so-called escorts. Women street prostitutes are more often trading money for sex as a matter of survival to feed their drug habit. In a large study of female crack addicts (*N*=4,667), women who traded sex for crack had more partners, had sex more often, used drugs before and during sex more often, and had higher rates of STDs (Logan, 2000).

In addition to their challenges with substance abuse, women sex workers bring painful personal histories into their profession. Studies show that up to 95% of prostitutes were victims of childhood sexual abuse (WomensLaw.org, n.d.). Clinically, this history raises the question about repetition compulsion and other forms of trauma reactions.

Working in the sex industry presents unique challenges if a woman decides to quit. Ninety-two percent of prostitutes reported they desired to leave prostitution but couldn't because of a variety of reasons (WomensLaw.org, n.d.). They had no other way to support themselves financially and lacked basic job skills and experience, they were homeless or at the mercy of their pimps, they were chemically addicted and had no way to access treatment, or they were afraid they'd be harmed by their pimp if they attempted to leave the sex industry and deprived the pimp of his income. Clearly a comprehensive approach is needed to help these women.

Health care, educational, and social services are crucial for their success. Most women also need instruction with basic life skills such as budgeting, nutrition, and parenting. It's important to be familiar with resources that can help with these myriad issues. WomensLaw.org provides a state-by-state listing of resources, and some faith-based organizations also offer practical assistance, job training, and counseling.

Even if a woman is able to successfully navigate these practical challenges, her clinical path involves unusual hurdles. Former sex workers may be uncomfortable in Twelve Step meetings, a key element of recovery, because of the potential awkwardness of interacting with addicts who have used their former services. Other women may be judgmental of sex workers and not welcome them into the fellowship of recovery. Clearly, developing deep relationships with other women is often extremely challenging for female sex workers.

Clinicians who work with sex and love addiction in women need to be aware of this information about sex workers so that they can challenge the fantasies that occur in those who participate in addicted behaviors, including sex with prostitutes or others working in the sex industry or personally offering sex for sale. Addictive or not, engaging in prostitution for many women requires detachment and compartmentalization, which erodes their self-worth and places them at serious risk for injury and disease.

Prostitution is a means to an end in which the means is one of the most intimate of human behaviors and the end is economic survival. For most women, whose social roles are inconsistent with money-sex exchanges, prostitution can lead to social stigmatization, alienation, and despair. Further research is needed to add to the literature and help clinicians understand the prevalence of sex addiction in women who engage in prostitution. At a minimum it's important for clinicians to be mindful of the dynamics of degradation, abuse, addiction, power, control, and desperation that exists for women in the sex trade business.

INTIMATE PARTNER VIOLENCE (IPV)

A painful reality is that women in American culture are victims of violence, which sadly often occurs within their homes by partners and spouses. Intimate Partner Violence (IPV) has costly and serious consequences to society as a whole, including the costs associated within the legal system, medical costs, and lost productivity within work places. Violence against women is a significant social problem with research suggesting that as many as 22% to 29% of women report histories of intimate partner violence, and that IPV remains the leading cause of injuries to women (Tjaden & Thoennes, 2006). The associated costs of IPV exceed $5.8 billion annually (National Center for Injury Prevention and Control, 2003).

In his Proclamation for National Domestic Violence Awareness Month (2011), President Obama stated,

> The ramifications of domestic violence are staggering. Young women are among the most vulnerable, suffering the highest rates of intimate partner violence. Exposure to domestic violence puts our young men and women in danger of long-term physical, psychological, and emotional harm. Children who experience domestic violence are at a higher risk for failure in school, emotional disorders, and substance abuse, and are more likely to perpetuate the cycle of violence themselves later in life. (Obama, 2011)

Clinicians working with FSLAs need to be familiar with IPV issues and how they relate to FSLAs and their partners. Without this understanding, the clinician may not have sufficient knowledge to formulate questions, understand the types of IPV, or appreciate when IPV makes it prohibitive for the FSLA to co-habit with her partner or engage in conjoint therapy. Females struggling with sex and love addiction are possibly at greater risk due to the intensity of eroticized rage within the romantic partnership and the presence of addiction within the couple system. Data from the Women's Sexuality Survey showed that 71% of FSLA survey respondents stayed in a relationship even after abuse, compared to 43% of non-FSLA women who remained in abusive relationships (Corley & Delmonico, 2011).

Typically, women are perceived as the victims of interpersonal violence, and statistics confirm that is more often the case. The occurrence of abuse perpetrated by female partners is controversial and requires additional inquiry especially as it relates to female sex and love addiction (Langhinrichsen-Rohling, 2010). Sometimes the interpersonal violence is bidirectional, which means both partners are perpetuating violence toward each other. Male victims of IPV may need additional supports, as the legal system doesn't always view men as victims of violence perpetrated by women.

Comparing IPV to Process Addictions

Domestic violence, in its cyclic presentation, is a form of pathological violence. Biological research into aggression and violence has found associations with the reward cascade that are also seen in addiction and compulsive behaviors including sexual addiction, compulsive gambling, and eating disorders (Buckholtz, 2010; Coupis, 2008). The reward cascade is recognized as the mood-altering pathway that initially stimulates arousal and pleasure. When this process is corrupted, the brain becomes hijacked (Volkow, 2011). However, for some individuals, the experience of withdrawal requires again accessing the pathway to dampen the pain and discomfort. Accessing this pathway in alternative or interactive approaches results in a type of speedball in which the addicted person combines uppers and downers to manage mood. The addicted individual becomes highly adept at regulating mood through a series of behaviors that occupy an increasingly greater amount of time. Because this becomes an addictive process, he or she is unable to stop despite negative consequences. In this sense, for some individuals, IPV may become an addiction. Further research is needed to support this hypothesis.

Inter-partner violence conforms to what's known about the two-fold nature of the neurobiology of addiction. In the acquisition phase (Wikler, 1961), the addict is motivated by the rush of pleasurable feelings that arise from the activation of dopamine reward centers in the brain (Milkman & Sunderwirth, 2010; Ozelli, 2007). The environment plays a role by becoming associated with the thrill, and the addict can no longer resist the set of conditioned cues that result in the dopamine stimulating behavior. For the alcoholic, this event may be entering a bar; for the FSLA, it may be the presence of the computer and associated pornography access. For the person addicted to IPV, it's the circumstances and antecedent behaviors that flood the nucleus accumbens in the reward center of the brain with dopamine.

For some IPV addicts, the acquisition phase of pleasure seeking may be characterized by behaviors such as bullying, teasing, or unwanted rough housing. The arousal of these activities results in feelings of euphoria, power, and release. The abuse of others becomes a type of conditioned desire, and the IPV addict develops tolerance to the stimuli, which results in the need for greater intensity of IPV. The IPV addict progresses to more abusive behavior to obtain the same pleasure response. The jokes and teasing become crueler. Hitting, pushing, and bullying occur, in addition to rape and other sexually sadistic behaviors. IPV becomes an extreme form of gambling in which the bet is often the IPV addict's life or the life or wellbeing of his or her partner.

In the second phase of addiction, the person is no longer gaining pleasure from the experience but is now focused on the relief of unwanted feelings of despair, inadequacy, anxiety, fear, and shame. The IPV addict is now trapped in a pattern of arousal and activation as a means of quieting the panic that's triggered by the withdrawal of the drug. Similar to the manner that amphetamine addicts start to drink or use benzodiazepines to manage the now intolerable rush, IPV addicts display a type of compulsive attachment. While medicating with the pleasurable high of power and control, the IPV perpetrator is concurrently activating a type of love-addicted downer that's accessed to moderate the intense rush of violence. In traditional domestic violence paradigms, this process is referred to as the honeymoon phase in the abuse cycle (Walker, 2009).

People who perpetrate IPV see nothing but their fear of losing the other, and they're willing to destroy the other in order to always keep him or her. For the victim, feelings of shame contribute to the problem by reinforcing the belief that "I deserve it." The literature about IPV often describes it as a disorder of power and control, which is descriptive of all addictions. The FSLA or her partner will do anything to control the intolerable feelings within.

Classifications of IPV

It's important to recognize that not all IPV is the same. Johnson proposed a classification system for differentiating IPV that ranges from a single event to a chronic pattern in which IPV is triggered by tension and stressors that impact the relationship (Johnson, 2010). Examples include lost employment or when a sex or love addict returns home after acting out and is discovered by the partner. Johnson also identified that one or both partners may act out upon each other. Violent resistance occurs when a partner attempts to fight back for a variety of reasons including defense, revenge, or escape. The movie *The Burning Bed* (Goldenberg & Greenwald, 1984) exemplifies this type of IPV. Less dramatic examples include partners of sex addicts who engage in "payback" behaviors. Although not necessarily physically violent, some partners engage in rageful resistance, which is described as violating the rights of the other and justifying the boundary violations out of revenge and blind anger. Refusing child visitation is a good example of rageful resistance.

As described by Narro and Schwartzberg (2007), revenge may have several functions that range from normative to pathological. Restoration of self-esteem and rearranging a power balance can be a non-pathological defense against feelings of hurt, disappointment, and vulnerability. Small acts of revenge, in which the revenge-seeker feels a renewed sense of power balance without engaging in grossly destructive behavior, can be understood and sometimes applauded. The partners of FSLAs will engage in revenge behaviors such as disclosing the addict's behaviors to friends and family without consulting her, engaging in public humiliation, or holding onto pornography as a means of blackmail. An FSLA's behavior can be revengeful when her sexually addictive behavior has indications of eroticized rage.

Couple and Family Therapy for IPV Systems

It is long recognized that addicted family systems need therapeutic assistance to heal the maladaptive patterns of family dysfunction and trauma. Residential or inpatient treatment programs often offer family week experiences to help educate and encourage therapeutic support for all members of the family. The IPV addicted family system also needs intervention; however, family therapy may be more problematic and difficult for IPV addicted family systems due to the duplicitous social messages about violence and the psychological experiences of shame, betrayal, and perceptions of inadequacy. For the perpetrator, violence serves to shift shame, despair, helplessness, and depression into grandiosity and euphoria, and eventually into a state of numbness. Couples therapy may be contraindicated in romantic relationships with strong markers of IPV. Therapists considering couples therapy with both partners need to evaluate for possible violence and postpone or defer couples sessions until both partners demonstrate the capacity to interact in non-violent ways. Proactive couples contracts in which consequences are clearly stated can assist with boundary setting and accountability.

Families in which IPV occurs are at risk in several ways (Cook, 2005). Children raised in violent families can experience attachment wounds including insecure and disorganized attachment styles (van der Kolk, 1989). Children who experience terrible humiliation learn that violence is a method of distancing themselves from re-experiencing those feelings (Gilligan, 1996). Humiliation and shame lead to belligerence,which manifests by projecting shame on others, which tragically is the seed of violence in children. Violence, when myelinated into early neural circuitry, is fused with the childhood feeling of being a powerless victim,thereby making any threats to the ego a reason to defend against feelings of shame.

Treating Interpersonal Violence

Using an addiction model as a method of treating IPV requires thorough assessment to determine levels and degrees of behaviors that are part of the addiction cycle. Clinicians are encouraged to work initially as if the IPV is "intimate terrorism" until collateral information is obtained and safety demonstrated. Sobriety in every form is essential. IPV addicts must eliminate drugs and other mood altering behaviors (including sports or martial arts that may be healthy in a different context) from their addiction profile. Clear rules and boundaries are needed with high levels of accountability, including legal responsibility.

Group therapy to address addictive behaviors is necessary to challenge chameleon behaviors and "gaslighting," a term taken from the movie *Gaslight* (Hornblower & Cukor, 1944), wherein the male antagonist manipulated the female protagonist's reality to the extent that she doubted her intuition, perception, and reality. Like a chameleon, some people will change their personality presentation to be what they believe the other person wants them to be, and they use this behavior to groom their partners and sometimes their therapists. Gaslighting occurs when an intimate partner repeatedly denies another's reality, leaving the person fragile and unsure of whether his or her perceptions can be trusted. Abused partners begin to question their feelings about what's happened to them, and they become increasingly disconnected with themselves and reality.

It's believed that IPV improves with group therapy compliance. According to Marshall (2010), group therapy can be more effective than individual therapy when working with offenders who exhibit similar behaviors. Individual therapy is also encouraged to explore underlying cognitive distortions, create affect regulation, and eventually address trauma and family of origin issues. Be mindful, however, that research suggests that among some abusive IPV clients, therapy has little effect beyond the impact of legal accountability (Babcock, 2004). It's also concerning that among couples' therapists, only a minority are considering the victim's safety as a factor in their selection of a treatment modality. According to Schacht and colleagues, therapists who work with couples may be under-identifying domestic violence, and they may be using conjoint therapy when it's contraindicated because of relationship violence (Schacht, Dimidjian, George, & Berns, 2009).

Like all recovering persons who must avoid people, places, and things associated with an addiction, FSLAs who are also IPV addicts will need to alter social networks that reinforce misogynistic perspectives. Help the FSLA identify healthy and supportive persons from whom she can get experience, strength, and hope. Referrals to medical professionals are also important since self-care is usually lacking, and the FSLA may have been exposed to diseases that have untoward effects for her and her partners. Medications may be warranted to decrease underlying anxiety and emotional reactivity.

Safety Issues

Another important intervention is to develop a safety plan (Baly, 2010; DeKeseredy, 2008). Safety plans can include identifying alternate safe living arrangements; locating local shelters; placing cash, medications, and other necessary items in a safe and accessible location; and keeping copies of important documents in a safety deposit box or other place so that returning to an abusive situation isn't necessary in order to obtain basic needs. Local police departments are often willing to do what's referred to as "civil standby" while an IPV victim retrieves her possessions from an unsafe environment.

Clinicians must always assess for the risk of violence when discussing disclosure with any FSLA. Keep in mind that disclosures about acting out behaviors and reporting relapses may not be appropriate when either partner has a history of violence (Corley & Schneider, 2012). Risk for violence is increased during disclosure when it's done as an act of malice, when the client or spouse is known to be lying, and when the partner doesn't want disclosure. If there's a history or fear of IPV within the relationship, disclosure is contraindicated. Insist on meeting with the domestic partner first to assess about his or her ability to refrain from violence when hearing difficult, upsetting information. Encourage the partner to be in his or her own therapy before receiving disclosure. If the FSLA client decides she wants to disclose, proceed very cautiously and be certain a comprehensive safety plan is in place. Insist that the disclosure occur in a therapist's office so that reactions can be safely processed and contained. It's valid to use informed consent with both partners to clearly affirm a no-violence contract before a disclosure session. Be aware, too, that the risk for IPV often increases when the abused person attempts to leave the relationship. Studies from a number of countries show that 40-70% of female murder victims were killed by a husband or boyfriend, usually as part of an on-going violent relationship (Hayward, 2000; Karch, Logan, & Patel, 2011; Paulozzi, Saltzman, Thompson, & Homgreen, 2001).

Legal Issues

Clinicians working with FSLAs with IPV issues must also be cognizant of legal issues such as mandated reporting laws. As noted previously, the majority of FSLAs endorse questions indicating that they remain in hurtful relationships. The clinician is encouraged to explore IPV fully since many FSLAs may not recognize their behaviors or their partners' behaviors as abusive. Several states have mandated reporting laws regarding partner abuse (Coulter & Chez, 1997), and therapists must be aware of their state regulations. Warrantless arrest statutes are in effect in all 50 states so that police officers can arrest abusers on probable cause (Zeoli, 2011). Therapists working with FSLAs who are in IPV relationships may need to work collaboratively with police, probation officers, and other members of the legal system. Obtaining releases of information to contact police and other relevant agencies is important with this population. This practice can be especially useful when an FSLA misses an appointment and you have safety concerns. The FSLA who is a parent may have reporting issues when her children are in proximity of abusive behavior (Tufford, 2010). Again, the need for reporting on this issue varies by state.

When the FSLA is the abuser or she facilitates the abuse of her children by not protecting them, then boundaries will need to be clearly articulated. Protection of children and vulnerable dependents is imperative when the FSLA is abusive. Reporting her abuse to appropriate agencies according to state laws is a priority when others are at risk. Informing the FSLA up front about reporting issues is important so that she has informed consent regarding reporting IPV and doesn't feel betrayed by your legal obligations. Facilitating the FSLA in self-reporting her abusive behaviors can be highly therapeutic as an act of taking responsibility. When permitted by law, calling appropriate agencies together can provide an alliance. If you make a joint report, it's critical to document the reporting process, including the name and case number, if available. If it's later asserted that the FSLA failed to take action, your records will be an assurance of her ownership of abusive behaviors and hopeful progress in treatment.

Female Sex and Love Addicts and IPV

Enormous confusion is associated with relationships plagued by IPV. During the honeymoon stage, hope springs eternal, and the victim clings to the encouraging signs of "love." Yet the abuser may quickly flip into violence, and the relationship morphs into a war zone. Hedges observes,

> In the beginning, war looks and feels like love. But unlike love, it gives nothing in return but an ever deepening dependence, like a narcotic, on the road to self-destruction . . . it takes a higher and higher dose to achieve the thrill . . . finally, one ingests war to remain numb. (Hedges, 2002, p. 162)

FSLAs likewise often experience shame, anger, and hostility that resemble a personal war. Female addicts, especially female sex addicts, are not immune from this risk. Further research is needed to answer questions and explore relationships among biogenic, social, and psychological factors associated with IPV. It appears that some IPV may be addictive and a disorder independent of other addictive processes such as chemical addiction. For others, IPV may be part of an interactive compulsive process that may be best described as addictive. For still others, it may not be addictive at all and may be part of a personality or behavioral disorder.

Awareness, discernment, and safety are critical factors for clinicians who work with female sex and love addicts who are also living with interpersonal violence. You must notice the signs and ask the questions that identify IPV as an issue for an FSLA. You need to cautiously assess the risks to all within her family system and perform your clinical due diligence to keep family members, especially vulnerable children, safe. Specific training for treating IPV is essential as this issue greatly complicates clinical work with women who struggle with sex and love addiction.

Writers

Susan Campling - Female Sex Offenders, Female Sex Workers, Inter-Partner Violence
Jill Vermeire - Lesbian SLAs
Robin Cato - collaboration and editing

REFERENCES

Babcock, J. G. (2004). Does batterers' treatment work? A meta-analytic review of domestic violence treatment. *Clinical Psychological Review, 23*(8), 1023-1053.

Baly, A. (2010). Leaving abusive relationships: Construction of self and situation by abused women. *Journal of Interpersonal Violence, 25*(12), 2297-2315.

Buckholtz, J. T. (2010). Mesolimbic dopamine reward system hypersensitivity in individuals with psychopathic traits. *Natural Neuroscience, 13*(4), 419-421.

Carnes, P. (1983). *Out of the shadows: Understanding sexual addiction.* Center City, MN: Hazelden.

Cole, J. (2011, May). Speech presented at the National Strategy Conference on Combating Child Exploitation, San Jose, CA. Retrieved from http://www.justice.gov/iso/opa/dag/speeches/2011/dag-speech-110517.html; see also http://www.justice.gov/criminal/ceos/subjectareas/prostitution.html

Connelly, R. (2011, May 12). The 10 hottest women on the Texas sex offender list. *Houston Press.* Retrieved from http://blog.houstonpress.com/hairballs/2011/05/hot_female_sex_offenders.php

Cook, A. E. (2005, May). Complex trauma in children and adolescents. *Psychiatric Annals*, 390-398.

Corley, M. D., & Delmonico, D. (2011, September). *Closing the gap: Results from Women's Sexuality Survey on Female Sex and Love Addicts.* Presentation at the Society for the Advancement of Sexual Health Conference, LaJolla, CA.

Corley, M. D., & Schneider, J. P. (2012). *Disclosing secrets: An addict's guide to when, to whom, and how much to reveal.* Tucson, AZ: Recovery Resources Press.

Cortoni, F. H. (2010). Recidivism rates of female sexual offenders are low: A meta analysis. *Sex Abuse, 22,* 387-401.

Coulter, M. C. & Chez, R. (1997). Domestic violence and mandatory reporting laws. *Journal of Family Violence, 12*(3), 349-356.

Coupis, M. (2008, Spring). The rewarding effects of aggression is reduced by nucleus accumbens dopamine receptors antagonism in mice. *Psychopharmocology, 197*(3), 449-456.

DeKeseredy, W. S. (2008). *Dangerous exits: Escaping abusive relationships in rural America.* New Brunswick, NJ: Rutgers University Press.

Farley, M. (2004). Bad for the body, bad for the heart: Prostitution harms women even if legalized or decriminalized. *Violence Against Women, 10*(10), 1087-1125.

Farley, M. (2006). Prostitution, trafficking, and cultural amnesia: What we must not know in order to keep the business of sexual exploitation running smoothly. *Yale Journal of Law and Feminism, 18,* 101-136.

Fazel, S., Sjöstedt, G., Grann, M., & Långström, N. (1971). Sexual offending in women and psychiatric disorder: A national case-control study. *Archives of Sexual Behavior, 39*(1), 161-167.

FBI. (2006). *Crime in the United States 2005: Uniform crime reports.* U.S. Department of Justice. Washington, DC: Federal Bureau of Investigation.

Gilligan, J. (1996). *Violence: Our deadly epidemic and its causes.* New York, NY: G.P. Putnam and Sons.

Goldenberg, R. L. (Teleplay), & Greenwald, R. (Director). (1984, October 8). *The burning bed* [Made for TV movie]. United States: National Broadcasting Company.

Hayward, R. F. (2000). Breaking the earthenware jar: Lessons from South Asia to end violence against women and girls. New York, NY: UNICEF.

Hedges, C. (2002). *War is a force that gives us meaning.* New York, NY: First Anchor Books.

Hornblower, Jr., A. (Producer), & Cukor, G. (Director). (1944). *Gaslight* [Motion picture]. United States: Metro-Goldwyn-Mayer.

Ibanez, A. C. (2001). Victims, perpetrators or actors? Gender armed conflict and political USDOJ violence. In C. Sweetman& G. B. Oxfam (Eds.), *Gender, armed conflict and political violence* (pp. 117-140). London, UK: Zed Books.

Jeffreys, S. (2007). Double jeopardy: Women, the US military and the war in Iraq. *Women's Studies International Forum, 300*(1), 16-25.

Jervis, R. (2011, February 1). Child sex rings spike during Super Bowl week. *USA Today.* Retrieved from http://www.usatoday.com/news/nation/2011-01-31-child-prostitution-super-bowl

Johnson, M. F. (2010). Research on domestic violence in the 1990s: Making distinctions. *Journal of Marriage and Family, 62*(4), 948-963.

Karch, D., Logan, J., & Patel, N. (2011, August 26). Surveillance for violent deaths, national violent death reporting system, 16 states, 2008. Washington DC: Center for Disease Control, 60(SS10), 1-54. Retrieved from http://www.cdc.gov/mmwr/preview/mmwrhtml/ss6010a1.htm?s_cid=ss6010a1_e

Kasl, C. (1990). *Women, sex, and addiction: A search for love and power.* New York, NY: Ticknor & Fields.

Kristoff, N. (2012, March 17). Where pimps peddle their goods. *New York Times.* Retrieved from http.//www.nytimes.com/2012/03/18/opinion/Sunday/kristof-where-pimps-peddle-their-goods

Langhinrichsen-Rohling, J. (2010). Controversies involving gender and intimate partner violence: Response to commentaries. *Sex Roles, 62*(3-4), 221-225.

Lawson, L. (2008). Female sex offenders' relationship experiences. *Violence Victimology, 23*(3), 331-343.

Laws.com. (n.d.). *Laws.com.* Retrieved from http://sex-rimes.laws.com/prostitution/prostitution-statistics

Lee, A. (2011, October 10). Officer teaches language of the prostitution industry. *Sun Herald.* Retrieved from http:///.sunhearld.com/2011/.../officer-teaches-language-of-prostitution .html

Lever, J., & Dolnick, D. (2000). Clients and call girls: Seeking sex and intimacy. In R. Weitzer (Ed.), *Sex for sale* (pp. 187-204). New York, NY: Routledge.

Logan, T. L. (2000). Sexual and drug use behaviors among female crack users: A multi site sample. *Drug and Alcohol Dependence, 58*(3), 237-245.

Marshall, W. B. (2010).The importance of group process in offender treatment. *Aggression and Violent Behavior, 15*(2), 141-149.

Mathews, R. M. (1989). *Female sexual offenders: An exploratory study.* Brandon, VT: Safer Society Press.

McClanahan, S. M. (1999). Pathways into prostitution among female jail detainees and mental health services. *Psychiatric Services,50*(12), 1606-1613.

McDaniel, K. (2012). *Ready to heal: Breaking free of addictive relationships* (3rd ed.). Carefree, AZ: Gentle Path Press.

McGee, H. O. (2011, August). Rape and child sex abuse: What beliefs persist about motives, perpetrators and survivors? *Journal of Interpersonal Violence, 26*(17), 3580-3593.

Milkman, H. S., & Sunderwirth, S. G. (2010). *Craving for ecstasy and natural highs: A positive approach to mood alteration.* Thousand Oaks, CA: Sage Press.

Miller, H., Turner, K., & Henderson, C. (2009). Psychopathology of sex offenders: A comparison of males and females using latent profile analysis. *Criminal Justice and Behavior, 36*(8), 778-792.

Narro, L., & Schwartzberg, S. (2007). *Envy, competition and gender.* New York, NY: Rutledge.

National Center for Injury Prevention and Control. (2003). *Costs of intimate partner violence against women in the United States: Centers for Disease Control and Prevention.* Atlanta, GA: Centers for Disease Control and Prevention.

Nelson, S. (2009). *Care and needs: Support of male survivors of child sexual abuse.* Edinburgh, Scotland: University of Edinburgh Center for Research on Family and Relationships.

Ngo, D. (2011, May 11). *Lovebuz.* Retrieved from Your Tango: www.yourtango.com

Obama, B. (2011). National Domestic Violence Awareness Month 2011 by the President of the United States of America. Washington, DC, Federal Registry: Proclamation number 8727 DCPD 201100713

Ozelli, K. (2007, September). This is your brain on food. *Scientific American, 297*,884-885.

Paulozzi, L., Saltzman, L., Thompson, M., & Homgreen, P. (2001, October 12). Surveillance for homicide among intimate partners, United States, 1981–1998. Washington, DC: Centers for Disease Control,50(SS03),1-16. Retrieved from http://www.cdc.gov/mmwr/preview/mmwrhtml/ss5003a1.htm

Pearson, E. (2012, Febuary 17). Disturbing subhuman tricks of sex slavery. *New York Daily News.* Retrieved from ttp://www.nydailynews.com/new-york/sex-slave-story

Romans, S. P. (2001, February). The mental and physical health of female sex workers: A comparative study. *Australian and New Zealand Journal of Psychiatry, 35*(1). 75-80.

Russo, T. (2012, January 6). *Department of Justice: Justice Blog.* Retrieved from An Updated Definition of Rape: www.DOJ.

Sandler, J., & Freman, N. (2009, December). Female sexual offender recidivism: A large scale empirical analysis. *Sex Abuse, 21*(4), 455-473.

Schacht, R., Dimidjian, S., George, W., & Berns, S. (2009). Domestic violence assessment procedures among couple therapists. *Journal of Marital and Family Therapy, 35*(1), 47-59.

Sickmund, M. (2006). Juvenile residential facility census 2002: Selected findings. National report series bulletin. U.S. Department of Justice, NCJ 211080.

Silbet, M. P. (1982). Substance abuse and prostitution. *Journal of Psychoactive Substances, 14*(3), 193-197.

Stemple, L. (2009, February). Male rape and human rights. *Hastings Law Journal, 60*(605), 605-647. Retrieved fromhttp://uchastings.edu/hlj/archive/vol60/Stemple_60-HLJ-605.pdf

Strickland, S. (2008). Female sex offenders: Exploring issues of personality, trauma and cognitive distortions. *Journal of Interpersonal Violence, 23*(4), 474-489.

Tjaden, P. T., & Thoennes, N. (2006). Extent, nature, and consequences of rape victimization: Findings from the National Violence Against Women Survey. U.S. Department of Justice & Center for Disease Control. Retrieved from http://www.ncjrs.gov/app/pubications/abstract.aspx?id=210346.

Tufford, L. M. (2010). Mandating reporting and child abuse exposure to domestic violence: Issues regarding the therapeutic alliance with couples. *Clinical Social Work Journal, 38*(4), 426-434.

UNICEF.org. (n.d.). Retrieved from htt://www.unicef.org/protection/index_exploitation.html

United States Department of Justice. (2003). *Recidivism of sex offenders released from prison in 1994.* Bureau of Justice Statistics, Washington, DC: Office of Justice Programs.

United States Department of Justice. (2007). *Female sex offenders.* Center for Sex Offender Management. Washington, DC: Office of Justice Programs.

United States Department of Justice. (2008, June 25). *3.2 percent of inmates report sexual victimization in local jails.* Bureau of Justice Statistics. Washington, DC: Office of Justice Programs.

van der Kolk, B. (1989). The compulsion to repeat the trauma. *Psychiatric Clinics of North America, 12*(2), 389-411.

Vandiver, D. (2006). Female sex offenders: A comparison of solo and co-offending offenders. *Violence and Victim, 21*(3) 339-354.

Volkow, N. B. (2011). Addiction: Pulling at the neural threads of social behaviors. *Neuron, 69*(4), 599-602.

Walker, L. (2009). *Battered women.* New York, NY: Springer.

Walker-Rodriquez, A., & Hill, R. (2011, March). Human sex trafficking. *FBI Law Enforcement Bulletin*. Washington, DC. Vol. 80, #3.

Weitzer, R. (2006, March-April). Moral crusade against prostitution. *Society*, 33-38.

Wijkman, M. J. (2010). Women don't do such things: Characteristics of female sex offenders. *Sex Abuse, 22*(2), 135-156.

Wikler, A. (1961). On the nature of addiction and habituation. *British Journal of Alcohol and Other Drugs, 57*(2), 73-79.

Wilber, D. Q. (2011, November 13). MS-13 Gang. *Washington Post*. Retrieved from http./ /www.washingtonpost.com/local/ms-13-gang-is-branching-into-prostitution-authories

WomensLaw.org. (n.d.) Retrieved from http://www.womenslaw.org/simple.php?sitemap_id=148

Wormer, V. (2010). *Working with female offenders*. Hoboken, NY: Wiley.

Young, V. (1994). Feminist View. In M. Eliott (Ed.), *Female sexual abuse of children* (pp. 100-115). New York, NY: Guilford Press.

Zeoli, A. (2011). A summary and analysis of warrantless arrest statutes for domestic violence in the United States. *Journal of Interpersonal Violence, 26*(14), 2811-2833.

Zollman, P., Frederick, B., Townsend, J., & Werth, M. (2011, February 24). Crimes and Craigslist: A sad tale of murder and more. AIM Group. Retrieved from http://www.aimgroup.com/files/2011/02/Craigslist-Report.pdf

Part Three

Living in Grace and Integrity

CHAPTER 10

Healthy Relationships

Marnie Ferree, Alexandra Katehakis, Jill Vermeire
with contribution by Deborah Corley

The greatest gift the recovering female SLA can give herself is to reach out to others so that she can have the experience of getting her needs met, feeling she's lovable and worthy, and that others are reliable and will show up for her. She'll also learn that by setting good boundaries in relationship with others, she doesn't have to be sexual to be lovable. She'll experience that she's good enough as she is and that she deserves intimacy and safety in all of her relationships.

Ferree (2010) asserts that sex and love addiction is best conceptualized as an "intimacy disorder," and the best antidote is building healthy relationships. In other words, the only way to practice healthy intimacy is through relationships with self and others. This chapter is dedicated to assisting the FSLA in having the courage to be authentically who she is and in developing genuine relationships. With your guidance, she'll have the experience of coming "home" to loving herself and developing healthy relationships with others, including friends and her family of origin. These processes will ultimately create an integrated self that is the foundation for choosing well when it comes to sharing intimate love with another.

The Most Important Relationship of All

Self-love is the most important love the recovering female sex and love addict can experience. It's a love that can't be taken from her, and as healthy individuals well know, there can be no love of *other* without this foundation. The love of self is a paradoxical conundrum in that it requires self-care in the form of boundaries so that a woman can create or strengthen her belief that she deserves to be cared for. Self-love requires that she knows who she is, exercises her voice, and honors herself by forgiving herself and making amends to those she has wronged.

Defining herself

As the recovering FSLA begins to define herself, start with conversations about what she values and what integrity means to her. Help her to construct statements, if necessary, that illustrate those values. For example, if she values honesty then remind her that she can be honest about her feelings in all of her relationships. This doesn't mean being hurtful to others; instead it means being sensitive to what she really needs while being considerate of the other person. Challenge her to be mindful about whether she is acting out any of her addictive patterns of the past by doing such things as trying to impress by overpaying or paying all the time, care-taking a family member or boss' emotional needs to the exclusion of her own, and so forth. If so, have her identify the unhealthy behaviors and agree to stop them.

Knowing who she is and isn't, what she believes, what she thinks, what she feels, and what she likes and wants means that relationships can develop in a healthy way, and that her needs can be communicated clearly and met.

Finding her voice

Part of the FSLA's recovery is learning to be direct, versus passive aggressive, even if she's afraid that if she speaks her truth, people won't like her. Encourage her to speak up in the moment during therapy sessions, even though she might not get what she wants or fears she might offend you or hurt your feelings. Having the experience of healing such ruptures with you in therapy will give her the internal knowledge that things can work out. Over time, she'll learn that when she's truthful, she may get what she wants or else she can learn to tolerate disappointment in a healthy way. Practicing with you (presumably a healthy person capable of honest dialogue) allows her to expand her experience by being direct in her friendships and other relationships, which is explored later in this chapter.

Forgiving herself

Part of defining herself and developing a healthy self-love is to forgive herself, which for many recovering FSLAs is a difficult task. As outlined throughout this book, many grew up in unhealthy families where they experienced abuse or significant attachment injuries. This foundation builds self-hatred and shame, which are the antitheses of self-love. When combined with the behaviors and destruction of FSLA, a woman carries an enormous burden of guilt that hinders her growth.

Encourage the FSLA to go through a process of grieving her addiction and what it cost her. Forgiveness is costly and the price is feeling the full weight of how she's harmed herself. Help her identify the negative self-talk she entertains. Experiential techniques are particularly well-suited to help her externalize her addiction and separate it from her worth as a person. For example, invite her to envision her addiction as an entity outside of herself such as a mask she's used to hide her pain. Suggest she create a collage or drawing or something else tangible to represent the behaviors she now regrets. Use a Gestalt technique and have her place this representation in a chair and invite her to talk to it. Then ask her to "role reverse" and speak from the place of her addiction. Remind her that it's okay to honor what she did to survive, and that today she has other, healthier options for meeting her needs.

Encourage the FSLA to embrace the spiritual practices that are meaningful to her. Judeo-Christian faith, for example, asserts that we are "fearfully and wonderfully made." Other spiritual traditions have similar beliefs about the inherent worth of the human soul. Both Native American and Buddhist traditions/spirituality hold that everything and everyone in the universe is interconnected and related. Buddhism teaches that an individual inherently has value and worth just by existing, and that internal change (in thoughts and attitude) can create external change. Native American tradition believes that everything is sacred, and that everything has a purpose and can teach a lesson if the person will learn. The Quakers teach there is an Inner Light (an element of God's own Spirit and divine energy) that resides in each person, and thus everyone is inherently valuable and equal. Goddess or Feminine Divine spirituality embraces basic beliefs such as change begins with the self, behaviors serve a purpose and can be let go when no longer needed, and it's important to release unhelpful anger and to forgive self and others. Ask the recovering woman to explore her own spiritual teachings for tenets that affirm her intrinsic value apart from her behavior.

Making amends

Working through the Twelve Steps provides another avenue for forgiving herself, especially as she completes Steps Eight and Nine. In Step Eight she identifies the people she's harmed through her addiction and develops a willingness to make amends to them. Step Nine is the active process of making those amends, when possible. This Step purposely comes after the first eight Steps because it requires the humility, maturity, and community that develop through working the prior Steps. Because of her shame, an FSLA sometimes wants to jump ahead and make amends in an effort to release some of her guilt. It's important to help her wait until she's done the preliminary work first and developed a deeper awareness of how she's harmed others and cultivated more personal integrity.

Making direct amends involves overt contact with someone she's harmed. The contact can be through a face-to-face conversation, a phone conversation, or some form of written expression of amends. Sometimes the FSLA intentionally initiates that contact; at other times she walks through an open door of unexpected opportunity. In either case, the recovering woman humbly takes full responsibility for her part in harming another and ignores any hint of blame. She chooses to focus on herself and her own injurious behaviors and purposely ignores the part the other person played in the situation. Making amends is about cleaning her own "side of the street" no matter how trashy the other side may be.

An FSLA must have appropriate expectations for the encounter when she makes amends. The point is to take responsibility and offer an apology without expectation of receiving forgiveness. The other person's reaction isn't the FSLA's concern; her own actions are her sole focus. She'll need the support of her recovery community to help her if someone refuses to accept her genuine amends or worse, responds with attack. Even in that painful scenario, the FSLA's responsibility is discharged, and most women find their guilt and shame still lift.

An important caveat is the wisdom of the second part of Step Nine that advises avoiding making direct amends when doing so "would injure the person or others." This idea is confusing for many recovering women and seems to provide an easy out that avoids the hard work of taking responsibility and making amends for wrongs. Direct amends is contraindicated if the person owed an amends is unaware of how he or she has been harmed, and learning about the infraction will be damaging or inappropriate. An example is when an FSLA has acted out with a married man. That man's wife would be included in the list of those harmed (Step Eight), and the recovering woman must be willing to make amends if that becomes appropriate. However, it's the straying husband's responsibility to inform his wife of his infidelity, not the FSLA's responsibility as the affair partner. Unless the FSLA is absolutely certain the wife is already aware of the betrayal, the FSLA should not initiate an amends with the wife because to do so would injure her.

Indirect amends is the solution to this kind of situation. Through indirect amends a recovering person makes a gesture that offers symbolic recompense for the wrong. In the example above, the recovering FSLA might volunteer or make a donation to a women's shelter to help other women who are in painful situations. She could coordinate with her counselor to purchase or provide books about addiction and recovery for clients' use. The point is for the FSLA to be specifically aware of how she's harmed others and to consider how she might take some tangible step to right her wrongs. It's also best to only make indirect amends to former acting out partners. While the FSLA has, indeed, likely harmed those she was involved with, it's risky to have direct contact with former addictive cohorts. It's too easy to reconnect in an unhealthy way through what was intended as a positive process. Encourage her to let go of her need to "make things right" with former partners and trust the God of her understanding to share that message.

Living amends is a final category, which means making amends through a vicarious process of simply living life differently. In the prior example the recovering FSLA who acted out with married men would practice living amends by connecting only with available, unmarried partners. She would be active in a Twelve Step S fellowship and support or sponsor other women on the journey of recovery.

Combined with the gift of sobriety and the benefits of living in healthier ways, making amends is a powerful healing force for the recovering woman. Through this process she frees herself from much of the shame she's carried and creates internal space for grace and peace.

Healthy Friendships

Many FSLAs learned through the neglect or trauma they experienced in their families of origin to get their needs met by being seductive and manipulative in relationships with others. Relating to people with sexual energy gave them a false sense of power and control. Since the FSLA's commodity is sexuality, her motives are often to control the outcome of a situation for self-gratification, whether it's with a boss, someone behind a checkout counter, or a lover.

As a recovering person, the FSLA must learn additional ways to relate to people. Normal dealings with friends help the recovering woman practice interacting with integrity instead of manipulation or sexualization. Her self-valuation rises as she presents her authentic self and sees herself as more than just a sex object. Without her obsessive, fear-based focus on being accepted by others, she learns her own likes and dislikes, her opinions, values, and dreams. As her view of herself blossoms, she can tolerate compliments by simply saying, "thank you" instead of responding with self-deprecation. Over time, healthy friendships assist a woman in opening her heart to the normal ebb and flow of relationships.

Developing healthy friendships, though, is much easier said than done for the recovering woman. In active sex and love addiction, most women don't form relationships with other women unless they're in service to her addiction. Heterosexual women will often say they prefer male friends because they're not catty like females or because males are more trustworthy. Female SLAs often have ex-lovers as "friends," which can serve the purpose of continuing to operate out of power and control instead of true intimacy. The FSLA will know exactly how to seduce and manipulate these partners into getting what she wants and needs, which allows her to be in control of her friendships. A general principle of FSLA recovery is that it's unwise to maintain a friendship with a former acting out partner. In fact, many recovering people and clinicians who treat them view these lingering relationships as a breach of sobriety. At the very least this kind of friendship is usually a violation of the FSLA's primary relationship if she has one. If she only wants to have friendships with the opposite sex, former partners, or potential sex partners, it's time to challenge her to rethink her friendships.

A big step toward intimacy is making friends (of the opposite gender if the FSLA is heterosexual or the same gender if she's lesbian) without sexualizing them or having sex with them. Encourage the recovering woman to have open and honest conversations with friends about how she feels and what she enjoys about their company. This practice will help her become more assertive and authentic. Remind her to listen to how her friends respond even though they may say things she doesn't want to hear. Having explicit conversations about the boundaries and expectations of both parties is vital to her friendships' success.

Help the FSLA understand that it's okay to expect mutuality from friends. It's even okay to get into arguments if she's unhappy or has a misunderstanding. Remind her to stand up for herself and learn to repair misunderstandings in safe and constructive ways. The goal for healthy relationships is to stay out of isolation so that she has people who will genuinely be there for her.

The power of female friendships

Taylor (2002) reveals some age-old mysteries of women and how we're biologically wired for relationships. It turns out that women have a biological imperative, encoded in our DNA, for community with other females. Not only is this true in the United States, but studies show that women's desire to connect with one another crosses cultures and even shows up in the animal kingdom. Taylor uses research from many fields to make a case for why women are more community focused, less competitive, more collaborative and social, and more in need of girlfriends.

Stress causes human beings to fight, flee, or seek comfort from affiliation depending on the circumstances. Under extreme duress, the organism will engage the fight or flight response, which is likely how most FSLAs learned to manage early stressors in their families. However under normal, everyday stress, most women will seek affiliation. Taylor uses the metaphor of "tend and befriend" (2006, p. 273), which describes our natural instincts to tend to our young and be with our friends. In other words, women naturally turn toward their friends for comfort and support.

For years we've known that married men live longer than single men. But, women who aren't married but have female friends and family members live longer than their male counterparts. Studies show that when women are with girlfriends, their bodies release oxytocin, the attachment hormone, which relieves everyday stress (Taylor et al., 2000). While in her addiction, the typical FSLA didn't prioritize her relationships with girlfriends, but instead, substituted intrigue and sex with men for stress relief. Spending time with girlfriends is the easiest, most cost effective way of reducing everyday stress, but it takes time and effort to make healthy girlfriends.

Another remarkable benefit of women spending time with women is the effect women have on each other's self-esteem. Women in recovery state that their female friends make them feel pretty and good about themselves, whereas in their addiction, those same women report that males made them feel sexy but often left them feeling dirty or bad about themselves.

For example, when Emily came into treatment she didn't have any female friends. One of her destructive patterns was to have sex with her girlfriends' boyfriends and then turn the former lovers into "friends." Emily had a slew of ex-lovers around and a lot of angry ex-girlfriends, and therefore she received no real nurturing from women. It took her a while to develop trust with women given her betrayal by her mother when she was a teen. Emily was an athlete, and devoted to gymnastics from the time she was a very young child. Her father abandoned Emily and her mother when she was five years old; her male coach became her surrogate father and she trusted him implicitly. Over time, her mother began to travel with the gymnastic team and when she was 14 years old, Emily discovered that her mother was having an affair with her coach days before she shattered her wrist, and therefore, her gymnastic dreams. This perfect storm devastated her and fueled her insatiable need to be loved and desired by males, while simultaneously creating a gross anger and mistrust of women. Thus began her sex and love addiction and her inability to trust women to take care of her. Making and keeping female friends in recovery was a monumental task for Emily and a pivotal point in her recovery.

It turns out that female friendships are hard to make and hard to keep for all women, not just women in recovery. A survey from Duke University (McPherson, Smith-Lovin, & Brashears, 2006) showed a sharp decline in friendships in our nation. This finding points to an increasingly isolated culture where we don't have others to rely on during tough times like natural disasters, relationship changes, losses of health, or financial difficulties. Without communities of women, very little will get accomplished in our towns and cities, and women need other women in order to flourish. Where would we be without a hug or a friendly smile from another woman on any given day? The FSLA needs to be reminded what being a good girlfriend means, and she'll have to practice how to incorporate this important part of her changing life.

Failure to develop same-sex friends can be a trap for FSLAs in recovery and a way to avoid dealing with intimacy issues. Learning to trust women, asking them for nurturing, and relying on them for support can be difficult but ultimately healing for FSLAs.

The value of male friendships

The heterosexual FSLA may wonder if she can ever befriend males again, and the answer is *yes*, but it won't be easy. Challenges will arise, so clear intentions and boundaries must be stated and adhered to. Making good choices will likely take her a long time. O'Meara (1989) offers a helpful guide through his landmark study on the top hurdles to opposite sex friendship. Pay attention to the following challenges when your client begins to tell you about a new male friend she's met.

For starters, help her to *define the relationship* as a friendship. Platonic relationships can be difficult to discern because we develop feelings for those we care about. Since the FSLA has a history of sexualizing or fantasizing about males, she may not be able to make the distinction between friendship and romance, and she'll have to seek advice from you. Pay attention to why she thinks this man would make a good friend and whether or not she's sexually attracted to him.

Sexual attraction is the next hurdle in opposite sex relationships. Studies show that men choose female friends based on attraction, while women struggle with the sexual tension that can invade a platonic relationship (Chatterjee, 2001). Your client has to be in reality about the males she chooses for friends. What are their intentions and hers? Why choose the friendship? How much affection is appropriate and at what stage of the relationship is a simple hug upon saying "hello" or "goodbye" okay?

She'll also have to manage the *power differential* that is inherent in male/female friendships. O'Meara (1989) found that even though we live in a world that aspires to equality between the sexes, males still dominate, and females have a tendency to take a submissive role no matter how equal their education or financial status. The FSLA has to be mindful of her patterns and how she's taken a submissive position as a form of seduction in the past. Query her about the power differentials in the relationship. Is he older, financially more solvent, extremely handsome, or does he have a higher level of education? If so, how does that make her feel? Where are the points of bona fide equality between them, and how will she negotiate differences without putting herself in a one-down position and thereby denigrating her self-esteem?

The next challenge comes from the *cultural pressure*. Many times older people or friends will make innuendo about an opposite sex friendship and insinuate that there must be something else going on or suggest that something else should be going on since they're "such great friends." If the FSLA is considering romantic involvement with her friend, make sure she processes her intentions with you and her sponsor first so as not to ruin the relationship. That said, sometimes the most successful love relationships evolve out of a long-term friendship.

Finally, pay close attention to the *meeting places* where the recovering SLA chooses her male friends. Does she meet them in "the program," at a recovery convention, or in a bar? Is she mingling alcohol with socializing and choosing friends while under the influence, or does she choose male friends she meets while giving community service, at work-related gatherings, or through her spiritual community?

Challenges for Healthy Female/Male Friendships

1. Define the relationship
2. Pay attention to sexual attraction
3. Mind the power differential
4. Stay aware of cultural pressure
5. Choose sober meeting places

Chatterjee, 2001

Boundaries in relationships

The first introduction to boundaries the female SLA will experience is in creating her sobriety plan (see chapter 6 for details). This plan helps her keep straight the sexually destructive behaviors she chooses to abstain from (bottom lines), the behaviors that could trigger her to want to act out on her bottom lines (middle lines), and the behaviors she wants to engage in that are life affirming and esteem building, known as top lines. Over time, however, she'll need assistance in understanding all sorts of boundaries. Teaching the female SLA to set clear emotional, psychological, and physical boundaries is essential to insure that she protects more than her recovery progress. Boundaries are necessary in order to feel separate from other people and to get her needs met in healthy ways. The language of boundaries can initially feel stilted or awkward, but over time, she'll experience the benefits—one of which is integrity.

Healthy boundaries will help her know who she is and help her maintain a sense of reality. If boundaries define who we are, then remind your client that she'll need to decide what she's going to do in a variety of social situations. One of the important choices she must consider is what she'll do in an environment where alcohol is present. Alcohol and recreational drug use will quickly derail her sobriety because of their disinhibiting properties. Have her talk about holidays and social events and her plan for navigating them long before the event. Who else does she need to check with? Does she need to "book-end" the event, meaning does she need to call someone in the program before she arrives at the event and again upon leaving? These types of boundaries will assist her in defining who she is in relationship to other people in her life and protect her from doing things that will harm her.

Continue to monitor her reports of how she interacts with others by paying attention to how she uses her sense of humor and whether it's appropriate. Remind her to talk about interests and hobbies or things that make her feel good about herself, especially when interacting with new people. You can also have the recovering FSLA create a collage of her boundaries in order to visualize what her ideal self and relationships would look like. Encourage her to pay attention to who she is becoming and what her vision is for how she'll develop healthy relationships over time.

Good emotional boundaries remove walls of defensiveness so that the recovering FSLA is free to explore and be who she really is. This type of exploration will allow her to have the experience of being vulnerable and will enable her to be more accepting of others who are different from her. Healthy boundaries build upon themselves. When the FSLA defines what she really needs for herself and from others, she can then ask to have her needs met and be able to meet others' needs. That process will empower her to have intimacy in her relationships and bring a new kind of order into her life. Gone is the chaos and uncertainty; she'll have a good sense of how she'll be treated by others and know how she will treat others. Setting boundaries and living by them requires self-discipline and maturity. No longer will she allow herself to be manipulated by others, nor shirk responsibility or accountability in her own life. She will be an adult woman, living in integrity and with dignity.

Close, loving friendships create a personal support network that are crucial to your client's well being over time. Ferree (2010) emphasizes that no one can recover alone. She asserts that we're made for relationship and need healthy relationships in order to thrive. Moral support and accountability experienced in a healthy relationship will open a woman's heart and keep stress at bay. Contemplative practices like meditation, prayer, and deep breathing are skills that will help her put distress to rest. As she learns to focus on the present and to depend on herself to make good choices, she'll feel stronger, more confident, and more open to connections with herself and others.

Relationships with a Supportive Community

One of the benefits to recovery from sex and love addiction is that women who participate in Twelve Step programs can end up with life-long friendships. For many, it takes an addiction to awaken them to the reality that they can't handle life alone. Participating in Twelve Step meetings creates opportunities to make friends of the same gender. Sitting in meetings day after day, week after week, and hearing one another's stories is a bonding experience and a reminder that a hug, a friendly smile, or a simple acknowledgment of another is a moment of intimacy and healing. The fellowship encourages "program calls," meaning that an FSLA reaches out to other women when she's scared, lonely, or thinking about contacting a former acting out partner. This simple act of calling a woman when in need and expecting to get her needs met is a new and essential ingredient to the FSLA's recovery. She may struggle with this practice initially because she was either emotionally abandoned or enmeshed by her mother and doesn't trust women. As she has more and more positive experiences, she'll eventually come to rely on her female friends in the program. Encourage her to go to coffee before or after a meeting, to invite women to her home for Step work, or to arrange a girls' movie night. Soon she'll come to see that whether she's struggling with her difficulties or has something to celebrate (like 90 days of sobriety in the program) she'll want to share with a friend.

Since she won't be that skilled at recognizing healthy women, remind her to seek out women who have good recovery in the program and women who, when they share, engender an experience of hope for her own future. Women who appear stable, happy, content with themselves or in committed relationships, and who have time in the program are good choices. A recovering FSLA should also pay attention to how she's responded to. Do the people she reaches out to return her calls in a timely fashion? Are they keeping commitments to meet her and do they arrive on time? This is a chance for her to practice healthy boundaries and have the experience of expecting people to do what they say they're going to do and choosing not to be in relationship with people who don't.

This goal is where group therapy can also be a very helpful practice ground for a recovering woman. Group is a safe place for the FSLA to clearly state her needs, express her fears and concerns, and share her victories. Here she can learn how powerful it is to give voice to her truth and to learn to take constructive criticism so she can grow and change. Don't be afraid to have her grapple with having to hear difficult things about herself in service of continuously breaking through her denial mechanisms. Critical thinking and self-reflexivity are necessary components for integration and becoming a more authentic woman.

Healthy Dating Relationships

As difficult as it is for most women recovering from sex and love addiction, the best practice is to wait until after at least 12 months of solid sobriety before starting to date. Remind your client that she's been impaired with an attachment-based intimacy disorder, and she needs time to heal before again delving into the world of potentially romantic relationships. She needs an extended period of time practicing healthy relationships with women and friends in recovery circles before she joins the dating platforms. Eventually, though, a point comes in the treatment process for the single recovering FSLA to address dating. One of the common sayings in the Twelve Step communities is, "The best way to see your character defects is to get into a relationship!" A sense of humor can be helpful, as dating usually has a lot of missteps and blunders. Setting realistic goals and having a positive, healthy attitude will be fundamental for the FSLA in this stage of her process.

When a clinician is starting to dialogue with a client ready to embark on dating, it's helpful to review the key elements of intimacy, which include vulnerability, boundaries, self-esteem, moderation, and the concept of "progress not perfection." Pay special attention to any areas the FSLA has struggled with in the past. For example, if she normally falls "head over heels" for someone and becomes consumed with a potential partner, she'll have to work and use her recovery tools to maintain balance. If she's never practiced having sexual boundaries, then she can expect some anxiety and confusion when she's actually setting boundaries with another human being.

It's also important to emphasize the word *dating*. At first this concept can cause confusion because the FSLA probably associates dating with sex and/or commitment. The dichotomous thinking of the addict will automatically assume *dating* means *relationship*. Although it's a matter of semantics, these are very important distinctions to make. The clinician needs to illuminate the value in going on actual dates that have a starting point and stopping point, which is new territory for most recovering women.

Talking about dating as a recovering FSLA and actually *doing* it are two different things. It might be helpful to role-play possible scenarios that might arise. Role-playing lets the FSLA find and practice specific words and sentences she can use in the moment and lessens the fear of implementing them when the time actually comes. Help her stay attuned to her bodily based feelings and trust her intuition, which keeps her empowered and focused on recovery.

The client should work with you on designing the kind of relationship she wants to develop. Many recovering FSLAs find it very helpful to create "The Lists," which are informal inventories or registers developed anecdotally among recovering people to catalogue a variety of things. In terms of healthy dating, helpful lists should include the "deal breakers" and the "wish" list. Deal breakers are those traits or characteristics that would cause a recovering FSLA to run away if they show up anytime in the dating process. A wish list is a registry of things the client knows for sure she must have in her partner. There are many varieties on this concept. For example, Katehakis (2010) outlines a Personal Inventory that uses what she calls the Green Light, Yellow Light, Red Light system. She asserts that a healthy process for choosing a dating partner and exploring a relationship is something many FSLAs have ignored in their active addiction. Katehakis' two-point Recovery Dating Plan describes a suitable or unsuitable partner and details an appropriate timeline for healthy dating behavior.

The first section of the Recovery Dating Plan, called a Personal Inventory, has to do with the FSLA:

- Green represents your client's ideal qualities.
- Yellow represents warning signs that she's being triggered in old ways or in her middle circle behaviors.
- Red represents her deal-breakers or ways she may be acting out.

Personal Inventory

GREEN (Ideal qualities)	YELLOW (Warning signs)	RED (Deal-breakers)
• I genuinely look forward to seeing the person. • I tell the truth. • I take an active interest and ask questions to get to know them. • I compliment from a solid place in myself, not out of need. • I say "good night" in an appropriate way that feels good for me.	• I overspend to impress my date. • I obsess about what was said and examine every nuance. • I find myself trying to "fix" the other person or their problems. • I value the other's opinion or time more than my own. • I fantasize about our future together. • I rationalize not getting my needs met.	• I miss work or meetings to be with the person. • I lie about myself. • I lie by omission. • I become more isolated and my social circle is diminishing. • I rationalize a lot of middle-circle activity. • I find I'm not that interested in the person but go out anyway because I don't have any other prospects. • I have sex because I haven't in a long time.

Source: Reprinted with permission from *Erotic Intelligence: Igniting Hot, Healthy Sex While in Recovery from Sex Addiction* by Alexandra Katehakis (Deerfield Beach: HCI Publications) Table 6.1, p. 123.

Figure 15

No matter which terminology or system is used, it's important for the client to have a clear list that includes deal breakers and red flags, the absolute "must haves," and a third section that includes things she'd like to have and things that are possible flags but need further investigation. The therapist's role is to help the client have a realistic mindset that avoids fantasy or unrealistic ideas and to serve as an accountability checkpoint.

Dating plan

Before the FSLA actually begins having dates she should have a solid dating plan in place. Addicts don't do well without structure. A dating plan acts as a compass to keep the FSLA pointed in the right direction—the direction of recovery. She'll need reminders about the woman of grace and integrity she is becoming. The dating plan is basically her rules or boundaries she's setting for herself with the guidance of her therapist. Looking back on her past dating disasters, the clinician and client work together to construct the dating plan from what they know hasn't worked in the past and the behaviors that have contributed to her addiction. This process relies on the therapist acting as a healthy role model and the client learning to re-parent herself. It's a co-creative process with the therapist guiding the way.

There are a variety of things to consider when helping the client make her dating plan. Evaluate matters such as her age, phase of life, dating goals, ability to share intimately at an appropriate pace, and a general dating timeline. As a guideline the first date should be focused on general commonalities and discovering if there's enough resonance between the two people for a second date. Second and third dates *can* be appropriate for sharing general recovery information, perhaps limiting it to revealing she's *in* recovery and that it's an important part of her life. By the fourth, fifth, or sixth date important information about sexual matters such as birth control and STDs could be revealed.

Why? If a sixth date has occurred it should mean these two people are really beginning to know and like each other. If things continue to go well, the relationship could naturally lead to more physical contact, depending on what boundaries the FSLA and you have discussed. A woman in recovery conducts herself with integrity and honesty, and she can't move into a sexual relationship without disclosing important health information to her partner. By having the courage to share this information up front rather than in-the-moment as an "*Oops, by the way . . .*" the FSLA will know where her partner stands on the issue and whether or not the relationship can continue to grow or if it needs to end. There's never a good time to have that kind of discussion, but having it is mandatory. (See the section Disclosing in a New Love Relationship.)

By the time a client has been going on multiple dates consistently with a specific person, things such as lifestyle, education, sense of humor, religious/spiritual beliefs, values, future dreams and goals (including having children or not), and more specifics about addiction and recovery will most likely be out in the open. If these topics haven't been shared in the relationship, explore why. Again, many FSLAs find it much easier to be sexual with a partner than to be emotionally vulnerable. Remind your client to position "first things first" (a recovery slogan) and to share *herself* with someone before sharing her body. Any other important information, such as something that would affect the partner's health or right to informed consent, needs to be shared before the couple decides to move into a committed relationship.

A woman and her dating partner need to specifically consider various activities in their relationship. How often will they go on dates? What about other contact like texts, phone calls, and emails? Although texting and other electronic methods are now standard ways of communicating, they can easily create a false sense of intimacy. Advise the FSLA to be aware of the limitations of these methods, and suggest she restricts their use to routine matters. This practice forces her to come out from behind the seductive wall of anonymity, and be relational, instead. This boundary also supports the FSLA in having a relationship with a person rather than with an electronic conduit. Remind the FSLA that in-person interactions are best for building intimacy.

Expect the clever addict to find loopholes in the dating plan. Newly recovering addicts released into the dating world can be very much like teenagers who need to test boundaries. This is why the dating plan is subject to revision at the discretion of the therapist. Just as a thorough history of the client's past and acting out behaviors was a necessary part of initial treatment, details of her dates are important now. You'll need to get a clear picture of the dates from beginning to end . . . down to where the dating partners slept. Sometimes a client might omit the part where they fell asleep at her date's house. It's your role to process this behavior with the client and bring attention to any contradictions, old patterns, or possible self-sabotaging behaviors she's presenting.

Following is Katehakis' (2010) chart detailing a healthy dating timeline as the second part of a Recovery Dating Plan.

Dating Timeline

Dates 1-4 (1st month)	**Dates 5-8 (2 months)**	**Dates 9-15 (3 months)**
• Talk on phone or computer 1-2x/week max • No text messages • Dating others • No serious talk about your history or past relationships • Hug, kiss on cheek • Both take cars, meet there • Spending <$100 on a date	• "Light" petting, above the waist (hands), outside clothes • French kissing • Talking on phone or computer <2x/week • Text messages used sparingly, if at all • Seeing each other's house/home • Physically affectionate • Spending > $100 on a date	• Discontinue dating others before having intercourse discussion • Disclosure about sexual history and addiction (before intercourse!) • Discussion about STDs and birth control • Intercourse with condom only • Oral sex • Sleep over at each other's house • Short vacations (i.e., weekends away)

Source: Reprinted with permission from *Erotic Intelligence: Igniting Hot, Healthy Sex While in Recovery from Sex Addiction* by Alexandra Katehakis (Deerfield Beach: HCI Publications) Table 6.3, p. 126

Figure 16

Disclosing in a new love relationship

When an FSLA begins a new relationship, she wants to know if or when she should tell the new person in her life about her addiction. It's a tricky situation. She might want to wait to tell until she's sure this is a serious relationship, but she also fears that waiting can be viewed by the potential partner as being dishonest or untrustworthy. Suggest that she "test-the-water" by mentioning that she attends Twelve Step meetings or that she works a program of recovery as a way to open the door for further discussion down the road. Although most people are fairly accepting of recovery from alcohol or drug addiction, attending Al-Anon for family situations, or dealing with food or weight challenges, dating partners are less likely to respond positively to sex addiction.

Have the FSLA practice talking about issues related to her value that committed relationships start with best friendships, and best friends have enough trust in each other to tell the truth and not keep secrets. Preparing a disclosure letter will help her formulate her thoughts about what to say. A letter might offer general information about her addiction and the types of acting out she once engaged in, her willingness to answer other questions, and what she does on a regular basis that helps her stay sober. She can also include what expectations she has of the new partner or boundaries she needs if they become serious. Examples include matters such as her recovery is her first priority, that she desires monogamy, that she intends to use condoms or safer sex practices for a period of time, that she won't use recreational drugs and desires a partner who follows the same practice, that she favors responsible and limited use of alcohol, and so forth. She should also determine what information she wants to keep private at this juncture and possible consequences for this boundary. Planning for possible rejection from the dating partner is useful as a relapse prevention step.

If a recovering FSLA is uncomfortable disclosing her addictive history to a dating partner, you and she can discuss her reluctance and what circumstances might make her more open to disclosure. For example, she may share that she needs her partner *not* to inquire about her past and instead allow her to reveal herself as she feels comfortable. The partner may decide he or she needs to know more information, in which case, ideally, the couple agrees that questions about prior history are addressed within the safety of couples counseling. These are delicate and difficult issues, yet navigating them successfully bodes well for the health of the relationship—or provides the recovering FSLA important information about whether she wants to pursue the relationship.

Keep in mind these issues could be valuable to address within non-romantic relationships as well. Disclosure isn't limited to a committed romantic relationship. The FSLA has most likely impacted other relationships in her life, and it's important to examine each one to discover if a disclosure and boundary discussion is necessary.

Healthy Committed Partnership

An FSLA may come to treatment already in a committed partnership, just having ended one (possibly as a consequence of her acting out), or having difficulty finding and/or maintaining partnership. Committed partnership may not be the goal for the client depending on her values, beliefs, and the status of her current life situation. On the other hand, commitment or marriage may have been the sole focus of her entire existence. Regardless of her situation, committed partnership will likely be a subject discussed in the treatment setting.

As a reminder, if the FSLA is newly in recovery, it's best to wait at least a year or two before starting a dating relationship. The task at hand is learning first to be friends with herself and others. When the time is right, remind the recovering woman that finding, entering, or maintaining a committed partnership presents unique opportunities for anyone, addict or not. For the FSLA, commitment can be either a main goal or her biggest fear. Mindfulness and ongoing dialogue around her past experiences, trauma, triggers, and recovery will be necessary. As the treating clinician you play a large part in supporting the FSLA as she navigates the often confusing but rewarding path toward partnership, intimacy, and commitment.

It's possible the FSLA has never experienced a committed partnership. She may have some fears or negative beliefs about what a partnership means, whether she deserves love, or her ability to create and sustain healthy intimacy. She might want to avoid the idea altogether, and mistakes isolation for healthy living. All of these issues are clinically relevant and should be processed in therapy. The better her support system, the stronger her foundation in recovery, and her amount of clarity regarding her vision for her future will all support her transition into a committed partnership when the time comes. You'll have ample opportunity to support, guide, reframe, and redirect the client as she explores commitment and what role it will play in her life.

A good exercise would be to discuss some "predictions" or "anticipations" about what she might do or how she may react in the presence of commitment. Based on her past history (if you're aware of her former patterns) it could be predicted that some clients in a committed relationship may feel instantly suffocated and want to push away. This reaction will provide an opportunity to look at the characteristics of healthy intimacy and determine whether the recovering FSLA is reacting to real intimacy, or if, in fact, she's in an enmeshed situation that requires more boundaries and communication.

Some clients have a history of entering a committed relationship and collapsing into it, neglecting anything outside of the relationship. This is a potential slip into old love addict behavior and can be remedied with some accountability and focus on maintaining hobbies, commitments, and relationships outside of the partnership. Learning how to be balanced and moderate within a committed partnership will take time and accountability for the FSLA to explore this territory from a recovery standpoint.

Not losing herself in a love relationship is quite challenging, especially if she identifies as a love addict. Standing on her own two feet in relationship to another requires the important process of learning differentiation. In other words, maintaining her sense of self while attaching to another in a healthy way requires a balance between her individuality and unhealthy dependence on validation from another. Tolerating the natural transitions from closeness to distance without being threatened or terrified she'll be abandoned is a new skill the recovering woman has to hone. Living with the natural tension and anxiety that accompanies loving is an adult developmental task, and at this stage of her recovery, she's ready for it. The work she's done in the program and the habits she's developed, like making program calls while under duress and calling her sponsor when she needs comfort and soothing, will help her regulate during difficult times in her relationship. Recovery and healthy dependency demands self-confrontation. When the recovering FSLA is clear that she is responsible for her happiness, then she'll stay vigilant about repairing old disconnecting patterns that leave her feeling alone and lonely.

Benefits of a committed partnership

Human beings are wired for attachment and connection, both of which fuel our life force. The power of touch, love, and laughter can't be underestimated, which is why the FSLA has sought these missing experiences through her misguided foray into sex and love addiction. She was "looking for love in all the wrong places" and hurting, instead of healing herself along the way.

Luckily, our brains are rewiring themselves daily, and there's nothing like a healthy love relationship to speed up that process. Brain circuitry that shapes memories, experiences, and the self are in a constant change process, especially when we're involved in an intimate relationship. The infant bonds with her mother in ways that she remembers, ultimately, in her neural circuitry and body. This feeling state is set, like a compass guiding us forward as we seek a mate with whom to spend our lives (Ackerman, 2002).

We now know that long-term relationships predict good health and happiness over the life span. We also realize that a loving relationship is the most challenging experience we can have because it forces us to grow. When the FSLA falls in love (sometimes for the first time), she exposes herself to a myriad of new experiences that range from tasting new foods to dealing with old emotional patterns, to travelling to new places and making new friends and family members. All of these experiences, whether easy or difficult, serve to rewire her brain in new and robust ways that contribute to an earned secure attachment.

Attaching in a committed partnership changes the immune system, too, and the partners' bio-rhythms literally sync up when they sleep. At the same time, loving another person can be painful where there's discord or upset. The pain centers in the brain are activated by social rejection, which is why an argument can feel physically painful to lovers (Eisenberger, 2012). However, unlike new lovers who feel threatened during an argument, people who love over time have less activation in the fear centers of their brains, and instead have activation in the calm centers of the brain (Acevedo, Aron, Fisher, & Brown, 2012). In other words, those who enjoy a positive, long-term partnership are securely attached enough that their brains literally have a calming reaction to conflict, as if to reassure them, "Hey, we'll figure this out. It's okay."

One of the final goals of recovery from sex and love addiction is helping your client find a love that's restorative, healing, and challenging in productive ways so that she can begin to reach her full potential as a woman and as a human being. Although relationships aren't the "be all, end all," when healthy, they do facilitate change and increase our capacity for intimacy and for loving more deeply.

Relationship With Family of Origin

After developing a relationship with a partner who was harmed by the FSLA's behavior, one of her most difficult challenges is developing a healthy relationship with her family of origin. From an attachment perspective, family members were her primary and probably deepest source of wounding, and navigating a different kind of relationship with them is usually complicated and painful. Disengaging from an enmeshed family system, connecting within a distant family system, and setting boundaries in a boundary-less system all present significant challenges. This lengthy process requires maturity, perseverance, and strong support. At this stage of her healing, a recovering woman will greatly benefit from participating in a Twelve Step group such as Codependents Anonymous, Al-Anon, Adult Children of Alcoholics, S-Anon or Co-SA. These programs help her focus on herself in relationship with less-than-healthy people and offer specific strategies for "detaching with love." Encourage her to broaden her healing by intentionally working a program that focuses on the significant others in her life.

As McDaniel explains (2012), there's a fine, often blurry line between sex and love addiction and co-sex and love addiction in women. Especially with regard to family of origin, recovering addicts also possess many codependent traits. FSLAs are familiar with the dances of avoidance, anger, enabling, placating, denying, distancing, and the myriad others that make up her rhythm with her family. As the recovering woman explores her current patterns with her family through therapy and a Twelve Step fellowship for codependents, she'll discover new insights and choices for revamping these relationships.

Forgiving those who hurt her

Forgiveness is the FSLA's first step in forming a healthy relationship with her family. This idea may be confusing for her and even distasteful. Help her explore the truths about forgiveness—what it means, what it involves, and what it *isn't*. Often the best place to start is to address typical misconceptions about forgiveness.

Forgiveness doesn't mean the client glosses over the wounds she's experienced. She doesn't give the perpetrators a pass or let them off the hook. It doesn't mean the ones who've harmed her have acknowledged their wrongs, asked for forgiveness, or deserve forgiveness. It doesn't mean there's necessarily a restoration of the relationship. And it doesn't mean the perpetrators aren't held accountable for their actions.

Rather, forgiveness is solely for the benefit of the recovering woman. It's a gift she gives herself. Forgiveness doesn't depend on anyone or anything other than her own desire for deeper healing. Choosing to forgive moves the client from a victim to a survivor. She's no longer shackled by the painful chains of her past; she's free to embrace her identity as a woman of grace and integrity. Forgiveness is a process of valuing herself first, exercising her voice, and making the choices that empower her transformation process.

Forgiveness requires the FSLA to examine the ways she was harmed and grieve them fully. She must forgive with her eyes wide open instead of shaded with denial or minimization. Many of the processes and techniques described in chapter 7 for healing from trauma are effective in this grieving process. In fact, one of the benefits of addressing her trauma and attachment injuries is that as the FSLA understands these issues, she often develops compassion for her parents and others in her family of origin. She may come to understand how they, too, were wounded, and she is better able to see their hurtful behavior as their forms of unhealthy coping for their own wounds. This process potentially forms a healing circle of grace as the FSLA's understanding and forgiveness of self leads to an understanding and forgiveness of others.

Eventually, the client makes a conscious choice to forgive. This decision is formed by her will more than by her emotions. She doesn't have to be free from the pain or the scars of her wounds to choose to forgive. She simply has to be willing to make the paradigm shift to embrace life and healing rather than focusing her energy on her hurts. She chooses to relinquish her need for retribution to her Higher Power.

Forgiveness is a specific process about individuals, not a global step that lumps together all who've wounded her. The FSLA was wounded by specific people and specific instances, therefore, forgiveness requires equally specific intention. When she's ready, encourage her to take a specific step to symbolize her letting go of her bitterness and desire for revenge. Gestalt or experiential techniques are helpful as she releases the power she's given to those who have hurt her. If those who have wounded her are no longer alive, these symbolic practices are very helpful to cut the ties that capture her from beyond the grave.

Forgiveness, like surrender, is also an on-going, repetitive process. Just because the FSLA has forgiven someone once doesn't mean she won't have to revisit the pain she experienced at that person's hands. At different stages of her life and journey she'll likely have to choose to forgive again. It isn't necessary for her to specifically share her choice with those who have hurt her. In fact, that step is often not in her best interest if the perpetrator hasn't shown any awareness of how he or she has wounded the client. Forgiveness is a private matter between the healing woman and her Higher Power. It represents the woman's choice to take responsibility for her current actions and relationships and to turn her energy toward health.

Healthy boundaries with family

Most FSLAs find it important to establish strong boundaries with family members, especially early in the healing process. Kay, for example, needed several months without contact from her family while she processed her parents' failure to protect her from sexual abuse at the hands of a dear family friend and their on-going relationship with the perpetrator even after she disclosed the abuse. She found she had to repeatedly and firmly hold the boundary and screened her calls, blocked their email addresses, and left their mailed letters unopened. Eventually, Kay grew stronger in her truth and her ability to maintain her differentiation while in the presence of her family. She chose to slowly re-establish contact with them that still allowed her to protect herself and her children. Kay found she could best handle family gatherings in small doses, and she book-ended those visits with supportive friends. Eventually, Kay and her parents forged a respectful, though cautious relationship, which she came to find meaningful. They weren't able to discuss fully her abuse and her journey of recovery, but they grew to enjoy social contact and could celebrate holiday meals together. Kay gave herself permission to keep the relationship on a surface level and to accept this as the limit of her parents' ability or willingness.

Kay's story illustrates creating a healthy relationship with family of origin. She had to forgive them for the ways they wounded her, and she chose to maintain a relationship with them. At the same time, she set strong boundaries she was able to enforce. She didn't leave her children in their care and she left if her parents were abusing alcohol, which had been a pattern during her childhood abuse.

Often FSLAs long for their families to understand their journey and to embrace a healing path for themselves. Certainly, this is a legitimate desire. Unfortunately, however, few families are willing to adopt recovery principles for themselves. This reality doesn't mean the FSLA must cut off all contact with her family. That stance reflects the black and white thinking that characterizes addiction. Like Kay, the recovering woman can accept her family for who, what, and where they are, and she can make choices about interacting with them in ways that affirm her own healing.

In a practical sense, the FSLA can drive separately to family events, can limit the time she spends with family members, can refrain from inviting family members into her own living space, or can leave if people are abusing alcohol or other drugs.

She can change the subject if she's peppered with intrusive inquiries about her life and request that others stop being critical or judgmental. If they refuse, she can politely remove herself from the situation. She can work the Steps in relation to her family and surrender her unmet expectations for them.

The good news is that as the healing woman changes, her family members sometimes follow. Even if they don't fully embrace recovery, they may get better at respecting her boundaries. As the years go by and the recovering FSLA moves beyond sobriety to serenity and acceptance, often family tensions ease. The family itself may not be significantly different, but the FSLA finds she is different and better able to detach from the dis-ease of her family.

Relationships with adult siblings are often easier to restore. The FSLA can slowly explore the history she shares with her siblings and test the waters to see if their life experiences were similar. She may be surprised to discover her siblings are relieved to talk more openly about their childhood experiences. As adult siblings face the role reversal of caring for aging parents, they may find common ground for a healthier relationship. If not, the FSLA now has a "family of choice" in her supportive friends to help her navigate on-going difficult waters.

Healthy relationships provide the antidote to the attachment and abuse injuries that are the set-up for sex and love addiction. As the recovering woman develops a healthier relationship with herself, she's better equipped to expand those skills to her friendships, dating and committed partners, and even her family of origin. These new or renewed relationships provide signposts of the power and progress of her healing journey.

Contributing Writer

Deborah Corley - Disclosing in a New Love Relationship

REFERENCES

Acevedo, B. P., Aron, A., Fisher, H. E., & Brown, L. L. (2012). Neural correlates of long-term intense romantic love, *Social Cognitive and Affective Neuroscience Advance Access, 7*(2), 145-159. doi:10.1093/scan/nsq092

Ackerman, D. (2002, March 24). The brain on love [Opinion page]. *New York Times.* Retrieved from http://www.opinionator.blogs.nytimes.com/2012/03/24/the-brain-on-love/

Chatterjee, C. (2001, September). Can men and women be friends? Male-female friendship can be tricky, but both benefit from cross-sex buddyhood. *Psychology Today, 34*(5), 60.

Eisenberger, N. (2012). The neural bases of social pain: Evidence for shared representations with physical pain. *Psychosomatic Medicine, 74,* 126-135.

Ferree, M. C. (2010). *No stones: Women redeemed from sexual addiction* (2nd ed.). Downers Grove, IL: Intervarsity Press.

Katehakis, A. (2010). *Erotic intelligence: Igniting hot, healthy sex while in recovery from sex addiction.* Deerfield Beach, FL: Health Communications.

McDaniel, K. (2012). *Ready to heal: Breaking free of addictive relationships* (3rd ed.). Carefree, AZ: Gentle Path Press.

McPherson, M., Smith-Lovin, L., Brashears, M. E. (2006). Social isolation in America: Changes in core discussion networks over two decades. *American Sociological Review, 71*(03), 353-375.

O'Meara, D. J. (1989). Cross-sex friendship: Four basic challenges of an ignored relationship. *Sex Roles, 21*(7-8), 525-543.

Taylor, S. E. (2002).*The tending instinct: How nurturing is essential to who we are and how we live.* New York, NY: Henry Holt & Company.

Taylor, S. E. (2006).Tend and befriend: Biobehavioral bases of affiliation under stress. *Current Directions in Psychological Science, 15*(06), 273-277.

Taylor, S. E., Cousino-Klein, L, Lewis, B. P., Gruenewald, T. L., Gurung, R.A.R., & Updegraff, J. A. (2000). Biobehavioral responses to stress in females: Tend and befriend, not fight or flight. *Psychological Review,107*(3), 411-429.

CHAPTER 11

Healthy Sexuality

Alexandra Katehakis
with contribution by Jill Vermeire

Although the issue of sex and love addiction in women is best viewed as an unhealthy coping mechanism rooted in disrupted attachment which leads to problems of dysregulation of the autonomic nervous systems and functional problems in the central nervous system, FSLA obviously involves . . . well, *sex*. Unlike recovering from substance addiction, which means simply eliminating the use of alcohol or drugs, eliminating sex isn't the goal of recovery from sex and love addition. Although an initial period of celibacy is recommended to achieve sobriety, abstinence isn't the long-term solution. It's easy to let the pendulum swing its full arc from sexual acting out to sexual anorexia, and your job is to help the recovering woman avoid this common trap.

If a woman can hide her fear of intimacy behind the cloak of recovery, she doesn't have to risk the discomfort required in order to restore her sexuality. Paradoxically, what the FSLA wants lies beyond her fear. In order to achieve a connected and intimate relationship with another, she must understand and take measures to walk directly through the "fire" of her fear.

Denying sexuality creates the same havoc in a woman's body, mind, and spirit as does sexually acting out. It's easy to deal with co-occurring disorders, attachment injuries, family of origin issues, and a host of other symptoms and ignore sexual numbness. Sexual shame can remain so intense that your client won't mention it in therapy, and her core pain will continue until it's identified and robustly explored. If women aren't taught new ways of sexually expressing themselves, they're likely to believe they just haven't found the right person, which may persuade them to return to their love-addicted behavior. The healing outlined in the preceding chapters equips the recovering woman to break through the wall of fear and learn to experience healthy sexuality. She must explore what the concept means for her and how it gets expressed in her life whether she's single or coupled. The clinician's role is to assist the FSLA in grappling with these important issues in her healing journey.

Definition of Healthy Sexuality

Intimacy refers to a woman's ability to be close and have a deep, honest rapport with another person. The term "sexuality" refers to her capacity for sexual feelings. More than that, these concepts provide the foundation on which you'll help your client build, explore, and develop a healthy, erotic sex life. Most female sex addicts hold the cultural belief that they have to have sex in order to be loved. They frequently associate sex with love, self-worth, and a way to feel alive or experience intensity. Healthy sex includes intensity, but "intensity with connection" is where you want to direct the recovering FSLA.

As you work with your client, keep in mind that healthy sex is SAFE. The characteristics and key points involved in healthy sex are:

- Healthy sex is not *Secretive* or shameful to herself or the other person.
- Healthy sex is not *Abusive* in any way.
- Healthy sex is not used to ignore or escape her *Feelings*.
- Healthy sex requires an *Emotional connection* of some sort with the other person.

Healthy sex is about love, respect, mutual caring, giving and receiving pleasure, and a desire to know herself and her partner in a deeper way. Healthy sex can be intense, but the afterglow and heat remain instead of dissolving into the next rush. The simple pleasures that express or celebrate the love she shares is what connects her with herself and her partner over time (Katehakis, 2010).

Consider these actions that make up the aspects of sexual health when helping your client understand what healthy sex will eventually involve. Healthy sex adds to a person's well-being and is therefore free from behaviors or energy that creates destruction to her psyche, feelings, and physical body. There's a feeling of wholeness and a sense of being restored to a wholesome person. Engaging in healthy sex can have a tone of innocence and simplicity that feels beneficial, healthful, and sound. A person might feel she is restoring her character as a result of the sexual act because it feels good in the moment and leaves her feeling good afterward. Healthy sex is free from shame and pain and doesn't create disorder or drama in the woman's life.

By now you and your client have discussed her attachment style , so remind her that she's going to come up against the limitations of her autonomic nervous system again and again. No matter how much her psychological issues have been ironed out, the patterns in the body are tenacious and need constant attention in order to re-pattern them. You'll remind her that one of the challenges of being a woman in sexual recovery is to use all of her tools all of the time. In this case, mindfulness of what happens to her as she begins to get closer to another is crucial to both changing her nervous system and her capacity for intimacy.

For example, Wendy had an anxious, avoidant attachment style due to the family with which she grew up. Her mother was very anxious and avoidant of intimacy and her father had a pre-occupied style of attachment and was a sex addict. Wendy's mother, through no fault of her own, didn't have the "equipment" in her own nervous system for being affectionate, warm, and physically nurturing, which left Wendy with essentially the same anxious and avoidant imprints in her own system. Her father was ambivalent in his attachment style, wanting closeness when it suited him, then pushing it away when he no longer needed it. Wendy's father was her only source of warmth and affection, but he ran "hot and cold" which left her feeling insecure and uncertain about being lovable.

As an adult, Wendy desperately wanted to be loved and touched, but she always used sex as a way to get those needs met. Naturally, she chose men like "dear old dad" who would give her pseudo-love and attention, but leave her in the end. Now in recovery, Wendy has a new compass for choosing men. In early recovery, as a way to avoid past patterns, she always went with the guy who didn't feel right and stayed away from the guy who seemed right. Over time, she learned to tolerate her discomfort with the "good" guy, in other words, the guy who didn't give her mixed messages, was nice to her, and who was emotionally available. Through therapy, she learned to track the sensations in her body so that she was well aware when she started to withdraw in reaction to emotional closeness. She could literally feel the avoidant set-up in her body. This feeling of emotional withdrawal was Wendy's cue to move in closer to him by accepting his compliment while making eye contact and remembering to breathe in those moments. Slowly but surely, she was able to expand the capacities in her autonomic nervous system for true love and affection by using her partner as an interactive regulator that included long, regulatory hugs. These simple, but often not easy moves are the foundations for life-long connections, which are the foundations for healthy sexuality.

Probably the most important piece of information you can give your female clients is to let them know that sexual activity is not fixed or simply primal. The latest sexuality research shows that human beings are capable of talking, delaying orgasm, having a sense of what their partner is thinking, and more during the sexual act. This information points to the possibility that "the central control mechanisms of sexual activity are quite flexible and susceptible to learning mechanisms" (Georgiadis, 2012).

What this means is that the cerebral cortex is interacting with the more primitive areas of the brain so it's completely possible for her to make informed decisions about what's sexually healthy for her and what isn't. This kind of informed decision is the result of the FSLA's diligent therapeutic work that has restored some of these higher cortical functions that lead her to her own personal sense of morality and the capacity for self-referential thinking. Like all human beings, the female SLA's sexuality is highly influenced not just by primitive drives, but by societal rules, mores, and other cultural forces. How we learn about sex, namely the reward aspects of sex, like sexual preferences and pleasure, reinforces future sexual behavior (Georgiadis, 2012). The recovering woman's early imprints influenced her to become a SLA, and her work in therapy is imprinting her to become a sexually healthy woman in recovery.

Healthy Sexuality Models

Many excellent models have been constructed to describe healthy sexuality. Two paradigms have long been used in the sex addiction treatment community and are helpful because of their simplicity. Ginger Manley (1995) developed a five-dimensional model that's illustrated below.

Manley's Healthy Sexuality Model

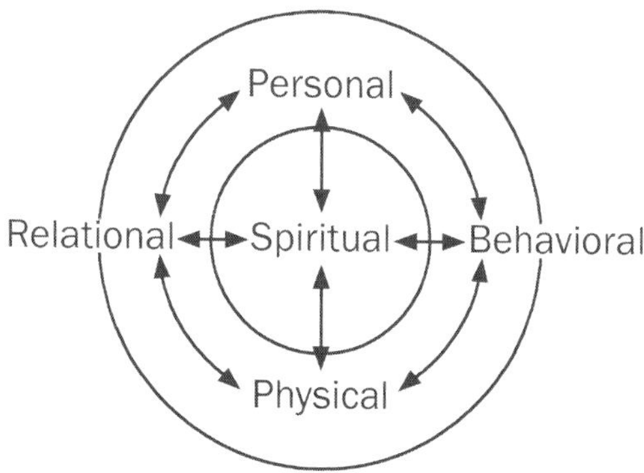

Source: Adapted from *Healthy Sexuality: Stage III Recovery* by Ginger Manley, *Sexual Addiction & Compulsivity*, 2(3), 157-183. Reprinted with permission from Taylor and Francis.

Figure 17

The ***behavioral*** dimension identifies what healthy sexuality is *not*. Manley asserts that healthy sexuality requires freedom from sexually or relationally addictive behaviors. In other words, healthy sexuality is based on sexual and relational sobriety. This point illustrates the importance of helping the FSLA determine her personal bottom line behaviors and sobriety definition before she starts to think about resuming sexual activity.

The ***physical*** dimension refers first to an individual's physical health. When illness or other physical impairment is at play, sex is often affected. If a woman fails to practice good self-care, is morbidly obese or chronically underweight, or is over-extended and exhausted, her sex life will be impacted negatively. This dimension also includes the mechanics of sexual functioning—whether or not the body parts work right. If dysperunia, meaning any genital pain with sexual intercourse such as vaginismus; or vulvadynia, meaning pain in the vulva area; lubrication problems; or other issues of sexual dysfunction persist; then healthy sexuality is impaired. The physical dimension also involves a person's body image, which is discussed more at length in a following paragraph.

The ***personal*** dimension is defined as the absence of significant after effects of trauma, both overt abuse and attachment injuries. This area is most closely associated with issues addressed in psychotherapy. An untreated sexual trauma survivor, for example, will likely dissociate during sex. A woman with poor differentiation of self may use sex to get or keep a partner or feel responsible for her partner's sexual issues. Again, this dimension illustrates why considerations about healthy sexuality come at this later stage in the recovering FSLA's process.

The ***relational*** dimension concerns the partnership in which sexual activity is taking place. Is the relationship founded on trust? Is there an emotional connection? Are there consistent expressions of non-sexual intimacy? Are both partners relatively healthy emotionally and psychologically? Is sex an affirmation of the coupleship rather than a way to define or maintain the relationship?

The ***spiritual*** dimension identifies that healthy sexuality is congruent with a person's value system. Sex is a life-affirming act that conforms to a woman's values regarding appropriate expressions of sexuality. She engages in sex without shame.

A second widely-used model of healthy sexuality is the CERTS paradigm, developed by Wendy Maltz (2012). This model also has five characteristics as outlined following.

CERTS Model of Healthy Sexuality

C = Consent. Both parties are adults who are able to freely consent to sexual behavior without coercion.

E = Equality. The partners enjoy equality within the relationship, meaning that there isn't an imbalance of power or exploitation.

R = Respect. Individuals engaging in sex respect themselves and each other and behave accordingly. This description means the sexual experience isn't shaming or degrading or humiliating to either person.

T = Trust. Sex occurs within a framework of trust. Those being sexual trust each other physically, emotionally, relationally, and sexually.

S = Safety. Healthy sex occurs by choice and mutuality. A woman can engage in sex without fear of physical harm or exposure to sexually transmitted diseases.

Source: "*The sexual healing journey: A guide for survivors of sexual abuse*" (3rd ed.) by Wendy Maltz. (New York, NY: William Morrow).

Figure 18

Foundation for Healthy Sexuality

Women recovering from sex and love addiction often ask, "When can I have sex again?" A better way to frame this question is to have her ask herself, "When can I trust *myself* again?" When can she trust that she's being true to herself and not wanting to have sex out of fear or a need to take care of her partner? Have her do the work to forgive herself before she considers resuming sexual practices. Remind the FSLA that she didn't know why she was acting out, she didn't think she was good enough, and she never learned how to ask to get her needs met. All these factors contributed to her sex and love addiction, and she deserves to heal these issues before she resumes being sexual. Be sure that she's experienced a total abstinence period (following disclosure if she has a partner) before she re-engages in sexual activity.

Sexual choice

Create conversations that challenge her to take loving care of herself first, then ask herself whether her desire to have sex with her partner is really a desire for him or her or driven by her need to try and put things back together again or for validation that she's lovable. Encourage her to take the time she needs to make decisions to ensure that she is safe, loved, and wanted by her partner and that she really wants her partner. Help her to slow things down and allow herself the dignity of her process so that she can wait until her intuition tells her it's the right time to resume sexual activity.

Sex then becomes a celebration of herself and her connection with another instead of old compulsive or destructive behaviors. Ask her what the purpose of sex is for her today and what she hopes to get out of a sexual relationship. Suggest she do some reading and writing on this topic so that she has clear intentions about what sex means to her today. Then she can begin to have conversations with her partner about what she wants and desires in her sexual relationship, which is an adult task she'll have to tackle. When sex is no longer used for purposes of power, control, validation, and manipulation, what is its purpose? When the female SLA comes to understand that she gets to say *yes* or *no* when it comes to having sex and mean it, then she's on the road to sexual health.

Sexual information and attitudes

It's important to intentionally address the term "sexuality," which can mean much more than specifically intercourse. Sexuality can be anything from kissing and hugging to massaging, sexual touching, and oral play, as well as intercourse. Be explicit with her about the exact behavior that's being discussed and never assume that you and the client are on the same page.

Consider that talking about sexual health with you will help decrease shame and prepare her to talk about it with a sexual partner. Start by having her define sexual acts she's comfortable with and those she's not and why. Have her explore her sexual identity and how it came to be in relation to the culture in which she grew up. Does she have a clear understanding of sexual anatomy and its function for both genders? On occasion, check in with her on how she's doing with her self-care habits and how she feels and perceives her body. Can she accept it without shame? Because so many female SLAs have used sex in negative ways and felt spiritually bereft due to their sex and love addiction, having conversations with her about sexual health will give you a good idea of whether she sees sex as a positive, spiritual act or whether she's still stuck in her traumatic use of it. Proceed slowly. These are tender areas and may be difficult for her to explore depending on her sexual past.

This is a good time in her treatment to include experiential exercises like making a collage of what her healthy sex life would look like. Colors, moods, or nature scenes may exemplify concepts she can't put into words. Encourage feelings states so she can practice talking to you about sexual matters that are difficult for her. Let her know that there's nothing sexual she can't talk about, and give her a sense that you champion and support her. Think about communicating with her by using metaphors like the caterpillar's transformation into a butterfly to remind her of her struggle through the cocoon of addiction to sobriety. Don't be afraid to use your sense of humor. Sexual conversations can be profound, profane, and funny.

Sexual presence

Healthy, intimate sex emphasizes empathy for her partner. No longer driven by the chemical high of falling in love, intimacy and love become a choice. A recovering woman should be clear that she is choosing her partner and putting into place the practices of connection she's learned, like being very intentional about having sex. This is the time to create a space for closeness so she can begin to really see her partner and be seen. Staying present during sex may be a new experience for her which creates a vulnerability, builds on the disclosures she's offered, and encourages a candor and truth about who she really is. This process creates an intimate, sexual charge born of truth and sensuality that encourages her to stay in her body and to feel and share all of her feelings. Help her to remember that she can no longer hide out during sex through fantasizing about others or dissociating. Healthy sex means staying present with herself and her partner so she can begin to recognize her sexuality as a sacred space for healing.

One of the quickest ways to ensure she is present with herself and with her partner is the mindfulness practice of being present, breathing, and making eye contact. Staying relational, meaning out of her head and *with* her partner will change her experience of sex and her sexuality. Chapter 7 describes a grounding exercise wherein you instructed the client to scan her body for tension and other sensations. Now that the recovering FSLA is more conversant in the language of her own body, encourage her to use her bodily-based cues as her navigator. Remind her to trust her gut if she's uncomfortable or if something feels wrong. Likewise, if she's not lubricating and not ready for intercourse she must be honest with herself and her partner —no excuses or denying. The more honest she can be with how her body is informing her, the better for her and ultimately for her relationship.

Meditation is an easy, effective relaxation technique that cultivates pure, present awareness. It's also been shown to have some wonderful effects on the central and autonomic nervous systems. Here are some specific suggestions for the recovering woman about enjoying a sensual meditation:

- Adjust the temperature in her house to the setting that's most comfortable. Most women tend to like their environments a little warmer than men. Body temperature and comfort are essential to feeling present and comfortable sexually.
- Have a cup of tea. Warm tea can be a natural aphrodisiac and feel like a treat at the same time.

- Light a candle and take a bath. Sensual experiences like bathing can be a time for self-reflection and a mindfulness practice. Suggest she be aware if she's actually enjoying the feel of the water, its temperature, and the smell of the bubble bath, or is she anxiously chewing on her thoughts about yesterday or tomorrow?
- Follow the bath by getting into bed naked and listening to some sensual music.

Body image

As the FSLA explores her newfound sober sexuality, the issue of body image will often present itself. A woman's beliefs and attitude toward her body have everything to do with her sexuality. A large percentage of woman fall somewhere on the spectrum of having a negative body image that ranges from either mildly critical to extreme body dysmorphia. Thinking about sexuality can trigger many FSLAs into old behavior or thinking even if they've constructed a strong foundation in their sobriety. Hopefully if there have been any disordered eating or dysmorphic traits, they've been addressed in the treatment process. Moving into sexuality will be a good way to gauge what's truly been healed in these areas and where there's room for improvement.

A simple exercise for her to get more comfortable with her body is called "Mirror, Mirror" (Bercaw & Bercaw, 2010). Designed for her to get present about her thoughts and feelings about her body, she can do this exercise alone or with a partner, depending on what stage of her recovery she's in. Standing naked in front of a full-length mirror, instruct her to take a deep breath, make eye contact with herself and say, "I love who you are." Have her notice any resistance or any other feelings that may arise. She should start at the top of her head and work her way down her body all the way to her toes without skipping any part. With each feature, she should speak out loud how she feels about that feature. For example, starting from the crown of her head would have her expressing how she feels about her hair (its color, texture, thickness, graying, etc.), then on to details about her ears, eyes, skin texture and tone, teeth, lips, and so forth. Remind her to be as specific as she can be and to notice if some part of her body she once liked has changed and if other parts she hadn't previously liked now look better to her.

If a partner is present, they should sit lovingly silent and then give feedback at the end of the body monologue. If the female is willing to hear constructive feedback, she can tell her partner. Her partner should reflect what he or she heard and only offer support if the partner wants to add to what he heard. It's recommended that your client create a list of affirmations for the body parts she is at odds with so that she can begin to speak positively about herself and so that she can share these with her partner down the road. (For complete instructions for partner involvement see Bercaw & Bercaw, 2010, p. 99-100).

Sexuality With Herself

Sometimes an FSLA doesn't have a sexual partner or finds herself in a relationship where her partner is unwilling or unable to have sex. Help your client grasp that she doesn't forfeit her sexual pleasure just because she doesn't have a partner with whom to share sexual experiences. Some women choose not to have a partner for a variety of reasons; other women would prefer to have a partner but haven't connected with someone they decide is right for sharing the intimacy of sex. Some women in recovery are willing to live in a sexless relationship or marriage because the overall value of the relationship supersedes the loss of a sexual connection. For example, consider the couple who has been together for 35 years, built a home, family, and business together, are active in their community, and are good companions and friends. The comfort of this woman's circumstances and positives in the relationship may supplant her need for sex when her partner is intractable about getting counseling for the issues that prevent them from being sexual together. Another case may be the woman whose partner has a long-term terminal illness or a serious medical or physical condition that leads to problems of sexual impairment or desire. Unless both parties are willing to explore alternate ways of being sexual, they'll lapse into a sexless relationship.

For a woman without a partner, healthy masturbation, if not previously problematic, can be a form of self-care like washing her hair or shaving her legs. Healthy masturbation isn't dissociative, a repetition of past trauma, or used to alter her mood repeatedly. For the single woman in recovery, masturbation may be the only sex she's having. A woman in a relationship may find that masturbation is pleasurable, but she wonders if she's being unfaithful to her partner. If she finds masturbation is replacing sex with a willing partner or results in her reverting to the compulsive behaviors of the past, she should stop masturbating. Advise her to consult her sponsor, talk to her partner, and sort this issue out with others in her program before she resumes the practice.

Self-pleasuring for the woman without an available partner need not be relegated to simple masturbation. When her desire is to awaken her sexuality for self-expression and gain knowledge about her body, mind, and soul, then she can embark on sexuality as a personal art form.

Breathing

For starters, simple deep-breathing exercises can assist her to begin a sexual practice with herself. Fully breathing into the abdomen is a way to relax and open the body, focus energy intention, and re-energize the body and mind. Point out that most of us take short, shallow breaths, so begin by having your client practice taking elongated, deep breaths. Start with breathing from the chest and move down into the belly and pelvis, reminding her to keep her focus on her breathing. Tell her to practice deep breathing daily until she can do it with ease. (This exercise can also be used in an all-female group. For complete instructions, see Katehakis, 2010, p. 219-222.)

Once she's familiar with the rhythm of her breathing and can sustain it, give her permission to move her body with her breath in the ways it naturally or spontaneously wants to move. Gently instruct her to allow all feelings and emotions, impulses, and sensations to guide her so that she becomes familiar with her interoceptive cues, that is, the cues arising from her body, which can include sensations in her muscles, internal organs, and joints. Naturally, when the body moves, the expression of that movement follows as sound. Sadly, women are often taught to be "good girls" or to be "seen and not heard" from the time they're very young. Exhaling loudly, moaning, sighing, singing, and laughter are some of the natural sounds that reveal inner pleasure (Schulte, 2005).

Once the client is at home in private, encourage her to practice breathing and moving and to add sounds with every movement she makes. Her own sounds will lead her to experience a full-body expression of her sexuality and to become familiar with the sounds of her own personal pleasure. Activating our bodies through sound and movement leads to sexual arousal.

Kegel exercises

Kegel exercises for toning the pelvic floor are another simple exercise she can do to increase her sexual desire and pleasure. By squeezing the pubococcygeus, often called the PC muscle or the pleasure muscle, she's activating a major part of the pelvic network. By working out or training this muscle, she's toning it for better, more powerful orgasms. In general, this muscle begins at the pubic bone and travels down to the coccyx, surrounding both sides of the vaginal area. Alternating squeezing or contracting this muscle with releasing or relaxing it is a way to exercise the muscle and to experience pleasure. When breath is deliberately added to this exercise, arousal will increase (Schulte, 2005). Suggest she read some books on female sexuality (listed in the appendix) as a way to introduce herself to this area of her body. Most basic books have instruction on how to comprehensively activate and strengthen this area (see Northrup, 2010, p. 237).

There are many complex, rich, and wonderful ways a recovering FSLA can discover her own personal sexuality. Whether with or without a partner, your clients can become intimately involved with their bodies and sexuality so that they can express it as a form of self-love and/or share it with a lover.

Sexuality for the Single Woman

Working with a single woman in recovery presents its own set of unique issues around sexuality. Many single FSLAs have never had any positive sexual experiences. Many times she's never had sober sex, especially if she's cross-addicted with alcohol or drugs. Preparing the female client for a renewed, healthier sexual life will require some groundwork, anticipation, and education around the realities of this new venture.

Moving a relationship from platonic to a sexual one will most often bring up a lot of fear and anxiety for the FSLA. Like dating in recovery, sex in recovery can be a positive or anxiety provoking experience depending on many factors such as her support system, strength of sobriety, and safety in talking about her successes and challenges. This will be another area where your own comfort level with using overt terminology like vagina, penis, or ejaculation will be an important factor in how well the client acclimates to this new lifestyle.

Most clients struggle when it comes to physical expressions of intimacy. Again, based on the recovery plan and past acting out behaviors of the FSLA, the client/therapist team can incorporate sexuality into her dating plan in a way that contains the client, keeps her safe, and allows her to have some fun as well. Most recovering sex and love addicts commit to a definition of sobriety that restricts sexual intercourse to a committed relationship. Be certain she's determined what sobriety means for her and which behaviors fall into her plan for healthy sex.

As previously mentioned, you must get specific about the physical expressions of intimacy in which the client will be engaging. You may have to confront some countertransference here. Deciding together when the client will be able to kiss, when to touch specific body parts, or when to engage in certain sexual acts such as mutual masturbation or oral sex can incite some discomfort for the therapist who hasn't reconciled his or her own sexual blocks and preferences. It's important that you're comfortable talking about explicit behaviors while containing sexual energy around the discussion. If you feel any resistance, discomfort, or countertransference in discussing this type of material, consultation or supervision is advisable.

It's equally important to keep your own values around morals and sexuality out of the discussion. The client's best interest, health, and recovery come first. Viewing these issues through a recovery rather than a moral lens is important when helping the client navigate through this process. Choices about what sexual behaviors she'll explore belong to the recovering FSLA, not to the therapist.

Certain questions can help her exploration process. Ask, "Can you engage in this behavior with integrity or is this moving too fast with possible triggers into your addiction?" Since FSLAs tend to be more comfortable sexualizing everything rather than being intimate in the absence of sex, inquire whether this is "addict" or "recovery" behavior. It's best that you and the client decide together—up front—how far sexually she can appropriately go without threatening her recovery. You might also find it useful to speak with other therapists regarding various ideas about sexuality and timelines with FSLAs.

Just as the dating plan can be constructed in a very deliberate way, so can a plan in relation to sexuality. For a recovering FSLA, intercourse will be saved for committed relationships unless there's some good reason why it might be healthy to have intercourse without commitment. That decision will truly be between the clinician and client. Be aware, however, that for a woman in recovery from sex and love addiction, intercourse can intensify and complicate things and is best left for the client's committed relationship. Other sexual acts can be left open and available for exploration within healthy, non-committed relationships.

Sexuality is such a personal and subjective experience that sensitivity to an individual's values will play an important part during re-entry into sexual relationships. Keeping the focus on her recovery and setting up a plan that keeps her away from her bottom line or inner circle behaviors is the best place to start. The recovering woman usually has many questions about what's healthy or appropriate. Again, the best way to navigate through the dialogue is to help her discover what's right for her. Questions about behaviors or experiences might include:

- Could this sexual activity bring joy and/or pleasure or will it lead to feelings of shame or guilt?
- Could this activity be triggering or cause you to disconnect/check out?
- Is this sexual expression nurturing, spiritual, and pleasurable, or is it destructive, sabotaging, or manipulative?

Ultimately it's up to the recovering FSLA to find the answers within herself, but she'll look to you for support, role modeling, or guidance as she navigates these very confusing but important questions.

Sexuality Within a Coupleship

When your client is beginning a healthy sexual relationship after recovery, you can support her by encouraging her to take a sexual leap of faith. Remind her that sexual change is gradual, not sudden. It's a process she has to trust and believe will happen. One of the most often used phrases in the Twelve Step programs is "Let go and let God." Attempts to do otherwise and control outcomes can destroy her sexual experience.

Because FSLAs can confuse sex with intimacy in their addictions, they have to be reminded to sustain sex with intimacy in recovery. Sexual vitality comes from relationships. The challenges of closeness renew sexual interest and deepen the meaning of sex. One of the best ways to do this is to encourage the recovering FSLA and her partner to talk before, during, and after sex. Verbalizing passion, needs, and fears is perhaps the best way of facilitating sexual intimacy.

A useful way to get started having explicit conversations with her partner is to share the sexual messages they grew up with by talking through these kinds of questions:

- What were the messages you got from your family about sex and sexuality?
- What kind of messages did you get about sex from your community?
- What do you consider to be "normal" sexuality?

Unhealthy shame around one's sexuality is one of the greatest barriers to vitality states in the body and in having a full life. Recovering couples have to overcome unhealthy sexual shame through affirmation of themselves and each other. Couples that do the best in restoring their sexuality emphasize the strategy of mutual affirmation. If you're seeing the couple, remind both parties to compliment each other. When both affirm all the positive things they can see about each other's sexuality and about their sexuality together, healing is under way.

Extinguishing unhealthy shame is no easy feat and can take a lifetime of practice to heal. For starters, eye contact and mutual gazing will bring up shame and thus quickly allow the couple to move into vulnerable and intimate spaces without ever taking their clothes off. The eyes are the windows to the autonomic nervous system, meaning that bodily-based feelings such as shame are easily evoked through eye contact. Looking into each other's eyes also produces a high level of novelty in the system, which gives the couple the opportunity to see one another in new ways and to also "see" the person with whom they first fell in love.

A particularly effective practice for reducing unhealthy shame is the following couple's exercise of affirmation. Instruct the couple to start by sitting knee-to-knee in a relaxed position for both. One person volunteers to be seen and the other to be the witness. The person witnessing begins by saying, "I see who you are." The person being seen says, "Thank you." The witness repeats the words, "I see who you are," and the person being seen responds again with, "Thank you." This process is repeated for anywhere from 3-to-10 minutes and participants don't deviate from the script.

Both parties will notice feelings arising in themselves and in their partners. They may begin with nervous laughter or feeling silly. Encourage them to invite all responses and not judge any of them. The couple should stay with the exercise and breathe as they notice feelings of joy, sadness, pain, hope, sorrow, excitement, and so forth arise. Remind them to let themselves "be" without judgment. Partners should switch roles so both have the experience of witnessing and being seen. Each round can end with a few moments of silence and a deep, body-to-body hug for co-regulation and connection.

When the process is complete for both, they may process their feelings and what they learned about themselves and each other. Affirmations can be constructed out of this exercise and the mirror exercise that both can share with each other. Turning their partner's affirmations into compliments is a loving and supportive gift they can give themselves, each other, and the coupleship.

Boundaries and limits are new for most FSLAs in recovery, which is why building trust helps heal the sexual wounds of the past. Both partners need permission to say *no* to sex without fear of reprisal or abandonment. Remind the couple to give profound respect to the other's vulnerabilities and wishes, even when they don't fully understand them, like them, or approve of them. Remember, trust is the goal. To seduce, manipulate, or test the other's boundaries is extremely destructive. Healing will shift perspectives and boundaries. Breaking the trust again may lead to irreparable damage.

For the codependent female SLA, saying *no* and meaning it can be a major boundary accomplishment and one she must achieve for her sexual well-being. Likewise, saying *yes*, being acknowledged, and following-through is part of being a healthy sexual adult. Some ways she can practice boundaries when it comes to her sex life are to:

- Listen to her partner's needs, wants, and desires with an open mind and heart.
- Take time to appreciate her partner's desire to try something new even if she may not be in the mood.
- Never place judgment on her partner's preference for sexual acts. Instead, remain curious and honest about what works for her and what doesn't.
- Always believe it's okay to say *no*. How she says it and the tone she uses is what matters.

Help your recovering client pay attention to feelings. Addicts and partners learned to sexualize their needs and pain; yet their needs remained unfulfilled, their pain went unattended to, and their sexuality was stifled. Couples in recovery should attend to their feelings and be honest about them. Instruct your client to begin by just labeling her feelings. With time she'll get better at sorting them out.

Having explicit conversations about sex is part of expressing feelings and experiencing an adult sexuality. The recovering FSLA should talk about her personal experiences and what she feels and needs in order to keep the sexual interaction and conversation open. Sensitive to rejection, she must remember that just because her partner isn't available for sex or for specific acts doesn't mean that it's a rejection of her. Managing her anxiety and staying connected with her partner is an opportunity for her to practice empathy for her partner's feelings and preferences. Tools that will be of assistance to both parties in expressing their feelings are:

- Using the language of "I" statements to express her truth and feelings without judgment.
- Speaking from the heart so she comes across as sincere and not rejecting or judgmental.
- Asking her partner about his or her feelings and expressing her own will open the door for intimate and empowering conversations.

Ask your clients if they can begin to see sex as legitimate joy. It's time to abandon the grim rules they learned that kept them in addictive and co-addictive obsession. Remind them to have fun and play. One of the functions of having a sobriety plan and boundaries is to allow for spontaneity and experimentation while still staying safe. Recovery is about sexual growth, which requires risk. The recovery principles a couple has learned will carve out an area of safety so that they can risk themselves sexually in new, positive and rewarding ways.

Finally, remind the couple to take care of their physical health because it's basic to sexual health. Exercise, proper eating habits, and good sleep hygiene are essential components to having a healthy sex life. Limiting the use of drugs like alcohol, nicotine, and caffeine should go without saying. Taking care of themselves will allow the couple to have the kind of sex life they're hoping for over a lifetime.

Contributing Writer

Jill Vermeire - Sexuality for the Single Woman

REFERENCES

Bercaw, W., & Bercaw, G. (2010). *The couples guide to intimacy: How sexual reintegration therapy can help your relationship heal.* Pasadena, CA: California Center for Healing.

Georgiadis, J. R. (2012). Doing it…wild? On the role of the cerebral cortex in human sexual activity, *Socioaffective Neuroscience & Psychology, 2,* 17337. doi: 10.3402/snp.v2i0.17337

Katehakis, A. (2010). *Erotic intelligence: Igniting hot, healthy sex while in recovery from sex addiction.* Deerfield Beach, FL: Health Communications.

Maltz, W. (2012). *The sexual healing journey: A guide for survivors of sexual abuse* (3rd ed.). New York, NY: William Morrow.

Manley, G. (1995). Healthy sexuality: Stage III recovery, *Sexual Addiction & Compulsivity, 2*(3), 157-183.

Northrup, C. (2010). *Women's bodies, women's wisdom: Creating physical and emotional health and healing* (revised ed.). New York, NY: Bantam Books.

Schulte, C. (2005). *Tantric sex for women: A guide for lesbian, bi, hetero, and solo lovers,* Alameda, CA: Hunter House.

CHAPTER 12

Healthy Living Practices

Linda Hudson, Kelly McDaniel, Anna Valenti-Anderson, Jill Vermeire
with contributions by Marnie Ferree, Alexandra Katehakis

Recovery from sex and love addiction is about much more than stopping addictive behaviors. Sobriety is merely the starting point that provides the gateway into living life differently. Living life well. If recovery is simply about not doing certain behaviors, an addict will almost surely relapse. A life based on *don'ts* replicates the deprivation most addicts experienced in their childhoods, which isn't an appealing existence. Recovery involves living "happy, joyous and free" as the *Big Book of Alcoholics Anonymous* (Alcoholics Anonymous World Services, Inc., 1976) terms it. Simple healthy practices like those outlined below will restore the recovering woman's sense of vitality, optimism, and overall well-being.

SELF-CARE

Self-care is an enormous component of healthy living. In fact, it provides the crucial foundation for sustaining a new way of life. Assisting your clients with self-care requires that you personally practice healthy living. A key tenet of helping others is that you can't take someone farther than you've gone yourself. How do you nurture your best self? What do you do for fun? How often? Do you take regular vacations? What exercise do you do routinely? Do you nourish yourself with healthy nutrition and your own therapy? Are you making time for friends and loved ones? Do you seek consultation when you struggle with a decision or loneliness? Keep your own self-care in mind as you encourage your clients in the practice.

If self-care is automatic for you, take time to consider where you learned healthy habits. From your mother, father, friends? If you had healthy modeling for taking care of yourself, you may not immediately resonate with the incredible energy and focus it takes to create this practice from scratch. When you suggest that a recovering

FSLA practices healthy living, you may as well be speaking a foreign language. Even if she has the desire to live in a healthier way, she often simply has no idea what that looks like or where to start. Just as you had to help her deconstruct the behaviors and wounds associated with her acting out and then address each element, you'll need to take a similar approach in outlining the positive aspects of her recovery. Suggest taking small steps at first to keep her from being overwhelmed.

Self-neglect is a by-product of shame, which is at the core of sex and love addiction. Therefore, self-care is one of the first steps toward self-love. When your client starts taking care of her health and her body she's declaring that she matters to herself. The process of recovery will change her brain function and neurochemistry, and within short order, many women report feeling less depressed and anxious.

For some of your clients, you'll need to outline and direct specific positive behaviors. While this is best done after a trusting relationship is established, some physical concerns may need to be addressed early in the therapy process. For example, you may need to suggest a client gets a thorough medical check-up. Many FSLAs struggle with disordered eating, so a nutritional consultation can be an early addition to her healing plan. Encourage dental health and overall physical fitness. Challenge her to make adequate sleep a priority.

Practical and Nurturing Steps

Some of the recovering woman's self-care will probably involve very practical matters. Encourage her to make a list of messes she needs to clean up like straightening or painting a room that's been unattended, balancing her checkbook, or cleaning out her refrigerator or closet. As she completes a task, her sense of accomplishment will motivate her to tackle other things on her list. The renewed order in her surroundings will soothe her and reduce some of the internal clutter that accompanies an out-of-control environment. Suggest she invite a supportive friend to help her with big or overwhelming endeavors and to share her celebration of finishing the project. Help her develop a plan for maintaining order in her home.

Suggest the FSLA examines her wardrobe and discards items that were part of her acting out. During active addiction many women wear clothes or accessories that flaunt their sexuality or availability. Invite her to consider each questionable item and determine if it sends the message she now wants to convey. At the same time, encourage her to wear clothes that reflect her sense of herself and make her feel beautiful and dignified. Remind her that her choices are less about the items themselves as they are about how they make her feel inside and how they reflect the image she wants to project.

Encourage her to incorporate nurturing activities into her life like buying herself flowers, taking bubble baths, having a monthly massage,or having a manicure or pedicure. Typically sex and love addicts have lost touch with hobbies and activities that build their self-esteem and make them feel dignified. Now is the time to help her solidify who she wants to become and the lifestyle she'd like to have. Dream with her about what she would like to do with free time. Support her as she returns to healthy activities she once enjoyed or explores new ones. Remind her she doesn't have to be an expert in these activities. Encourage her to play golf for enjoyment rather than keeping score, to paint or compose music or write for self-expression instead of focusing on perfection. Suggest she tries dancing or kick-boxing or hiking—anything that interests her. Prompt her to invite friends over for a simple cookout or a potluck meal. Remind her of the importance of balance in life, which means she needs to avoid over-working and make time for other activities (Muller, 2000). This kind of healthy focus on self is foreign to many FSLAs, and she'll need your patient reminding that nurturing herself is not only appropriate, but vital to her long-term healing.

Emotional Self-Care

Remind the recovering FSLA to also attend to her emotional health. Sobriety and healing will cause her to feel more alive, more like the woman she has desired to be. She'll need to nurture herself emotionally as well as physically. If she doesn't already have some kind of daily meditation practice, this is a good time to implement one. How she structures the time and the materials she uses are less important than simply making quiet time each day for self-reflection. Many women enjoy one of the recovery meditation books; others use a religious or spiritual guide; still others find a time of journaling and silence is most helpful. Suggest she explores which avenue works best for her and remains open to changing her practice if she needs a fresh approach.

Completing a daily gratitude list is another way to maintain optimism and perspective. Recovery from sex and love addiction is difficult and often discouraging, even after the client achieves sobriety. Practicing gratitude is an important way to solidify her positive self-talk after years of shame. If she's overwhelmed with problems or on-going consequences, suggest she start her gratitude list with simple, tangible things: the roof over her head, the food on her table, the pen and paper she's writing on, the phone that connects her to supportive friends. It's important that she actually writes down the things for which she's grateful, because the concrete list provides a record of the blessings in her life when she's discouraged. Practicing gratitude is one way of working Steps One, Two, and Three as she trusts her Higher Power to handle her life.

Play, Breathe, Serve

Most traumatized women don't know how to play, which is an emotionally nourishing exercise. Again, suggest she start with something simple like riding a bike or swinging at the park. She could invite friends over for interactive games or cards or a "makeover" evening. Help her find things that encourage laughter. A good belly laugh is great medicine for the soul, especially when it's shared with a friend. Suggest she dance outside in the rain or do whatever lightens her heart.

Intentional breathing is another great way to nurture herself as well as support brain health. Teach her abdominal breathing and show her that just a few deep belly breaths will help regulate her brain when she's anxious or stressed. A good practice is to wake slowly each day and practice half a dozen deep breaths before she even gets out of bed. Intentional breathing is also a helpful practice in conjunction with meditation.

If her living situation and circumstances permits, suggest your client explores getting a pet. Many women in recovery find the unconditional love a pet offers (especially a dog or cat) is very affirming. Pets also provide an outlet for healthy touch and a way the FSLA can nurture herself as she lovingly and consistently cares for her pet. Many clients report that a pet was a significant source of comfort during childhood, and having a pet becomes an especially meaningful part of her recovery journey.

Being of service to others is another important platform of recovery. The last of the Twelve Steps suggests a recovering woman shares the message of healing and offers service to those in need. Helping someone else is one of the best strategies for combating self-pity or discouragement. Obviously, a recovering FSLA can do service work at S meetings by setting up chairs, making coffee, maintaining the phone list, or doing similar duties. She can sponsor other women or donate literature to those who can't afford it. Suggest, though, that she broaden her horizons to service work outside the normal recovery circles. She can volunteer at a women's shelter, a food bank or kitchen, as a mission worker in an area of need, at her local library, as a Big Sister, or with her church or synagogue. Getting outside herself and making a tangible difference in even a small corner of the world reminds her that she is more than her addiction and that she can be successful in ways beyond her personal recovery.

Menstrual Health

Our culture minimizes and misunderstands the impact of a woman's menstrual cycle. As you help your clients take care of their bodies and health, education about the hormone fluctuations during the cycle is imperative. A recovery plan that takes hormones into account better equips your clients for success. Following are some helpful strategies outlined by Northrup (2010) for various phases of the menstrual cycle. (Be aware that women on birth control pills are in a state of pseudo pregnancy and will not experience their natural cycle. Their bodies don't send the signals to males that women who cycle naturally do.)

During ovulation, the fertile phase of the cycle, women have more energy and clarity about themselves, their sexuality, and their attractiveness. This is a wonderful time of the month to explore creative pursuits, plant a garden, plan a party (for her girlfriends), and excel at work. Men are drawn to women who are ovulating, which means this may be a risky time for the FSLA as sexual energy is pouring through her body. Help your client chart her cycle to know when ovulation occurs so she'll be better prepared for the sexual challenges she may experience. McDaniel (2012) offers more information about navigating sexual boundaries during the fluctuations of the menstrual cycle.

During the second half of the menstrual cycle, known as the luteal phase, women experience a rise in progesterone that often brings fatigue and a desire for more quiet. Our culture doesn't allow a change in pace to honor this shift, so the FSLA is often taxed at work, with children, and managing life during this time. Again, this is a risky time for clients in early recovery. Women frequently compensate for hormonal shifts with cravings for sugar, caffeine, and sex during the luteal phase. Identify and encourage her need for extra care and support in this phase of her cycle. Help her make healthy food choices, schedule an extra session if needed, give her reading suggestions, and/or encourage her to plan a safe massage. It's also important for her to get plenty of sleep.

MEANINGFUL WORK OR PURPOSE

For women in recovery, building a life of meaning promotes joy. In order to live a meaningful life, women must first have the ability to envision goals. In active addiction, most women lose sight of who they could be. Abused as children, many women never imagined who they might become. Recovery is a woman's chance to reclaim, design, and live her best life. She is creating a self to love, to enjoy, and to be proud of.

According to Cameron (2002), "Each of us has an inner dream that we can unfold if we will just have the courage to admit what it is" (p. 193). Similarly, Csikszentmihalyi (2008) says, "If goals are well chosen, and if we have the courage to abide by them despite opposition, we shall be so focused on the actions and events around us that we won't have the time to be unhappy" (p. 227). FSLAs must replace the flow of addictive highs with the flow of meaningful life activity. In order to stay sober, life must have moments that feel as good as addiction once felt.

Part of healing an addiction is the return of choice and voice. Your client will discover stirrings of delayed or forgotten hopes and dreams. In early recovery, she may not have much capacity for creative thinking because even after her acting out is arrested, her trauma still hijacks her energy for dreaming. Expect clients to be confused and discouraged. Identifying wants and needs after a lifetime of ignoring them through addiction and dissociation takes time and support. Healing restores the gift of hope, and at that point you can help her explore a variety of options for meaningful work and purpose.

Meaningful Work

Sometimes an FSLA is under-employed as a result of her addiction. She may have settled for a job that enabled her acting out or she may have been unable to keep meaningful work as a consequence of her addiction. Your client may not be employed and decides she wants to re-enter the work force. If she's ready to explore different job options, it might be helpful for her to take some aptitude tests. Many free or inexpensive questionnaires are available online or through a community college. Perhaps her education didn't prepare her for her current interests, and she decides to go back to school. Or she may want to turn a hobby into an entrepreneurial adventure. Many women find their recovery inspires a career change. It's not unusual for former FSLAs to enter a helping profession as a result of their personal healing. Some women find it helpful to work with a life coach as they explore educational and employment opportunities.

Other clients may choose to stay at home with their children and need help determining how to make that option work financially. Or an FSLA may already be a stay-at-home mom and wants to find more fulfillment in that role. Help her reframe the mundane tasks of home-making as an investment in her children's emotional health. Remind her about healthy attachment practices, and support her in valuing these unassuming gifts. Suggest she join a parents' cooperative or playgroup to forge connections with others. Because homemakers don't have the luxury of scheduled lunch breaks or designated ending times for their work day, reinforce the importance of good self-care and outside activities. Encourage your client to work closely with a sponsor in this process of re-evaluating her circumstances. Suggest she finds women she admires and study them or contact them for mentoring purposes. Women benefit from using other women as positive role models.

Life Purpose

Many people believe in the importance of finding purpose beyond their work. Ultimately, an individual's sense of worth springs from a reason beyond any vocation, no matter how prestigious or even rewarding. Closely associated with spirituality, which is explored in the next section, finding purpose in life is a higher calling that evolves for many recovering women.

Frankl (2006) offers a poignant and powerful look at this idea as framed by the background of the atrocities of a Nazi concentration camp. In the Foreword to the fifth edition, Rabbi Harold Kushner writes,

> Terrible as it was, [Frankl's] experience at Auschwitz reinforced what was already one of his key ideas: Life is not primarily a quest for pleasure as Freud believed, or a quest for power as Alfred Adler taught, but a quest for meaning. The greatest task for any person is to find meaning in his or her life. (p.x)

While Frankl recognized meaning could be derived from work or from love, he believed one could potentially find the deepest meaning through facing difficult times with courage.

This idea seems particularly applicable to recovery from sex and love addiction and the wounds that lie beneath it. Though certainly not on the level of a concentration camp, women suffer horribly with this malady and they suffer more when they realize the pain they've inflicted on those around them. How does a woman keep from being swallowed by the sinkhole of this sickness? What reframe allows her to find meaning in this sorrow? Ferree (2008) speaks of what she calls "redeeming the pain," which is how she refers to the process of finding meaning in difficult experiences. She describes a variety of ways she converted the trauma of attachment injuries, abandonment, sexual abuse, and sexual addiction into positive avenues of healing for herself and especially for others.

While most recovering FSLA's stories will be less public, many other women find similar ways to find meaning in painful experiences. This concept is at the heart of the Twelve Step programs, which promote "paying it forward" by "carrying the message to others." Much as cancer survivors often describe, enduring and surviving a life-threatening illness changes your perspective. The patient often becomes more grateful, more present, more compassionate, or more supportive of others. She uses the things she's gone through to help others, and in so doing, she finds purpose in her suffering.

This paradigm shift doesn't usually occur until several years into the healing process, but the reflective clinician can help an FSLA begin to look for these "miracles" of perspective. One practical way to reflect this thinking is to ask the client to construct an "angel" egg that compliments the trauma egg she created earlier in her process. The angel egg identifies people or events that offered help or hope during challenging times. As the recovering FSLA explores these instances, she recognizes that indeed, she was protected or affirmed in ways she may not have been aware of at the time. In similar fashion, she eventually may see how her experiences uniquely position her to offer the same angel touch to others, and she finds a point to her suffering.

HEALTHY ONLINE BEHAVIOR

When the FSLA has arrested all of her unhealthy behaviors, including online behaviors,it's important to explore what healthy online behaviors might look like. The best way to decide what's healthy for the FSLA is to go back and review what she was doing that was unhealthy. This particular treatment issue will have to evolve as time moves on and as technology advances. Keep in mind that a number of devices are now capable of accessing the Internet. Healthy online practices encompass smart phones and electronic tablets as well as desktop and laptop computers.

Practical Steps

Remember that sex and love addiction is an intimacy disorder, and the Internet *is not* intimate. The Internet provides a false sense of intimacy and FSLAs need to always be cognizant of that reality. Setting up healthy practices for using the Internet without jeopardizing recovery is a sometimes overlooked aspect of treatment for females. Obviously, if part of the acting out behavior was online pornography, then a filter is mandatory with someone other than the client holding the password. If an FSLA participated in sexual acts via a webcam, then it might be necessary to disable the camera when possible. Interventions to support discontinuation of any acting out behavior involving the Internet are mandatory. A common healthy practice is to put any computer into a public area like the living room or kitchen until an FSLA's recovery is solid enough to consider relocating it.

Participating in social networking sites such as Facebook and Twitter will be more challenging. Healthy behavior involving these types of sites needs to have some kind of accountability built into her recovery. As a general rule of thumb, it's recommended that a client never have ex-lovers or "qualifiers" (former acting out partners) as friends on any site. The treating clinician must be familiar with how these sites work to know what kinds of questions to ask and what kind of parameters are needed. Never leave it solely up to the client to decide what her boundaries should be because she might not know what she needs or be willing to admit to it.

If the client is single and dating, she should take special care to curb the desire to obsess, stalk, manipulate, or seduce via social network postings. Additionally, if the recovering woman has a rich fantasy life, she should avoid people on these sites who arouse fantasy thinking. Help her see the difference between participating in the cultural norms regarding social networking and slipping into old, unhealthy behaviors.

Chatting and instant messaging, which are also hard to avoid in today's culture, are practices to be addressed. Although they can be useful at times, when it comes to being relational, they can prohibit intimacy and connection. It's wise to structure use of these communication modalities in some way, and the guidelines may depend, in part, on the client's lifestyle and needs. She might need to use these forms of communication in work-related situations or with family, but when it comes to any relationship that involves building intimacy and connection, it's advisable to limit the chats and messages to communications such as confirming plans, saying a quick hello, and requesting to talk by phone.

Online Guidelines for Couples and Households With Children

Clients who are married or in committed relationships need to negotiate their expectations regarding accountability and transparency about using the Internet and other electronic devices. Help them establish concrete parameters for healthy use that both parties will follow, including exchanging passwords for voicemail, email, and other online accounts. Inquire also into the use of texting and emailing between the partners, and discuss the difference between a quick exchange and potentially hiding from each other through the use of less personal forms of communication. For example, if a clinician learns that a husband and wife maintain contact almost solely using their phones and computers, explore if they're avoiding a closer connection through the use of their electronics. Suggest that the couple agrees on some limits about their use of non-verbal forms of communication that are similar to those used with single and dating clients. Boundaries such as texting only to confirm plans, coordinate children's activities, and so forth would be acceptable. Having an argument or trying to convey attachment needs and wants would involve in-person conversations.

Similar practices are recommended for clients with children. The FSLA can role model healthier behaviors to her children by practicing these newfound recovery behaviors. Again, using technology only for things such as confirming plans, checking schedules, or giving a quick check in are all perfectly fine. When it comes to actually connecting, attuning, and being involved in her children's lives, the recovering mom should engage in face-to-face communication to avoid emotional disconnection. This can prove to be challenging given the extreme dependence on texts and emails; however, it's easier when the client prioritizes her goal of staying emotionally connected.

One caveat could be families with teenagers. The typical teenager doesn't want to talk to grown-ups. Technology can actually prove useful with this age group because it allows teens to open up more and allows the parent to know her child in a way that perhaps past generations haven't. However, everything is best in moderation. If the only way a parent is communicating with her teen is via texting, then it's best to incorporate some in-person contact, at least by phone or webcam if the teen is away from home for school or work.

The younger FSLA may need to be guided on how to deal with virtual worlds such as Second Life. She may need to completely avoid those types of sites if they're directly related to the addiction (fantasy, acting out, obsessing). However, if complete abstinence isn't indicated (for example, an FSLA enters Second Life just for fun once in a while or has a business set up there), then creating limits to the types of rooms she visits, the language she uses, how she dresses her avatar, and the amount of time she spends may be the more achievable option. The recovering woman will need to honestly and continually examine her reasons and motivation for going into virtual worlds.

Internet Health Plan

Curtailing online behavior might be a challenging process due to the tide of dependency that most people have developed on the Internet in today's world. It's critically important to understand the client's reality and normal use of technology in order to help her devise a solid plan of recovery. Edwards, Delmonico, and Griffin (2011) developed an Internet Health Plan shown below that uses the familiar three-circle model to categorize online behaviors.

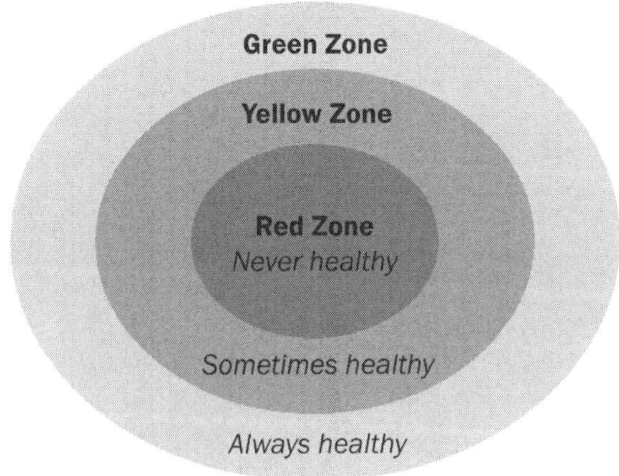

From "Cybersex Unplugged: Finding Sexual Health in an Electronic World" (p. 203) by Edwards, Delmonico, and Griffin, 2011, Charleston, SC: Create Space. Reprinted with permission.

Figure 19

"Red zone" or inner circle behaviors include ones that the client determines are never healthy such as viewing certain images, accessing sexual material, or going online during the middle of the night. "Yellow zone" or middle circle behaviors are those that are sometimes healthy and sometimes not, or behaviors the client hasn't yet made a decision about. Examples include using the Internet when the recovering FSLA is alone or when she's aware she's already triggered into a vulnerable state. "Green zone," outer circle behaviors, are those that are always healthy for the client such as remaining accountable for online use or accessing recovery resources via the Internet. Help your client get very specific about her Internet health plan and review it periodically as she progresses in recovery.

PREVENTING SEX AND LOVE ADDICTION

The path from childhood though adolescence and into adulthood is not often an easy one. At any point in the process a girl may find herself faced with emotional, physical, psychological, and sexual challenges. Nature and nurture dovetail in a complicated dance that creates various experiences and varying degrees of drama, danger, and divinity. If sex and love addiction is best conceptualized as an intimacy disorder whose roots lie in disruptions of early attachment, the best prevention is obviously to support parental attachment and the creation of healthier families. A woman's earliest interactions in her family can become protective factors or can put her at a higher risk for becoming an FSLA. Having a strong and positive attachment to nurturing parents or caregivers, experiencing effective parenting with involved parents, receiving clear and consistent messages around limits and discipline, and seeing healthy interpersonal behaviors modeled by those primary caregivers all help the young female learn positive social skills, manage stress, and choose friendships more wisely.

One of the primary avenues for rearing a healthy woman is to encourage her ability to bond, play, explore, and set limits with others in her life. Simply put, good-enough caregivers help a child and adolescent connect with herself and others in healthy and non-destructive ways. To that end, young women need to be provided healthier messages about who they are as females, as women, and as partners. Disempowering messages that base a female's happiness and fulfillment on having the perfect body, or being sexually available all the time, or needing validation about her desirability, or thinking she needs someone to be (or make her) happy are not constructive (Ferree, 2010). Instead, young women need messages that tell them they are inherently valuable, worthwhile, and precious just for having been born. Zoldbrod (2005) argues that goals for sexual actualization include learning about love, touch, empathy, trust, the ability to relax and be soothed, positive body image and gender identity, comfort in one's sexual orientation and self-esteem, a healthy sense of power and control, and having permission to explore and experience socialization.

Parents Set the Stage

Parents can help a young female be less susceptible to sex and love addiction through gaining a positive sense of self (self-esteem), learning how to set limits for herself and with others, and maintaining boundaries. Parents can further help girls learn how to participate in healthy interpersonal relationships, achieve social competency, and find interdependent balance by mastering the separation and individuation phases of their development. Females who are able to internalize the message that they're inherently valuable, vulnerable, imperfect, and okay, have reasonable needs and wants that they can meet themselves and ask others to meet, and can express spontaneity in healthy ways reduce their risk to codependency and addiction (Mellody, Wells Miller, & Miller, 1989).

Teaching adolescent females about healthy sexuality and practices, therefore, rests for the most part on appropriate role modeling from their parents. If you're working with a young woman as a client, it's likely necessary to involve the parents or guardian in some aspect of the therapy in order to support them in becoming good role models. Oftentimes this is the most challenging part of treating adolescents, yet involving the parents usually yields the best outcome for the client.

If the parent of an adolescent female is the client and wants to teach his or her child about healthy sexuality, clinicians can help by supporting the adult in becoming a great role model. This objective is achieved by guiding the client through his or her own beliefs and values around sexuality and helping the parent find a level of comfort and self-acceptance. Just changing the parent's energy around sex, addressing fears and concerns, and improving overall attitude about sexuality can cause a shift at home. Teaching an adolescent about healthy sexuality means the adult must know what he or she believes first and then allow the daughter to explore issues and ask questions as they arise.

In the event that an adult can't or won't be part of the treatment process, you must proceed with the girl or adolescent in a supportive manner while always keeping ethical and legal boundaries in mind. Be mindful of the laws and ethics in your state regarding what is allowable to discuss with an under-age client. If possible, it's also helpful to know what an adolescent client's parents or guardians feel is appropriate when it comes to talking about sex or sexuality.

Cultural, religious, and generational issues will need to be considered as well. You must understand the client's values, morals, and beliefs as you discuss the subject of healthy adolescent sexuality. Where one client might believe masturbation is a sin, another might believe it's healthy and a better option than pre-marital sex. Some clients' cultures favor abstinence-based sex education, whereas others are more liberal and will teach safe sex guidelines. You must be mindful about your own bias and values and seek supervision or consultation if any countertransference issues arise.

Explore Healthy Relationships and Sexuality

It's important that young girls learn that healthy sexuality doesn't involve shame, guilt, or negative consequences. You can introduce and explore concepts like integrity and grace and what they look like in your client's mind. Exploring who she looks up to and what she believes represents a real woman helps you navigate through a dialogue while maintaining appropriate clinical boundaries. Find out about her social system and what she sees among her peer group regarding sexuality. Sexuality is a sensitive subject and adolescent girls need a safe place to talk about it without feeling shamed. You can be a very important role model or confidant for a young girl, even within the ethical limits.

As female adolescents begin to experience puberty and hormonal changes, myriad chemicals can cause mood swings, create anxiety, and increase depression. Most teens struggle and are sometimes overwhelmed with romantic and sexual thoughts and feelings. They experience normal sexual curiosity about their own and others' bodies. They must learn how to navigate relationships while coping with peer pressure and their longing to fit in. This is a challenging and exciting time where both biological and psychological changes occur. During this stage female teens begin to "hard-wire" their expectations and skills for expressions of love, romance, and sexuality.

Most young girls learn to expect that they will someday find someone with whom they will "fall in love" or at least establish a romantic union. This may or may not include marriage, and it may or may not include children. Although many women say they're most happy and fulfilled when in relationships, they must be taught to experience self-intimacy (having a relationship with themselves) before they're able to have an intimate relationship with another.

The intensity of a new relationship can release neurotransmitters such as endorphins and dopamine that temporarily help some teens fill an emotional void that developed through less than nurturing relational experiences in their childhood. Even well-adapted, healthy individuals enjoy the high of a new romance. If a female adolescent becomes used to mood-altering fantasy, she may continue using intensity to escape underlying depression or using masturbation to numb out from an uncomfortable home environment.

Although most adults can challenge themselves to change self-defeating thoughts and maladaptive behaviors, what was learned in early childhood and through adolescence is intricately wired into the brain. As a clinician you can educate a female adolescent in simple terms about the neurochemistry of attachment and addiction and help her explore the differences between healthy relationships and unhealthy ones. You can talk about the symptoms of dependent/codependent relationships and unhealthy attachment and explore if any of these challenges are present in her life. Schaeffer (2009) and Maltz (2012) have written material on healthy relationships and sexuality that are easy-to-read and widely available.

Outline Healthy Beliefs

To combat the unhealthy cultural messages that inundate today's young females, invite an adolescent to consider alternative beliefs such as the ones below:

- Sex does not equal love.
- Even if I love you or you love me, we don't necessarily have to be sexual.
- Just because you have sex with me doesn't automatically mean you love me.
- I can choose to be sexual if and when I want to.

When a young female develops a positive sense of self and is equipped to maintain healthy boundaries, she's less likely to be used sexually or to accept negative core beliefs about herself and her sexuality.

Teach a young female client how to feel, identify, and regulate her emotions so she doesn't experience flooding, and instead, develops positive coping mechanisms that build healthy internal and social skills. Explore how to deal with depression, anxiety, loneliness, fear, and other uncomfortable feelings through talking to trusted others, journaling, breathing, and seeking healthy expression through the arts, music, or similar ways. Help her explore and define her value system and faith in God or a Higher Power. Determine what she knows in terms of sex education and, if necessary, instruct her about sexuality, including about pregnancy, abortion, and sexually transmitted diseases, including HIV. Encourage her to set a goal of financial self-sufficiency so that she doesn't become dependent on someone else for her survival. Even if her eventual desire is to stay home and raise children, encourage her to finish school so that if she ever had to earn an income for herself (or her children) she could do so without having to take a job that provided inadequate financial resources or resorting to working in the sex industry. Teach her there is risk in mixing romance with business and a risk in using her sexuality to earn favoritism or to exploit others.

An adolescent female on the road to sex and love addiction is most likely looking outside herself for validation, affirmation, and esteem. She's attempting to feel good about herself though self-defeating or destructive means. Your job is to help her find ways to love, accept, affirm, validate, and esteem herself from within so she no longer seeks external ways of soothing her emotional discomfort through intensity and escape.

The best way to prevent adolescent females from becoming sexually addicted is to address the role modeling and parenting they're receiving, because children learn what they live. Helping parents understand the etiology of FSLA and the various ways it manifests is the best place to start supporting the generations to come. If adults realize the roots of sex and love addiction lie in attachment and intimacy issues from childhood, they can begin to heal their own injuries, break the cycle, and create healthier attunement and bonds with their children. With parents or role models who are present and available, one by one, adolescent girls can begin to develop into empowered women of grace and integrity.

Spirituality

Developing a personal spirituality is one of the most important aspects of healthy living, yet it's often much more difficult than many might think. The last of the Twelve Steps talks about a "spiritual awakening," and the program is described as deeply "spiritual." For the recovering female SLA, though, this concept is little more than an abstract notion when she's struggling with the challenges of sobriety and healing. Most clients haven't explored many of their personal beliefs, especially about God or a Higher Power. Many were raised in religious traditions that spelled out, quite literally, who God is and how he is working in their lives. Sometimes clients have had no religious or spiritual experiences or education. God or a Higher Power is absent or irrelevant. The therapist's task is to help the recovering FSLA define who or what she believes and how that force is active in her life. Does she trust in a power greater than herself? How does any unbelief in a Higher Power play out in her life?

One barrier to spirituality for many FSLAs is their experience with organized religion. People within the various religious communities make up the rules, interpret the holy texts or scriptures, and tell others how to behave. Typically these leaders are male—priests, ministers, rabbis, monks, and mullahs from every religious tradition—who are working to create a stable group or community of faith. Whether the leaders are benevolent or abusive, they are in charge. In order to be a part of any religious tradition, following the rules is required so that the group maintains the stability of the whole. Women who've struggled with sex and love addiction have broken the rules, and not infrequently they bear the judgment of the religious leaders.

Religiosity is not spirituality, yet many clients in early recovery don't understand the difference. Spirituality is more about the internal presence of God or a Higher Power, not the external rules of an institution. People who are involved in a spiritual experience are encouraged to follow principles, recognize the compassion of the Universe, challenge the rules of the group, and explore their individual experiences of the Divine. There's no judgment attached to a person's experience of the Divine. Guidance comes through intuitive experience, quiet contemplation, and prayerful awareness. There are no rules that must be adhered to—only experiences that encourage oneness with all that is.

Clients need to understand the difference between religiosity and spirituality and explore those differences. Many clients will report they have a belief in God but see him as an external force. As long as God can be kept "out there," he can't really be all that relevant—he "can't get to me." When clients are encouraged to see God as an internal force rather than an external force, their resistance often shifts. The idea that we co-create our realities is much more palatable than an active force that's out there somewhere pulling strings.

In this way the Twelve Step programs of S recovery offer the expansion of a spiritual worldview. Rather than fight against a set of preordained rules and structures, the program encourages the development of a relationship with a Higher Power. In working the first three Steps clients begin to realize that recovery is a journey of healing for all the relationships in their lives, beginning with their concept of God. A woman realizes she isn't in this world alone. She begins to repair her relationship with the Universe, whatever that relationship may be. She learns to trust in the truth that she won't be abandoned and that if she asks for help, assistance comes. Repair work with an internal power leads her to a co-creation process that heals the distortions promised by her addiction.

Seen in this light recovery is more rewarding than resisting yet again some external source that's seen as limiting. The focus shifts from having a moral judgment that "I shouldn't do this behavior" to experiencing an internal connection to that still small voice that stirs within. The internal guiding force becomes more personal, more insistent. As the pain, fear, and resistance is stilled, the recovering woman becomes more aware of the urge to open up to her heart's desire. She longs to rest in the care of One who doesn't abandon, isn't abusive, and doesn't ask her to abandon herself.

The spiritual journey in recovery brings each woman to the crossroads she perhaps has been circling her entire life. She can no longer pretend that her addictive behaviors have been beneficial. Face-to-face with the consequences of running from her internal Source, that guiding principal that no one else describes or defines for her, she finds that she has exhausted her spirit. As she turns into the road of healing, Spirit comes to her patiently as a friend, offers comfort as an intimate companion, and provides far more love than the last sexual partner. Spirit doesn't leave her and offers a warm embrace and encouragement as she journeys deeper into becoming a woman of grace and integrity.

Contributing Writers

Marnie Ferree - Emotional Self-care; Play, Breathe, Serve; Life Purpose
Alexandra Katehakis - Practical Self-care

REFERENCES

Alcoholics Anonymous World Services, Inc. (1976). *Alcoholics anonymous* (3rd ed.). New York, NY: Author.

Cameron, J. (2002). *The artist's way: A spiritual path to higher creativity.* New York, NY: Tarcher Putnam.

Csikszentmihalyi, M. (2008). *Flow: The psychology of optimal experience.* New York, NY: Harper and Row.

Edwards, W. M., Delmonico, D., & Griffin, E. (2011). *Cybersex unplugged: Finding sexual health in an electronic world.* Charleston, SC: Create Space.

Ferree, M. C. (2008, September). *Redeeming the pain.* Presentation at Society for the Advancement of Sexual Health Conference, Boston, MA.

Ferree, M. C. (2010). *No stones: Women redeemed from sexual addiction* (2nd ed.). Downers Grove, IL: InterVarsity Press.

Frankl, V. (2006). *Man's search for meaning* (5th ed.). Boston, MA: Beacon Press.

Maltz, W. (2012). *The sexual healing journey: A guide for survivors of sexual abuse* (3rd ed.). New York, NY: William Morrow/Harper Collins.

McDaniel, K. (2012). *Ready to heal: Women facing love, sex, and relationship addiction* (3rd ed.). Carefree, AZ: Gentle Path Press.

Mellody, P., Wells Miller, A., & Miller, J. K. (1989). *Facing codependence: What it is, where it comes from, how it sabotages our lives.* New York, NY: Harper Collins.

Muller, W. (2000). *Sabbath: Finding rest, renewal, and delight in our busy lives.* New York, NY: Bantam Books.

Northrup, C. (2010). *Women's bodies, women's wisdom: Creating physical and emotional health and healing* (revised ed.).New York, NY: Bantam Books.

Schaeffer, B. (2009). *Is it love or is it addiction?* (3rd ed.). Center City, MN: Hazelden.

Zoldbrod, A. P. (2005). *Sex smart: How your childhood shaped your sexual life and what to do about it.* Otsego, MI: Page Free Publishing.

Appendices

APPENDIX A – Assessments

Attachment Style Assessment
Adapted by M. Deborah Corley from Bartholomew, K. & Horowitz, L. M. (1991). Attachment styles among young adults: A test of a four-category model. *Journal of Personality and Social Psychology, 61*, 226-244. Assessment is included in Sample Forms section.

Compulsive Sexual Behavior Inventory (CSBI)
Available through Dr. Eli Coleman, Center for Sexual Health
1300 2nd Street S., Suite 180, Minneapolis, MN 55454. Phone 612-625-1500.
Available at **http://www.uofmmedicalcenter.org**

Hypersexual Behavior Inventory (HBI)
Reid, R., Garos, S., Carpenter, B. (2011). Reliability, validity, and psychometric development of the hypersexual behavior inventory in an outpatient sample of men. *Addiction & Compulsivity, 18*, 30-51.
Available at **http://www.rory.net/Pubs/HBI.pdf**

Internet Sexual Screening Tool Revised (ISST-R)
Delmonico, D. L., & Miller, J. (2003). The Internet Sex Screening Test: A comparison of sexual compulsives versus non-sexual compulsives. *Sexual and Relationship Therapy, 18*(3), 261-276.
Available at **http://www.internetbehavior.com/isst**

Love and Relationship Addiction Questions
Available through Brenda Schaffer's website **http://www.loveaddiction.com**

Sexual Addiction Screening Test Revised (SAST-R)
Women's Sexual Addiction Screening Test (W-SAST)
Psychometrics of both are reviewed in:
Carnes, P., Green, B., Carnes, S. (2010). The same yet different: Refocusing the sexual addiction screening test (SAST) to reflect orientation and gender. *Sexual Addiction & Compulsivity, 17*(1), 7-30.
Both instruments and the article are available on the IITAP website:
http://www.iitap.com/documents/SDI-R%20The%20Same%20Yet%20Different.pdf

Sexual Compulsivity Scale (SCS)
A copy and psychometric information is located in:
Kalichman, S. C., Rompa, D. (1995). Sexual sensation seeking and sexual compulsivity scales: Reliability, validity and HIV risk behavior. *Journal of Personality Assessment, 65*, 586–601.

Sexual Dependency Inventory (SDI-R)
Delmonico, D. L., Bubenzer, D. L., & West, J. D. (1998). Assessing sexual addiction with the sexual dependency inventory-revised. *Sexual Addiction & Compulsivity,* 5(3), 179. Restricted in use. Contact the International Institute for Trauma and Addiction Professionals at **http://www.iitap.com**

APPENDIX B – Sample Forms

Assessing Attachment Style

Using a scale from 0-5 with *0 = not at all like me*, and *5 = very much like me*, rate yourself for each of the descriptions of attachments styles listed below. Make a note if it is different if you are under significant stress.

A. "I am comfortable without close emotional relationships. It is very important to me to feel independent and self-sufficient, and I prefer not to depend on others or have anyone depend on me."

0 1 2 3 4 5
Not at all like me *Very much like me*

B. "I want to be completely emotionally intimate with others, but I often find that others are reluctant to get as close as I would like. I am uncomfortable being without close relationships, but I sometimes worry that others don't value me as much as I value them."

0 1 2 3 4 5
Not at all like me *Very much like me*

C. "I am uncomfortable getting close to others. I want emotionally close relationships, but I find it difficult to trust others completely or to depend on them. I worry I will be hurt if I allow myself to become too close to others."

0 1 2 3 4 5
Not at all like me *Very much like me*

D. "It is easy for me to become emotionally close to others. I am comfortable depending on others and having others depend on me. I don't worry about being alone or having others not accept me."

0 1 2 3 4 5
Not at all like me *Very much like me*

Adapted from Bartholomew & Horowitz (1991) by Corley, Santé Center for Healing

Assessing Attachment Style
Scoring Information

Likert Scale: 0-5 with *0 = not at all like me*, and *5 = very much like me*

The higher the score on the item, the more the type is dominant. If the client uses more than one primary attachment style (as indicated by a high rating on more than one item), determine the circumstances that influence which style is used.

Statement A = Avoidant Dismissing Style Client's score _______

A. *"I am comfortable without close emotional relationships. It is very important to me to feel independent and self-sufficient, and I prefer not to depend on others or have anyone depend on me."*

Statement B = Anxious (sometimes called Preoccupied) Client's score _______

B. *"I want to be completely emotionally intimate with others, but I often find that others are reluctant to get as close as I would like. I am uncomfortable being without close relationships, but I sometimes worry that others don't value me as much as I value them."*

Statement C = Avoidant Fearful Client's score _______

C. *"I am uncomfortable getting close to others. I want emotionally close relationships, but I find it difficult to trust others completely or to depend on them. I worry I will be hurt if I allow myself to become too close to others."*

Statement D = Secure Client's score _______

D. *"It is easy for me to become emotionally close to others. I am comfortable depending on others and having others depend on me. I don't worry about being alone or having others not accept me."*

Adapted from Bartholomew & Horowitz (1991) by Corley, Santé Center for Healing

Boundaries and Consequences Analysis

BOUNDARY ANALYSIS		
OK	Questionable	Not OK

Prepared by Linda Hudson, Hudson Consulting Associates

Contract for Group Therapy

This contract for group therapy is in addition to the Informed Consent and Practice Policies you have received. Please read this agreement thoroughly, initial each item, and sign and date the contract where indicated.

____ 1. **Confidentiality**. I will maintain the confidentiality and anonymity of each person participating in group therapy. I will not reveal in any way another person's identity or what she has said or done. Confidentiality also extends to other clients I may see at the group therapy location.

____ 2. **Group Fees**. Each group member pays the same amount for group. Payment is required in monthly increments by check, cash, or credit card at the first group of every month. If needed, I may discuss an alternate payment arrangement with my group therapist.

____ 3. **Attendance**. Absences impact everyone in the group, and I must pay for my space in group therapy whether or not I attend. I will be prompt to all group meetings. If I miss a group session, I will call my group therapist as soon as possible. I understand that it's not acceptable to make contact through other group members.

____ 4. **Time Commitment**. This therapy group is a (----) month commitment and I am expected to attend all group meetings. Exceptions are made for religious or national holidays, major sickness, loss, or emergency, or if my group therapist cancels a group. I will make every effort to notify my group therapist in advance if I know I will miss a group session.

____ 5. **Early Termination.** I have a choice to leave group before the time commitment is over, though early termination is discouraged. I am requested to have at least one transition session with the group to process my choice to terminate and to provide closure.

____ 6. **Sexual Contact**. I will refrain from sexual or romantic contact with other group members to preserve the integrity and safety of the group. Sexual or romantic involvement with another group member may result in termination from group. This extends to sexual or romantic contact with anyone I meet on these premises (i.e. waiting room).

____ 7. **Assignments**. Assignments may be given during group. I will follow through with any commitments I make to the group regarding completion of assignments.

_____ 8. **Respect the Process**. Any concerns should be communicated directly with the group therapist. I will refrain from devaluing or gossiping about the group therapist or other group members while not in group therapy.

_____ 9. **Release of Information**. If I would like my group therapist to consult with other professionals on my behalf, I must complete a separate release for consultation, which is available through my group therapist.

I have read, understand and agree to the information and guidelines stated in this Group Therapy Agreement.

____
Signature

____
Printed Name

____
Date

Adapted from Group Contract used by Center for Healthy Sex

Diagnostic Interview Questions with an FSLA

General

1) What are the problems for which you are seeking help?
2) How often have they occurred?
3) How long have the behaviors existed?
4) Has there been an escalation?
5) What has caused you to seek treatment now?
6) Has the behavior resulted in losses related to family, career, finances, etc?
7) How much time is spent engaging and recovering from the behavior?
8) Do your behaviors alter your mood?
9) Do you believe you have a problem?
10) Do others believe you have a problem?
11) How ready are you for change?
12) Have you been in treatment before for this problem?

Other Compulsive Behaviors

13) What other problematic behaviors interact with sex and romance for you?
14) How often do you drink alcohol, smoke or use drugs?
15) How are your eating habits and appetite?
16) Do you ever use food to medicate feelings?
17) How often do you exercise?
18) Have you ever taken laxatives or vomited because you felt overfull or to avoid gaining weight?
19) Have you ever had cosmetic surgery?
20) Do you use cosmetic fillers or Botox?

Relationship History

21) How many significant relationships have you had and how long have they lasted?
22) Why and how did previous relationships end?
23) Have you ever lived with a romantic partner?
24) What is your marital status? Is your relationship still intact?
25) Does your partner know about your problems?
26) What role does power and control play in your relationships?
27) At what point did serial relationships commence?
28) What length of time did you spend in between relationships?
29) What is it like to be alone once a relationship ends?
30) Have you ever been with another person sexually or romantically during a committed relationship?
31) Have you had a history of emotional affairs?
32) Tell me about your mother, father, siblings, and friends.
33) Is there a history of addiction in your family? What kinds? What about your partners?

Sexual History

34) When was your first sexual experience?
35) How old were you when you began masturbation and fantasy?
36) What did/do you fantasize about?
37) How often do you masturbate now?
38) Do you masturbate with objects?
39) Do you view pornography?
40) What kind of pornography?
41) Have you ever traded sex for money, goods or services?
42) What is enjoyable about sex for you?
43) What makes you uncomfortable sexually?

Trauma History

44) Did you experience physical, sexual, or verbal abuse in your childhood?
45) Did you experience physical or emotional abandonment in your childhood?
46) Was there ever a time in your childhood that you felt special or different?
47) What were the significant losses in your childhood?
48) What was school like?
49) What would you do to make your child's experience better than your own childhood?

Medical and Reproductive

50) What medications do you take?
51) What is your medical history for illness and surgery?
52) Have you had any surgery that has impacted you sexually?
53) Have you ever had an STD such as Chlamydia, herpes simplex I or II, or HPV?
54) Have you been tested for HIV?
55) Have you ever had a head injury?
56) How many hours do you sleep per night?
57) What form of birth control do you use?
58) How many times have you had unprotected sex?
59) Do you have any living children?
60) Do you have a history of abortions, miscarriages or adoptions?
61) Have you ever experienced fertility problems?
62) Have you experienced the death of a child?

Violence

63) Have you ever had sex when you did not want to?
64) Did anyone ever do anything to you sexually as a child that made you uncomfortable?
65) What is the most painful thing a partner has ever said to you?
66) Have you ever been assaulted?
67) Have you ever coerced someone to be sexual with you when she/he didn't want to?

68) Have you ever crossed someone's boundaries by reading mail, listening to messages, or otherwise invading his or her personal space?
69) Have you ever hit, pushed or spit on another person?

Legal

70) Do you have a criminal record?
71) Have you ever been sued?
72) Have you received sanctions against a professional license?
73) Have you ever had a DUI?
74) What behaviors do you fear might be illegal?
75) As an adult have you ever been sexual with a minor?
76) Have any of your partners been sexual with a minor?

Prepared by Susan Campling, Psy.D.

Disclosure/Amends Letter from Addict

Bob,

Thank you for being part of this session with me today. My goal for this letter is to be accountable for my behavior and finally tell you the whole truth. I have betrayed you in many ways. I violated our marital vows, have had several emotional and sexual affairs over the past 15 years, and most recently I've had a sexual affair with our friend John.

I started it by emailing him and making flirtatious and sexual comments – those were the ones you found on the computer. I lied to you about that, but your suspicions were correct. After several emails containing sexual fantasy, we started getting together at a hotel downtown. I had unprotected oral, vaginal and sometimes anal sex with him on a weekly basis over a six-month period. I met him for sex after I went to my art class and sometimes in place of the class. I betrayed you by lying, telling him about our marital problems, and by spending money on these encounters for alcohol and sometimes for the hotel room, food, sex toys, and lingerie. While I was spending this money on the affair, I tried to make you feel guilty about betting on horses. I only ended the affair when you found the emails and threatened to leave me.

I've engaged in similar behaviors in the past even before I met you. In the last 10 years since we've been married I've had sex with over a dozen men that I knew or met online. I was ashamed and didn't admit this to you for fear you'd leave me. John is the only person I've been with that you know. I've also masturbated compulsively when alone and while using pornography online and then refused sex with you because I was sore or had no desire.

These behaviors were about me, not about you. While we've had our problems, I am responsible for what I did, and it's not your fault. I didn't treat you like my best friend. When I had problems, instead of trusting that you'd help me, I turned to others or to porn and masturbation to make me stop feeling.

All of this was wrong of me, and I am sorry. You have every right to be angry and confused by my actions. I'm telling you these things because I want to have a relationship with you based on honesty, and because you have a right to know before we can ever heal our relationship. I know it will be hard if not impossible for you ever to trust me again. I will accept whatever consequences come as a result of my behavior. I'm willing to tell you anything else you need to know as long as we talk about it with a therapist.

I do love you. Sarah.

Prepared by Deborah Corley, Ph.D.

Fire Drill

1. STOP – do something different. The solution is not to try harder!!

2. Make a phone list of at least 5 people. When you're tempted to act out, call everyone on the list. If you don't connect in person leave a message stating your commitment to do whatever you need to do to stay sober. This practice helps hold you accountable. Call the person back and discuss whether or not you were able to keep your word to yourself.

NAME	PHONE NUMBER
______________________	______________________
______________________	______________________
______________________	______________________
______________________	______________________
______________________	______________________

3. Write a letter to yourself. What is motivating you to recover? Include both positive or negative consequences. On the flip side of your letter make bullet points to remind you of your motivation.

4. List Affirmations that support your plan.

____

____

____

____

____

Prepared by Linda Hudson, Hudson Consulting Associates

Session Rating Scale (SRS V.3.0)

Name: ______________________	Age (Yrs): ______________
ID#: ______________________	Sex: M / F
Session #: ______________________	Date: ______________

Please rate today's session by placing a mark on the line nearest to the description that best fits your experience today.

I did not feel heard, understood, and respected.	**Relationship** 1 – – – – – – – – – – – – – – – – – 5	I felt heard, understood, and respected.
We did *not* work on or talk about what I wanted to work on and talk about.	**Goals & Topics** 1 – – – – – – – – – – – – – – – – – 5	We worked on and talked about what I wanted to work on and talk about.
The therapist's approach is not a good fit for me.	**Approach or Method** 1 – – – – – – – – – – – – – – – – – 5	The therapist's approach is a good fit for me.
There was something missing in the session today.	**Overall** 1 – – – – – – – – – – – – – – – – – 5	Overall, today's session was right for me.

The Heart and Soul of Change Project • www.heartandsoulofchange.com

To download a working copy of the SRS (free for personal use) go to the website, www.heartandsoulofchange.com. The citation to the original validation article about the SRS:

Duncan, B., Miller, S., Sparks, J., Claud, D., Reynolds, L., Brown, J., & Johnson, L. (2003). The Session Rating Scale: preliminary psychometric properties of a "working" alliance measure. Journal of Brief Therapy, 3(1), 3-12.

Two other sources can help you understand more about how to use the SRS:
Duncan, B. (2010). On becoming a better therapist. Washington, DC: American Psychological Association.
Duncan, B. (2012). The partners for change outcome management system (PCOMS): The heart and soul of change project. Canadian Psychology, 53, 93-104.

You can download the two articles from the Heart and Soul of Change Project (www.heartandsoulof changeproject.com) as well as over 200 other free resources to help you improve both your alliance and outcomes with your clients.

APPENDIX C – Characteristics of a Sex and Love Addict *

The following are some characteristics of sex and love addiction that we have used to hide the progressive loss of self, which is the heart of the disease:

1. Having few healthy boundaries, we become emotionally and sexually involved with people without knowing them.

2. Out of fear of abandonment or loneliness, we stay in or return to painful, destructive relationships, always struggling to conceal our dependency. Real intimacy is rare, if it has ever existed.

3. Fearing emotional or sexual deprivation, we compulsively pursue and involve ourselves with one relationship after another, sometimes having more than one sexual or emotional affair at a time.

4. We confuse love with such things as neediness, intensity, pity, sexual or physical attraction, being a victim or being a rescuer.

5. We feel empty or incomplete when we are alone. Though we fear both intimacy and commitment, we continually search for relationships or sexual contacts.

6. We sexualize stress, guilt, loneliness, anger, fear and envy. We use sex or emotional dependence as substitutes for nurturing, support and understanding.

7. We manipulate and control others with drama and sexuality.

8. We become immobilized or seriously distracted by sexual or romantic obsessions and fantasies.

9. We avoid personal responsibility by attaching ourselves to people who are emotionally unavailable.

10. We stay in denial about our addiction to emotional intensity, romantic intrigue and compulsive sexual activity.

11. To avoid feeling vulnerable, we may retreat from all intimate involvement, mistaking sexual and emotional anorexia for recovery.

12. We assign magical qualities to others. We idealize and pursue them, then we blame them for not fulfilling our fantasies and expectations.

* The Characteristics are typically read at meetings of Sex and Love Addicts Anonymous.

APPENDIX D – The Twelve Steps of S.L.A.A.*

1. We admitted we were powerless over sex and love addiction - that our lives had become unmanageable.
2. Came to believe that a Power greater than ourselves could restore us to sanity.
3. Made a decision to turn our will and our lives over to the care of God as we understood God.
4. Made a searching and fearless moral inventory of ourselves.
5. Admitted to God, to ourselves, and to another human being the exact nature of our wrongs.
6. Were entirely ready to have God remove all these defects of character.
7. Humbly asked God to remove our shortcomings.
8. Made a list of all persons we had harmed, and became willing to make amends to them all.
9. Made direct amends to such people wherever possible, except when to do so would injure them or others.
10. Continued to take personal inventory, and when we were wrong promptly admitted it.
11. Sought through prayer and meditation to improve our conscious contact with a Power greater than ourselves, praying only for knowledge of God's will for us and the power to carry that out.
12. Having had a spiritual awakening as the result of these steps, we tried to carry this message to sex and love addicts, and to practice these principles in all areas of our lives.

APPENDIX E – Twelve Step Programs

FOR SEX ADDICTS

Sexaholics Anonymous (SA)
www.sa.org; Telephone: 866-424-8777; E-mail: saico@sa.org

SA is a 12-step program for sex addicts and sex offenders. Most meetings are attended primarily by men, though women are welcome. SA bases its definition of sobriety on traditional concepts of marriage, and is the least gay-supportive of the 12-step recovery programs for sex addiction. However, individual groups vary widely in their degree of openness to GLBT issues. Phone and on-line meetings are available.

Sex Addicts Anonymous (SAA)
www.sexaa.org; Telephone: 800-477-8191; E-mail: info@saa-recovery.org

A 12-step program for sex addicts and some offenders, SAA offers a good mix of gay- and straight-oriented meetings. Women frequent some meetings, and on-line and phone meetings are available (see www.saatalk.org).

Sexual Compulsives Anonymous (SCA)
www.sca-recovery.org; Telephone: 800-977-HEAL (800-977-4325)

A 12-step program designed primarily for sex addicts, SCA is concentrated mostly in major urban areas. Its meetings often reflect a sizable gay presence. Women frequent some meetings.

Sex and Love Addicts Anonymous (SLAA)
www.slaafws.org; Telephone: 781-255-8825

A 12-step program designed for sex addicts and individuals with patterns of unhealthy romantic relationships, SLAA has a greater female presence than many other recovery programs. Some meetings are for women only, and phone and on-line meetings are available.

Sexual Recovery Anonymous (SRA)
www.sexualrecovery.org; Telephone: 212-340-4650; E-mail: info@sexualrecovery.org

SRA is a 12-step program similar to SA except that the phrase "committed relationship" is used instead of "marriage." Meetings are limited in number but open to everyone in sexual recovery.

FOR SIGNIFICANT OTHERS OF SEX ADDICTS

S-Anon International
www.sanon.org; Telephone: 800-210-8141 or 615-833-3152; E-mail: sanon@sanon.org

A companion program to SA, S-Anon is a 12-step program for spouses/partners of sex addicts and sex offenders. Most meetings are primarily attended by married women.

Codependents of Sex Addicts (COSA)
www.cosa-recovery.org; Telephone: 763-537-6904; Email: info@cosa-recovery.org

A companion program to SAA, COSA is a 12-step program for partners and significant others of sex addicts and sex offenders. Both men and women attend groups, and phone meetings are available.

CO-Sex Addicts and Love Addicts Anonymous (COSLAA)
www.coslaa.org; Telephone: 860-456-0032

COSLAA is a 12-step support group for the recovery of family, friends, and significant others whose lives have been affected by their relationship with someone addicted to sex and love. COSLAA, also known as CO-Sex and Love Addicts Anonymous, reaches out to the suffering individual, 18 years or older, regardless of sexual orientation, gender, or relationship status.

SRA-Anon
http://sexualrecovery.org/sra_anon.html;
Telephone: 646-450-9690 (NY area) or 323-850-8565 (LA area)
E-mail: sraanon@verizon.net

A program for spouses, relatives, friends, and significant others - when the sexual behavior of someone you love troubles you.

FOR COUPLES

Recovering Couples Anonymous (RCA)
www.recovering-couples.org; Telephone: 510-663-2312

This 12-step program focuses on recovery issues experienced by couples affected by sex addiction. Both partners (addict and co-addict) are encouraged to attend. All committed couples are welcome, and phone meetings are available.

APPENDIX F – Resources for Female Sex and Love Addicts

Only a limited number of treatment centers offer dedicated programming for female sex and love addicts and their partners. Below are three programs connected to members of the steering committee of the Women's Study Group, the writers of Making Advances.

Bethesda Workshops
Nashville, TN

Bethesda Workshops provides a place of healing for those damaged by sexual addiction. We offer four-day clinical, faith-based intensive workshops for female sexual addicts, male sex addicts, partners of sex addicts, and couples. Using the best clinical strategies coupled with Christian principles, we help clients begin a process of spiritual, emotional, behavioral, and relational healing. Under the direction of Marnie C. Ferree, MA, our staff are licensed clinical professionals with specific training in treating sexual addiction, co-addiction, and trauma according to a systemic model, along with a strong emphasis on the Twelve Steps. Visit www.bethesdaworkshops.org for complete information.

Center for Healthy Sex
Los Angeles, CA

Center for Healthy Sex (CHS) is an out-patient treatment center in Southern California, under the direction of Alexandra Katehakis, MFT, specializing in providing treatment for issues related to sexual addiction and sexuality. CHS offers Intensive Out-Patient Programs (IOP) for sex and love addiction to local and national clients. IOPs are gender specific and accommodate females, males, and partners of sex addicts. Other services include individual, group therapy, couples therapy, workshops, and continuing education courses for the professional. Visit http://centerforhealthysex.com for more information, articles, and resources.

Santé Center for Healing

Argyle, TX

Santé Center for Healing outside Dallas offers treatment and rehabilitation for those suffering from sexual addiction, eating disorders, compulsive gambling/gaming, and drug and alcohol addiction. Santé also offers a Professional Health Program designed to meet the specific needs of the impaired physician. Patients at Santé receive a spectrum of addiction treatment that addresses the whole person- mind, body and emotions. Under the direction of Deborah Corley, Ph.D., co-founder and co-owner, Santé offers a wide range of clinical settings (from supportive living environments to intensive outpatient programs to residential treatment) to meet the needs of any individual, including those suffering from complex behavioral health issues. Visit http://www.santecenter.com/ for more information about this comprehensive treatment center.

The premier non-profit resource organization in the field is the Society for the Advancement of Sexual Health. SASH has supported the Women's Study Group and this book, and all proceeds from its sale benefit SASH.

Society for the Advancement of Sexual Health (SASH)

The Society for the Advancement of Sexual Health (SASH) is a nonprofit multidisciplinary organization dedicated to scholarship, training, and resources for promoting sexual health and overcoming problematic sexual behaviors. In addition, SASH maintains a searchable database of members, most of whom are clinical professionals. All proceeds from *Making Advances* are being donated to SASH. Visit www.sash.net for information.

APPENDIX G – Suggested Reading

Assessment & Diagnosis

Carnes, P. J., & Adams, K. A. (2002). *Clinical management of sex addiction.* New York, NY: Brunner-Routledge.

Greene, R. L. (2003). *The MMPI-2 and MMPI-2-RF: An Interpretive Manual (3rd ed.).* Boston, MA: Allyn and Bacon.

Johnson, S. M. (1994). *Character Styles.* New York, NY: W. W. Norton.

Johnson, S. M. (1987). *Humanizing the Narcissistic Style.* New York, NY: W. W. Norton.

McGoldrick, M., Shellenberger, S., & Gerson, R. (1999). *Genograms: Assessment and Intervention.* New York, NY: W.W. Norton.

Meloy, R. (1993). *Violent Attachments.* Northvale, NJ: Jason Aronson.

Attachment Theory

Brisch, K. H. (2002). *Treating attachment disorders: From theory to therapy.* New York, NY: Guilford Press.

Cassidy, J., & Shaver, P. R. (2008). *Handbook of attachment: Theory, research, and clinical applications (2nd ed.).* New York, NY: Guilford Press.

Flores, P. (2011). *Addiction as an attachment disorder (2nd ed.).* Landham, MD: Jason Aronson.

Schore, A. N. (2003). *Affect dysregulation and disorders of the self.* New York, NY: W. W. Norton.

Schore, A. N. (2003). *Affect regulation and repair of the self.* New York, NY: W. W. Norton.

Boundaries & Codependency

Beattie, M. (1986). *Codependent no more: How to stop controlling others and start caring for yourself.* Center City, MN: Hazelden.

Brown, B. (2007). *I thought it was just me: Telling the truth about perfectionism, inadequacy and power.* New York, NY: Gotham Books.

Katherine, A. (2000). *Where to draw the line: How to set healthy boundaries every day*. New York, NY: Fireside Books.

Katherine, A. (1994). *Boundaries: Where you end and I begin* (2nd ed.). Center City, MN: Hazelden Educational Materials.

Lerner, R. (1995). *Living in the comfort zone: The gift of boundaries in relationships*. Deerfield Beach, FL: Health Communications.

McBride, K. (2008). *Will I ever be good enough? Healing the daughters of narcissistic mothers*. New York, NY: Free Press.

Mellody, P., Miller, A. W., & Miller, J. K. (1989). *Facing codependence: What it is, where it comes from, how it sabotages our lives*. New York, NY: HarperCollins.

Couples

Gottman, J. M. (2011). *The science of trust: Emotional attunement for couples*. New York, NY: W.W. Norton.

Gottman, J. M. (2000). *The seven principles for making marriage work*. New York, NY: Three Rivers Press.

Johnson, S. M. (2005). *Emotionally focused couple therapy with trauma survivors: Strengthening attachment bonds*. New York, NY: Guilford Press.

Leadem, J., & Leadem, E. (2010). *One in the spirit - Meditation course for recovering couples*. Toms River, NJ: Leadem Counseling.

Mellody, P. & Freundlich, L. S. (2004). *The intimacy factor: The ground rules for overcoming the obstacles to truth, respect, and lasting love*. New York, NY: Harper Collins.

Schnarch, D. (1991). *Constructing the sexual crucible: An integration of sexual and marital therapy*. New York, NY: W.W. Norton.

Solomon, M., & Tatkin, S. (2011). *Love and war in intimate relationships: Connection, disconnection, and mutual regulation in couple therapy*. New York, NY: W.W. Norton.

Dating

Binazir, A. (2010). *The tao of dating: The smart woman's guide to being absolutely irresistible*. Santa Monica, CA: Elite Communications.

Cloud, H., & Townsend, J. (2010). *Boundaries in dating: Making dating work.* Grand Rapids, MI: Zondervan.

Kasl, C. (1999). *If the buddha dated: A handbook for finding love on a spiritual path.* New York, NY: Penguin Group, Inc.

Woodward-Thomas, K. (2004). *Calling in 'the one': 7 weeks to attract the love of your life.* New York, NY: Three Rivers Press.

Disclosure

Corley, M. D., & Schneider, J. P. (2012). *Disclosing secrets: An addict's guide for when, to whom, and how much to reveal.* Tucson, AZ: Recovery Resources Press.

Schneider, J. P., & Corley, M. D. (2012). *Surviving disclosure: A partner's guide for healing the betrayal of intimate trust.* Tucson, AZ: Recovery Resources Press.

Group Therapy

Maguire, J. (1998). *The power of personal storytelling: Spinning tales to connect with others.* New York, NY: Penguin Putnam.

Velasquez, M., Gaddy Maurer, G., Crouch, C., & DiClemente, C. C. (2001). *Group treatment for substance abuse: A stages-of-change therapy manual.* New York, NY: Guilford Press.

Yalom, I. D., & Leszcz, M. (2005). *Theory and practice of group psychotherapy* (5th ed.). New York, NY: Basic Books.

Interpersonal Neurobiology

Badenoch, B. (2008). *Being a brain-wise therapist: A practical guide to interpersonal neurobiology.* New York, NY: W. W. Norton.

Cozzilino, L. (2010). *The neuroscience of psychotherapy: Healing the social brain* (2nd ed.). New York, NY: W. W. Norton.

Marks-Tarlow, T. (2012). *Clinical intuition in psychotherapy: The neurobiology of embodied response.* New York, NY: W. W. Norton.

McGilchrist, I. (2009). *The master and his emissary: The divided brain and the making of the western world.* New Haven and London: Yale University Press.

Schore, A. N. (2012). *The science of the art of psychotherapy*. New York, NY: W.W. Norton.

Siegel, D. (2012). *Pocket guide to interpersonal neurobiology: An integrative handbook of the mind.* New York, NY: W. W. Norton.

Mothering and Friendship

Chesler, P. (2009). *Woman's inhumanity to woman.* Chicago, IL: Lawrence Hill Books.

Cori, J. L. (2010). *The emotionally absent mother: A guide to self-healing and getting the love you missed.* New York, NY: The Experiment.

Edelman, H. (2006). *Motherless daughters - The legacy of loss* (2nd ed.). Cambridge, MA: De Capo Press.

Hunter, B. (2006). *In the company of women; Deepening our relationships with the important women in our lives.* New York, NY: Random House.

Northrup, C. (2006). *Mother daughter wisdom: Understanding the crucial link between mothers, daughters, and health.* New York, NY: Bantam Books.

Valen, K. (2010). *The twisted sisterhood: Unraveling the dark legacy of female friendships.* New York, NY: Ballentine Books.

Parenting

Haffner, D. W. (2008). *What every 21st-century parent needs to know: Facing today's challenges with wisdom and heart.* New York, NY: Newmarket Press.

Newton, R. (2008). *The attachment connection: Parenting a secure and confident child using the science of attachment theory*. Oakland, CA: New Harbinger Publications.

Nogales, A., & Golden-Bellotti, L. (2009). *Parents who cheat: How children and adults are affected when their parents are unfaithful.* Deerfield Beach, FL: Health Communications.

Siegel, D. J., & Bryson, T. P. (2011). *The whole-brain child: 12 revolutionary strategies to nurture your child's developing mind.* New York, NY: Delacorte Press.

Siegel, D. J., & Hartzell, M. (2003). *Parenting from the inside out: How a deeper self-understanding can help you raise children who thrive.* New York, NY: Penguin.

Partners of Sex Addicts

Black, C. (2009). *Deceived: Facing sexual betrayal, lies and secrets.* Center City, MN: Hazelden.

Carnes, S., Lee, M., & Rodriguez, A. (2012). *Facing Heartbreak: Steps to recovery for partners of sex addicts.* Carefree, AZ: Gentle Path Press.

Carnes, S. (Ed.). (2011). *Mending a shattered heart: A guide for partners of sex addicts* (2nd ed.). Carefree, AZ: Gentle Path Press.

Corcoron, M. (2011). *A house interrupted: A wife's story of recovering from her husband's sex addiction.* Carefree, AZ: Gentle Path Press.

Glass, S. L., & Staeheli, J. (2003). *Not Just Friends: Rebuilding trust and recovering your sanity after infidelity.* New York, NY: Free Press.

Schneider, J. P., & Corley, M. D. (2012). *Surviving disclosure: A partner's guide for healing the betrayal of intimate trust.* . Tucson, AZ: Recovery Resources Press.

Steffens, B., & Means, M. (2009). *Your sexually addicted spouse: How partners can cope and heal.* Far Hills, NJ: New Horizon Press.

Sexuality

Bercaw, W., & Bercaw, G. (2010). *The couples guide to intimacy: How sexual reintegration therapy can help your relationship heal.* Pasadena, CA: California Center for Healing.

Berman, J., Berman, L. & Bumiller, E. (2001). *For women only: A revolutionary guide to reclaiming your sex life.* New York, NY: Henry Holt.

Jonnaides, P., & Gross, D. (2011). *The guide to getting it on* (6th ed.). Oregon: Goofy Foot Press.

Katehakis, A. (2010). *Erotic Intelligence: Igniting hot, healthy sex while in recovery from sex addiction.* Deerfield Beach, FL: Health Communications.

Komisaruk, B. R., Bayer-Flores, C., & Whipple, B. (2006). *The science of orgasm.* Baltimore, MD: John Hopkins University Press.

Maltz, W. (2012). *The sexual healing journey: A guide for survivors of sexual abuse* (3rd ed.). New York, NY: William Morrow.

Rankin, L. (2010). *What's up down there? Questions you'd only ask your gynecologist if she was your best friend.* New York, NY: St. Martin's Press.

Schulte, C. (2005). *Tantric sex for women: A guide for lesbian, bi, hetero and solo lovers.* Alameda, CA: Hunter House.

Zoldbrod, A. P. (1998). *Sex smart: How your childhood shaped your sexual life, and what to do about it.* Oakland, CA: New Harbinger Publications.

Sex and Love Addiction

Carnes, P. (1997). *Sexual anorexia: Overcoming sexual self-hatred.* Center City, MN: Hazeldon.

Delmonico, D. L., Griffin, E., & Moriarty, J. (2001). *Cybersex unhooked: A workbook for breaking free of compulsive online sexual behavior.* Wickenburg, AZ: Gentle Path Press.

Delmonico, D., Griffin, E., & Moriarity, J. (2001). *In the shadow of the net.* Center City, MN. Hazelden.

Ferree, M. C. (2010). *No stones: Women redeemed from sexual addiction* (2nd ed.). Downers Grove, IL: InterVarsity Press.

Kasl, C. S. (1990). *Woman, sex, and addiction: A search for love and power.* New York, NY: Harper & Row.

Maltz, W., & Maltz, L. (2008). *The porn trap: The essential guide to overcoming problems caused by pornography.* New York, NY: Harper Collins.

McDaniel, K. (2012). *Ready to heal: Breaking free of addictive relationships* (3rd ed.). Carefree, AZ. Gentle Path Press.

Mellody, P. (1992). *Facing love addiction: Giving yourself the power to change the way you love.* New York, NY: HarperCollins.

Milkman, H., & Sunderwirth, S. (1987). *Craving for ecstasy: The consciousness and chemistry of escape.* San Francisco, CA: Jossey-Bass.

Norwood, R. (1985). *Women who love too much.* New York, NY: Pocket Books.

Peabody, S. (2005). *Addiction to love: Overcoming obsession and dependency in relationships.* New York, NY: Celestial Arts.

Peele, S., & Brodsky, A. (1991). *Love and addiction.* New York, NY: Taplinger Publishing Co.

Resnick, R. (2008). *Love junkie: A memoir.* New York, NY: Bloomsbury.

Schaeffer, B. (2009). *Is it love or is it addiction?* (3rd ed.). Minneapolis, MN: Hazelden.

Silverman, S. W. (2008). *Love sick: One woman's journey through sexual addiction.* New York, NY: W.W. Norton.

Vare, E. A. (2011). *Love addiction: Sex, romance, and other dangerous drugs.* Deerfield Beach, FL: Health Communications.

Spirituality

Chodron, P. (1997). *When things fall apart: Heart advice for difficult times.* Boston, MA: Shambala Classics.

Kurtz, E., & Ketcham, K. (1992). *The spirituality of imperfection.* New York, NY: Bantam Books.

Monk-Kidd, S. (1990). *When the heart waits: Spiritual direction for life's sacred questions.* New York, NY: Norton Press.

Myss, C. (2001). *Sacred contracts: Awakening your divine potential.* New York, NY: Harmony Books.

Newberry, T. (2007). *The 4:8 principle: The secret to a joy filled life.* Carol Stream, IL: Tyndale House.

Tolle, E. (2005). *A new earth: Awakening to your life's purpose.* New York, NY: Plume.

Vanzant, I. (1998). *One day my soul just opened up: 40 days and 40 nights toward spiritual strength and personal growth.* New York, NY: Fireside.

Survivors of Incest

Adams, K. (2012). *Silently seduced: When parents make their children partners* (2nd ed.). Deerfield Beach, FL: Health Communications.

Bass, E., & Davis, L. (1988). *The courage to heal: A guide for women survivors of child sexual abuse (3rd ed.).* New York, NY: Harper Collins.

Love, P. & Robinson, J. (1990). *Emotional incest syndrome.* New York, NY: Bantam Books.

Maltz, W. (2012). *The sexual healing journey: A guide for survivors of sexual abuse (3rd ed.).* New York, NY: William Morrow.

Trauma

Carnes, P. (1997). *The betrayal bond.* Deerfield Beach, FL: Health Communications.

Courtois, C. A., Ford, J. D., Van der kolk, B. A., & Herman, J. D. (2009). *Treating complex traumatic stress disorders: An evidence-based guide.* New York, NY: Guilford Press.

Emerson, D., Cooper, E., van der kolk, B. A., Levine, P. A., & Cope, S. (2011). *Overcoming trauma through yoga: Reclaiming your body.* Berkeley, CA: North Atlantic Books.

Levine, P. A. (1997). *Waking the tiger: The innate capacity to transform overwhelming experiences.* Berkeley, CA: North Atlantic Books.

Murray, M. (1991). *Prisoner of another war - A remarkable journey of healing from childhood trauma.* Palo Alto, CA: PageMill Press.

Ogden, P., Minton, K., & Pain, C. (2006). *Trauma and the body: A sensorimotor approach to psychotherapy.* New York, NY: W.W. Norton.

Rothschild, B. (2000). *The body remembers: The psychophysiology of trauma and trauma treatment.* New York, NY: W. W. Norton.

Women's Health and Psychology

Brizendine, L. (2006). *The female brain.* New York, NY: Broadway Books.

Miller, J. B., Kaplan, A., Jordan, J., Stiver, I. P., & Surrey, J. (1991). *Women's growth in connection: Writings from the Stone Center.* New York, NY: Guilford Press.

Northrup, C. (2010). *Women's bodies, women's wisdom: Creating physical and emotional health and healing* (revised ed.). New York, NY. Bantam Books.

Pipher, M. (2002). *Reviving Ophelia: Saving the selves of adolescent girls.* New York, NY: Ballentine Books.

APPENDIX H - Acknowledgements

We are grateful to all the female sex and love addicts who have shared their stories and their recovery process with us over the years. Thanks, also, to the women who joined us at the first Women's Summits and who brought clinical observations, opinions, ideas, and wished us well on this writing adventure. A special thank you to Rob Weiss for initiating the first Summit discussions, to Drs. David Delmonico and Joshua Hook for helping us with data analysis from the Women's Sexuality Survey, and to Life Healing Center, Santé Center for Healing, and SASH for sponsoring the first Women's Summit meetings.

A number of individuals were instrumental in bringing this project to fruition. Natalie Finegood, M.A., provided helpful research assistance. Sharon Smith was invaluable as a copy editor, and Susan Thompson offered expert formatting and graphics. They were a joy to work with during the last, pressured days of completing the manuscript.

Without the support of the administrative staff at Bethesda Workshops, I would never have been able to complete this undertaking. Nicole Hobson, the director of workshop operations, stood in the gap while I devoted month after month to *Making Advances*. She provided laughter and cookies when I needed them, and I'm extremely grateful for her support and friendship. Administrative assistants Rebecca Agee and Emily Husbands worked extra hours and kept the office running smoothly in my absence.

My family also bore the burden of my unrelenting focus on this book. I rarely strayed from my editing post during June and July, and I bowed out of a family vacation when the work proved more time-consuming than I had planned. I'm grateful that my husband David and I have enjoyed many years on the healing side of this journey, and I'm blessed by his constant support of my efforts to help women, including during the long days and nights of working on this book. My daughter E.A. spent hours proof-reading during her one short visit home this summer, which kept me from going over the edge.

The steering committee for *Making Advances* included Deb Corley, Linda Hudson, and Alex Katehakis. These strong women guided this project, did an immense amount of writing and editing, consulted for hours about various issues, and offered unwavering support. Deb Corley provided financial underwriting for the Women's Sexuality Survey and the costs associated with publishing *Making Advances*, and it was her suggestion to donate the book's proceeds to SASH.

With gratitude to you all,
Marnie C. Ferree, Editor

APPENDIX I - Writers

Susan Campling, R.N., Psy.D.

Dr. Susan Campling has worked in the field of trauma and addiction for over 20 years. Dr. Campling is a founding member of Fairview Counseling, a nonprofit program for abused children, and has served on the Advisory Board for SASH, IITAP, Spirit2Spirit and Alvernia University graduate psychology programs. She is a Certified Sex Addiction Therapist-Supervisor, Certified Domestic Violence Therapist, Certified Sexual Offender Therapist, and Certified Trauma Therapist. She also is certified in the area of telemental health and chemical addiction. Dr. Campling is key faculty for the Advanced Training in Problematic Sexual Behavior (ATPSB) certificate program. She previously served as the Director of the Keystone Center ECU, and Gentle Path. Dr. Campling has presented extensively on the topics of sexual addiction, sexual offending, domestic violence and trauma. She was the recipient of Caron Foundation's Health Professional Award.

Contact Information: Email: Drcampling@live.com

Robin Cato, J.D.

Robin Cato is the Executive Director for The Society for the Advancement of Sexual Health (SASH). She is also an Attorney in the State of Georgia where she has practiced in both civil and criminal areas of law. Prior to her law career, she taught high school English in Orlando, FL. She earned her B.A. in English from Stetson University in Deland, FL, and her J.D. from Mississippi College School of Law, Jackson, MS. She also serves on the local school board in her county in Georgia.

Contact Information: SASH, Royston, GA
www.sash.net , 706-356-7031, Email: sash@sash.net

M. Deborah Corley, Ph.D.

M. Deborah Corley, Ph.D. is co-owner and co-founder of Santé Center for Healing in Argyle, TX, a poly-addiction residential treatment center that also treats mood disorders co-occurring with chemical and behavior addictions. A licensed marriage and family therapist, sex offender treatment provider, chemical dependency counselor, and certified sex addiction therapist, she has been a popular presenter at many national conferences for the past 30 years. Dr. Corley spearheaded the data analysis from the Women's Sexuality Survey and co-authored two articles on female sex and love addicts. She has also written articles on related topics such as disclosure, resolution of trauma, restoring trust after betrayal, and treating sexual addiction.

She designed and developed the Maintaining Proper Boundaries Course at Santé in 2003 in collaboration with Vanderbilt's Center for Professional Health and continues as faculty. Dr. Corley has co-authored three books: *Embracing Recovery, Disclosing Secrets and Surviving Disclosure.*

Contact Information: Santé Center for Healing, Argyle, TX
www.santecenter.com, 800-258-4250

Marnie C. Ferree, M.A.

Marnie C. Ferree, M.A., is a licensed marriage and family therapist in Nashville, Tennessee, where she is the founder and director of Bethesda Workshops, a clinical intensive workshop program for sex addicts, their partners, and couples affected by sexual addiction. The treatment program she established in 1997 for female sex addicts was the first of its kind in the country. Her book, *No Stones: Women Redeemed From Sexual Addiction*, was the first to address sexual addiction in women from a Christian perspective, and she has also authored clinical articles in peer-reviewed journals and numerous articles in Christian periodicals. Marnie is a Certified Sex Addiction Therapist (CSAT) and serves on the editorial board of the *Sexual Addiction & Compulsivity Journal.* She is a frequent speaker at professional and recovery conferences, churches, and schools, and has been featured on *Dateline* and in other media.

Contact Information: Bethesda Workshops, Nashville, TN
www.bethesdaworkshops.org, 866-464-HEAL (866-464-4325)
Email: mferree@bethesdaworkshops.org

Linda Hudson, M.S.

Linda Hudson is a Licensed Professional Counselor, past President of the Society for the Advancement of Sexual Health (SASH), the recipient of the first Merit Award for Outstanding service to SASH, and currently serves as Board Advisor. Trained as a family systems and addictions therapist she believes in a strong integration of body, mind and spirit and works to assist all clients in clarifying and integrating their spiritual beliefs into their lives. During her 28 year career, she has earned a reputation as one of the nation's foremost authorities in her field and assisted hundreds of clients in resolving a multitude of problems through intensive one-on-one counseling as well as workshops and group sessions. Linda is a frequent speaker and trainer on issues of sexuality, spirituality and relationships.

Contact Information: Hudson Consulting Associates, Dallas, GA
www.hudsonconsulting.info, 678-363-3561

Alexandra Katehakis, M.A.

Alexandra Katehakis, M.F.T., is Founder and Clinical Director of the Center for Healthy Sex in Los Angeles, California, a private agency dedicated to the treatment of sex addicts, their partners, and couples via individual, group, and intensive outpatient programs. In addition to being author of *Erotic Intelligence: Igniting Hot Healthy Sex While in Recovery From Sex Addiction*, Ms. Katehakis is an international speaker at conferences and has written numerous clinical articles for professional journals including "Affective Neuroscience and the Treatment of Sex Addiction" in the *Sexual Addiction & Compulsivity Journal*. Ms. Katehakis is a Certified Sex Addiction Therapist/Supervisor and AASECT Certified Sex Therapist/Supervisor. She has specialized in the treatment of sexual addiction and other sexual disorders for fifteen years.

Contact Information: Center for Healthy Sex, Los Angeles, CA
www.centerforhealthysex.com, 310- 843-9902

Kelly McDaniel, M.A.

Kelly McDaniel, L.P.C., NCC, CSAT, maintains a private practice in both San Antonio and Fredericksburg, Texas, where she specializes in the treatment of women who are searching for greater meaning, peace, and connection in their lives. As a Certified Sex Addiction Therapist (CSAT), and a Post Induction Therapy (PIT) trained therapist, McDaniel also pulls from Relational/Cultural theory in her work with women. In 2008, she published *Ready to Heal: Women facing Love, Sex, and Relationship Addiction* that is currently available in its new edition called *Ready to Heal: Breaking Free of Addictive Relationships*.

Contact Information: Kelly McDaniel, San Antonio, TX
www.kellymcdanieltherapy.com, 210- 826-8377

Anna Valenti-Anderson, M.S.S.W.

Anna Valenti-Anderson holds professional licenses as a Clinical Social Worker and Independent Substance Abuse Counselor, and certifications as a Certified Sex Addiction Therapist-Supervisor (CSAT-S), Post Induction Therapy (PIT) trained therapist, and Adoption Service Provider. She maintains a private practice in Phoenix, Arizona. As founder of SANEResources.org and Clinical Director at Crosswinds Counseling Services, she helps clients address issues related to trauma and abuse, sexuality and intimacy, codependency and courtship, and cross addictions. Anna also works part-time in the area of independent adoptions. She has been published in *Newsweek*, and the *Sexual Addiction & Compulsivity Journal* for "Use of Object Relations and Self-Psychology as Treatment for Sex Addiction with a Female Borderline Patient." She wrote the first CSAT Instructor's Manual to

Dr. Carnes' *Recovery Start Kit: The First 130 Days* and also contributed to *Making Marriage a Success: Pearls of Wisdom from Experts Across the Nation.*

Contact Information: SANE Resources, Phoenix, AZ
www.SANEResources.org or www.annavalenti.com, 623-695-0064

Jill Vermeire, M.A.

Jill Vermeire, M.F.T. completed her Masters degree in Clinical Psychology at Pepperdine University and in 2000 began her private practice in Los Angeles, specializing in sex, trauma, and addictions. In 2009 Jill appeared with Dr. Drew Pinsky in VH1's *Sex Rehab*, which she later discussed on a number of programs including T*he Oprah Winfrey Show*, *Extra*, *Issues with Jane Velasquez*, and on HLN, NBC News, the TV Guide Network, and KROQ's *Loveline*. In 2011 Jill decided to combine her love for travel and helping others by creating Love Rehab for Women via her company, Red Lotus Way. She now helps women heal their hearts and gain clarity about their relationships during retreats in exotic destinations around the world.

Contact Information: Jill Vermeire, Los Angeles, CA
www.love-rehab.com, 310-751-0509

Sonnee Weedn, Ph.D.

Sonnee Weedn, Ph.D., is a clinical and forensic psychologist in Novato, CA, where she has maintained a general practice for 32 years that includes five weekly therapy groups. She is certified by the American Psychological Association in the Treatment of Alcoholism and Other Chemical Dependencies, and is a Certified Sex Addiction Therapist. Dr. Weedn consults to numerous entities and treatment facilities in the area of continuing education. She is a columnist for the online magazine, *Doctora Ana* (in Spanish and English), a regular contributor to the *Marin Medical Journal*, and the author of the award winning book, *Many Blessings: A Tapestry of Accomplished African American Women*. Her workshops and trainings have been presented internationally, and she is the founder of the Sonnee Weedn Institute for Integrative Therapy (SWIIT), which advances training for professionals in alternative and holistic treatment.

Contact Information: Dr. Sonnee Weedn, Novato, CA
www.drsonneeweedn.com, 415-883-7758

Made in the USA
San Bernardino, CA
13 January 2014